GENOCIDE

The Cultures and Practice of Violence Series

Series Editors:
Neil L. Whitehead, University of Wisconsin, Madison
Jo Ellen Fair, University of Wisconsin, Madison
Leigh Payne, University of Wisconsin, Madison

The study of violence has often focused on the political and economic conditions under which violence is generated, the suffering of victims, and the psychology of its interpersonal dynamics. Less familiar are the role of perpetrators, their motivations, and the social conditions under which they are able to operate. In the context of postcolonial state building and more latterly the collapse and implosion of society, community violence, state repression, and the phenomena of judicial inquiries in the aftermath of civil conflict, there is a need to better comprehend the role of those who actually do the work of violence—torturers, assassins, and terrorists—as much as the role of those who suffer its consequences.

When atrocity and murder take place, they feed the world of the iconic imagination that transcends reality and its rational articulation; but in doing so imagination can bring further violent realities into being. This series encourages authors who build on traditional disciplines and break out of their constraints and boundaries, incorporating media and performance studies and literary and cultural studies as much as anthropology, sociology, and history.

GENOCIDE

TRUTH, MEMORY, and REPRESENTATION

Edited by
Alexander Laban Hinton
and Kevin Lewis O'Neill

Duke University Press
Durham and London   2009

© 2009 Duke University Press

All rights reserved

Printed in the United States of America
on acid-free paper ∞

Designed by Heather Hensley

Typeset in Minion Pro by Achorn
International

Library of Congress Cataloging-in-
Publication Data appear on the last
printed page of this book.

CONTENTS

ACKNOWLEDGMENTS

This book began to take form at several interrelated panel discussions on genocide, truth, memory, and representation, including those held at meetings of the American Anthropological Association, the Society for Psychological Anthropology, and the International Association of Genocide Scholars. We are grateful to the participants in these sessions and to our other contributors for being so responsive to our queries and suggestions and so patient during the review process. In addition, we would like to thank the series editors of The Cultures and Practice of Violence Series, Neil L. Whitehead, Jo Ellen Fair, and Leigh Payne, and our editors at Duke University Press, Valerie Millholland and Miriam Angress. We appreciate their support for and encouragement about the volume. Last, we are grateful for the efforts of Molly Balikov, Heather Hensley, and Petra Dreiser during the production process.

Kevin Lewis O'Neill and Alexander Laban Hinton

GENOCIDE, TRUTH,

MEMORY, AND REPRESENTATION

An Introduction

Tomorrow
you will walk toward other evenings
and all your questions
will flow like the last river of the world.
—Herberto Padilla, "History"

Genocide staggers the imagination. It staggers us with numbers. In the 20th century alone, 65,000 Hereros, 1 million Armenians, 6 million Ukranians, 6 million Jews, 3 million Bangladeshis, up to 1 million Indonesians, 100,000 Hutus, 2 million Cambodians, 200,000 East Timorese, 200,000 Guatemalans, 800,000 Tutsis and moderate Hutus, and countless numbers of indigenous peoples have been annihilated.[1] And this is a partial list. It staggers us with images: Armenian death marches into the desert, Nazi crematoriums and concentration camps, Cambodian killing fields, Interahamwe roadblocks and rape pens in Rwanda, Sudanese refugee camps, Sarajevo besieged, and Kurdish villagers in Iraq gassed to death. Some of these images have become iconic of genocide: emaciated prisoners staring from behind the wires of a concentration camp, mass graves packed with corpses, and the fleeing or suffering refugee. With the power of these numbers and images genocide also staggers us with questions: How can such events happen? What motivates people to commit these heinous crimes against humanity? What is it like to endure horrors of this type? How do survivors cope? Can they ever? Why could the violence not be stopped? And why does genocide happen time after time?

Questions such as these motivated the Polish jurist Raphaël Lemkin to seek the creation of new international law that would punish the perpetrators of mass murder. Writing in the shadow of the Holocaust, Lemkin coined the term *genocide*—a hybrid word taken from the Greek *genos* (race, tribe) and the Latin *cide* (killing)—to denote a crime that involved "a coordinated plan of different actions aiming at the destruction of essential foundations of life of national groups, with the aim of annihilating the groups themselves" (1944:79). Just two years after Lemkin published this definition, the United Nations General Assembly passed Resolution 96-1, which states: "Genocide is a denial of the right of existence of entire human groups, as homicide is the denial of the right to live of individual human beings.... Many instances of such crimes of genocide have occurred, when racial, religious, political and other groups have been destroyed, entirely or in part" (Kuper 1981:23).

In 1948 Resolution 96-1 became international law, with genocide referring to "acts committed with intent to destroy, in whole or in part, a national, ethnical, racial or religious group, as such." These acts include both outright "killing" and "causing serious bodily or mental harm" or creating "conditions of life" intended to physically destroy the members of a group. The definition of genocide in Resolution 96-1 also encompasses attempts to eliminate a group's survival by "preventing births" or "forcibly transferring [their] children" to another group. Yet it is clear that some key elements of Lemkin's original conceptualization of genocide were left out of Resolution 96-1.

Why? The contours of the legal definition of genocide shifted as United Nations (UN) delegates debated the wording of the convention for two years (Kuper 1981). Certain types of groups (national, ethnical, racial, or religious) were included. Others, such as economic and political groups, were eventually excluded for a variety of reasons ranging from the conceptual (e.g., some argued that political and economic groups were not enduring) to the pragmatic (e.g., many states feared interference in their internal political affairs and some, such as the Soviet Union, feared accusations they had committed genocide against such groups).

Similarly, in *Axis Rule in Occupied Europe*, Lemkin, reflecting on Nazi atrocities, argued that there were political, social, cultural, economic, biological, physical, religious, and moral "techniques of genocide" (1944:82). While physical, biological, and cultural acts appeared in the initial draft of the convention, the broader sense of "cultural genocide" was eliminated from the final text (Kuper 1981). Cultural genocide, for example, includes curtailing or banning a language, traditional socialization practices, artistic endeavors, ritual practices, social institutions, and so forth. The framers of the 1948 Convention on the Prevention and Punishment of the Crime of Genocide erased these aspects from the text for conceptual and legal reasons (some argued that cultural genocide was already prohibited in international law) and practical reasons (colonial powers, for example, likely feared accusations of cultural genocide). There were similar debates over issues of motivation and intent, the scale of destruction, and punishment and enforcement.

The very conception and legal definition of genocide was forged in a highly politicized atmosphere, one that resulted in inclusions and exclusions and a moral gradation of atrocity. The destruction of political groups, while abhorrent, was written out of the convention and became something else, an implicitly lesser crime; cultural genocide similarly dropped from sight, eventually reemerging in popular discourse as "ethnocide."

It is precisely these sorts of processes of inclusion and exclusion that are at the core of this book. Moreover, this book addresses acts of discursive privileging and moments of silencing that complicate and constitute issues of truth and falsity. While some of the essays in this volume grapple with the genocide convention directly (e.g., Pamela Ballinger's essay), most carry these themes far and wide to consider how genocide is itself represented and remembered in a variety of contexts.

Along these lines, while this book examines several cases commonly regarded as genocide, it includes other cases in which the application of the term remains contested such as the North-South conflict in Sudan and Guatemala, where debate continues over whether civil conflict reached genocidal proportions. The Guatemalan case also illustrates how such views change over time, as many more people came to view the violence against the indigenous Maya as genocide following the findings of the Commission for Historical Clarification (Comisión para el Esclarecimiento Histórico,

CEH) in 1999. Such moments and these more contested cases are revealing about the ways in which horrific violence is represented, remembered, and linked to truth claims about genocide. Accordingly, the essays in this volume do not just explore the relationship of genocide to truth, memory, and representation; they are also concerned with how *discourses about* genocide, truth, memory, and representation are interlinked. This issue emerges perhaps most clearly in Conerly Casey's essay on Nigeria. While some scholars suggest that Nigeria has been the site of genocide or genocidal massacres (see Kuper 1981; Chalk and Jonassohn 1990),[2] others would argue that genocide has not taken place there. Casey's essay explores the ways in which discourses about genocide in Nigeria are bound up with issues of representation, memory, and truth claims, particularly with regard to the media.

At the same time, several of the essays in this volume are directly concerned with issues of truth, memory, and representation in the aftermath of what most people would agree is genocide. These chapters ask: What happens to people and the societies in which they live after genocide? How are the devastating events remembered on the individual and collective levels, and how do these memories intersect and diverge as governments in postgenocidal states attempt to produce a more monolithic "truth" about the past? How are representations of a violent past structured by one's positioning as a survivor, perpetrator, witness, government official, scholar, activist, legal professional, journalist, or ethnographer? And, what are the epistemological, ethical, and empirical entanglements in which researchers find themselves enmeshed in postgenocidal contexts?

Central to the book is the notion that socially and historically located cultural practices construct postgenocidal contexts and that these practices are best observed through experience-near qualitative research methods. Indeed, one of the major ways in which anthropology can contribute to the field of genocide studies is through this experience-near, ethnographic method of data collection. Extended face-to-face engagements with communities yield textured, thick descriptions that macro-analyses of genocide overlook. To this end and through these means, this book asks, what do cultural practices and lived experiences look like in postgenocidal contexts—spaces in which trauma, grief, and fear, as well as power and state control, frame and at times define the contours of everyday life for survivors and perpetrators alike?

The "truth" of genocide, for example, often becomes a power-laden tool over which politicians, activists, and the international community wrestle by asserting and contesting representations cobbled together from the often fragmented and clashing memories of survivors, perpetrators, witnesses, and bystanders. While scholars can make distinctions between truth, memory, and representation for the sake of analytical clarity, these divisions frequently become problematic on the ground. This conceptual unsteadiness can prove troubling for those who want to definitively explain how, why, and when mass murder takes place.

The stakes are high here as various individuals, groups, governments, and institutions vie to map out a narrative of the past that legitimates their agendas or desire for justice, assert or reject the right to legal redress for and moral outrage about "the crime of all crimes," and acknowledge or disavow memories, experiences, suffering, and losses linked to mass murder. These often fiery debates rage around us in the world today, ranging from the Turkish government's continuing denials of the Armenian genocide to the debate over whether or not a genocide has taken place in Darfur.

Such issues have also arisen in the two countries in which the co-authors of this introduction have conducted ethnographic fieldwork, Guatemala (O'Neill) and Cambodia (Hinton). The politics of memory have been particularly contested in Cambodia, where, during Democratic Kampuchea (DK), Pol Pot's Khmer Rouge enacted policies resulting in the death or execution of 1.7 of Cambodia's 8 million inhabitants—almost a quarter of the population—from 1975 to 1979 (Hinton 2005).

After a Vietnamese-backed army overthrew the Khmer Rouge in January 1979, the sands of memory began to shift (see Hinton 2008). In Cambodia, the People's Republic of Kampuchea (PRK) (ironically, many of the top officials in the PRK were former Khmer Rouge who had been purged by the DK regime) lambasted the genocidal policies of the Khmer Rouge, established the Tuol Sleng Museum of Genocidal Crimes, wrote school texts detailing the atrocities, held public events to commemorate the genocide, and even put on a weeklong tribunal (August 15–19, 1979) that convicted Pol Pot and his deputy, Ieng Sary, of genocide in absentia. Over the ensuing decade the PRK repeatedly called for a UN-sponsored trial of the "Pol Pot–Ieng Sary–Khieu Samphan clique."

Due to geopolitics the international community would have none of it (see Fawthrop and Jarvis 2004). Not only did China and a coalition of

Western powers led by the U.S. refuse to hold such a tribunal, but they allowed the DK regime to hold onto Cambodia's seat at the UN while rearming and supporting the Khmer Rouge in the fight against the PRK, which was portrayed as a puppet of Vietnam. Meanwhile, former DK leaders made speeches in which they asserted that PRK genocide memorials were fabrications and, even more strikingly, that the Vietnamese were perpetrating a genocide in Cambodia. With a handful of exceptions, the international community remained largely mute on the topic while providing the Khmer Rouge with a forum to continue their denials. Even after a peace accord was reached and UN-backed elections were held in 1993, many officials continued to refer to the genocide using the phrase "the unacceptable practices of the recent past."

Ironically, after the 1993 election the U.S. and other governments began to openly use *genocide* to describe the actions of the murderous group that they had directly and indirectly supported since 1979. In fact, in 1994 the United States passed the Cambodian Genocide Justice Act, which prohibited further cooperation with the Khmer Rouge and provided funds for the collection of evidence for a possible tribunal. Only recently, in 2006, was a UN-sponsored tribunal finally set up to bring the surviving leaders of the Khmer Rouge to justice and to pass judgment on whether or not evidence exists to convict former Khmer Rouge leaders of genocide (in the legal sense of the Genocide Convention). Even as these state-level and international-level contestations over the genocide unfolded, individual Cambodians found their own memories and suffering framed first in terms of the genocidal policies of the "Pol Pot–Ieng Sary–Khieu Samphan clique" (during the PRK), then in terms of a public need for forgetting and reconciliation (just after the UN-sponsored election in 1993), and most recently in terms of the need for "truth" that will be revealed by the UN-sponsored tribunal (Hinton 2008).

Guatemala provides another vantage on such shifts in the politics of truth, memory, representation, and genocide, one in which truth commissions have played a prominent role. As we see in the present essays by Victoria Sanford and Debra Rodman, the country's 36-year civil war began after the failure of a nationalist uprising by military officers in 1960. It formally ended on December 29, 1996, with the signing of a peace agreement between the military and counterinsurgent forces in Guatemala City. The roots of the war, however, took hold in 1954 with a U.S.-backed coup of the then democratically elected government. President Jacobo Arbenz's practice of land redistribution—accentuated by a Cold War fear of communism—threatened the United Fruit Company, a U.S.-based corporation and Guatemala's biggest landowner. Following the coup, Guatemala's government became increasingly militarized, while other Ladinos (Guatemalans of "mixed" descent) formed counterinsurgent guerrilla forces.

The struggle between the government and the guerrillas was at first articulated through the language of class conflict. In the 1960s, however, Ladinos incorporated Maya communities, historically excluded by Ladinos, through an ethnic analysis of Guatemala's struggle over freedom of organization, land rights, and democracy. The government's response to these demands throughout the 1960s, 1970s, and 1980s was absolutely brutal, especially between 1978 and 1982. Large-scale massacres, scorched-earth tactics, and massive acts of disappearances and displacements aimed at annihilating Guatemala's Maya population riddled the country with what would later be understood as acts of genocide.

Global awareness of such systematic, large-scale human rights violations forced the Guatemalan government by the mid-1980s to adjust its tactics to continue receiving international aid. Under the protective umbrella of general amnesty and impunity, civilian rule slowly began to shape the agenda alongside the military, while human rights abuses increased and went unpunished. Guatemala's peace process, however, slowly began in 1986, amid political unrest, with a series of talks and accords that ultimately led to a UN-mediated peace process (1994–96) and to the writing of two truth commission reports.

The Oslo Accord, signed in 1994 as part of the UN peace process, initiated the CEH, a project created to investigate human rights violations and to make recommendations on how to promote peace in postwar Guatemala. The Roman Catholic Church's Archbishop's Office for Human Rights (ODHA), motivated by the CEH, initiated its own Recovery of the Historical Memory Project (REMHI), a faith-based truth commission that sought to establish the history of Guatemala's civil conflict and to serve as a basis for justice and national reconciliation.

While they were two distinct projects, both the CEH and the REMHI came to strikingly similar conclusions. According to the CEH, more than two hundred thousand people died or disappeared as a result of the armed conflict, of which more than 80 percent were Maya; the report also establishes that 93 percent of these human rights violations can be connected to the state. In light of the Genocide Convention both projects establish that the Guatemalan state committed acts of genocide against Maya people.

The conclusion that periods of Guatemala's civil war are best understood as genocidal is not an uncontested argument (Nelson 2003). What this book aims to appreciate, however, is not whether Guatemala's civil conflict was or was not genocidal, but how both reports represent genocide. It is certain that both reports functioned as machines of documentation. The commissions collected, analyzed, edited, and published extraordinary amounts of data that form seemingly comprehensive histories of human rights abuses. A close textual analysis, for example, demonstrates that Christian frameworks motivate both representations of genocide (O'Neill 2005). The CEH's ostensibly secular report employs a Christian imagination through its reliance on a conspicuously Protestant image: the testifying individual who works toward reconciliation by giving truthful witness. This central figure condemns genocide as a kind of fallen event. The REMHI's Roman Catholic report, on the other hand, represents Guatemala's genocide analogically as a sacramental moment between Guatemala's communal body and the suffering body of Jesus Christ. While not a celebration of Guatemala's genocide by any stretch of the imagination, the report links the passion narratives to Guatemala's genocidal histories, cultivating religious meaning amid horrific moments: "Despite the profound sorrow with which we have heard these testimonies of human suffering, the memory and image of Christ crucified anew, we can do no less than hope that by renouncing this dark past of horror, and with our determination to rebuild our country, a new climate of hope will emerge with fraternity, solidarity, and understanding" (REMHI 1998:1:xi). Guatemala, then, becomes a case where we see how Christian imaginations inflect not just explicitly Christian truth commission reports but also secular, humanistic, democratic, and Western institutional attempts at remembering genocide.

While acknowledging that such tribunals and truth commissions are often very important to people who have been the victims of mass atrocity, this book nevertheless demonstrates that there are inevitably gray zones (see Sanford this volume; Levi 1989) and silences that are elided from these official accounts. The essays in this volume linger on the disorderliness of genocide, as well as on the inevitable incompleteness of any attempt to remember and represent the truth of mass killings, systematic torture, and deliberate attempts to annihilate a single group of people from the face of the earth.

Through the tools of experience-near, ethnographic methods, then, this volume demonstrates the enmeshments of truth, memory, and representation in genocidal and postgenocidal contexts. To emphasize this point, we have articulated these as a single block: truth/memory/representation. By doing so, we note that each essay, like the cases discussed above, speaks to questions of truth, memory, and representation, albeit in different ways and to different extents. Accordingly, for the sake of analytical clarity, we have compartmentalized each article in terms of emphasis, highlighting one dimension of each to create a coherent, stylized conversation that makes a significant contribution to the anthropology of genocide, genocide studies, and the history of anthropological thought. We do this through the use of boldface, darkening the analytical thread we want to emphasize while also allowing the other two themes to remain present: **truth**/memory/representation, truth/**memory**/representation, and truth/memory/**representation**.[3] The aim for this book's critical reader, then, will be to follow our organizational strategy—noticing the themes that we have selected—but also to read across these editorial decisions to see how each essay can be read in and through each subtitle.

This book also fulfills a research imperative. While scholars in fields such as history, sociology, and literature have increasingly struggled with questions of genocide, truth, memory, and representation, particularly in the context of the Holocaust (e.g., Diner 2000; Friedlander 1992; Hartman 1994; LaCapra 1998; Levi and Rothberg 2003; Postone and Santner 2003; Young 1993), anthropologists have only more recently begun to grapple with such issues, about which they have a great deal to say because of their engaged, experience-near perspective. The burgeoning anthropological interest in genocide has a number of roots, including a growing interest in both modernity and globalization, as well as in violence and terror, a shift from small village studies to those that examine the state-level dynamics in situations of upheaval, flux, and violence, and a greater commitment to reflexivity, historicity, and engaged anthropology. Our aim here is to advance this emerging research trajectory while also giving the conversation shape and structure. In this sense it is important to note the dearth of literature available to date on the anthropology of genocide as a research imperative.

As part of this growing engagement with political violence, a number of anthropologists began writing about genocide, particularly after the genocides of the 1990s in the former Yugoslavia and Rwanda. However, to date the nascent anthropological literature on genocide has been published in diffuse forums—articles, book chapters, a handful of ethnographies, and two edited volumes by Alexander Laban Hinton (2002a, 2002b). No book in anthropology has yet directly grappled with the complex yet crucial relationship of genocide, truth, memory, and representation from a comparative perspective. In doing so, this book fills an important gap while building on and contributing to a growing body of work that explores issues of truth, memory, and representation in relationship to political violence and terror (e.g, Besteman 2002; Das et al. 2000; Das et al. 2001; Feldman 1991; Ferguson 2003; Kleinman, Das, and Lock 1997; Malkki 1995; Nagengast 1994; Nordstrom and Robben 1995; Sanford 2003; Scheper-Hughes and Bourgois 2004; Sluka 2000; Taussig 1984, 1987; Whitehead 2004, Zulaika and Douglass 1996).

Pamela Stewart and Andrew Strathern (2002:3–14) have helped bring back into current anthropological discussion David Riches's earlier (1986) argument that violence is characterized by a structure (it involves a triad of actors: "performer, victim and witness"), competitive stakes ("contested legitimacy"), an aesthetics (it is "highly visible" and performative), and a semantics (as opposed to being "senseless," violence has crucial "expressive" properties and involves shared understandings). Expanding on and introducing some critical points regarding Riches's model, they further explore violence in terms of history, narrative, and performance, a move also influenced by Michael Taussig's (1984, 1987) concurrent work that foregrounded issues of representation, "epistemic murk," and the symbolic and mimetic properties of violence. Such notions were amplified by a number of subsequent ethnographies that focused more directly on political violence, such as Allen Feldman's (1991) analysis of the performative, embodied, and narrative aspects of violence in Northern Ireland, Liisa Malkki's (1995) discussion of "mythico-histories" in the aftermath of the 1972 Burundi genocide, Joseba Zualaika and William Douglass's (1996) work on narratives of terrorism, and E. Valentine Daniel's (1996) discussion of the silences, gaps of meaning, and limits of representation involved in the Sri Lankan conflict—though of course each of these scholars was influenced by other literatures as well.

More recently, several works have reframed such ideas in terms of the imagination, a notion that resonates with Riches's (1986) emphasis on the communicative dimensions of violence, Cornelius Castoriadis's (1987) concept of "the social imaginary," recent studies of globalization, modernity, and the effects of mass mediation (see Appadurai 1996; Anderson 1991; Goankar 2002), and the aftermath of 9/11 (Strathern, Stewart, and Whitehead 2006). What such diverse sources share is a view of the imagination as a creative force that both interprets events in terms of a set of existing cultural codes and generates new constellations of meaning in moments of transformation, chaos, and even radical change. With regard to violence, the imagination involves narratives, performances, embodiments, and symbols that infuse spaces of violence with meaning and communicative value but are creatively reworked through time (e.g., Aijmer and Abbink 2000; Hinton 2005; Schmidt and Schröder 2001; Strathern, Stewart, and Whitehead 2006).

All of this work, both new and old, has relevance for the articles in this volume, which explore how the genocidal past is represented and reimagined, asserted or elided through narratives and counternarratives, remembered or forgotten, avenged or unavenged, and coped with or silenced and ignored in different contexts and historical moments. With regard to Riches in particular, the two cases we discussed earlier and the essays in this book foreground how truth and legitimacy are asserted in postgenocidal contexts, how victims, perpetrators, witnesses, and outside observers may all imagine the past in very different ways, and how these contestations remain highly visible, particularly given the proliferation and rapidity of electronic media. Power remains central to this politics of memory, as some groups have the means—often through the control of government and media—to assert their genocidal imaginary and suppress that of others, even as this genocidal imaginary may be contested and resisted through local protests, ritual, personal remembrance, a lingering sense of wounding, and even silences that refuse to instantiate official narratives.

As this discussion suggests, the stakes involved and the issues discussed in this book are not just intellectual but also political. On the one hand, within anthropology, we intend this volume to fill a crucial gap in the anthropology of genocide by bringing together anthropologists who are conducting cutting-edge research on genocide, truth, memory, and representation in a variety of different contexts including Bali, Germany,

Guatemala, Nigeria, Rwanda, Sudan, East Timor, and the former Yugoslavia. On the other hand, this book intends to be a politically engaged contribution to work on and in postgenocidal contexts, ranging from that of scholars in the field of genocide studies and human rights to that of staff workers at nongovernmental organizations, of aid workers, and of development officers. Outside anthropology there is an urgent need for a book of this kind. Moreover, because of anthropologists' on-the-ground field experience and attunement to local understandings, they have a great deal to offer interdisciplinary discussions about genocide that have taken place in a variety of cultural contexts. This is to say that while scholars in other fields have conducted excellent analyses of the macrolevel factors facilitating genocide, fewer have been able to approach genocide from this type of local perspective. By filling this important niche, this volume is meant to appeal to a wide audience, ranging from scholars and teachers in a variety of fields to activists, legal professionals, and interested lay readers.

What can anthropology contribute to efforts at rebuilding, reconciliation, and relief? A great deal, we argue. The essays in this book attest to this argument, examining such topics as the friction between state discourses and personal experience; how people cope with, respond to, and remember genocide when the state foments a regime of silence or of forgetting about the events; how the state attempts to strengthen political identity (thereby increasing its popular support) by creating "emotive institutions" (White 2005) and discourses of remembering that link its followers through a shared suffering and outrage; how individual strategies of coping with trauma are affected and ruptured by such state initiatives or silences; how the very act of writing about or representing genocide both clarifies and occludes memories and understandings of the genocidal past; and how local frames for comprehending genocidal acts articulate with and diverge from global discourses.

PART 1: **TRUTH**/MEMORY/REPRESENTATION

> There are no whole truths: all truths are half-truths.
> —Alfred North Whitehead, *Dialogues*

It is difficult but important to approach the issue of truth in relationship to genocide. It is difficult because so many people were killed, suffered enormously, or remain enraged about the violence to which they were subjected. To avoid misinterpretation, we want to be clear that we fully recognize the reality of such mass violence, a reality that both of the authors have confronted directly in their fieldwork. Did the Holocaust really happen? Of course. Were indigenous peoples throughout the Americas victims of genocide? Yes.

Nevertheless, it is important that we remain open to exploring the ways in which *discourses about* truth have been deployed—including the manner in which dominant state discourses may silence or even deny the experiences and memories of victims. To this end, this volume risks for the sake of analytical sophistication a more nuanced understanding of truth within genocide and postgenocidal spaces. That is, this volume wants to sidestep "black-and-white" conversations to explore how the idea and felt-reality of truth within postgenocidal contexts come to be lived by survivors and perpetrators alike. As Whitehead suggests in the above epigraph, issues of truth and falsity are never simply black and white but involve shades of gray. Genocidal and postgenocidal spaces provide haunting examples of this.

Victoria Sanford's essay, "What Is an Anthropology of Genocide? Reflections on Field Research with Maya Survivors in Guatemala," turns this tension between truth and falsity into an ethnographic problematic through the work of Dominick LaCapra and Primo Levi. Drawing on over ten years of fieldwork with Maya survivors in postgenocidal Guatemala, Sanford addresses the question of truth along with questions of memory and representation. She asks: What do questions of truth and truthfulness mean for ethnographers whose very research depends on the collected stories and testimonies of survivors and perpetrators? Borrowing the concept from Levi, Sanford explores what she calls the "grey zone" of research, arguing that the memory of survivors and perpetrators in postgenocidal contexts will undoubtedly reveal ruptures and contradictions in communities of survivors.

Rather than as a methodological crisis, Sanford reads this predicament as a theoretical opportunity to "push and redefine the limits of anthropological research on genocide." Striking at the nature of testimony itself, Sanford argues that the truth of narrative—as well as the truth of memory and of representation—lies in its ability to unsettle more "authentic" accounts of genocide. The excavation of testimonies in postgenocidal contexts, for example, contributes to the reconstruction of political subjectivities. Sanford makes this point by drawing on her own research on the evacuation of clandestine gravesites in Guatemala. For Sanford and her informants the exhumation of remains contributes to the making of collective memories, as well as to the political will to resist more official and often state-sponsored truths. The grey zone of research is thus the answer to Sanford's own question, what is an anthropology of genocide? By her account, an anthropology of genocide involves the excavation of marginalized voices in postgenocidal contexts to contribute to the construction of political subjectivities and of unofficial, but no less true, political spaces of resistance.

In her essay, "Perilous Outcomes: International Monitoring and the Perpetuation of Violence in Sudan," Sharon E. Hutchinson undoes seemingly truthful assumptions about international human rights monitoring groups and the implied neutrality that these groups, as well as the truths they deliver, carry. Hutchinson's article points to gray half-truths. Based on fieldwork as an official monitor in the Sudan, Hutchinson's work provides a case study that writes against the assumption that international monitoring teams are essentially benign. In reality, these teams—and truths themselves—are never neutral, and well-intentioned efforts can have counterproductive outcomes. Monitoring teams may actually yield, as Hutchinson's title suggests, perilous outcomes.

Hutchinson enumerates many generalizable problems in her case study, providing points of reference for scholars in other postgenocidal contexts. For example, the international human rights monitoring team in Sudan did not address the issue of proportionality lying at the heart of international humanitarian law, failed to contextualize allegations of military violence, did not explain the criteria by which some incidents were selected for investigation rather than others, projected the "illusion of neutrality," did not document the military shifts of power and territory under the group's watch, and (implicitly) condoned the forward movement of government military troops despite the existence of several internationally brokered military stand-down agreements explicitly prohibiting such movement. The human rights field operation, Hutchinson argues, ultimately did more to excuse and condone military violence against southern Sudanese civilians than to restrain or rectify military violence. Hutchinson's essay, in all, raises the problem of international monitoring operations, including those in postgenocidal contexts. While the supposed truths of international human rights monitoring operations will always be incomplete, Hutchinson points to concrete investigative strategies and reporting priorities that could reduce the possibility that such missions will inadvertently reinforce an atmosphere of military impunity.

In her essay, "Whose Genocide? Whose Truth? Representations of Victim and Perpetrator in Rwanda," Jennie E. Burnet continues where Hutchinson ends, arguing that the Rwandan government's articulation of national unity through the commemoration of genocide has actually polarized survivors and stunted their ability to mourn. The polarization occurred during the discursive construction of victim and perpetrator in postgenocidal Rwanda. At the center of Burnet's ethnographic account is an annual day of remembrance that takes the form of a national mourning ceremony. The ceremony functions as a space where national discourses are made on and about the Rwandan genocide. In this space, there is an emphasis on a seemingly naturalized difference between victim and perpetrator—between Tutsi and Hutu.

Burnet argues that this representation of the Rwandan genocide fails to capture the complexity of the varied subject positions within postgenocide Rwanda and that this national discourse, in turn, marginalizes many of those who were victims of the genocide but who nonetheless do not fit within these two distinct categories. Moreover, Burnet shows how these national discourses structure the social reality that survivors must now negotiate in their daily lives. Hutu widows of the genocide, for example, find it difficult to get sufficient financial assistance from international relief organizations, noting that the government uses their plight to marshal aid but then fails to deliver that aid to them. Burnet makes the point that representations of the truth of genocide, especially state-sponsored attempts at mourning, have concrete effects on those who carry on in postgenocidal contexts.

PART 2: TRUTH/**MEMORY**/REPRESENTATION

> Memory may almost become the art of continually varying and misrepresenting the past, according to one's interests in the present.
>
> —George Santayana, *Persons and Places I*

Just as the production of truth in postgenocidal contexts is often cast in shades of gray, so, too, are memories in these traumatic spaces selective. Take, for example, truth and reconciliation commissions (TRCs), which now produce an established genre of human rights literature, the TRC report (Hayner 1994, 2002). Functioning as machines of documentation, these commissions collect, analyze, edit, and publish extraordinary amounts of data that form seemingly comprehensive histories of genocide. They do so with standard techniques of memory making: first-person testimonies, statistical analysis, charts, graphs, case studies, photographs, and historical periodization (O'Neill 2005). Anthropological theory, however, tells us that these acts of remembering yield "systems from chaos" (Taussig 1987:xiv) through objectivity (Rosaldo 1989), generalizations (Abu Lughod 1991), interview-based research (Dwyer 1982), notions of truth (Tyler 1986), and colonial relationships (Asad 1973).[4] The politics of memory, as Santayana explains, involves continually reworking the past "according to one's interests in the present."

Drawing on the experiences of Balinese in the aftermath of 1965–66, Leslie Dwyer's essay, "A Politics of Silences: Violence, Memory, and Treacherous Speech in Post-1965 Bali," explores the dynamics of presence and absence in this politics of memory. Although Bali is a well-worn anthropological space, most scholars who worked in Indonesia after 1965–66 rarely mentioned the country's history of genocide, concluding that Balinese no longer wished or perhaps were unable to speak about this troubled time. The national history textbooks also fail to reference a genocidal violence in which some 80,000–100,000 people were killed. Dwyer asks, placing the question of memory at the fore: Why had 1965–66 seemed to have disappeared not only from the popular imagination and from expert attention but from the lives of Balinese themselves? Dwyer's haunting insights suggest that acts of forgetting genocide must form a part of any study on and about remembering genocide. Dwyer advocates listening to the marginal stories that anthropologists are best able to engage through the practice of ethnography. There, in the margins of mass violence, anthropologists are able to begin to read silences and moments of forgetting.

Uli Linke's essay, "The Limits of Empathy: Emotional Anesthesia and the Museum of Corpses in Post-Holocaust Germany," also explores the dark side of memory: forgetting. She places at the center of her piece a tension between the unprecedented successes of "Body Worlds," an art exhibition comprised of stylized corpses, and memories of the Holocaust in postgenocidal Germany. What allows the display of dead bodies to be so successful in a space where dead bodies had long been painful referents to an even more painful past? Linke argues that a kind of coldness, a kind of forgetting, has allowed "Body Worlds" to become the most visited exhibit in Germany's history. Part of this forgetting, Linke continues, involves the sexualization of the bodies on display. Enlarged genitalia, distinctly gendered poses, and the housing of the exhibit in Germany's Erotic Art Museum exist as strategies to negate the humanity of the bodies on display. As Linke argues, objectified bodies have no history and, in turn, are not the subject of empathy. This process of dehumanization facilitated the success of "Body Worlds" in post-Holocaust Germany and raises questions about the limits of empathy and about strategies employed to cope and to forget in other postgenocidal contexts. How, her essay asks us, do sites of memorialization, like museums, serve as places of forgetting, where self-reflexivity and the engagements of feelings are numbed?

In her essay, "Forgotten Guatemala: Genocide, Truth, and Denial in Guatemala's Oriente," Debra Rodman explores areas largely unaffected by Guatemala's genocide, detailing how national and international media construct the memories of genocide for indigenous and nonindigenous (Ladino) persons alike in postwar Guatemala. Rodman pays particular attention to the oral histories that stand in stark contrast to how anthropologists and international observers remember Guatemala's genocidal history. Based on fieldwork in Guatemala's interior, Rodman focuses on the theme of denial, noting how a culture of fear and violence paradoxically allowed both Ladinos and Maya to deny the war and genocidal dimensions. For example, many Ladinos do not accept the concept of a civil war, choosing to believe instead that the army invented the guerrillas to maintain control of the indigenous population and to eliminate the Maya population. Rodman found that many in the region tend to accept the state-sponsored belief that the violence is not political but a result of delinquency. Rodman also provides examples of people attributing the civil war and the massacres that accompanied it to family feuds. In the end, Rodman lists several more ways in which Guatemala's genocidal civil war is denied or made neutral and then forgotten by many.

> Chaos is the score upon which reality is written.
> —Henry Miller, *Tropic of Cancer*

Representation, like truth, is a gray area and, like memory, is selective and constituted in part by the act of forgetting. As Miller suggests, representations of genocide are written against a backdrop of enormous upheaval, suffering, and chaos. This tension between (inevitably narrowed) assertions of reality and the enormity of genocide is evident in the attempts of scholars, government officials, survivors, and perpetrators—to name but a few—to represent what are otherwise ineffable crimes against humanity. The politics and poetics of writing about genocide thus produce situated knowledges that force us to ask how the act of representing genocide may make genocide itself into the cultural category we have come to know.

Elizabeth F. Drexler's essay, "Addressing the Legacies of Mass Violence and Genocide in Indonesia and East Timor," addresses this question, making clear that memories are never unmediated and that with issues of violence and genocide, the truth never simply awaits discovery. Drawing on her fieldwork in postgenocidal East Timor, Drexler explores the dense interconnections between institutions and representations, focusing most squarely on the inability of postindependence institutional responses to violence to curb genocidal state violence. Drexler writes, "The transitional institutions have failed not only to demonstrate how conditions of civil war could develop but also to hold the Indonesian military accountable for the violence it perpetrated."

Drexler's essay aims to reposition and, in some instances, refashion advocacy in postgenocidal contexts based on a greater awareness of how violence and genocide are represented. Drexler's ethnographic focus on transitional governments emphasizes the ad hoc, theatrical nature of representation within genocidal contexts and how tribunals and special panels, for example, create dubious histories of causation, conspiracy, and complicity. In the article Drexler also raises problems with the practice of transcription and translation—the very tools through which genocide is represented. In the case of East Timor these technical problems questioned the legitimacy and the promise of postgenocidal reconciliation. Through the lens of anthropological field methods, Drexler found that betrayal and collaboration, rather than reconciliation, colored the representation of official accounts of violence in East Timor. Drexler's argument recognizes the importance of representing violence in international forums, but it is also critical of representations of mass violence, suggesting that the very conditions that enabled mass violence to occur actually structure the representation of mass violence as well.

Conerly Casey's essay, "Mediated Hostility: Media, Affective Citizenship, and Genocide in Northern Nigeria," focuses on how national and transnational media contribute to the formation of new modes of citizenship—feelings of belonging with the state—in Nigeria against the backdrop of violent conflict. In Nigeria local media represent the political sentiments of majority ethnic groups (Hausa, Yoruba, and Igbo) and religions (Islam and Christianity) that are embedded in historical memories of communal violence and genocidal massacres. Focusing on instances of such violence and on perpetrators, Casey emphasizes that the construction of killers (subjects) and victims (objects) involves media as a mode of power.

Central to Casey's argument is the idea that media disrupts the temporality of history, creating entangled representations of social reality. In media-saturated places such as northern Nigeria, Casey argues, youths' uncertain experiences of local conflicts become placed next to regional and global media images of political unrest. The result is an affective citizenship constituted by "historical ruptures of identity, memory, emotion, and agency, processes that become sediment within the body and enacted by the body." The intent here is to make clear that media representations play an especially important role in the construction of political belonging among Nigerian youths who are (or who may become) perpetrators in genocidal massacres.

In her essay, "Cleansed of Experience? Genocide, Ethnic Cleansing, and the Challenges of Anthropological Representation," Pamela Ballinger asks the important question: What does the analytical category "ethnic cleansing" allow scholars of violence to see (and not see) as compared to the category of "genocide"? Engaging her fieldwork in the former Yugoslavia, Ballinger questions the very tools that scholars use to represent genocidal activities. The major concern here is with experience, particularly the kinds of experience the phrase *ethnic cleansing* brings into focus and the kinds of experience thus removed from critical analyses. Following a genealogical review of the term *ethnic cleansing*, Ballinger turns to a case study of what some scholars call Yugoslavia's first instance of ethnic cleansing:

Istria. This case study provides a number of details that strain the categories of both genocide and ethnic cleansing, demonstrating that scholars must be careful when representing mass violence. On the one hand, the Istrian case involves hundreds of thousands of refugees. Yet while *genocide* and *ethnic cleansing* suggest the production of complete victims, forced migration out of Istria happened over the course of several years and for multiple reasons. Genocide or ethnic cleansing did not happen all at once, nor did mass violence crash down on the population of Istria like a wave. The events were much more diffuse, much grayer. This case study challenges the implied structure and essence of common representations of genocide and ethnic cleansing. On the other hand, the term *ethnic cleansing* does refocus attention on the ethnic dimensions of violence in and beyond the Istria case. Ballinger's argument problematizes the classifications and analytical categories that scholars use, noting that scholarly representations of genocide have an effect as well.

CONCLUSION: TRUTH/MEMORY/REPRESENTATION AND IMAGINATION

> Some distortion is inherent in every attempt to achieve
> stability or closure, as history changes into memory and its
> institutionalization.
> —Geoffrey Hartman, "Darkness Visible"

Genocide staggers the imagination. On the one hand, victims, if not all of us, struggle to comprehend the enormity of genocide. On the other hand, genocide's very enormity provides potent fodder for imaginings (and the parallel silencings and forgettings that ensue) of the genocidal past—what we earlier referred to as the "genocidal imaginary." Truth, memory, and representation mix together in a given space and moment of time to construct a reality that, while partial and incomplete, nevertheless may have powerful effects on those interpellated into or subjugated by such a discursive regime.

Antonius C. G. M. Robben's epilogue, "The Imagination of Genocide," concludes this book by drawing out two key themes that cut through the essays: imagination and incomprehension. While anthropologists and other scholars pursue their research on and in postgenocidal spaces, most have never directly experienced genocide or lived through the chaos that they are trying to capture. Most scholars thus rely on their imaginations. The imagination, Robben makes clear, only takes us so far, as genocide itself is impossible to directly and fully know, comprehend, and represent. Genocide's ineffable qualities and the distances that exist between the anthropologist and genocidal events are thus poignant and powerful notions with which both to begin and to end this book.

Rather than seeking straightforward truths, memories, and representations, the reader is encouraged to follow the book's guiding problematics and questions, which focus not on veracity or realism but on the cultural work that practices of truth, memory, and representation do in postgenocidal contexts and on how that work differs from one social and historical space to another. Anthropologists, as this book in general and Robben's epilogue in particular demonstrate, rely on their imaginations to understand the incomprehensible, but in a way that uncovers how and why truth, memory, and representation exist as entangled efforts in spaces of such traumatic and horrific acts of mass violence.

NOTES

1. These numbers are taken from Charny 1999; Kuper 1981; and Totten, Parsons, and Charny 1997. It is notoriously difficult to determine the exact number of dead in genocide, a reality that has led to many controversies. As several of the essays in this volume demonstrate, such debates are often closely bound up with the politics of memory and representation.

2. Article 2 of the 1948 UN Genocide Convention defines genocide as follows: "In the present Convention, genocide means any of the following acts committed with intent to destroy, in whole or in part, a national, ethnical, racial or religious group, as such: (a) Killing members of the group; (b) Causing serious bodily or mental harm to members of the group; (c) Deliberately inflicting on the group conditions of life calculated to bring about its physical destruction in whole or in part; (d) Imposing measures intended to prevent births within the group; (e) Forcibly transferring children of the group to another group." In an effort to address the problem of numbers (i.e., how many people must be killed before mass murder may be considered genocide), Leo Kuper proposed that smaller-scale "genocidal massacres" are "expressed characteristically in the annihilation of a section of a group—men, women, and children, as for example in the wiping out of whole villages. This is in part because the genocidal massacre has some of the elements of genocide" (1981:10). Like many other scholars of genocide, the co-editors prefer a broad definition of genocide that encompasses a variety of collectivities, including political and economic groups as well as other sorts of groupings found in different cultural traditions. Along these

lines Helen Fein (1990) has proposed defining genocide as "sustained purposeful action by a perpetrator to physically destroy a collectivity directly or indirectly, through interdiction of the biological and social reproduction of group members, sustained regardless of the surrender or lack of threat offered by the victim" (1990:24; see also Chalk and Jonassohn 1990:23; Hinton 2002b).

3. See Dirks, Eley, and Ortner (1994) on this organizational strategy.

4. This particular constellation of critiques of anthropology comes from an article by Roy D'Andrade (1995).

REFERENCES

Abu Lughod, Lila
1991   Writing against Culture. *In* Recapturing Anthropology: Working in the Present. Richard G. Fox, ed. Pp. 37–62. Santa Fe: School of American Research Press.

Aijmer, Göran, and Jon Abbink, eds.
2000   Meanings of Violence: A Cross-Cultural Perspective. Oxford: Berg.

Anderson, Benedict
1991   Imagined Communities: Reflections on the Origins and Spread of Nationalism. Rev. 2nd edition. New York: Verso.

Appadurai, Arjun
1996   Modernity at Large: Cultural Dimensions of Globalization. Minneapolis: University of Minnesota Press.

Asad, Talal, ed.
1973   Anthropology and the Colonial Encounter. London: Ithaca.

Besteman, Catherine, ed.
2002   Violence: A Reader. New York: Palgrave Macmillan.

Castoriadis, Cornelius
1987   The Imaginary Institution of Society. Kathleen Blamey, trans. Cambridge: MIT Press.

Chalk, Frank, and Kurt Jonassohn
1990   The History and Sociology of Genocide: Analyses and Case Studies. New Haven: Yale University Press.

Charny, Israel W., ed.
1999   Encyclopedia of Genocide. 2 vols. Santa Barbara, CA: ABC-CLIO.

Comisión para el Esclarecimiento Histórico (CEH)
1999   Guatemala: Memoria del silencio. 12 volumes. Guatemala City: CEH.

D'Andrade, Roy
1995   Moral Models in Anthropology. Current Anthropology 36(3):399–408.

Daniel, E. Valentine
1996   Charred Lullabies: Chapters in an Anthropology of Violence. Princeton:
            Princeton University Press.

Das, Veena, Arthur Kleinman, Margaret Lock, Mamphela Ramphele, and Pamela
            Reynolds, eds.
2001   Remaking a World: Violence, Social Suffering, and Recovery. Berkeley:
            University of California Press.

Das, Veena, Arthur Kleinman, Mamphela Ramphele, and Pamela Reynolds, eds.
2000   Violence and Subjectivity. Berkeley: University of California Press.

Diner, Dan
2000   Beyond the Conceivable: Studies on Germany, Nazism, and the Holo-
            caust. Berkeley: University of California Press.

Dirks, Nicholas B., Geoff Eley, and Sherry B. Ortner, eds.
1994   Culture/Power/History: A Reader in Contemporary Social Theory.
            Princeton: Princeton University Press.

Dwyer, Kevin
1982   Moroccan Dialogues. Baltimore: Johns Hopkins University Press.

Fawthrop, Tom, and Helen Jarvis
2004   Getting Away with Genocide? Elusive Justice and the Khmer Rouge
            Tribunal. Ann Arbor, MI: Pluto.

Fein, Helen
1990   Genocide: A Sociological Perspective. Current Sociology 38(1):v–126.

Feldman, Allen
1991   Formations of Violence: The Narrative of the Body and Political Terror in
            Northern Ireland. Chicago: University of Chicago Press.

Ferguson, R. Brian, ed.
2003   The State, Identity, and Violence: Political Disintegration in the Post–
            Cold War World. New York: Routledge.

Friedlander, Saul, ed.
1992   Probing the Limits of Representation: Nazism and the Final Solution.
            Cambridge: Harvard University Press.

Goankar, Dilip Parameshwar
2002   Toward New Imaginaries: An Introduction. Public Culture 14(1):1–9.

Hartman, Geoffrey H., ed.
1994   Holocaust Remembrance: The Shapes of Memory. Oxford: Blackwell.

Hayner, Priscilla B.
1994   Fifteen Truth Commissions, 1974–1994: A Comparative Study. Human
            Rights Quarterly 16:597–655.

2002 Unspeakable Truths: Facing the Challenge of Truth Commissions. New York: Routledge.

Hinton, Alexander Laban
2005 Why Did They Kill? Cambodia in the Shadow of Genocide. Berkeley: University of California Press.
2008 Truth, Representation and the Politics of Memory after Genocide. *In* People of Virtue: Reconfiguring Religion, Power and Morality in Cambodia Today. Copenhagen: NIAS Press.

Hinton, Alexander Laban, ed.
2002a Annihilating Difference: The Anthropology of Genocide. Berkeley: University of California Press.
2002b Genocide: An Anthropological Reader. Malden, MA: Blackwell.

Kleinman, Arthur, Veena Das, and Margaret Lock, eds.
1997 Social Suffering. Berkeley: University of California Press.

Kuper, Leo
1981 Genocide: Its Political Use in the Twentieth Century. New Haven: Yale University Press.

LaCapra, Dominick
1998 History and Memory after Auschwitz. Ithaca: Cornell University Press.

Lemkin, Raphaël
1944 Axis Rule in Occupied Europe: Laws of Occupation, Analysis of Government, Proposals for Redress. Washington: Carnegie Endowment for International Peace, Division of International Law.

Levi, Neil, and Michael Rothberg, eds.
2003 The Holocaust: Theoretical Readings. New Brunswick, NJ: Rutgers University Press.

Levi, Primo
1989 The Drowned and the Saved. New York: Vintage.

Malkki, Liisa H.
1995 Purity and Exile: Violence, Memory, and National Cosmology among Hutu Refugees in Tanzania. Chicago: University of Chicago Press.

Miller, Henry
1961 [1934] Tropic of Cancer. New York: Grove.

Nagengast, Carole
1994 Violence, Terror, and the Crisis of the State. Annual Review of Anthropology 23:109–136.

Nelson, Diane
2003 The More You Kill the More You Will Live: The Maya, "Race," and Biopolitical Hopes for Peace in Guatemala. *In* Race, Nature, and the Politics of

Difference. Donald S. Moore, Jake Kosek, and Anand Pandian, eds. Pp. 122–146. Durham, NC: Duke University Press.

Nordstrom, Carolyn, and Antonius C. G. M. Robben, eds.
1995   Fieldwork under Fire: Contemporary Studies of Violence and Survival. Berkeley: University of California Press.

O'Neill, Kevin Lewis
2005   Writing Guatemala's Genocide: Christianity and Truth and Reconciliation Commissions. Journal for Genocide Research 7(3):310–331.

Padilla, Herberto
1993   History. *In* Against Forgetting: Twentieth-Century Poetry of Witness. C. Forché, ed. P. 602. New York: Norton.

Postone, Moishe, and Eric Santner, eds.
2003   Catastrophe and Meaning: The Holocaust and the Twentieth Century. Chicago: University of Chicago Press.

Proyecto Interdiocesano de Recuperación de la Memoria Histórica (REMHI)
1998   Guatemala: Nunca más. 4 vols. Guatemala City: Oficina de Derechos Humanos Arzobispado de Guatemala.

Recovery of Historical Memory Project (REMHI)
1999   Guatemala: Never Again. Gretta Tovar Siebentritt, trans. New York: Orbis.

Riches, David
1986   The Phenomenon of Violence. *In* The Anthropology of Violence. David Riches, ed. Pp. 1–27. Oxford: Blackwell.

Rosaldo, Renato
1989   Culture and Truth: The Remaking of Social Analysis. Boston: Beacon.

Sanford, Victoria
2003   Buried Secrets: Truth and Human Rights in Guatemala. New York: Palgrave Macmillan.

Santayana, George
1944   Persons and Places. New York: Scribner.

Scheper-Hughes, Nancy, and Philippe Bourgois, eds.
2004   Violence in War and Peace: An Anthology. Malden, MA: Blackwell.

Scheper-Hughes, Nancy, and Margaret Lock
1985   Speaking "Truth" to Illness: Metaphors, Reifications, and a Pedagogy for Patients. Medical Anthropology Quarterly 17(5):137–140.

Schmidt, Bettina E., and Ingo W. Schröder, eds.
2001   Anthropology of Violence and Conflict. New York: Routledge.

Sluka, Jeffrey A., ed.
2000   Death Squad: The Anthropology of State Terror. Philadelphia: University
            of Pennsylvania Press.

Stewart, Pamela J., and Andrew Strathern
2002   Violence: Theory and Ethnography. New York: Continuum.

Strathern, Andrew, Pamela J. Stewart, and Neil L. Whitehead, eds.
2006   Terror and Violence: Imagination and the Unimaginable. London: Pluto.

Taussig, Michael
1984   Culture of Terror, Space of Death: Roger Casement's Putumayo Report
            and the Explanation of Torture. Comparative Studies in Society and His-
            tory 26(3):467–497.
1987   Shamanism, Colonialism, and the Wild Man: A Study in Terror and
            Healing. Chicago: University of Chicago Press.

Totten, Samuel, William S. Parsons, and Israel W. Charny, eds.
1997   Century of Genocide: Eyewitness Accounts and Critical Views. New
            York: Garland.

Tyler, Stephen
1986   Post-Modern Ethnography. In Writing Cultures: The Poetics and Politics
            of Ethnography. James Clifford and George E. Marcus, eds. Pp. 122–140.
            Berkeley: University of California Press.

White, Geoffrey M.
2005   Emotive Institutions. In A Companion to Psychological Anthropology:
            Modernity and Psychocultural Change. Conerly Casey and Robert B.
            Edgerton, eds. Pp. 241–254. Malden, MA: Blackwell.

Whitehead, Alfred North
1954   Dialogues. Boston: Little, Brown.

Whitehead, Neil L., ed.
2004   Violence. Santa Fe: School of American Research Press.

Young, James Edward
1993   The Texture of Memory: Holocaust Memorials and Meaning. New
            Haven: Yale University Press.

Zulaika, Joseba, and William A. Douglass
1996   Terror and Taboo: The Follies, Fables, and Faces of Terrorism. New York:
            Routledge.

1   **TRUTH**/MEMORY/REPRESENTATION

Victoria Sanford

1   WHAT IS AN ANTHROPOLOGY

OF GENOCIDE?

Reflections on Field Research with Maya Survivors in Guatemala

Genocide is a problem not only of war but also of peace.
—Raphaël Lemkin, *Axis Rule in Occupied Europe: Laws of Occupation,
Analysis of Government, Proposals for Redress*

This essay draws on the work of Dominick LaCapra (2001) and
Primo Levi (1989) to consider the limits of memory and the
challenges of anthropological research on genocide. In particular, I borrow Levi's concept of the "grey zone" to consider the
lived experiences of Maya youth who were both victims and
victimizers in the Guatemalan genocide. Based on more than
a decade of field research on the exhumations of clandestine
cemeteries of Maya massacre victims,[1] I consider the excavation of individual and collective memory as a cultural and political act of community reconstruction. I suggest that both the
accretion of truth and political space in the exhumation of clandestine cemeteries are central to the processes of reclaiming
cultural memory and of contesting dominant metanarratives
that negate subaltern subjectivity and buttress official histories
of denial. I trace political agency and the development of new
subjectivities in Maya communities over time. I ask, "What is
an anthropology of genocide?" to provide a framework for my
reflections on field research with Maya survivors of genocide.
It is my hope that this framework is useful for reflecting on field

research on genocide and violence in other contexts (see also Strathern, Stewart, and Whitehead 2006; Riches 1991). This essay is my modest attempt to share both the survivor memories and the challenge they present to the researcher in the field who, while overwhelmed by the sensation of their immediacy and sorrow, seeks to understand the lived experiences of survivors in such a way that they might make sense to survivors, researchers, and readers.

THE LIMITS OF MEMORY AND RESEARCH

The Auschwitz survivor Levi wrote: "It is natural and obvious that the most substantial material for the reconstruction of truth about the camps is the memories of the survivors" (1989:16). Holding this same belief in the value of testimony a half century later and on a different continent, the Guatemalan anthropologist Ricardo Falla lived with survivors of Guatemalan army massacres who were still in flight from army attacks in the northern Ixcán region of the country.[2] While he accompanied Maya survivors in their hardship, he took their testimonies of survival. In 1992 Falla published *Masacres de la selva* based on some 700 testimonies. That same year I completed a yearlong project of taping the life history of Mateo, a Mam Maya child survivor of the Ixcán massacres, who had been recruited by the guerrillas, the civil patrols, and the army before reaching the age of 15. At the time of our project, Mateo was a 19-year-old refugee attending high school in San Francisco. Falla documented two survival stories that are of interest for our consideration of the limits of memory and of the challenge of research on genocide.[3] Mateo had never met Falla, nor had he read his work, yet he gave similar testimony regarding these two survivor stories.

Falla's witness remembers:[4]

> An 8-year-old girl survived because they tied a rope around her neck and tightened it, "they saw the tongue coming out of the girl and thought she was dead." An old man of 75 was cut in the neck by the soldiers, and he also lived because "the knife got stuck on a button in his shirt, and the soldiers thought they had hit the bone and there was blood, so they kicked him and left him for dead." A couple and their baby girl also survived. They threw themselves into the river from a bridge. She was carrying the baby of 1½ years and the woman was hit by a bullet from

the bridge, but she did not die, neither did her baby. "God is great," says the witness, because these five survived. (1992:57)

Mateo remembers what was recounted to his family by the survivors:

The army arrived to another center very close to our village. The people were at church praying. The soldiers surrounded the church, doused it with gas, and burned it with the people inside. Other families were burned too because the church was built with carton and palms and close to some other little, palm houses. So they caught fire and burned as well. There were about 10 families and the army captured them and put them into a line.

My father's compadre and comadre were in this line. One-by-one, the army would grab each person in line, beat them and ask them questions. The soldiers beat the campesinos and they killed them. But my father's compadre was old. They tied him up and they stabbed him three times in the neck and they cut him in other places, too. But because he was so old, his skin didn't break enough. First the soldiers were mad because he didn't die. Then when he looked bad off, they said, "Now, he is dead." Then, they threw him in a hole. He stayed there.

Next, the soldiers took his daughter and they tortured her with a rope. They put a rope around her neck and pulled the ends of the rope until they thought she was dead, too. Then, they threw her in the same hole. They told us later that the army left them there for dead.

Behind them, were some other friends waiting their turn. He was very religious and was with his wife and baby girl, maybe she was one year old. The baby was crying. The father said, "Why don't we pray? Let's give ourselves to God because our time has arrived. Only a few more people and it will be our turn and they will kill us." The soldiers were shouting, "This is what we are going to do to everyone!" They were killing people and chopping them up. They cut them up with machetes and they tortured them and raped the women.

So the man and woman gave themselves to God and as they were praying an idea occurred to them. They were very close to the river which was running very high because it was winter. The man said to the woman in their language, "Let's leave. We will try to escape and if they kill us, it is worth it because we will die from bullets. Because if they kill us like they are killing the other people, we are going to suffer a lot. We have seen how they are dying. They are going to kill us just like them."

They decided to escape and cross the river. Even if they drowned in the river, they would still suffer less. So they gave themselves to God because they had great faith. They had faith. He grabbed his wife's hand and they ran. When they reached the river, the army was firing at them. But as the family reached the water's edge, the river lowered its water and the family passed to freedom. When they reached the other side of the river, the water rose again.

The soldiers were chasing them, trying to catch them, and firing bullets. When the water rose again, it drowned some soldiers. But the family was safe on the other side. It was a miracle of God because they had faith in God and because no one else can lower the river. They came to our house at six in the morning because they were like family for us. The old man came with his daughter because he was my father's compadre. (Sanford 1993)

While Falla's witness corroborates Mateo's testimony, together Falla's witness and Mateo raise a number of issues about the limits of memory and of research on genocide. First, only the five survivors and the soldiers who committed the atrocities know exactly what happened because they are the only witnesses to this particular massacre. Second, everyone tries to make sense of terror in his or her own way. Falla's witness believes the man survived because a button protected him, while Mateo believes it was the old man's leathery skin that stopped the knife from getting down to the bone. Massacres are not neat enterprises. Perhaps it was a button or thick skin, but maybe it was just plain sloppiness in an assembly-line massacre.

Both Falla's witness and Mateo attribute the survival of these five people to the grace of God. The literary beauty and possible doubt raised by the river parting in Mateo's account is almost insignificant in the face of a horror so great that mere survival becomes a miraculous feat. To not die in the unbridled terror of a village massacre in Guatemala was so incomprehensible to both Mateo and Falla's witness that both had to use divine intervention as an explanation for the extraordinary phenomenon of surviving genocide.

In his work on the trauma and history of the Holocaust, LaCapra points out how testimonies "provide something other than purely documentary knowledge. Testimonies are significant in the attempt to understand experience and its aftermath, including the role of memory and its lapses, in coming to terms with—or denying or repressing—the past" (2001:86–87). As an example LaCapra cites the work of Dori Laub for the Yale Fortunoff collection of Holocaust survivor videos. LaCapra recounts Laub's story of a woman narrating her survival and her memories of witnessing the Auschwitz uprising: "All of a sudden, we saw four chimneys going up in flames, exploding. The flames shot in the sky, people were running. It was unbelievable" (LaCapra 2001:87). Laub recounts how this woman's testimony was screened "to better understand the era" several months later at a conference on education and the Holocaust. A heated discussion ensued because historians disputed the testimony, claiming that it was inaccurate because one chimney had blown up at Auschwitz, not four. This "error" in her testimony led many to conclude that all events recounted in her testimony were therefore inaccurate (LaCapra 2001:88).

Laub is a psychoanalyst and actually participated in the interview of this woman. He came to a different conclusion about the veracity of the testimony: "The woman was testifying," he says, "not to the number of chimneys blown up, but to something else, more radical, more crucial: the reality of an unimaginable occurrence. One chimney blown up at Auschwitz was as incredible as four. The number mattered less than the fact of the occurrence. The event itself was almost inconceivable. The woman testified to an event that broke the all compelling frame of Auschwitz, where Jewish armed revolts just did not happen, and had no place. She testified to the breakage of a framework. That was historical truth" (LaCapra 2001:88).

Laub's story, as LaCapra suggests, "prompts one to raise the questions of traumatic memory and its relation to memory both in the ordinary sense of the word and in its more critical sense insofar as it is tested and, within limits, controlled by historical research" (2001:89). When presenting ethnographic material and sharing the testimonies of massacre survivors in academic and policy venues, I have often been asked, "How do you know they are telling you the truth? How do you decide what is true?" While one might believe that these questions themselves reflect the disbelief of the person asking the question, I have come to believe that these questions more reflect a desire for an orderly and tangible world—a world that, if it ever existed, is turned upside down and made surreal by the obscenity of war and genocide. In her work on trauma and recovery, Judith Herman has observed: "Traumatic events destroy the victim's fundamental assumptions about the safety of the world, the positive value of self, and the meaningful order of creation" (1992:51). Thus memories of survival seem both obscene and surreal to those who have not experienced it or have not come close to it through its recounting by survivors. Conversely, those who have experienced and survived extreme state violence, regardless of place and time, often comment that the testimonies resonate with their own experiences of survival. Indeed, Indonesians, South Africans, Rwandans, Salvadorans, Argentines, and Chileans, among others, have often shared their own stories in public venues to contest those who have asked about the truth of the testimonies I have presented.

In his writing on the Vietnam war, Tim O'Brien offers, "You can tell a true war story by the questions you ask. Somebody tells a story, let's say, and afterward you ask, 'Is it true?' and if the answer matters, you've got your answer" (1990:89). This is not the glib response it may appear to be. He further explains: "In a true war story, if there's a moral at all, it's like the thread that makes the cloth. You can't tease it out. You can't extract the meaning without unraveling the deeper meaning. . . . It comes down to gut instinct. A true war story, if truly told, makes the stomach believe. . . . a true war story is never about war. . . . It's about love and memory. It's about sorrow. . . . You can tell a true war story by the way it never seems to end. Not then, not ever" (1990:83–91).

Indeed, it is from the seemingly never-ending testimonies of survivors that researchers seek to reconstruct genocide. The deluge of painful memories is shared by survivors who seek to reconstruct their personal and community histories and, at the same time, to communicate the experience and memory of these events to outsiders. It is from this deluge that can envelop the researcher, as well as those giving testimonies, that we seek to disentangle "facts" and, at the same time, to understand and respect the raw memories shared with us.

THE "GREY ZONE" OF RESEARCH

Further complicating testimony-based research with genocide survivors is the significant probability that one will take testimonies from "compromised" survivors or even out-and-out collaborators. Levi problematized this space as the "grey zone" constituted by "the hybrid class of prisoner-functionary" in which "the two camps of masters and servants diverge and converge" (1989:42). In the Guatemalan genocide Maya youth were forcibly recruited into the Guatemalan army and boys and men forced into army-controlled civil patrols. Sometimes the extreme marginalization and poverty experienced by Maya youth was enough to convince them to allow themselves to be recruited. Gaspar, a Tz'utijil-Maya who grew up in conditions of enslavement on a finca and in the streets of Guatemala City, recalls:

> The army was always recruiting in the park, at the cinema, and anywhere else where young men congregated. I always got away. I was good at slipping away because I had lived on the streets. I saw that the world was made up of abusers and abused and I didn't want to be abused anymore. So, one day when I was sixteen, I let the army catch me. But they didn't really catch me, because I decided I wanted to be a soldier. I didn't want to be abused anymore.
>
> I wanted a chance to get ahead. I saw what the soldiers did. I knew they killed people. But I wanted to see if in reality it could really be an option for me. If there would be an opportunity to get ahead, to learn to read and write. I always thought that it would be very beautiful to learn to read and write. I was always looking for a way to get ahead, to improve myself, but sometimes the doors just close and there is nowhere else to go. The army says we will learn to read and write, but when you go into the army, they teach you very little. They give you a weapon and they teach you to kill. They give you shoes because you don't have any. Many times, you join the army for a pair of shoes. When they grab you to recruit you, they say, "You don't have any shoes."
>
> In the army, I was full of hate. I used the weapons with the hatred I had carried inside of me for a long time. Even though the hatred can be strong, you are still a human being with the spirit of your ancestors, with the spirit of peace and respect. So, inside you have great conflict. It was very difficult for me to find an internal emotional stability.
>
> When I was recruited, there were a lot of indigenas recruited. They were beaten hard and called "stupid Indians" for not knowing how to speak Spanish. The soldiers who beat them were indigenous. The problem in the army is that no one trusts anyone else, even though most of the soldiers are indigenous.

After I was recruited, they told me that I could be a Kaibil because I was tall, fast, and smart.[5] But I wasn't so smart. They took us to the mountains. Each of us had to carry a live dog that was tied up over our shoulders. I was thirsty. There was no water. Well, we had no water and we were given no water. But our trainer had water. He walked ahead of us on the path spilling water to remind us of our thirst. I was innocent. When we were ordered to pick up the stray dogs on the street, I thought we were going to learn how to train them, that we would have guard dogs. But when we arrived to the camp, we were ordered to kill them with our bare hands. We had to kill some chickens, too. We were ordered to butcher the chickens and dogs and put their meat and blood in a big bowl. Then, we had to eat and drink this dog and chicken meat that was in a bath of blood. Whoever vomited had to vomit into the shared bowl and get back in line to eat and drink more. We had to eat it all, including the vomit, until no one vomited.

The army kills part of your identity. They want to break you and make you a new man. A savage man. They inspired me to kill. There was a ladino recruit who said that Indians were worthless and that we didn't go to school because we didn't want to. I pushed him off a cliff. I would have enjoyed it if he had died. This is how the army creates monsters.

You become very hard in the mountains and sometimes the only thing you feel is fear. You are afraid of any man, or every man. After my first battle with the guerrilla, I decided to escape, because I wanted to improve myself and found no way to do it in the army. (Sanford 2003:183–184)

Gaspar's story is, as Levi suggested of testimonies from the grey zone, "not self-contained. It is pregnant, full of significance, asks more questions than it answers, sums up in itself the entire theme of the grey zone and leaves one dangling. It shouts and clamors to be understood, because in it one perceives a symbol, as in dreams and the signs from heaven" (1989:66). In our meetings Gaspar expressed a deep commitment to the truth about what had happened. Each time he came to my house, he would begin by saying, "I am going to tell you everything. I am going to tell the truth. It is inhuman, but I will tell you what they made us do." In his sharing of these memories, his stories were always powerful and descriptive. I could see the place where the violence happened. I could hear the pleas of those who were injured or killed. I could feel his disgust and hatred, and also the power he felt at the moments he carried out these atrocities. Sometimes he would shake as he told me of these experiences. Sometimes I would shake after he left my home.

I believe that testimonies like Gaspar's, which emanate from the grey zone, at one and the same time push and redefine the limits of anthropological research on genocide and violence. They blur the neat categories of performer (perpetrator), victim, and witness as suggested by David Riches's triangular model of violence (1986). Further, they challenge the limits of research in postgenocidal contexts and force us to come to terms with representations of truth and memory as much as they do with contradictory representations of genocide after the fact. They demand that we heed LaCapra's insistence on the need for "empathetic unsettlement" when taking testimonies and for an inclusion of that unsettlement in our analyses (2001:xi). They also reaffirm the importance of such subjective qualities of research as "careful inquiry, specific knowledge, [and] critical judgment" (LaCapra 2001:xiii). And, rather than discount Gaspar's testimony for being outside the "authentic" victim-survivor experience or for being too tangential to the actual genocide, Philippe Bourgois suggests that it is "precisely the very peripheral qualities" of the survivor's testimony "that can teach us why genocides continue to be part of the human condition" (2005:90).

EXCAVATION AND RECONSTRUCTION

In her ethnographic work on Burma, the Australian anthropologist Monique Skidmore meticulously details the urgency to document lived experiences of ongoing state violence to prevent the academic dismissal of citizen subjectivity—a dismissal that ultimately supports the military regime's historical denial. Specifically, she sees ethnography as playing an important role in highlighting the various subjectivities recreated under authoritarianism to identify the potential forms of political agency (Skidmore 2006). Subjectivities are created by the human condition and constituted and reconstituted in daily life. Different types of situations can create, destroy, or diminish the human capacity to exercise subjectivities. Anthropology offers an opportunity to recognize the unique subjectivities of genocide survivors. Levi wrote: "We are slaves, deprived of every right, exposed to every insult, condemned to certain death, but we still possess one power, and we must defend it with all our strength for it is the last—the power to refuse our consent" (1993:41). In this context Levi points to the diminished capacity of survivors to exercise their citizen subjectivity. Yet even in the extreme conditions of the Holocaust, Levi identifies refusal of consent as the "one power" left to survivors. This power to refuse consent is remembered by survivors and can become pivotal not only for a collective memory of the past but also for collective action seeking redress. This collective action itself is the constitution of a new political subjectivity.

Listen to Pablo's testimony of the army occupying his newly repopulated village of Plan de Sánchez in 1984. Two years earlier the army had massacred 188 people, mostly women, children, and elderly. In 1984 the army was concentrating massacre survivors into army-controlled model villages that included the forced participation of all men as patrollers in army-controlled civil patrols and indoctrination projects to negate the very genocide committed by the army.[6] Pablo remembers the first such meeting he was required to attend:

> The army official said, "Welcome to all of you. I have called you here to ask you some questions. Do you deserve to have what happened in Plan de Sánchez happen again? Who of you here behaves like shit? Who of you here doesn't want to collaborate?" That's how he began. Then, he took off his jacket. He took off his machine gun. He took off his belt and threw it down in front of the people. "Who is opposed?" he shouted and picked up his machine gun and pointed it at all the patrollers. "Who is here who doesn't want to collaborate?" he said. "Whoever doesn't want to collaborate, I will finish him off right here with this," he said with his machine gun pointing out at the people. "Look here, what happened in Plan de Sánchez, please, no one is going to complain about it because whoever complains," he said holding up his machine gun, "this is what you get." By then he was really red in the face. He said, "Forget about everything that has happened. Your mothers, your fathers are dead. Leave it at that. Forget it."
>
> "Watch out!" he said, "If you start complaining. . . ." Then, he was right in front of me. He looked at me and said, "Do you hear me?" "Yes," I said. And then I guess because I was already conquered by death and I

felt no fear, I thought, "If they kill me, they kill me. But they are going to kill me for the truth." I looked up at him and said, "Excuse me sir, pardon my question. In my case, I was in the army in Jutiapa and the army killed my father. So, why do you say now that we have peace and should forget everything that has happened? Why has all this happened? Why did the army kill my father?"

The official shouted at me, "Shut your mouth!" But I said, "You can forget, but we are the ones in pain. We will never forget. What happened is written in our hearts. What would you do if they killed your whole family? Would you be capable of forgetting it? Look sir, the truth is that I am not afraid to declare and speak the truth. I was in the army. I was told that I was there to defend the patria, the land, and the family, and the army killed my family. And this sir, I will never forget. Maybe you can forget it, but we can't."

He shouted at the patrollers, "And is this true? Is that what happened in Plan de Sánchez?" All the patrollers were looking at the ground. He was expecting everyone to say, "No," that everyone would agree with him. Someone in the group softly said, "Yes, it is true." And others started to nod in agreement and say, "Yes, it is true. It is true." The official was still holding his machine gun, but he grabbed his jacket and belt and the rest of his things. He didn't say anything to us. He said to another officer, "Bring in the specialist to explain to this kid." Then, he left. (Sanford 2003:226–227)

"This kid" was Pablo. He was 16 and had already lost every member of his family except for his younger brother, who was the lone survivor of the massacre. Pablo's refusal to consent to forgetting the army massacre of his family and village led to a collective community refusal to consent to the army's indoctrination. It also marked the beginning of the reassertion of the community's collective memory of the massacre—one that would eventually lead the community to be among the first to have an exhumation in Guatemala. Pablo recalls: "After the meeting, lots of people congratulated me. They thanked me. They said, 'You are really aggressive. You declared the truth. We will never forget your courage'" (Sanford 2003:227). Indeed, as LaCapra suggests, establishing accurate shared memory of such past "limit events" plays a significant role in the development of a genuine political process for the collectivity (2001:96).

Still, Pablo's challenge to the army official in 1984 and the community's collective organizing for an exhumation of the clandestine cemetery of massacre victims in 1994 were not without incident. Pablo explains:

> The specialist was one of these people from civilian affairs who just said the same things that official had said, but in a softer voice. "We have to forget everything. What you said is true, but we can't bring back the dead. There is nothing to be done. We are with you now and you are with us," he said. . . . The patrols came through a few days later. They just kept walking around. They were always coming back and walking through here.
>
> They did that when you were here during the exhumation. They came at night. They wanted to know what was in the house where the forenses kept their tools. I told them we had loaned the house to people to store their belongings. That was the army's revenge against us—to send a platoon here. One of the soldiers came over to ask me questions. They asked me for a place to spend the night. I told them that we never refuse shelter to anyone and told them they could sleep in the corridor outside. "What about that house?" he asked. I told him there was no space there. . . . When the sun rose, they got up and stayed about two hours. They said they wanted to buy some food. But we didn't have enough food to sell. So I gave them each a tortilla. They left. But instead of taking the main road, they went to the path that leads to Juan Manuel's house. They were going there to investigate him. They were separating so they could surround his house. So, I went after them. I said, "Excuse me, I think you have lost your way. The path out of the village is up here. This path doesn't go anywhere." Then, they left. (Sanford 2003:227)

TRUTH AND POLITICAL SPACE

The army officer's attempt to institutionalize forgetting formed part of an official campaign to write the genocide victims out of Guatemalan history. As Levi wrote, "In an authoritarian state it is considered permissible to alter the truth; to rewrite history retrospectively, to distort the news, suppress the true, add the false. Propaganda is substituted for information" (1995:212). Fortunately, the Guatemalan army failed in its attempt to rewrite history in Plan de Sánchez the day Pablo challenged the officer and throughout Guatemala after the Archbishop's Office on Human Rights (Oficina de Derechos Humanos del Arzobispado de Guatemala, ODHA) published its 4-volume *Nunca más* report (1998) and the Commission for Historical Clarification (the Guatemalan truth commission, Comisión para el Esclarecimiento Histórico, CEH) published its 12-volume *Memoria del silencio* report (1999). Each report condemned the Guatemalan state for carrying out a premeditated campaign of violence against its own citizens. Significantly, the CEH concluded that the army had carried out genocidal acts, massacred 626 indigenous villages, displaced 1.5 million people, forced more than 150,000 people into refuge in Mexico, and left more than 200,000 people dead or disappeared (CEH 1999). These reports were possible because survivors like Pablo gave testimony to investigators. Indeed, Pablo participated in the third exhumation of a clandestine cemetery of massacre victims in Guatemala. This exhumation carried out by the Guatemalan Forensic Anthropology Foundation (Fundación de Antropología Forense de Guatemala, FAFG) took place before the peace accords were signed between the army and the guerrillas, before the army-controlled civil patrols were demobilized, before the United Nations established its presence in Guatemala with MINUGUA (Misión Naciones Unidas en Guatemala, UN Mission in Guatemala), and before international nongovernmental organizations (NGOs) came onto the Guatemalan scene.[7]

During the exhumation, the FAFG, the Guatemalan Human Rights Ombudsman and the survivors received threats: "Leave the Dead in Peace, Sons of Whores, or the Violence of the Past will Return." The survivors were undeterred. They knew the exhumation had to continue or they would lose what little political space they had. They were concerned for our safety because the local army commander had publicly stated that all the "anthropologists, internationals, and journalists in Plan de Sánchez are guerrillas." Nonetheless, Erazmo, who had lost his wife, eight children, and 80-year-old mother in the massacre, pointed to the open graves and said, "There, there is no lie. There you are seeing the truth." I asked what importance the truth could have 12 years after the massacre. Juan Manuel, who had also lost his wife and family, said, "We want peace. We want people to know what happened here so that it does not happen again—not here, not in some other village, department or country" (Sanford 2003:46–48).

My experience taking the testimonies of Pablo, Erazmo, Juan Manuel, and hundreds of others resonates with Levi's thoughts on memory. He wrote: "For these survivors, remembering is a duty. They do not want to forget, and above all they do not want the world to forget, because they understand that their experiences were not meaningless, that the camps were not accidental, an unforeseen historical happening" (1995:221). For Levi, as for O'Brien, remembering is part of grappling with the experience of surviving what others seem only able to doubt.

At the same time, those conducting research on genocide in postconflict situations, and sometimes during the conflict, must consider the security of those giving testimony because the narrators are real people who live and act in real social history of which the testimony is a part (Beverley 1996b:37). Although the majority of survivors with whom I have spoken have sooner or later chosen anonymity, not once has a single survivor asked me not to use their testimony. Indeed, when asking for anonymity, survivors emphasize that it is the story that has an urgent need to be known. As Doña Juanita explained after changing her mind about the use of her name, "I am afraid of what might happen to my children if I use my name. But if you need my name to give faith to my testimony, I give you my permission" (Testimony no. 7, September 7, 1997, Panzós, Guatemala). While survivors come forward and speak for many different reasons, common among them are the desire to unburden their pain, to share the content of their lived experience of violence, and to have their experiences validated by those who listen and by the wider audience they hope their testimony will reach. This is, after all, the essence of testimony—it is "an authentic narrative, told by a witness who is moved to narrate by the urgency of a situation" (Yúdice 1996:44).

In a certain way, regardless of the memories that are shared, each survivor and each witness must suspend his or her own disbelief to believe that the outside listener, whether national or international, a human rights worker or an academic researcher, might actually be able to comprehend personal representations and memories of terror. Then, in the giving of testimony or in responding to interview questions, the witness seeks to consciously represent the memories of terror that dominate the unconscious and to continue to shape daily encounters even absent the public acknowledgment of terror and its memory. As Jorge Luis Borges has noted, "Only one thing does not exist. It is forgetting" (Benedetti 1995:11).

While forgetting may not exist, remembering and the sharing of memories may not always be the same. In his work on oral history, Alessandro Portelli (1991) observes that the timing of the researcher in the life of the research subject can produce different outcomes, analyses, and reflections on the part of the research subject. Likewise, the "real world" political timing, as well as the timing in the life of the researcher, can also make significant and different contributions to political memory and to an understanding of the development of new subjectivities. For example, 20 years after having survived a Salvadoran army attack on civilians during his field research among revolutionary peasants during the 1980s, Bourgois revisited his field notes and wrote a poignant, self-reflective essay about the sanitizing effect the Cold War had had on his analysis at that time (2001). If both narrator and listener interpretations of events may shift over time, what is the validity of testimony? And, what is the contribution of an anthropology of genocide largely based on survivor testimonies?

Testimonies portray the experience of the narrators as agents of collective memory and identity, rather than as their representatives (Yúdice 1996). The accretion of marginalized voices transforms experience into collective memory. Anthropological representations of lived experience subvert official memory, institutional time, and homogenized culture. For the Guatemalan historian Sergio Tischler Visquerra (2005), this subversion of official time and official history opens the door to a multiplicity of time and experience that, in turn, allows for the inclusion of diverse subjectivities with new visions of the past, present, and future. In this way, changing political, economic, and cultural subject positions are central to both understanding past genocides and preventing new ones in the future. Anthropological research over time offers the possibility of developing theoretical explanations without losing the meaning of the experience of violence for social subjects. And, as Veena Das and Arthur Kleinman suggest, this anthropological work is critical because "the production of the subject in conditions of violence is largely invisible to public commissions and judicial inquiries about violence" (2000:13). Anthropological research on genocide can serve to mediate between politics and the economy, between the Cold War and globalization, and between neoliberal triumph and utopian dreams of revolution.

I first began working in Plan de Sánchez during the FAFG exhumation of the clandestine cemetery in 1994. I have continued to visit the village and meet with Juan Manuel, Erazmo, Pablo, and other survivors. On a visit to Plan de Sánchez in 1997, Juan Manuel recalled the October 1994 reburial of the massacre victims. The reburial began with a mass in the church in Rabinal and was followed by a public gathering in the plaza in front of the church. Thousands of Achi-Maya filled the plaza and streets of Rabinal to witness the burial procession. After the mass the crowd in the plaza listened to the words of the survivors from Plan de Sánchez, which were amplified throughout the community. Juan Manuel remembered the moment:

> After the exhumation, people had been congratulating me. They would say, "Congratulations Juan. You really have balls to declare the truth." But then they would tell me to be careful because everyone knew who I was and there were people who didn't like what I did. I was thinking about this as we carried the coffins to the church. After mass, when I was standing in front of everyone, I just wasn't afraid. I told the whole truth. I said the army should be ashamed. "How shameful for them to say that my wife with a baby on her back was a guerrilla. They dragged her out of my house and killed her. Shameful! They opened the abdomens of pregnant women. And then they said that they killed guerrillas. Shameful!" I said. I talked about the people in Rabinal who had collaborated with the army and how they walked through the streets with no shame for the killings they had done. In this moment, I had no fear. I declared the truth.
>
> Afterwards a *licenciado* told me, "What a shame that you are a poor peasant and not a professional. If you were a professional, there would really be change here."[8] I thought to myself, "I may be a sad peasant who can only half-speak, but I wasn't afraid and I spoke the truth." The entire pueblo was there. The park was completely full. Everyone was listening to what I was saying and I didn't feel embarrassed. I knew that afterwards maybe they would be waiting for me in the street somewhere and that that might be my luck. I said, "Believe me, the guilty think that with just one finger they can cover the sun. But with what they have done here, they simply can't." (Sanford 2003:230)

In my own experience, one of the most significant aspects of writing ethnographies of the Guatemalan genocide is the sharing of so many histories previously untold. Indeed, as Portelli notes, "Oral sources tell us not just what people did, but what they wanted to do, what they believed they were doing, and what they now think they did" (1991:50). As these experiences are made public (even when the identity of the speaker is protected in anonymity), each new story creates space for another survivor to tell his or her story. While testimonies represented an accretion of corroborating supposed facts for FAFG, ODHA, and CEH investigations, they also represented an expansion of individual agency in the giving of testimony that collectively created new public space for local community action. It is from the collectivity of the many fragments of community truth telling that new space was created during the exhumation and gave rise to survivors beginning to initiate conversations about the massacre in public at the exhumation and at reburial sites.

CONCLUSION

One of the effects of the massive violence of limit events is the indiscriminate taking of victims, and the namelessness this creates for victims and survivors as well as for the violence itself. Trying to locate those surviving the violence in Panzós, Doña Natalia explained, "You can count the families that weren't affected by the violence here. I don't know who they are, but there must be some. There were always dead" (Testimony No. 19, September 7, 1997, Panzós, Guatemala). Even in small communities, the numbers of victims and survivors are so numerous as to erase individual identity through the sheer quantity of stories because each story embodies another from which another unfolds. This erasure is, of course, compounded by the official silencing of victims and survivors through government disinformation and the negation of the violence—silencing that has been enforced by army acts and threats of continued violence. While meticulous note taking during testimonies can attach a name, an age, a sex, family information, a life history, physical characteristics, and personal demeanor to each individual, this descriptive approach belies the reality of the anthropologist, translator, and individual giving testimony, who are collectively seeking a vantage point from which to comprehend the continuum of extreme violence experienced, because the agency of survival is found in the fragmented memories invoked in the process. Portelli reminds us that "subjectivity is as much the business of history as are the more visible 'facts.' What informants believe is indeed a historical fact (that is, the fact that they believe it), as much as what really happened" (1991:50–51). In other words, agency and history are both found in the present act of remembering and giving testimony to past and present acts of survival.

For the anthropologist listening to some 20 emotionally wrenching testimonies each day, the absorption of the stories leaves one with blurred faces of survivors and powerful images of the events survived (including composite images of events that are also produced by the accretion of testimonies). Rather than names and other facts, the cold, the hunger, the fear, and the desperation of survival are the sensations invoked in encounters with survivors following the taking of testimony. Indeed, Levi reminds us that for survivors, "just as our hunger is not the feeling of missing a meal, so our way of being cold has need of a new word. We say 'hunger,' we say 'tiredness,' 'fear,' 'pain,' we say 'winter,' and they are different things" (1993:123). These sensations from the testimonies left an imprint in my memory.

When I would see the men and women who had previously given their testimony, I would sometimes remember their names. Always I would remember what they had survived, the cadence of their voice and their body language as they told me their stories, the circumstances of their personal loss and survival, the rivers in which they had submerged themselves as they fled the army, the kidnapping of a son, or that of a husband. I would always remember their pain, their hunger, their thirst. I remembered, and continue to remember, the individuals who trusted me with their testimony by what they suffered. Perhaps survivors taught this to me as they gave their testimonies—how they remember their experiences of violence as living memories, not as names and dates frozen in the past. Or perhaps they taught me to "forget" information that could potentially harm others; information such as knowing individuals by name. Indeed, with few exceptions, I was always instructed by my friends to never acknowledge our friendship or even acquaintance to *desconocidos* (strangers).

Still, as I finish this essay, carefully cross-checking names, dates, and places to testimonies, I am reminded of Carl Jung's words: "The finest and most significant conversations of my life were anonymous" (1989:134). None of the individuals who gave testimony are anonymous people. And despite their anonymity on the page, their silence and the namelessness of the violence is at least partially broken. It is not the identities of the survivors that need to be known to "give faith to their testimonies," as Doña Juanita queried. Faith is given to their testimonies by their words breaking the silence and asserting their right to speak out against the genocide they survived. In speaking out, they assert their agency and their right to be heard. In this process the identities of state institutions and individuals responsible for *La Violencia* are also revealed. Significantly, in breaking the silence and the namelessness of victims and survivors through testimony, their actions and lives are recognized—not as object victims of state violence, but as conscious subjects negotiating extreme and personal violence in their lives (Sanford 1997). This recognition of past and present lived experience, political consciousness, and action is, in fact, evidence that "political agency becomes the factored product of multiple subject positions" (Feldman 1991:4).

At an academic presentation about the Panzós massacre, an anthropologist in the audience challenged the authenticity of the community leader Maria Maquín's discourse because she had used the words *nunca más* (never again). The anthropologist said, "Those just aren't her words. That is the discourse of outsiders. That is human rights discourse." Another anthropologist added, "Someone else is talking through her." In other words, these anthropologists did not recognize Maquín as a conscious political subject capable of appropriating global human rights discourse for local use. Nor did they recognize the powerful identification massacre survivors can experience with discourses on human rights that resonate with their own experiences of survival.[9] Certainly, they had not considered the "counterpossibility of transculturation from below," which, as John Beverley suggests, should lead us to understand and appreciate how the subaltern appropriates us for his or her own purposes (1996a:272).

In *Book of the Embraces*, Eduardo Galeano notes that the root of *recordar*, to remember, is the Latin *re-cordis*, which means "to pass back through the heart." The public remembering of Juan Manuel, Pablo, and Maria, this passing back through the heart before their communities, is the very essence of the discourse and practice of human agency, political consciousness, self-representation, and action. Their stories are not the stories of dead people, though the dead are present. These testimonies from survivors of the Guatemalan genocide are stories of the living—of those who survived and have much to share when given the opportunity to speak. Pablo and Juan Manuel broke the silencing of massacre survivors with their public testimonies. At the collective level of the community, this expansion of individual agency through testimony created new public space for community discussions and action. Thus Juan Manuel was able to stand before his community condemning the massacre of his family and, despite the great risk he took, remember that he "just was not afraid." The accretion of agency and facts in the public space of the exhumations opened the political space seized by Juan Manuel, in which he fused discourse and practice when he declared the army guilty of massacres in his community. In this sense, his public speech represents the multitude of the previously silenced and nameless who can now stand before their communities and directly and publicly contest those who cast doubt on their credibility and disparage their lived experiences of survival. Borrowing from Hans Kellner: "Never again is now" (1998:235).

EPILOGUE

Clyde Snow always says, "The bones don't lie." Indeed they do not. The testimonies of survivors and the forensic analysis of the remains of massacre victims in Plan de Sánchez provided evidence for a petition filed by survivors with the Inter-American Commission on Human Rights in 1995 requesting that the commission pass the case on to the Inter-American Court of Human Rights. Over the years we have often discussed this case with survivors in Plan de Sánchez. While allowing for citizen petitions, the Inter-American process is slow. We would reassure one another that something was bound to happen—especially after we knew that the case had been passed on to the court. Cases can take up to ten years. "Sooner or later there will be justice" became the refrain for survivors.

On April 29, 2004, the Inter-American Court issued its condemnation of the Guatemalan government for the July 18, 1982, massacre of 188 Achi-Maya in the village of Plan de Sánchez in the mountains above Rabinal, Baja Verapaz. The Inter-American Court attributed the massacre to Guatemalan army troops. This is the first ruling by the Inter-American Court against the Guatemalan state for any of the 626 massacres carried out by the army in the early 1980s. The court later announced the damages the Guatemalan state will be required to pay to the relatives of victims at $7.9 million (www.corteidh.or.cr/seriecpdf/seriec_116_esp.pdf, accessed Oct. 14, 2006).

Beyond the importance of this judgment for the people of Plan de Sánchez, the court's ruling is particularly significant because the following key points were included in the judgment: (1) there was a genocide in Guatemala; (2) this genocide was part of the framework of the internal armed conflict when the armed forces of the Guatemalan government implemented its National Security Doctrine in their counterinsurgency actions; and (3) these counterinsurgency actions carried out within the Guatemalan government's National Security Doctrine took place during the regime of General Efraín Ríos Montt who came to power through a military coup in March 1982.

Further, regarding the massacre in Plan de Sánchez, the court indicated that the armed forces of the Guatemalan government had violated the following rights, each of which is consecrated in the Human Rights Convention of the Organization of American States: (1) the right to personal integrity; (2) the right to judicial protection; (3) the right to judicial guarantees of equality before the law; (4) the right to freedom of conscience; (5) the right to freedom of religion; and (6) the right to private property (www.corteidh.or.cr/seriecpdf/seriec_105_esp.pdf, accessed Oct. 14, 2006).

The Plan de Sánchez case was considered by the Inter-American Court at the request of the Inter-American Commission on Human Rights, which had received a petition from Juan Manuel, Pablo, Erazmo, and other relatives of the massacre victims. These survivors requested consideration in the court because of the lack of justice in the Guatemalan legal system. Since the Plan de Sánchez case was initiated in 1995, the FAFG has carried out more than 200 exhumations of clandestine cemeteries of massacre victims in Guatemala. Each of these exhumations has included the filing of a criminal case with forensic evidence against the Guatemalan army and its agents. To date, only the Río Negro case has been heard in a Guatemalan court, and no army officials were indicted in the case that found three civil patrollers guilty (see Sanford 2003). In July 2006 the Spanish court Juzgado Central de Instrución No 1, Audiencia Nacional, Ministerio de Justicia, Madrid, issued international arrest warrants for seven former military officials, including Ríos Montt, for genocide, terrorism, torture, assassination, and illegal detention (Pérez and Orantes 2006). In 2008 Ríos Montt continues to stay his extradition to Spain through appeals in local Guatemalan courts.

NOTES

Special thanks to Alex Hinton and Kevin O'Neill for including my work on Guatemala in this volume, as well as to the editors and the two anonymous reviewers at Duke University Press. My appreciation always to Raul Figueroa Sarti for his unconditional support, and to Valentina for teaching me that I could write and be a mother at the same time. This essay is dedicated to the survivors of the Guatemalan genocide. A U.S. Institute for Peace grant provided research support for this chapter. Any errors are my own.

1. I began collecting testimonies from Guatemalan refugees in the United States in 1990. I began working with the Guatemalan Forensic Anthropology Foundation (FAFG) in Guatemala in June 1994. I conducted field research during the summers of 1994 and 1995, the spring of 1996, from the fall of 1996 to the fall of 1997, and concluded in the summer of 1998, with annual follow-up visits to various communities each year since 2002. For Sanford 2003 I collected more than 400 interviews and testimonies with survivors of massacres in villages in Chimaltenango, San Martín Jilotepeque, San Andrés Sacabajá, Chinique, Santa Cruz del Quiché, Chichicastenango, Cunen, Rabinal, Nebaj, Chajul, Cotzal, Panzós, Salamá, Cobán, San Miguel Acatán, and San Miguel Chicaj. I carried out field research in communities before, during, and after the exhumation of clandestine cemeteries. I also led the testimonial and archival research and wrote the historical reconstructions for the FAFG's report to the Commission for Historical Clarification for massacres in Panzós and Acul (FAFG 2000).

2. The term *testimony* is used here to mean the narration of one's memories of a significant and traumatic event or events.

3. *Stories* is used here to refer to the plot and characters of the different, real-life events chronicled in a testimony.

4. *Witness*, as used in this context, refers to someone who saw (witnessed) an event, as opposed to the act of witnessing through the taking of testimony.

5. Kaibiles are the elite fighting forces of the Guatemalan army.

6. The term *genocide* is used here in the legal sense of the UN Convention on the Prevention and Punishment of the Crime of Genocide. Indeed, the Guatemalan Commission for Historical Clarification concluded that "genocidal acts" had taken place (CEH 1999). On April 29, 2004, the Inter-American Court of Human Rights condemned the Guatemalan state for genocide in the Plan de Sánchez case. See Corte IDH, Caso Masacre Plan de Sánchez v. Guatemala, Serie C No. 105, Sentencia de 29 de abril, 2004, and Dissenting Opinion of Judge Cancado Trindade. Furthermore, on July 7, 2006, the Spanish court Juzgado Central de Instrución No 1, Audiencia Nacional, Ministerio de Justicia, Madrid, issued international arrest warrants for seven former military officials for the crime of genocide, as well as for terrorism, torture, assassination, and illegal detention.

7. For more on the first exhumations in Guatemala, see FAFG 1997.

8. A *licenciado* is someone with a university bachelor's degree.

9. For more on Maria Maquín and the Panzós massacre, see Sanford 2000, 2001, 2003, and 2008. See also FAFG 2000.

REFERENCES

Benedetti, Mario
1995   The Triumph of Memory. NACLA Report on the Americas 29 (Nov/
            Dec):10–12.

Beverley, John
1996a   The Margin at the Center. In The Real Thing: Testimonial Discourse and
            Latin America. Georg M. Gugelberger, ed. Pp. 23–41. Durham, NC: Duke
            University Press.
1996b   The Real Thing. In The Real Thing: Testimonial Discourse and Latin
            America. Georg M. Gugelberger, ed. Pp. 266–286. Durham, NC: Duke
            University Press.

Bourgois, Philippe
2001   The Power of Violence in War and Peace: Post–Cold War Lessons from
            El Salvador. Ethnography 2(1):5–37.
2005   Missing the Holocaust: My Father's Account of Auschwitz from August
            1932 to June 1944. Anthropological Quarterly 78(1):90–123.

Comisión para el Esclarecimiento Histórico (CEH)
1999   Guatemala: Memoria del silencio. 2 vols. Guatemala City: CEH.

Das, Veena, and Arthur Kleinman
2000   Introduction. In Violence and Subjectivity. Veena Das, Arthur Kleinman,
            Mamphela Ramphele, and Pamela Reynolds, eds. Pp. 1–18. Berkeley:
            University of California Press.

Falla, Ricardo
1992   Masacres de la selva. Guatemala City: Editorial Universitario.

Feldman, Allen
1991   Formations of Violence: The Narrative of the Body and Political Terror in
            Northern Ireland. Chicago: University of Chicago Press.

Fundación de Antropología Forense de Guatemala (FAFG)
1997   Las masacres de Rabinal. Guatemala City: FAFG.
2000   Informe de la Fundación de Antropología Forense de Guatemala: Cuatro
            Casos Paradigmaticos Solicitados por La Comisión para el Esclare-
            cimiento Historico de Guatemala Realizadas en las Comunidades de
            Panzós, Acul, Chel y Belén. Guatemala City: FAFG.

Herman, Judith Lewis
1992   Trauma and Recovery. New York: Basic Books.

Jung, Carl

1989   Memories, Dreams, Reflections. Aniela Jaffé, ed., Richard Winston and
            Clara Winston, trans. New York: Vintage.

Kellner, Hans

1998   "Never Again" Is Now. *In* History and Theory: Contemporary Readings.
            Brian Fay, Philip Pomper, and Richard T. Vann, eds. Pp. 225–244.
            Malden, MA: Blackwell.

LaCapra, Dominick

2001   Writing History, Writing Memory. Baltimore: Johns Hopkins University
            Press.

Lemkin, Raphaël

1944   Axis Rule in Occupied Europe: Laws of Occupation, Analysis of Govern-
            ment, Proposals for Redress. Washington: Carnegie Endowment for
            International Peace, Division of International Law.   .

Levi, Primo

1989   The Drowned and the Saved. Raymond Rosenthal, trans. New York:
            Vintage.
1993   Survival in Auschwitz. New York: Simon and Schuster.
1995   The Reawakening. New York: Simon and Schuster.

O'Brien, Tim

1990   The Things They Carried. New York: Houghton Mifflin.

Oficina de Derechos Humanos del Arzobispado de Guatemala (ODHA)
1998   Guatemala: Nunca más. 4 vols. Guatemala City: ODHA.

Pérez, Sonia, and Coralia Orantes

2006   Ordenan la captura de Efraín Ríos Montt. Prensa Libre, July 8: A1.

Portelli, Alessandro

1991   The Death of Luigi Trastulli and Other Stories: Form and Meaning in
            Oral History. Albany: State University of New York Press.

Riches, David

1991   Aggression, War, Violence: Space/Time and Paradigm. Man
            26(2):281–297.

Riches, David, ed.

1986   The Anthropology of Violence. Oxford: Blackwell.

Sanford, Victoria

1993   Victim as Victimizer: Indigenous Childhood and Adolescence in Guate-
            mala's Culture of Terror. M.A. thesis, San Francisco State University.
1997   Mothers, Widows and Guerrilleras: Anonymous Conversations with
            Survivors of State Violence. Uppsala: Life and Peace Institute.

2000   The Silencing of Maya Women from Mama Maquin to Rigoberta
        Menchú. Social Justice 27(1):128–151.
2001   From *I, Rigoberta* to the Commissioning of Truth: Maya Women and the
        Reshaping of Guatemalan History. Cultural Critique 47:16–53.
2003   Buried Secrets: Truth and Human Rights in Guatemala. New York:
        Palgrave Macmillan.
2008   La masacre de Panzós: Etnicidad, tierra y Violencia. Guatemala City:
        F&G Editores.

Skidmore, Monique
2006   Scholarship, Advocacy, and the Politics of Engagement in Burma (Myan-
        mar). *In* Engaged Observer: Anthropology, Advocacy, and Activism.
        Victoria Sanford and Asale Angel-Ajani, eds. Pp. 42–59. New Brunswick:
        Rutgers University Press.

Strathern, Andrew, Pamela J. Stewart, and Neil L. Whitehead, eds.
2006   Terror and Violence: Imagination and the Unimaginable. London: Pluto.

Tischler Visquerra, Sergio
2005   Memoria, tiempo y sujeto. Guatemala City: F&G Editores and Instituto
        de Ciencias Sociales y Humanidades de la Benemérita Universidad
        Autónoma de Puebla.

Yúdice, George
1996   Testimonio and Postmodernism. *In* The Real Thing: Testimonial
        Discourse and Latin America. Georg M. Gugelberger, ed. Pp. 42–57.
        Durham, NC: Duke University Press.

Sharon E. Hutchinson

2   PERILOUS OUTCOMES

International Monitoring and the Perpetuation of Violence in Sudan

When allegations of genocidal violence become so forceful that they can no longer be ignored, the international community's first response is often to call for the rapid deployment of an international observer mission to monitor the violence. The guiding hope is that the very presence of an international monitoring team—roaming the countryside, asking difficult questions, and issuing critical reports—will succeed where more conventional appeals to distant international agencies so often fail. Yet even when such missions prove ineffective in quelling the violence, the default assumption would seem to be that they are benign. After all, how could the activities of an international observer mission possibly make matters worse?

This essay sets out to challenge this naive assumption by demonstrating how and why well-intentioned international monitoring missions sometimes produce perverse effects. Concentrating on recent developments in Sudan—one of the most politically precarious and militarily self-destructive states in the world today—this article explores some of the unintended consequences of a U.S.-led international human rights monitoring mission that operated in Sudan during the final years of Sudan's second (North/South) civil war (1983–2005).[1]

The Civilian Protection Monitoring Team–Sudan (CPMT) was first deployed in September/October 2002 and was responsible for monitoring all serious military attacks against civilians and/ or civilian property throughout lengthy peace talks that culminated in the signing of the Comprehensive Peace Agreement between the government of Sudan (GOS) and the Sudan People's Liberation Movement/Army (SPLM/A) on January 9, 2005. Drawing on investigative data collected in the field while serving as an official CPMT monitor for several months during 2002 and 2003 and, more concretely, on a close reading of the more than 100 investigative reports issued by the team prior to its dismantlement in September/October 2005, I argue that this mission did more during its first year to excuse and perpetuate military violence against southern Sudanese civilians than to curtail or remedy it.

Significantly, Michael Ignatieff (2003) has argued that in the context of internal armed conflicts, international humanitarian interventions are never neutral. He reasons that states will accept an intervention only "if the intervening party takes no steps to encourage insurgents against the ruling regime" (2003:68). "Thus neutrality," Ignatieff remarks, inevitably "means taking the state party's side in the conflict" (2003:68); "sometimes this makes an intervener complicit in repression. At other times, neutrality makes the intervener the hapless plaything of contending parties to a civil war" (2003:68). What Ignatieff is pointing to is the possibility that in certain political and historical contexts, humanitarian interventions may have counterproductive outcomes. Consequently, situations may arise in which well-intentioned international monitoring missions actually serve to increase the efficiencies of unjust, violent, and repressive state regimes.

There is, perhaps, no way to ensure that international human rights monitoring missions will remain entirely neutral in situations of internal armed conflicts. However, I think there are ways that such monitoring operations can minimize inherent tendencies toward state bias without risking expulsion and thereby better resist possible complicity in the human rights violations they seek to curb. It is toward a deeper understanding of these risks and corrective possibilities that this case study of the CPMT's early performance is directed. (Regrettably, a comparative assessment of the unintended consequences of a much larger and more recently deployed international monitoring mission to Darfur, Sudan's deeply troubled western region, would be too much to tackle in this context.[2])

HISTORICAL CONTEXT

Since achieving independence in 1956, Sudan has proven a fertile breeding ground for sectarian pathologies shared by many of the world's most intractable conflicts. At war with itself for 42 of the past 53 years, the country has a history dominated by two major North/South civil wars (1955–72 and 1983–2005), as well as by numerous spin-off insurgencies and more localized conflicts, including the devastating genocidal violence that began burning through Sudan's western region of Darfur in early 2003.[3] Sudan's most recent civil war has commonly been portrayed as rooted in identity clashes and power struggles between a majority population in the North, identifying itself as Arab and Muslim, and a politically and economically marginalized minority population in the South, identifying itself as black African and, increasingly, Christian. In reality, however, Sudan's unrelenting strife has been perpetuated by a small, savvy, and internationally connected government-military-religious-commercial elite concentrated in greater Khartoum. And it has been this tightly knit elite that has repeatedly and forcefully suppressed the legitimate political aspirations and material needs of ever-growing numbers of war-displaced subsistence farmers, impoverished shantytown dwellers, drought-stricken herders, marginalized ethnic and religious minorities, and the vast majority of Sudan's population of 39 million. Rather than accept the nation's richly diverse cultural heritage, Khartoum's ruling elite has periodically sought, with varying degrees of coercion, to impose its cultural, linguistic, and religious preferences on the nation as a whole.

Sudan's North/South violence has also been stoked by powerful economic forces, including competing regional, national, and international interests in (1) the vast and increasingly lucrative southern oil reserves; (2) the abundant gold deposits in the southern region of Equatoria; and (3) the strategically vital headwaters of the White Nile. To these economic incentives must be added the ruthless profiteering of thousands of soldiers, politicians, international companies, arms merchants, gangsters, and warlords who have all too often succeeded in transforming Sudan's regional and sectarian conflicts into a self-perpetuating industry.

More than 2.5 million southern Sudanese are thought to have perished in Sudan's second civil war. Some 400,000 others fled to Kenya, Ethiopia, Uganda, and other African states and beyond, with an additional 4 million southerners having become internally displaced during that conflict. More than a million of these are currently camped in squalid settlements scattered on the peripheries of greater Khartoum. (These figures do not include the hundreds of thousands of men, women, and children who have died in the ongoing genocide in Darfur. Nor do they include the millions of Darfuris who have been violently displaced since 2003.)[4]

Officially, Sudan's long and bitter second civil war ended on January 9, 2005, following the signing of a Comprehensive Peace Agreement between the Sudanese government, headed by Omar Hassan el Bashir, and the SPLM/A, then led by John Garang de Mabior. While it is too early to say for certain whether or not that agreement will hold, mounting evidence suggests considerable reluctance on the part of Khartoum's northern ruling elite to abide by its power- and wealth-sharing commitments to southern leaders. In principle, the peace agreement commits southern Sudanese to a six-year interim period of "national unity," after which they will have the opportunity to vote in a regionwide referendum on whether they wish to remain part of a united Sudan or split off to form an independent country.[5]

The first major test of the peace agreement's resilience occurred on July 31, 2005, when Garang, the long-reigning leader of the SPLM/A turned successful peacemaker, died in a tragic—and in the eyes of many southern Sudanese, a suspicious—helicopter crash, shortly after assuming his position as First Vice President of the interim Government of National Unity. News of Garang's death provoked days of rioting between southerners and northerners in Khartoum and in other major cities. Despite this blow and despite continuing violence in Darfur, the implementation of the North/South peace agreement was continuing to move forward, if far too slowly and tentatively, as of the time of writing (May 2006).

THE CPMT'S FOUNDING MANDATE

The CPMT was born during the throes of the lengthy peace negotiation process between the GOS and the SPLM/A and was gradually phased out after the January 2005 signing of the Comprehensive Peace Agreement. Bankrolled entirely by the U.S. State Department, the CPMT was mandated "to investigate, evaluate, and report on alleged incidents involving serious violations of obligations or commitments [made by the GOS and the SPLM/A] to take constant care to protect the civilian population, civilians and civilian objects against the danger arising from military operations" (Civilian Protection Agreement 2002:1, art. 1, sec. 1). "Serious violations" included, but were not limited to, "grave breaches" of international humanitarian law as defined by the 1949 Geneva Conventions, including Common Article 3 (Civilian Protection Agreement 2002:2, art. 2, sec. 1a).

Initially, the CPMT was hailed as a tremendous step forward. Numerous human rights organizations, humanitarian agencies, and state actors had earlier accused the Sudanese government and the SPLM/A of intentionally targeting or failing to protect civilians in the civil war. The government, in particular, was heavily criticized for carrying out indiscriminate bombing raids against southern Sudanese civilians, for arbitrarily restricting or endangering humanitarian relief operations to vulnerable populations, and for waging a so-called scorched-earth campaign against southerners living in strategic regions of the Upper Nile to facilitate oil exploration and extraction activities in the South.[6] Despite the growing number and alarming consistency of these reports, there was as yet no monitoring team on the ground that could verify their accuracy. Humanitarian aid organizations active in the region were generally reluctant to speak out publicly for fear of being expelled by the GOS or the SPLM/A. The investigative reports of independent human rights organizations, moreover, were easily ignored or denied by the warring parties.

What made the CPMT's deployment so important was its potential to influence decisions at the international policy level. Ideally, it would provide a channel through which the Sudanese government, the SPLM/A, humanitarian and human rights organizations, and southern Sudanese civilians themselves could all voice their allegations and concerns. Here was a monitoring mechanism that—at least on paper—could move at will across enemy lines and expect full cooperation from both warring parties. With several airplanes at its disposal (in addition to numerous cars, satellite telephones, and computers), the CPMT enjoyed unprecedented logistical capacities. Capable of collecting hard military forensic evidence and diverse eyewitness accounts in a timely manner, the CPMT, it was hoped, would be able to cut through the propaganda wars and exaggerations of the warring parties to reveal what was really happening on the ground.

The CPMT's extraordinary investigative promise, however, was circumscribed by two formal agreements, potentially subject to diverse interpretations. On October 15, 2002, the GOS and SPLM/A signed a formal Cessation of Hostilities Agreement (officially known as the Memorandum of Understanding) aimed at creating a more conducive atmosphere for on-going peace talks. Both parties agreed to adhere to a "period of tranquility" (which went into effect on October 17, 2002) by undertaking a complete "military stand-down" of their respective forces (including allied militia forces) in "all areas of Sudan" (Cessation of Hostilities Agreement 2002:2–3, art. 2). Although both parties reserved the right to act in "self-defense" against hostile actions initiated by the other party (and/or its military allies), the agreement required the GOS and SPLM/A to maintain their current military positions and refrain from all offensive action. The agreement further stipulated that both warring parties must immediately cease the laying of landmines, refrain from occupying new areas, cease resupplying their troops with weapons and ammunition and, most important, desist from all acts of violence or abuse against the civilian population. Guarantees to ensure unimpeded humanitarian access to all areas and people in need and calls to freeze media wars and establish more effective channels of communication completed this military stand-down agreement.

Enforcement of this agreement, however, was ultimately stymied by the fact that no timely map was created by negotiators at the peace talks to indicate where the parties' respective troops were located on October 17, 2002. Without such a map or even a summary list of key locations occupied, it became much too easy for one or the other of the warring parties to counter subsequent allegations of offensive military action by claiming that it was legitimately defending areas previously held. This diplomatic lapse undercut the CPMT's investigative authority and impact.[7] Moreover, it was soon apparent that the GOS had no intention of abiding by the military stand-down agreement when it came to expanding and reinforcing its lucrative oil development operations on the Upper Nile.

The second agreement framing the CPMT's deployment was signed on March 30, 2002, when John Danforth, President George W. Bush's special envoy for peace in the Sudan, succeeded in persuading the GOS and SPLM/A to accept four "confidence-building measures" or "tests" in preparation for more serious, U.S.-supported peace negotiation efforts in the future. One test required both warring parties to refrain from intentionally attacking civilians and/or civilian property, with the added provision that an independent monitoring team would be created within two months of the agreement's signing (i.e., by June 2002) to check compliance. The resulting Civilian Protection Agreement became the CPMT's founding mandate, although the team's decreed deployment deadline was missed by many months.

The mandate was generally well conceived. It tasked the CPMT with investigating allegations of "serious violations" of international humanitarian law resulting in the loss of civilian lives or property. The mission was to be headquartered in Khartoum and to maintain a separate field office in the SPLM/A-controlled southern town of Rumbek. "Under the overall leadership of the Chief of the Khartoum Office, both the Chief of the Khartoum office and the Chief of the Rumbek Office are empowered to decide when an alleged incident . . . warrants investigation" (Civilian Protection Agreement 2002:2, art. 2, sec. 3a). All on-site investigations were to be carried out independently by team members. Once completed, each investigative report was to be submitted, first, to GOS and SPLM/A leaders, who would have a week to compose a written response, whereupon the final report, together with any official responses received, was to be released to the public. Eventually, an official Web site posting summaries and full reports was established.

Offered the choice of serving on the Khartoum or on the Rumbek subteam, I opted for the latter because it was much closer to the main battlefront, which was concentrated at that time in Nuer areas of the Upper Nile. Like all other CPMT monitors, I was issued a diplomatic visa and assured that I could never be searched or detained. And in a previously unheard-of concession made by both warring parties, CPMT members were granted the right to cross enemy lines at will, provided that they first "notified" the GOS and other concerned parties of their flight plans.

As things turned out, the team's diplomatic immunities and day-to-day movements were far more circumscribed than official documents decreed. Even so, my period of service on the CPMT allowed me to gain rapid access to people and places caught up in the immediate violent undertow of Sudan's two-decade-long civil war. Sometimes the team's plane touched down only hours after a major military assault, whereupon the team's medic usually took charge of bandaging up wounded civilians and soldiers brought in on makeshift stretchers, while I generally concentrated on interviewing civilian eyewitnesses, local military personnel, newly captured prisoners of war, and the like. Because nearly all the fighting that erupted during this time period was connected to a violent government military campaign to extend its oil exploration and development activities in Nuer regions of the Western Upper Nile and because I was the only team member who spoke Nuer (or, for that matter, Sudanese Arabic), I played a central role in gathering oral evidence during nearly all on-site investigations carried out by the CPMT-Rumbek. Furthermore, because Nuer speakers were fighting on all sides of this conflict, I had direct access to all kinds of information that other team members did not.

However, it was my experience that the CPMT's project managers often took a more restrictive view of the team's mandate than official documents proclaimed. Consequently, much of the oral testimony I collected about specific military abuses against civilians was ultimately deemed to fall outside the team's scope of action. For example, although there were no restrictions placed on the geographical scope of the CPMT's investigative mandate within Sudan, and both the Civilian Protection Agreement and the Cessation of Hostilities Agreement applied to all areas of the country, the CPMT's program managers rejected internal and external appeals to launch a formal investigation into the rapidly expanding violence in Darfur on the grounds that the CPMT should concentrate its monitoring activities in the South. Similarly, extensive eyewitness accounts I collected that documented the routine torture and killing of southern civilians by GOS forces in several (newly identified) "ghost houses" in Khartoum and Bentiu were deemed to fall outside the team's mandate.[8] After a while I resigned myself to this situation but continued gathering firsthand information about numerous topics that I thought critical to an in-depth understanding of Sudan's rapidly evolving civil war.

It should be emphasized that the CPMT's mandate contained no enforcement provisions. Nor, as I later discovered, had the U.S. State Department developed a clear plan of action about how to respond in the event of egregious or systematic violations of the Civilian Protection Agreement or Cessation of Hostilities Agreement. Like so many international monitoring missions established before and after it, the CPMT was granted neither the right nor the might to intervene directly to protect civilians from wanton military attack. Rather, the CPMT's powers were directed toward inducing greater GOS and SPLM/A compliance with international humanitarian law by exposing false allegations, publicly condemning serious violations and, more generally, by intensifying the watchful gaze of the "international community."

A second weakness in the team's founding mandate revolved around definitional questions. According to the mandate, "military operations" included, but were not limited to, "air attacks, artillery attacks, ground attacks, ambushes and intentional military activity or other uses of force that could result in the killing or injury of persons or the damage or destruction of property" by either warring party or their allied armed forces (Civilian Protection Agreement 2002:1, art. 1, sec. 1d). "Civilian facilities" were also broadly construed to include "schools, hospitals, religious premises, health and food distribution centers, or relief operations or objects or facilities indispensable to the survival of the civilian population and of a civilian nature" (Civilian Protection Agreement 2002:1, art. 1, sec. 1b). However, the Civilian Protection Agreement failed to specify whether oil development facilities and operations manned by foreign civilian contractors and heavily guarded by GOS military forces were to be categorized as "civilian facilities" worthy of the CPMT's protection—the GOS position—or whether they were to be classified as "legitimate military targets," owing to the fact that they were among the most heavily fortified structures in the South and provided the Khartoum government with significant revenues used to purchase advanced military equipment (such as fighter planes, helicopter gunships, long-range artillery units, tanks, etc.) from abroad and to construct domestic arms factories—the SPLM/A position. What this meant was that future CPMT managers were basically free to adopt whichever position they wished on the matter. Since the vast majority of military attacks against civilians reported during my term of service on the CPMT (December 20, 2002–March 31, 2003) were carried out in conjunction with the government's expanding oil development activities in the greater Upper Nile region, this was not an insignificant issue.

OVERARCHING AND COMPETING POLITICAL AGENDAS

In addition to these framing agreements, a number of broader political agendas further circumscribed the CPMT's mission. The U.S. Department of State issued the most powerful of these. State Department officials no doubt held hopes that the CPMT's deployment would help shield southern Sudanese civilians from wanton military attacks, especially from indiscriminate GOS bombing raids and helicopter gunship attacks that were raining down on southern Sudanese communities with increasing intensity at that time. However, the State Department's default position, it seems, was to minimize the political fallout of any continuing violence so as not to complicate the already difficult peace talks.

The Khartoum government, in contrast, surely regarded the CPMT's deployment as a significant intrusion on its sovereignty rights. At the same time, it realized it could potentially exercise control over the team's movements and activities through the invocation of those same rights. Indeed, during the months that followed, the Sudanese government did not hesitate to obstruct, delay, or derail specific on-site field investigations by the CPMT when they cut too close to the bone. But by allowing the CPMT's deployment, the GOS also hoped to defuse mounting international condemnations of its military actions against civilian populations in the south.

Reportedly the SPLM/A initially hesitated to sign the Cessation of Hostilities Agreement for fear of weakening its negotiating leverage at the peace talks. There is a real inequality created whenever an insurgent army is forced to drop its weaponry during peace negotiations with a state power. Should the GOS fail to respect the military stand-down, the SPLM/A had little recourse other than to walk out of the peace talks, which was not in its interests. Consequently, the SPLM/A had to invest considerable faith in the goodwill of international peace negotiators, as well as in the CPMT's protective promise in accepting both framing agreements. Any failure to restrain GOS military attacks through diplomatic means could negatively affect not only the outcome of the peace talks but, even more critically, relations between the SPLM/A's leadership and its civilian support base.

The real wild cards in the peace process, however, were various GOS-allied regional militias. Over the years the GOS had recruited an array of southern and northern auxiliary forces to spearhead its counterinsurgency campaign against the SPLM/A. Ties between Sudan's army forces and these auxiliary groups were strong and complex. Army military intelligence armed and directed the militias, many of whose leaders held high-ranking positions in the national military. However, the GOS routinely asserted that its militia forces attacked civilians without its consent so as to maintain a degree of plausible deniability. Owing to the bipolar (GOS-SPLM/A) resolution model adopted at the peace talks, government-allied militia leaders were neither consulted nor requested to sign the Cessation of Hostilities Agreement or the Civilian Protection Agreement. Instead, the government signed for them.[9] Sidelined and resentful, several prominent southern militia leaders—including several GOS-allied Nuer warlords strategically located in oil-rich regions of the Upper Nile—took the position that they were under no obligation to respect either agreement since they had not signed them. Consequently, GOS-allied southern militias remained an unpredictable source of volatility throughout the lengthy peace negotiations and currently represent one of the most serious challenges to the successful implementation of the final agreement.

All of this created a major dilemma for the SPLM/A because it had no comparable auxiliary forces at its disposal. Throughout the lengthy peace negotiations the GOS routinely denied any involvement in alleged militia assaults against civilians in SPLM/A-held territories. This put the SPLM/A in a bind. Were the SPLM/A to counterattack the government's militias, the GOS could respond by suspending the peace talks. Genuinely seeking a negotiated settlement, the SPLM/A leadership reportedly ordered its regional commanders to refrain from initiating any attacks on government-held locations. This is not to say that those orders were universally observed. There were recurrent GOS allegations of SPLM/A military attacks and counterattacks received during my tenure on the CPMT. Most of these alleged attacks were directed against oil-development infrastructure and military personnel advancing into SPLM/A-held areas. However, from my position on the CPMT, it certainly seemed that local SPLM/A commanders often chose to withdraw their troops rather than forcefully resist GOS military advances into their areas lest the SPLM/A be accused of violating the Cessation of Hostilities Agreement.

Finally, one must consider the perspectives of southern Sudanese civilians themselves, many of whom were initially hopeful about the CPMT's protective abilities. The team's name itself proved falsely reassuring. Moreover, the fact that the overwhelming majority of the team's members were former military personnel, many of whom initially donned military uniforms, led many southerners to conclude that they came with sufficient military hardware to physically protect them—a serious misunderstanding that reportedly encouraged some civilians to return to areas that in reality remained highly vulnerable to GOS military attacks. The CPMT's honeymoon period with civilians did not last long, however, especially since the GOS appeared to make a point of encouraging its militia allies to attack several civilian locations shortly after the CPMT visited them during the mission's first months of deployment. Be that as it may, the overarching expectations and voices of southern Sudanese civilians were, in my experience, the least likely to be recognized and heard by the CPMT.

A SELECTION OF KEY INVESTIGATIVE REPORTS

A few days before I joined the team, the CPMT released its first investigative report,[10] which confirmed an NGO allegation that the government had dropped multiple bombs on a civilian cattle camp in the Mundri/Lui area, western Equatoria, on September 21, 2002. The attack resulted in the deaths of up to 12 civilians and scores of cattle. Nevertheless, the report concluded that this raid was militarily justified, owing to the presence of an abandoned and inoperative artillery piece located in the vicinity of the cattle camp. Basically, the investigative team defined all civilian losses as collateral damage and recommended that in the future, abandoned military equipment be removed from the area or painted with a black "X" to indicate that it was not serviceable. Although the GOS claimed that it was targeting a (nonexistent) footbridge on the far side of the cattle camp, CPMT members hypothesized that government bomber pilots were more likely aiming at an abandoned artillery piece located 130 meters from the camp. However, owing to presumed "pilot misjudgment," the report concluded that the bombs were "unintentionally" released "too early," missing the target and striking the cattle camp (CPMT 2002:1–2). In essence, the team's leader, who was himself an experienced fighter pilot, adopted the perspective of the attacking plane rather than that of the civilians attacked.

The Mundri/Lui report provoked strong negative reactions from international human rights activists on its release, who charged that its conclusions were based on an inaccurate reading of the Geneva Conventions, insufficient knowledge of the military history of the area, and a failure to follow up on major inconsistencies between oral statements made by the GOS and material and oral evidence collected on-site. Had these issues been more thoroughly addressed, it was argued, the investigative team might have come to a very different conclusion—one that found that the GOS had used "disproportionate" or "excessive" force to destroy a military target that posed no objective threat.

Significantly, the executive summary of the report released to the public failed to mention that the artillery piece in question and other rusting and inoperative military hardware in the surrounding region were all "probable GOS" equipment, abandoned by the government during the "mid-to-late 1990's" when it lost military control of the area to the SPLM/A (CPMT 2002:12). The report's summary remains silent on this matter, and the report's conclusions simply state that "the positioning of military hardware in close proximity to a Church, *regardless of when it was conducted or by whom,* was at that time and still is, in clear violation of the Geneva Convention" (CPMT 2002:15; emphasis added). The team leaders clearly assumed that had this artillery piece been removed or marked, no government bombing raid would have taken place. In essence, the report censured the SPLM/A, which maintained no forces in the area, for violating the Geneva Conventions by failing to remove or mark heavy military equipment previously abandoned by the GOS, while it explicitly condoned the government's attack on a civilian cattle camp. But the CPMT investigators never interviewed the pilots concerned to verify the team's assumption that the abandoned artillery piece rather than an imaginary footbridge or the very real cattle camp was the actual target of attack. Nor did they check with government officials about whether or not individual fighter pilots were authorized to bomb military "targets of opportunity" without prior approval. More seriously, the report's central hypothesis regarding the presumed target and motives of the government pilots concerned was based solely on the direction of strafing tracks running past the artillery piece toward the camp. However, the sole civilian eyewitness interviewed by the CPMT investigators stated that he heard no machine-gunning during the bombing raid. Since this area had been bombed and strafed by government pilots on multiple occasions during the previous five years, it is difficult to understand why the investigative team maintained its hypothetical reconstruction of the event without verifying its accuracy through multiple eyewitness testimonies.

For my purposes, the Mundri/Lui report reveals a number of investigative weaknesses and logical inconsistencies that were to recur in subsequent reports. Specifically, this report failed to examine the all-important question of "proportionality" lying at the heart of international humanitarian law. The rules of war are directed at minimizing civilian losses and avoiding unnecessary suffering. A military attack is only legally justified when possible civilian casualties and losses are deemed proportionate or nonexcessive in relation to the military advantage potentially gained by the operation. But there is no evidence that the CPMT investigators ever asked themselves the question of whether or not the deaths of 12 civilians and numerous cattle were proportional to the possible destruction of an inoperable artillery piece that posed no objective threat. Since the government had previously bombarded this area on several occasions, it most likely knew from experience that the artillery piece in question was incapable of firing back. Thus reasonable minds could conclude that this bombing attack, whatever its true target, involved excessive force.

The discarding of eyewitness testimony when it contradicted the team leader's hypothetical reconstruction of the attack based on military forensics was another weakness of this report that was to recur in subsequent investigations. While the collection of hard military evidence—also known as Battle Damage Assessment or BDA—can constitute an extremely powerful investigative tool, it is best used in conjunction with eyewitness testimonies. No examination of bullet casings or mortar splashes can definitively determine, for instance, the chronology of an attack, especially in areas subjected to multiple military assaults over decades. Nor can military forensic evidence definitively determine which party was the aggressor, nor how many civilians were killed, wounded, and displaced. Corroborating eyewitness accounts thus prove essential. Nevertheless, this type of evidence was repeatedly sidelined and ignored by the team's managers.

The second investigative report issued by the CPMT represented a major advance. It documented a long and intense series of GOS and GOS-allied militia attacks over a broad region of the oil-cursed Western Upper Nile during a monthlong period in early 2003 (CPMT 2003a). Highlighting two major vectors of GOS military violence, one accompanying the expansion of a new oil development road along the eastern segment of the region, the report rightly condemns repeated GOS military attacks against unarmed civilians and states that "there was no indication that the SPLM had attacked GOS or GOS-allied militias in the region" (CPMT 2003a:1–2). The report significantly watered down its conclusions, however, by noting that the the GOS had accused the SPLM/A of killing four civilian construction workers employed by an oil company, although the report adds that this allegation remains under investigation and has not been substantiated by the team. The implicit assumption is that, were this allegation to be subsequently verified (and no subsequent verification was forthcoming), it would in some sense counterbalance the long string of verified GOS military attacks and reported military buildup in the region carried out in direct violation of both framing agreements (CPMT 2003a:3). Nowhere is there evidence in the report that the team's managers actively grappled with the question of whether or not civilian oil contractors protected by advancing government troops could be considered "legitimate military targets" according to the Geneva Conventions (CPMT 2003a).[11] Nevertheless, on the basis of a single unconfirmed GOS allegation and on the unstated assumption that, were it confirmed, the SPLM/A could be charged with violating the Civilian Protection Agreement, the report's conclusions shift abruptly into the passive voice in an apparent attempt to project what I would term an "illusion of neutrality." The conclusion reads: "Regardless of which party may be responsible, the observed facts concerning attacks on the civilian population on their villages and facilities are that: many thousands of civilians have been forcefully displaced from their villages by direct military attack" (CPMT 2003a:5).

The report's strengths stem from its more comprehensive temporal and regional coverage, its willingness to foreground oil-development issues as a primary cause of escalating GOS military violence in the region, and the fact that it helped pressure the GOS into signing an "addendum" to the Cessation of Hostilities Agreement that explicitly prohibited any further work on a major oil development road advancing into SPLM/A-held territory in the Western Upper Nile until after the signing of a final peace agreement. This supplementary agreement, which definitely helped reduce GOS and GOS-allied military attacks on Nuer civilian populations located in the immediate vicinity of the road, was signed on February 4, 2003 (Addendum to the Memorandum of Understanding on Cessation of Hostilities Agreement 2003).

The report, however, also had noteworthy weaknesses. First, it failed to make note of eight new military garrisons established by government troops between late December 2002 and the end of January 2003 along the new oil road advancing into SPLM/A-controlled territories. All of these garrisons sprang up under the aerial gaze of the CPMT, and all were created in direct violation of the October 2002 Cessation of Hostilities Agreement. Second, by ultimately blaming both the SPLM/A and the GOS for civilian losses when the overwhelming evidence suggested systematic aggressions solely on the part of the government, the report conclusions could be— and were—used by the Khartoum government to justify its actions (CPMT 2003a).[12] In the official SPLM/A response to the Western Upper Nile report, (submitted in the form of a letter dated January 31, 2003), Commander Salva Kiir Mayardit, the SPLM/A chief of staff, took aim at the report's conclusions: "Apportioning the blame on both sides while things are very clear on the ground, leaves the culprits to get away with it and this is why the GOS has been committing this genocide on our people with impunity. The GOS plans to displace the whole civil population of the Western Upper Nile during the truce period so that the oil companies can extend their oil exploration to the areas now under the SPLM/A administration. In order to achieve this in the shortest time possible, the GOS orders its troops and militia to kill, loot, rape, abduct young men, children and young women who can be used by the army as sex workers and burn down all the villages" (CPMT 2003a).[13]

Third, the original version of the final report was subsequently modified by a leading U.S. consulate official in Khartoum through the insertion of several explanatory notes into the body of the text. Three of these notes significantly softened the general thrust of the report's criticisms of GOS military aggression. Indeed, two of these insertions directly echoed the official response to the report submitted by the GOS (CPMT 2003a:appendix).[14] The first note reassures readers that although a GOS garrison commander stationed along the new oil road had seriously impeded the CPMT's investigative access and, indeed, had threatened to shoot down the CPMT's plane if it flew over his garrison, "the Government of Sudan has provided assurance in Annex A that CPMT aircraft are safe from hostile action of GOS forces and associated militias enroute to and from the area of interest and mission area" (CPMT 2003a:4). The second inserted note is more perturbing in that it follows instantly on the report's concluding recommendation that the GOS immediately cease all attacks on civilians. That note reads: "The CPMT was informed on January 25 that the provincial authorities in Bentiu had been instructed to ensure that GOS allied militia . . . launch no new attacks. CPMT visits to the region have not documented any new attacks in the region since that time." This final assertion, regrettably, was untrue. A third CPMT report, confirming an allegation of a GOS military attack on the town of Leer, in the Western Upper Nile, on January 26, 2002, was released to the public simultaneously with the team's Western Upper Nile report. The Leer report also verified a second GOS and militia attack on the village of Luom on January 30, 2005, which injured and/or killed two children and a pregnant woman (CPMT 2003b).[15] That the CPMT simultaneously issued two reports that contradicted each other in this way speaks to the vital importance of international human rights monitoring missions maintaining their investigative independence, regardless of their funding sources, to guard against the possible intrusion of competing political agendas and, in this case, of a strong dose of state bias. I should perhaps note that, despite the February 4, 2003, signing of the addendum to the Cessation of Hostilities Agreement, requiring, among other things, a return of all forces to their former locations on October 17, 2002, none of the new government garrisons created along the Bentiu-Leer oil development road were removed.

The Western Upper Nile report was followed by a long CPMT silence that extended into a lengthy grounding of all CPMT aircraft by the GOS between March 17 and April 11, 2003. It was during this period that I voluntarily withdrew from the mission. This is not to say that no reports of continuing military violence reached the team during this time. Indeed, the CPMT-Rumbek was actively engaged in investigating 12 SPLM/A allegations of GOS violations of the Civilian Protection Agreement at the time all planes were grounded. The GOS had also forwarded one allegation of a SPLM/A attack. Investigations of several SPLM/A allegations were well advanced at the time the mission was forced by the GOS to stop flying. However, of all of these in-process investigations, some of which were nearing completion at the time, the only report eventually to be issued concerned a GOS allegation of an SPLM/A attack on a supposedly civilian cattle camp surrounding a major government garrison in Wangkai in the Western Upper Nile.

Before turning to that report, it is important to emphasize that once an international monitoring mission is established, it is very easy for interested state parties, human rights groups, and the general public to assume that if no reports of serious violations are issued, none occurred. In my experience, nothing could be further from the truth. I also found a serious organizational weakness in the basic structure of the CPMT in that the team's managers were not accountable to anyone—be they GOS or SPLM/A officials, southern Sudanese civilians, international peace negotiators, the U.S. State Department, or the general public—when deciding which allegations of military violence would be investigated and which would be ignored. There was no running tally of all allegations received by the CPMT available to interested parties. Consequently, the temporal framing and selection of specific incidents for investigative follow-ups could appear arbitrary, if not skewed in the direction of creating an illusion of impartiality by alternating between alleged incidents of military violence against civilians allegedly carried out by the GOS and by the SPLM/A.

Since the CPMT had just issued a major report documenting a long series of GOS transgressions, the CPMT's management appeared to prefer to concentrate on the sole allegation of SPLM/A violence the mission had received during this time, rather than follow up on any of the 12 allegations of continuing GOS aggression received—one of which represented a major GOS military assault supported by helicopter gunships. The result was a significant intrusion of state bias under the guise of neutrality.

The CPMT's Wangkai report, the next one issued, was problematic for other reasons as well. First, it failed to mention that the civilian cattle camp allegedly attacked by the SPLM/A forces was the dry-season home base of a notoriously mercurial and militarily aggressive Nuer GOS militia warlord named Peter Gatdet Yaka. In many ways the entire incident crystallizes the quandary of local SPLM/A commanders when faced with a southern GOS-militia leader who vehemently denied that he had any obligation to abide by the Cessation of Hostilities Agreement because he had not signed it.[16] The report substantiated that a group of SPLM/A soldiers had raided a cattle camp near a major government army garrison at Wangkai on March 9, 2003, resulting in an indeterminate number of civilians killed and wounded (estimated to be 18 and 20, respectively) and the loss of some 20 to 40 head of cattle (CPMT 2003e:1–5).

The local SPLM/A commander admitted conducting an ambush on Gatdet's cattle camp but justified his actions on the basis of numerous cattle raids previously carried out against civilians in his area by Gatdet's militia forces. The SPLM/A commander also said that "out of respect for the cessation of hostilities agreement the attacking force did not fire on the GOS army garrison at Wangkai, and instead concentrated on the cattle camp" (CPMT 2003e:4). The government's garrison troops, however, responded by firing on the attackers and by dispatching two so-called technicals armed with 12.7 mm machine guns (CPMT 2003e:4). During the attack, many of the camp's residents ran to the garrison. Although the report acknowledged that garrison troops subsequently shelled and fired in the direction of the cattle camp, it did not explicitly consider the possibility that some civilians were wounded or killed by so-called friendly fire. Indeed, the report fails to mention that two civilian casualties were close relatives of Gatdet and that both were killed by 12.7mm gunfire—weapons allegedly used in this region at the time by GOS-supplied troops only (UN security personnel, personal communication, March 12, 2003).

Instead of crediting the SPLM/A with adhering to the Cessation of Hostilities Agreement by refraining from targeting the government garrison itself, however, the report roundly condemns it, blaming it for all civilian deaths. The report reads: "It is clear from the deployment of the [SPLM/A] attack and the fact that none of the 170 men in the GOS army garrison, which was only 300 meters from the cattle camp, were killed or wounded, that the target of the attackers was the population of Wangkai" (CPMT 2003e:3). These issues run deep. Perhaps SPLM/A raiders were seeking to regain previously captured civilian cattle. The report continues: "It was widely assumed that Wangkai was selected for attack rather than Mankien [Gatdet's main militia garrison] with its large force of defenders since it was an easier target of attack" (CPMT 2003e:3). However, Gatdet held no cattle at Mankien. Finally, the report misleadingly characterizes what was in reality Gatdet's personal herd and family cattle camp as "an undefended displaced civilian population in an isolated cattle camp" (CPMT 2003e:1)— an inappropriate characterization considering both the presence and the active response of the 170 government troops stationed nearby.

The next investigative report released by the CPMT followed up on a GOS allegation that the SPLM/A had launched an attack in the Eastern Upper Nile, capturing the villages of Malwal and Jekau, which resulted in the deaths of 12 civilians and displacing up to 8,000 others. The report concluded that the SPLM/A had attacked on March 17, 2003, but found "no evidence to substantiate the allegation" of mass civilian displacement nor "to support the claim that as many as 12 civilians were killed" in the operation (CPMT 2003d:6). However, the CPMT also found during the course of its investigations that "GOS militia forces in the area also conducted military operations" in "mid-March," resulting "in the beating of civilians, the looting of civilian property," as well as at least four rapes and "a list totaling 46 persons by name . . . killed during the GOS military attack" (CPMT 2003d:6.) The CPMT investigators also interviewed approximately 50 eyewitnesses, "representing an equal composition of political affiliation[s] in the area," who "unanimously identified their attackers as the 'GOS militia', not the SPLM/A" (CPMT 2003d:5). Despite the complete unanimity of all 50 eyewitnesses, the report weakly concludes that "it is likely that some civilians were killed as the result of attacks undertaken by both Parties" (CPMT 2003d:6). Here again CPMT investigators attempted to project an illusion of neutrality while indirectly introducing a significant element of state bias.

More disturbingly, the Pagak-Malwal Area report failed to make any determination about which attack—whether the GOS militia attack in "mid-March" or the SPLM/A attack on March 17, 2003—took place first. Surely this was a question that could have been asked of the 50 eyewitnesses interviewed.[17] Nor did the report attempt to reconstruct the military history of the area back to the start of the Cessation of Hostilities Agreement on October 17, 2002, to determine which warring party was seeking to advance territorially at the expense of the other. It also did not make any mention of the fact that regular GOS troops, working in tandem with a Malaysian oil company, were in the process of extending a new oil development road in the direction of Malwal during this same time period—though this fact was subsequently acknowledged by the CPMT in a later investigative report on the Longochok area (see CPMT 2003c:1).[18] By avoiding all these issues and simply asserting that civilians deaths were "likely" to have been perpetuated by both sides—despite the unanimous testimonies of 50 eyewitnesses to the contrary—the Pagak-Malwal report implicitly condoned and reinforced an atmosphere of military impunity in the region. In an apparent effort to project an image of neutrality, the CPMT's report indirectly rewarded the most territorially aggressive warring party and did little or nothing to ensure the future safety of civilians in the area.

This same region of the Eastern Upper Nile was the subject of another CPMT report that also reflects elements of state bias. "The Report of Investigation: Longochok Area" (CPMT 2003c) is one of the most convoluted, confusing, and unpersuasive reports issued during the CPMT's first year of deployment. The initial allegation, which originated with an international humanitarian agency active in the area, alleged that a GOS-allied militia attacked the village of Longochok and nine other neighboring villages, resulting in the deaths of 59 persons and the wounding of an indeterminate number of others, on May 22, 2003 (later dated in the same report as May 27).

The report opens by suggesting that recent political defections of senior military from government-backed militia forces to the SPLM/A and vice versa are the root cause of turmoil in the region. It further notes the presence of Fellata, or nomadic pastoralists originating from Fulani groups from West Africa, who move into the area during the dry season (November to June) to graze their cattle (CPMT 2003c:1). To its credit, the report mentions regular GOS forces and Petrodar Oil Company personnel carrying out road work in the area. However, it does so only to certify that they had withdrawn from the area prior to the attack in question, owing to the start of the rains. Contradictory civilian accounts attributed the attack to the Fellata, the GOS-allied militia forces, a combination of both these progovernment forces, and the SPLM/A. Officials of the SPLM/A claimed to have reached one of the villages (Wan Tau) the day after it was attacked and to have aided the villagers in burying the dead.

All eyewitnesses interviewed at Wan Tau stated that they were attacked by the Fellata. However, on the assumption that "the entire area" was controlled by the GOS-allied forces of a certain Commander Nyang Chatyout and that "he would have no reason to attack his own villages," the report concludes by "strongly suggesting"—but not confirming—"that it was the SPLM/A and an element of the Fellata . . . *not* the GOS or its militia that contributed to the death of . . . an indeterminate number of people, the displacement of civilians, and the destruction and looting of civilian property" (CPMT 2003c:5; emphasis original). Once again, there was no apparent attempt by the CPMT investigators responsible for the final form of this report to systematically reconstruct the recent military history of the area. Indeed, their central historical assumption—that the entire area was controlled by GOS-allied militia forces prior to this attack—was undercut by a logical inconsistency. The report explains that the Fellata "pay taxes each year to the appropriate authorities depending on their location, either the SPLM/A or the GOS, for [seasonal access to] water and grazing rights" (CPMT 2003c:4). But the report then notes that during the dry season in question, the Fellata paid taxes to the SPLM/A (CPMT 2003c: Consideration of Evidence, sec. P). This in itself is strong evidence that the SPLM/A controlled at least some of the area in question when the Fellata entered the region in November 2002—which, it should be stressed, postdates the official Cessation of Hostilities Agreement.

Nor did the CPMT investigators offer any explanation about why they decided to select and isolate this particular allegation of military violence when the team had received a series of unconfirmed allegations of military violence in the immediate area dating back to the beginning of January

2003—most of these being SPLM/A allegations of GOS military activity carried out in tandem with the expanding oil road. This is a problem. If international monitoring teams are not transparent about why they prioritize some allegations of violence and disregard others, it is very difficult for them to maintain the confidence and cooperation of all parties concerned. Indeed, even before the release of the Pagak-Malwal and Longochok area investigative reports, many SPLM/A commanders had lost confidence in the mission's objectivity and efficacy and had ceased forwarding any allegations.

CONCLUSIONS

To recapitulate, I have argued that (1) by refusing to address the issue of proportionality lying at the heart of international humanitarian law; (2) by decontextualizing allegations of military violence into isolated incidents while simultaneously failing to explain the criteria by which some incidents were selected for investigation and not others; (3) by striving to project an illusion of neutrality through frequent recourse to the passive voice and a seeming preference for no-fault violence; (4) by failing to keep a running tab of the military shifts of power and territory under its watch; and (5) by implicitly condoning the forward movement of government military troops in conjunction with expanding oil-development infrastructure (despite the existence of the Cessation of Hostilities Agreement and despite SPLM/A arguments that oil-development operations constituted legitimate military targets)—the CPMT did more during its first year of deployment to excuse and perpetuate military violence against southern Sudanese civilians than to restrain or curtail it.

In many ways the CPMT's most significant contribution during its first year of operation was to legitimize and perpetuate a limbolike state of "no peace/no war" that ultimately resulted in a major shift in the military balance of power in favor of the Sudanese government. Could one discern this result from a close reading of the investigative reports the CPMT issued during the mission's first year? One could not, owing to the mission's failure to provide any periodic updates or comprehensive overviews of the shifting territorial holdings of the warring parties.

What the CPMT actually monitored during its first year was a rapid territorial expansion of government military forces, especially in the oil-rich southern region of the Upper Nile. In some ways it actually proved easier for government forces to advance territorially at the expense of the SPLM/A after having signed the Cessation of Hostilities Agreement and the Civilian Protection Agreement than before. This was because the SPLM/A was more reticent to engage with advancing GOS troops lest it be accused of breaching these agreements and thereby of providing the Sudanese government with a pretense for abandoning the peace talks. Because the CPMT's presence helped prolong this inherently unstable military situation, it may have contributed—albeit inadvertently—to an intensification of both military impunity and civilian vulnerability. Could things have turned out differently? Perhaps, but that would have required the CPMT's managers to acknowledge and counter internal and external pressures to veer toward state bias. This case study analysis would seem to confirm Ignatieff's pessimistic assessment that in the context of internal armed conflicts, international interventions are never neutral.

NOTES

1. Sudan's first North/South civil war (1955–72) ended in a negotiated peace agreement that granted the southern third of the country considerable regional autonomy. However, following the discovery of large oil deposits in southern Sudan during the late 1970s, the 1972 Addis Ababa Peace Agreement was immediately and unilaterally abrogated by the central government in Khartoum, headed at that time by Jaafar Numeiri, thereby precipitating the re-eruption of full-scale civil war in the South.

2. I am referring to the 7,700-member-strong African Union Mission in Sudan (AMIS) which has struggled—wholly unsuccessfully—to curtail the genocidal violence waged since 2003 by Khartoum's armed forces and their Janjaweed auxiliary forces against the Fur, Zhagawa, Masalit, and other non-Arabized African populations in Darfur. The U.N. Security Council authorized a joint African Union / United Nations Hybrid operation in Darfur (UNAMID) to replace AMIS on July 31, 2007. Effective deployment of this much larger and better-mandated force of 26,000 members, however, has proven extremely difficult, given continued resistance from Khartoum. For a concise and penetrating analysis of the rapidly changing situation in Darfur, I recommend a 2008 report by Human Rights First, titled "Investing in Tragedy: China's Money, Arms and Politics in Sudan," available online at www.humanrightsfirst.info/pdf/080311-cah-investing-in-tragedy-report.pdf. Other important resources can be found in various reports issued by international Crisis Groups (www.crisisgroup.org). The African Studies Center Library at the University of Leiden, the Netherlands, has also posted an excellent bibliography on the Darfur crisis online (www.ascleiden.nl). For a concise history of the Darfur region, see Flint and de Waal (2005).

3. Solid historical analyses of Sudan's wars are numerous. Among the most accessible and comprehensive works are Deng 1995; Johnson 2003; Lesch 1998; Human Rights Watch 2003.

4. Estimates of the numbers of Darfuris who have died or have been displaced since 2003 vary. However, recent estimates of the total number of war-related deaths in the Darfur conflict range from more than 200,000 to closer to 450,000 (see Hagan and Palloni 2006; Reeves 2006).

5. The Comprehensive Peace Agreement is a collection of agreements between the GOS and the SPLM/A completed on December 31, 2004, and signed in a formal ceremony on January 9, 2005.

6. Various international human rights groups, other NGOs, and national and international commissions have documented the increasing intensity and geographical scope of GOS and GOS-allied military attacks on southern Sudanese civilians during this period. Especially helpful sources include the official Web sites of Human Rights Watch (www.hrw.org) and the International Crisis Group.

7. Some CPMT personnel, however, had collected considerable information about the military locations of both warring parties as of late October 2002. But there was no apparent will within the team's management to compile this information for purposes of reinforcing the Cessation of Hostilities Agreement or the Civilian Protection Agreement.

8. "Ghost houses" are secret locations where GOS security forces interrogated, tortured, and often killed citizens suspected of being disloyal to the state.

9. Page 2 of the Cessation of Hostilities Agreement explicitly stipulated that it encompassed all military forces, "including allied forces and affiliated militias."

10. The CPMT maintained a publicly accessible Web site for much of its duration, which contained versions of all published reports. Unfortunately, between the period of drafting this article and its publication, the CPMT's Web site was removed and these documents are no longer readily accessible online. Presumably, copies may be obtained by contacting the U.S. State Department.

11. Significantly, the official response letter of the GOS, which is included as an appendix of the report, acknowledges that the oil road that the civilian contractors were constructing at the time of the alleged attack "is considered a legitimate military target by the SPLA." January 5, 2003, letter from the Ministry of Foreign Affairs, the Republic of Sudan, to Brig. General (Retd) Herbert J. Lloyd, Project Manager, Civilian Protection Monitoring Team.

12. See the official response letter of the government's Ministry of Defense at the conclusion of CPMT 2003a.

13. January 31, 2003, letter from Cdr. Salva Kiir Mayardit, SPLA Chief of General Staff, to Brig. General (Retd) Herbert J. Lloyd, Project Manager, Civilian Protection Monitoring Team. This letter was the official response of the SPLM/A to the CPMT's Western Upper Nile report (2003a). Although it reportedly arrived too late to be included in the final binding of the report, I obtained a copy of it together with that report of February 6, 2003.

14. January 5, 2003, letter from the Ministry of Foreign Affairs included as an appendix in CPMT 2003a.
15. This was a special report produced by the CPMT for the purposes of monitoring the Cessation of Hostilities Agreement by the Intergovernmental Authority on Development (IGAD) peace negotiators. It is not numbered like other CPMT reports referred to in this article.
16. My knowledge of Gatdet's position in this regard stems from a lengthy interview I had with him in the Nuer language during one of the CPMT's on-site investigations.
17. The report's claim that the lunar calendar was generally utilized in this area is weak, and the statement "it [was] extremely difficult to tie an event to a specific calendar date" is even weaker (CPMT 2003d: 4). Whether or not the CPMT investigators were capable of identifying the date of the full moon during March 2003, it should have been possible for them to elicit clear statements from eyewitnesses about which attack occurred first.
18. Also see the SPLM/A's official response to the Pagak-Malwal area report of May 23, 2003, which is included at the end of that report.

REFERENCES

Cessation of Hostilities Agreement
2002   Memorandum of Understanding between the Government of Sudan and the Sudan People's Liberation Movement/Army (SPLM/A) on Resumption of Negotiations on Peace in Sudan. October 15.
2003   Addendum to the Memorandum of Understanding on Cessation of Hostilities between the Government of Sudan (GOS) and the Sudan People's Liberation Movement/Army (SPLM/A). February 4.

Civilian Protection Agreement
2002   Agreement between the Government and the Republic of Sudan and the Sudan People's Liberation Movement to Protect Non-Combatant Civilians and Civilian Facilities from Military Attack. March 31.

Civilian Protection Monitoring Team–Sudan (CPMT)
2002   Final Incident Report: Mundri; Report 1. Khartoum: Civilian Protection Monitoring Team–Sudan. December 15.
2003a   Final Report of Military Events in the Western Upper Nile, 31 December 2002 to 20 January 2003: Report 2. Khartoum: Civilian Protection Monitoring Team–Sudan. February 6.
2003b   Report for IGAD Special Envoy Lt. Gen. Lazaro Sumbeiywo, Alleged Attack on Leer, WUN, 26 January 2003. Delivered to him in Nairobi on 3 February 2003. Released by Permission of Lt. Gen. Sumbeiywo. Khartoum: Civilian Protection Monitoring Team/Verification Monitoring Team–Sudan. February 6.
2003c   Report of Investigation: Longochok Area; Report 11. Khartoum: Civilian Protection Monitoring Team–Sudan. May 23.

2003d   Report of Investigation: Pagak-Malwal Area; Report 4. Khartoum: Civilian Protection Monitoring Team–Sudan. May 17.

2003e   Report of Investigation: Wangkai Cattle Camp; Report 3. Khartoum: Civilian Protection Monitoring Team–Sudan. April.

Comprehensive Peace Agreement

2005   Comprehensive Peace Agreement. Electronic document, http://www.usip.org/library/pa/sudan/cpa01092005/cpa_toc.html, accessed July 7, 2005.

Deng, Francis M.

1995   War of Visions: Conflict of Identities in the Sudan. Washington: Brookings Institution.

Flint, Julie, and Alex de Waal

2005   Darfur: A Short History of a Long War. London: Zed.

Hagan, John, and Alberto Palloni, eds.

2006   Death in Darfur. Science (Sept. 15):1578–1579.

Ignatieff, Michael

2003   Human Rights, Sovereignty, and Intervention. In Human Rights, Human Wrongs: The Oxford Amnesty Lectures 2001. Nicholas Owen, ed. Pp. 49–88. Oxford: Oxford University Press.

Johnson, Douglas H.

2003   The Root Causes of Sudan's Civil Wars. Oxford: James Currey.

Lesch, Ann Mosely

1998   The Sudan: Contested National Identities. Bloomington: Indiana University Press.

Reeves, Eric

2003   Sudan, Oil, and Human Rights. New York: Human Rights Watch.

2006   Quantifying Genocide in Darfur. Electronic document, http://www.sudanreeves.org/PrintArticle102.html, accessed April 29, 2006.

Totten, Samuel, and Eric Markusen, eds.

2006   Genocide in Darfur: Investigating the Atrocities in Sudan. New York: Routledge.

Jennie E. Burnet

3   WHOSE GENOCIDE? WHOSE TRUTH?

Representations of Victim and Perpetrator in Rwanda

A little over twelve years ago, an estimated eight hundred thousand Rwandans, primarily Tutsi, but also politically moderate Hutu, were massacred in a state-sponsored genocide in Rwanda.[1] A major concern for the post-genocide Rwandan government, as well as for the international community, has been the sorting of victims and perpetrators for the purposes of justice. Yet the Rwandan government has also faced the challenge of rebuilding the nation and of promoting peace in a deeply divided society. To this end the government adopted a policy of "national unity" and abolished ethnicity as an official factor in bureaucratic life. This essay argues that despite official policy, state practices of national memory have maintained an ethnic dichotomy (Hutu-Tutsi) by politicizing victimhood and emphasizing the distinction between victim and perpetrator in national ceremonies commemorating the genocide.[2] The state's power to define who is "innocent" and who is "guilty," who is "victim" and who is "perpetrator," in public discourse has penetrated society so pervasively as to become hegemony. As a result, Hutu who did not participate in the genocide, as well as Rwandans in ethnically mixed marriages and families, were erased from the national imagination. Thus nationalized mourning for the 1994 genocide and its victims has limited the possibility of publicly mourning all victims of violence associated with the civil war (1990–94), genocide (April-July 1994), and insurgency (1997–2000). This essay is based on 31 months of ethnographic research in rural and urban Rwanda between April 1997 and November 2003.[3]

HETEROGENEOUS VICTIMS: POLITICAL POWER AND THE STRUCTURE OF VIOLENCE IN THE 1990S

While the 1994 genocide may be the best-known violent episode in Rwandan history, it was but one concentrated period of violence in a decade characterized by armed conflict. During the 1990s changing political contexts and regimes created a situation in which state-sponsored violence targeted different categories of people. As a result, a variety of Rwandans feel that they have been victims, although many of them are not publicly recognized as victims in post-genocide Rwanda.

In October 1990 the Rwandan Patriotic Front (RPF), a rebel movement composed predominantly of Tutsi who lived in exile, attacked Rwanda with the intention of liberating the country from President Juvénal Habyarimana's dictatorship. This civil war continued throughout the early 1990s and shaped the emerging rhetoric of ethnic hatred used by Hutu extremists who controlled the reins of power. The early 1990s in Rwanda also brought democratization and the rise of opposition parties to the country's political scene. The Habyarimana regime was eventually forced into peace negotiations with the RPF, from which emerged a power-sharing agreement between the regime, opposition political parties, and the RPF. Between 1990 and early 1994 the Rwandan state under the Habyarimana regime, as well as the Rwandan military, known by its French acronym FAR (Forces Armées Rwandaises), targeted Tutsi and opposition politicians, human rights activists, and journalists critical of the regime.[4]

In April 1994 Hutu extremists opposed to the power-sharing agreement seized power following Habyarimana's assassination.[5] They immediately began to execute their genocidal plan, a final solution to eliminate "Tutsi opposition" to Hutu rule. Between April and July 1994 all Tutsi were targeted for killing, while Hutu members of opposition parties, human rights activists, and anyone opposed to the genocide also became targets for elimination. The genocide ended when the RPF took military control of the majority of the territory, driving the Hutu-extremist government into exile, along with over a million civilians.

The RPF has remained in control of the government since 1994, first under a "consensual dictatorship" (1994–2003) and then under a nominal democracy following presidential and parliamentary elections in 2003. While the RPF and its members have been frequently portrayed as saviors and peacemakers, the party's rule has not been a universally positive experience for Rwandans regardless of their ethnicity. In 1994 and 1995 the RPF's military wing was responsible for killing unknown numbers of civilians, both Hutu and Tutsi (interviews by author 1999, 2000, 2001, 2003, 2004, 2006; Degni-Segui 1996; Des Forges 1999:705–714; HRW 1996; MSF 1995; Pottier 2002; Reyntjens 2004).[6] In 1996 the RPF forced the repatriation of nearly a million refugees living in eastern Zaire and organized the massacres of hundreds of thousands more under the guise of a "Banyamulenge rebellion" in eastern Zaire. Between 1997 and 1999 Rwandans inside the country found themselves caught between RPF soldiers and an insurgency, primarily composed of former Interahamwe militiamen and FAR soldiers, as well as some recruits from the refugee camps.[7] Both sides committed brutalities against the population that included killings, rapes, and torture. In 1999 the RPF changed its counterinsurgency tactics by relocating the civilian population in northwestern Rwanda so as to physically separate them from the insurgents. The RPF then succeeded in pushing the insurgency into eastern Democratic Republic of Congo (formerly Zaire).

In the ten years since the genocide the RPF has been the primary arbiter of political power within the state. After the RPF came to power in July 1994, the rebel movement turned ruling party faced the stark reality of creating a state in a territory devastated by war and genocide. Initially Rwandans opposed to the genocide (of all ethnic groups), whether inside or outside the country, were hopeful that the RPF would lead the effort to create a unified Rwandan state in which ethnic identity played an inconsequential role in political and economic life. Thus the RPF regime undertook a nation-building project, referred to by some as the "New Rwanda" (e.g., de Lame 2005; Jefremovas 1995, 2000, 2002; Pottier 2002). This nation-building project was intended to overcome the divisions between Hutu and Tutsi that were rendered violently material in the 1994 genocide. Yet it also had to cope with differences generated by waves of migration that were tied to Rwanda's violent political history.

Following the RPF victory in July 1994, Rwandans who went into exile in the 1950s, 1960s, or 1970s, or who were born and grew up in exile in Uganda, Kenya, Tanzania, Burundi, or then Zaire, began to return to Rwanda.[8] They were motivated by varying degrees of marginalization in their countries of asylum, as well as by fond memories of life "back home" (Kumar and Tardif-Douglin 1996; Kumar et al. 1996:91). This category of Rwandans became known as "old caseload refugees," in the parlance of the office of the United Nations High Commissioner for Refugees (UNHCR), or "returnees" in the language of Rwandans. Many of these returnees perceived the RPF as "their army," and thus they shared the victors' attitude of many RPF soldiers. Furthermore, these returnees were suspicious of Rwandans who had grown up inside the country, for these latter (be they Tutsi or Hutu) must have been collaborators in the genocide to have survived. Yet conflicts sometimes emerged even among returnees since they shared different experiences of exile and often belonged to different linguistic communities according to their countries of exile.

The shared experiences among individuals within each of these categories shape distinct subject positions from which people view the world and negotiate their way in it. The heterogeneity of individual citizens' experiences of marginalization (political, economic, or social), exile, identity-based violence, and state-sponsored violence before, during, and after the genocide, as well as language communities makes a unified national identity difficult (if not impossible) to imagine, in the sense of Anderson (1991).

For Rwandans who grew up inside Rwanda, the RPF takeover was at first a relief as it brought an end to the genocide, but they sometimes felt that the new government did not protect their interests, or they faced political repression (interviews by author 1997, 1998; HRW 2000, 2003, 2004). Tutsi genocide survivors sometimes bore the disdain and threats of returnees or RPF soldiers who assumed that they must have participated in the genocide to have survived. Hutu were presumed to be genocide perpetrators and risked being killed or arrested. Furthermore, Rwandans who lived through the genocide had usually suffered the total destruction of their financial lives, as well as psychological trauma and physical injuries.

The deteriorating situation inside Rwanda in 1995 and 1996 made it difficult for the 1.5 million refugees living in camps in eastern Zaire and western Tanzania to come home (UNHCHR 1997:13). Violence in Rwanda legitimated the fears of those living in the camps (Pottier 1996). The refugees returned in a flood in late 1996 and early 1997 when the RPF attacked the refugee camps in eastern Zaire under the guise of a Banyamulenge rebellion to force the disbanding of the camps that posed a security threat to the new government in Kigali (HRW 1997:10).[9] These "new returnees" faced many difficulties and a great deal of discrimination on their return. They usually found their homes occupied by "old" returnees or genocide survivors. Most new returnees found it extremely difficult to find employment since they were suspected of being genocide perpetrators, collaborators, or, at the very least, sympathizers. Thousands of them were arrested on charges of genocide. While many of these arrests were probably justified, an unknown number were based on false accusations.

"NATIONAL UNITY": PROMOTING UNITY OR ERASING DISSENT?

Since its formation in the late 1980s the RPF promoted an ideology of ethnic inclusion, which it called "national unity." The RPF emphasized unifying aspects of Rwandan history and culture (i.e., shared language, culture, and religious practices) and blamed the country's "ethnic problems" on colonialism, arguing that colonialists had created and perpetuated the divisions within Rwandan society (Pottier 2002:109–129). When the RPF took power in 1994, it created the Government of National Unity, which purported to follow the power-sharing agreements outlined in the Arusha Peace Accords. The RPF promised that after a transitional period of five years, national elections would choose a new government.[10] Based on these initial actions, the RPF appeared to be committed to its ideology of national unity, and Rwandans inside the country (whether Hutu or Tutsi) remained hopeful that the genocide had marked the end of political dictatorship and ethnic discrimination. The RPF regime took several steps to de-emphasize ethnic identity.

First, the government decreed that ethnic identity could no longer be an official factor in employment practices or in admission decisions to institutions of higher learning. This move marked a significant departure from government policy of the 1970s and 1980s. When he came to power though a coup d'état in 1973, Habyarimana instituted a policy of "ethnic equilibrium," which allocated positions in educational institutions and in the state apparatus on a quota system to correct the favoritism toward Tutsi in the Belgian colonial system. The RPF opposed the policy of ethnic equilibrium and advocated instead a system in which each individual was recognized for his or her individual qualities and skills (National Unity and Reconciliation Commission 2000:13, 20). Among numerous policies intended to promote national unity, a second important step was to remove ethnicity from the national identity cards.[11]

During the genocide national identity cards had played an important role in identifying targets of the genocide. At the infamous roadblocks anyone with "Tutsi" marked on his or her card was immediately killed; a person with "Hutu" or "Twa" marked on the card would be allowed to live unless he or she "looked" Tutsi, was known to be sympathetic to Tutsi or the RPF, was a member of an opposition political party, or otherwise raised the suspicions of the militiamen manning the barrier. In April 1996 the RPF regime issued new national identity cards that did not mention ethnicity (UN IRIN 1996). With the exception of soldiers who held military IDs, citizens above the age of 15 were required to exchange their old identity cards; if they did not have an ID card, they were required to get one. Rwandan citizens, including old returnees who had ID cards or laisser-passers from Burundi, Congo, Uganda, or Tanzania, had only a few weeks to apply for a new card to replace the old ones. The new identity cards eliminated the bureaucratic manifestation of "genocidal ideology," as the postgenocide government has labeled it, in the form of the official record of a citizen's ethnic identity.

Yet the new national identity cards served a second purpose. As part of the continuing armed conflict against insurgents, as well as against genocide perpetrators, Interahamwe militias, FAR soldiers, and Rwandan civilians who had gone into exile, the new identity cards aided in the policing of identity and in the weeding out of insurgents attempting to hide among the populace. Identity checks formed a normal part of daily life in postgenocide Rwanda. Security checks and roadblocks at the entrances to most provincial towns on the national highways allowed police or military personnel to verify the identities of all passengers in vehicles going through the checkpoints. All taxi buses and most private vehicles were stopped at these roadblocks, while vehicles belonging to the United Nations or to international humanitarian agencies, especially if they were carrying white passengers, were often allowed to pass without any identity controls. Beyond policing passengers in vehicles, government officials, soldiers, policemen, or members of the local defense could check pedestrians' identities at any time. This policing of identity, which also existed before the genocide under the Habyarimana regime, extends into the civilian sphere as well. Local government administrators down to the level of *nyumbakumi* police individuals' identities, and families are obliged to register any overnight visitors with local authorities (either the *nyumbakumi* or the head of the cell) and record their stay in a household registry, a notebook containing the names, birth dates, and communes of origin of household members and authorized by a local authority's signature.[12]

The new identity cards, which required all citizens to reregister in their communes of origin, helped ensure that insurgents could not use their old national identity cards to hide among the civilian population inside the country. The registration process allowed local officials to arrest individuals suspected of genocide who had been residing (or hiding) in other regions of the country. Individuals who failed to reregister and get new identity cards were immediately identifiable during identity checks. Once identified, these suspicious individuals could be arrested or detained for questioning. Portrayed alternately as a step toward national unity or a national security issue, the new identity cards were not always perceived as anodyne by citizens.

Although ethnicity was no longer officially part of bureaucratic life, it still played a role in the policing of identity, among other practices and policies of the state. During the insurgency from 1997 through 1999, many males between the ages of 15 and 60 left the northwestern prefectures of Ruhengeri and Gisenyi to avoid "getting caught up in" the struggle between insurgents and the Rwandan Patriotic Army (RPA) (interviews by author 1999, 2000, 2001).[13] As the insurgency became widespread and spilled into neighboring regions, people's fears increased that "infiltrators-*abacengezi*" (presumed to be exclusively Hutu), as the insurgents were commonly called by the government and the population, were spreading throughout the country and living among citizens. As a result, men, especially those between the ages of 16 and 30, faced increased scrutiny during identity checks (interviews by author 1999, 2000, 2001). Young men who did not present a military or a student ID card were often questioned about what they did and were berated by soldiers or police for not undertaking military service. Some of them found themselves immediately conscripted into the army, sent for military training, and deployed to Democratic Republic of Congo within a few months (interviews by author 1999, 2000, 2001). Furthermore, those who "looked Hutu" or who presented national identity cards issued in the northwestern prefectures of Ruhengeri and Gisenyi— where a greater percentage of the population is Hutu—frequently found themselves questioned extensively and were sometimes arrested or forced into military service (interviews by author 1999, 2000, 2001). This policing of identity was perceived by Hutu (as well as certain Tutsi) to single out Hutu. In this way identity checks served as a site for sorting "victims" (Tutsi) from "perpetrators" (Hutu).

The first commemoration of the genocide in April 1995 promoted the ideology of national unity through its representation of both Tutsi and Hutu as victims of the genocide. Held at the National Amahoro Stadium on the outskirts of Kigali, the memorial service saw about six thousand anonymous victims of the genocide interred alongside several well-known Hutu victims.[14] President Pasteur Bizimungu, a Hutu and a member of the RPF, and Vice President Paul Kagame, a Tutsi and also a member of the RPF, accompanied the coffin of a well-known Hutu victim and a coffin containing an unknown victim to their graves (Vidal 2001:6). Additional unknown victims were placed in the graves, which were then consecrated in an ecumenical ritual by a Catholic priest, a Protestant pastor, and a Muslim imam. In this way Hutu and Tutsi received joint recognition as victims of the genocide. The association of Hutu and Tutsi victims of the genocide held a powerful symbolism for the Rwandan population. As Claudine Vidal explains: "It was to recognize that some Hutu had also been targeted by the genocide organizers. Such a recognition was not self-evident: it had emerged after debates in the government council [i.e., the ministerial cabinet]. The government, in having nonetheless imposed it, was officially refusing to criminalize Hutu globally, was accepting that status as a genocide victim was not limited to Tutsi alone, and was not erecting a monopoly on suffering" (2001:7).[15]

Thus the ceremony communicated that leaders at the upper echelons of the new government believed that building a durable peace should be the main political objective of state power (Vidal 2001:7). This message was important to communicate to the population, which was overwhelmed by fears of becoming the targets of armed groups. Hutu who had remained in Rwanda feared becoming the victims of a "second genocide," as some of them labeled it. To some extent, these fears were justified, as the RPA had perpetrated extrajudicial killings and small-scale massacres against civilians in communities throughout the country (interviews by author 1999, 2000, 2001, 2002, 2004, 2007; Degni-Segui 1996; Des Forges 1999:705–714). Furthermore, in many communities Hutu faced acts of revenge by genocide survivors and old returnees (HRW 1995, 1996). Tutsi, on the other hand, feared that the FAR, along with the Interahamwe militia and new recruits from among the refugees, would attack from their bases in refugee camps in eastern Zaire. These fears were also justified as attacks targeting genocide survivors, potential witnesses in genocide trials, and Tutsi returnees were launched throughout 1996 and continued in 1997 (UNHRFOR 1997a, 1997b).

Despite the messages of national unity communicated during the first national genocide commemoration, as time passed Rwandan citizens began to doubt the RPF's commitment to an ethnically and politically inclusive society. Although the regime promoted national unity on an ideological level and through state rituals, the actions of its representatives (e.g., local government administrators and soldiers) contradicted this policy. Only three weeks after the national commemoration ceremony in 1995, thousands of Hutu civilians were massacred by RPA soldiers at internally displaced person camps in southern and northwestern Rwanda (Lorch 1995; MSF 1995; UNDHA 1995). Faced with mass arrests of Hutu accused of genocide, extrajudicial executions of Hutu and Tutsi perceived as potential challengers to RPF political power, and massacres of Hutu civilians, several Hutu politicians in the coalition government began to criticize the dominance of the RPA.[16] In response, they faced public campaigns to impugn their characters as well as death threats. Throughout 1995 prominent Hutu members of the transitional government resigned their posts, and many fled the country.[17] In the resulting cabinet reorganizations, additional Hutu were appointed to key posts, but the real power lay with RPF members appointed to lower positions in the ministries (Reyntjens 1995).

POLITICIZING VICTIMHOOD: A MONOPOLY ON SUFFERING

In postgenocide Rwanda the term *survivor* (shorthand for *genocide survivor*) had many different meanings depending on the context. Yet virtually all these meanings were political in the sense that they were shaped by social, economic, and political contexts and involved the staking out of political territory because the term's usage classified certain categories of suffering as more legitimate than others. While initially *survivor* could also apply to Hutu targeted during the genocide, over time the term became synonymous with *Tutsi*. The transformation in this word's referent evolved through the changing national (nationalized and nationalizing) discourses vis-à-vis the genocide.

Under the RPF's policy of national unity, open discussions about ethnicity became taboo, and using the terms *Hutu*, *Tutsi*, or *Twa* was considered politically incorrect.[18] Nonetheless, Rwandan society was far from unified, and ethnic distinctions have remained salient for Rwandans. Within this context a new language for discussing ethnicity emerged. Rwandans and foreigners working in Rwanda began to talk about ethnicity in terms of experiential categories focused on the 1994 genocide and two major refugee flows—the first mainly Tutsi refugees who left between 1959 and 1964 and returned after the 1994 genocide and the second mainly Hutu refugees who left in 1994 and returned in 1996 or 1997. Terms synonymous with Tutsi include victims (*inzirakarengane*), survivors (*abarokotse*), widows of the genocide (*abapfakazi b'itsembabwoko*), and old returnees (*abarutashye*, literally, "the people who returned"). Terms synonymous with Hutu include perpetrators (*abicanyi*), prisoners (*abafunze*), infiltrators (*abacengezi*), and new returnees (*abatahutse* or *abatingitingi*).[19]

While this new constellation may have been more accurate in that it focused on individuals' experiences rather than on imagined, innate ethnic essences, it polarized discussions of the genocide by leaving no room for Hutu victims and by globalizing blame on Hutu, regardless of whether they participated in the genocide. For Rwandans in ethnically mixed families, this polarizing discourse excluded their experiences of violence at the hands of the genocide perpetrators, as well as of the RPF, from the national imagination entirely.

In April 1995 Kagame summarized the double bind of Hutu opponents of the genocide in his response to a *Le soir* journalist's question about rumors of imminent massive reprisals against Hutu, which were circulating widely in April 1995: "There are many ways to analyze this phenomenon. First is that this fear could be justified. A lot of people know that they committed or were complicit with some crimes, and they are afraid of being held responsible. The second explanation is a long history of intoxication—they always told the population that Tutsi are dangerous, that they wanted power" (Vidal 2001:8).

Whether the first or the second explanation proposed by Kagame was correct, the (presumably Hutu) people were to blame—either for their participation in or complicity with the genocide or for their willingness to believe propaganda against Tutsi and the RPF. The vice president did not propose a third explanation: that the fears were justified because RPA soldiers had been killing civilians (both Hutu and Tutsi) since at least July 1994. Although these killings were well known among Rwandans inside the country, they were rarely reported by human rights organizations (interviews by the author 1998, 1999, 2000, 2001, 2005). The most that international human rights monitors and humanitarian aid workers could do was report that the RPA tightly controlled access to local communities throughout 1994 (see, e.g., HRW 1995, 1996). Rwandan citizens opposed to the killings kept their mouths shut to avoid becoming victims as well (interviews by author 1997, 1998, 2000, 2005). Under this discursive regime even prominent Hutu dissidents who had been targeted for killing in the genocide were vulnerable to accusations of genocide. Numerous Hutu politicians included in the postgenocide government between 1994 and 2005 have faced accusations of genocide (some justifiably) when they criticized the RPF or when they were no longer politically valuable to the regime (Dialogue 1995a, 1995b; HRW 1996).

A Hutu woman I interviewed in 2000 made a strong case for the inclusion of Hutu in the category of genocide survivors. When the genocide began, Seraphine, a Hutu, lived in a suburb of Kigali with her husband, a Tutsi, and their four children.[20] Within 24 hours of Habyarimana's plane going down, Seraphine's husband was called to a meeting where the Tutsi were taken away to be killed. Late that night some neighbors brought Seraphine's husband home, unconscious and with deep wounds on his head from the blows of a spiked club. He had been found in a pile of dead bodies. Seraphine spent the next few months with her husband hidden in the storeroom of their home. She encouraged rumors that he had been killed so that no one would come looking for him. Within a few days of her husband's "killing," a FAR officer began coming to Seraphine's house on a regular basis to rape her. Fearing for her husband's and children's lives, Seraphine did not resist him. Seraphine and her family survived the genocide and remained in the country when the RPF took power. Seraphine's husband partially recovered, but he was "not right in the head," as Seraphine put it. His ability to work or contribute to the upkeep of the household remained limited.

Despite Seraphine's emotional and physical suffering, she was not perceived as a genocide survivor for two reasons—because she was Hutu and because her husband did not die. Furthermore, with the polarizing ethnic discourse in postgenocide Rwanda, because she was not a "survivor," Seraphine became classified, by default, as a perpetrator. Because Seraphine, aware of the negative social repercussions for a "spoiled" woman, had remained silent about the rapes she endured, the FAR officer's frequent visits to her house in May and June 1994 incited rumors that she had been complicit in the genocide. Why else would she have "entertained" a powerful FAR officer known to be a member of an extremist Hutu political party that led the genocide?[21]

Seraphine drew my attention to her ambiguous status—caught between the categories of victim and perpetrator in public discourses about the genocide and national history. Explaining why she had shared her story with me, Seraphine said: "I wanted you to hear how it was for us [I understood "us" to be Hutu women married to Tutsi men.] I am a survivor, even if people don't see it. Since the genocide, my husband isn't right in the head. That's why he acts so strange [referring to his behavior earlier that day.] He still has problems, he can't concentrate; he can't work. So everything is up to me. I have my husband—and I thank God for that—but it's up to me to find the children's tuition and everything else."

Beyond the polarizing ethnicized national discourses, the ways people label the violence that occurred in 1994 are indicative of a political or ideological point of view. The labels mobilized by the RPF regime have further shaped Rwandans' views of national history and the significance of ethnic labels. In 1994 at least three different forms of violence with different motivations occurred simultaneously: (1) killings, rape, torture, and other acts of violence perpetrated against civilians (specifically Tutsi and politically moderate Hutu) by the Interahamwe militias, the FAR, and some of the population as part of the genocide; (2) intentional killings of soldiers and accidental killings of civilians in the course of combat between the RPA and the FAR; and (3) killings perpetrated by the RPA against civilians. In addition, there were cases of the settling of scores and of straightforward murder motivated by theft that took place in the midst of the chaos (interviews by author 1998, 1999, 2000). In postgenocide Rwanda, killings in the third category are very rarely discussed publicly, and then only at great peril. Thus, they remain unnamed, erased from the national imagination. Yet the ways people label the other two categories often reflect something about their political points of view.

In this essay and elsewhere I use the single term *genocide* to refer to killings in the first category (Burnet 2005:6–8). Defining the tens of thousands of Hutu who died as victims of this category as genocide victims is important because these survivors' experiences are excluded from public, collective memory by the Rwandan state's practices and its historiography of the genocide (see Vidal 2001:7). While my use of the term diverges from that of some genocide scholars such as Barbara Harff and Ted Robert Gurr (1998), who adhere to the limited, legal definition of genocide given in the 1948 UN Convention on the Prevention and Punishment of the Crime of Genocide and label this "ancillary" violence "politicide," my usage is in line with that of others, like Helen Fein (1990), who adopt more open definitions that include social or political groups as potential victims of genocide.[22] In the Rwandan case, defining genocide to include political groups is appropriate because it mirrors the way in which the genocide organizers defined their targets. Hutu members of moderate political parties, Hutu journalists critical of the extremist Hutu Power movement, and Hutu human rights activists were among the first to be killed as the genocide plan was implemented (Des Forges 1999; Prunier 1997). Furthermore, the Hutu Power propaganda before and during the genocide encouraged the population to seek out "enemies" of the state, "accomplices" (*ibyitso*) of the RPF, and infiltrators-*abacengezi* including Tutsi who had changed their ethnic identification to Hutu (Des Forges 1999:15, 75, 202–203; Prunier 1997:171).[23] While these labels became focused solely on Tutsi as the genocide progressed, in the initial days of killing they included prominent Hutu likely to oppose the genocide (Des Forges 1999:202–203). In addition, under the Hutu Power propaganda any Hutu who showed "too great a tolerance for Tutsi" or a "lack of commitment to Hutu solidarity" was presumed a Tutsi who had successfully disguised himself or herself as Hutu (Des Forges 1999:75). Finally, my usage coincides with that of many regional specialists including Alison Des Forges (1999:199–205), Catharine Newbury (1995, 1998; Newbury and Newbury 1999, 2000), David Newbury (1997, 1998), Johan Pottier (1996, 1997, 2002), and Claudine Vidal (1998; 2001), among others.

During my research in Rwanda between 1997 and 2001, I found that Rwandans who lived inside the country referred to the genocide as *les événements de 1994* (the events of 1994), *le génocide, la guerre* (the war), or simply *en 1994* (in 1994) when speaking in French. The two most frequently used expressions were *les événements de 1994* and *en '94*. When I asked informants why they chose this terminology, they explained, "*les événements* covers everything that happened in 1994, not just the genocide." Thus *les événements de 1994* included victims of the genocide, civilians caught in the crossfire between the FAR and the RPF, and civilians killed by the RPF. In contrast to the Rwandans I interviewed, most official state discourse between 1995 and 2002 referred to the first category of killings discussed above as *itsembatsemba n'itsembabwoko*—massacres and genocide. This official state discourse "maintains in practice the ethnic division which the RPF-led government denounces in theory," writes Pottier (2002:126), citing Nigel Eltringham and Saskia Van Hoyweghen (2000:226). Only Tutsi were victims of genocide. Hutu opposed to the genocide or Rwandans from ethnically mixed families were victims of massacres. While some Tutsi genocide survivors approved and advocated for this distinction, many Hutu targeted by the genocide perpetrators, tortured and raped alongside Tutsi, such as Seraphine, have perceived themselves as and have been perceived by others as genocide survivors. For example, a Hutu widow, whose Tutsi husband was murdered during the genocide, led a prominent, regional widows-of-the-genocide association in Butare prefecture between 1995 and 1999 when she was appointed mayor (interviews by the author 1999, 2000).

A third way that state practices have undermined national unity is through the Genocide Survivor Funds, known by their French acronym, FARG (Fonds d'Assistance pour les Rescapés du Génocide). Created by the Rwandan government and financed by international donors, these funds were intended to assist genocide survivors, in particular orphans of the genocide, with education expenses. To access the funds a person must be officially recognized as a genocide survivor by the FARG administration. Official recognition requires an individual to secure signatures from local representatives of a genocide survivors' organization and at least two personal witnesses. While the FARG is ostensibly intended to help all genocide survivors (meaning anyone targeted during the genocide) regardless of ethnic identity, these funds in many communities have been overwhelmingly channeled to Tutsi at the exclusion of genocide victims from mixed families or of Hutu ethnicity. While it would be reasonable and accurate to argue that Tutsi who survived the genocide bore the greatest burdens and suffered the most dramatic consequences of the genocide, some old returnees (Tutsi), who were not in Rwanda during the genocide, have also benefited from the FARG. As some university students and genocide survivors I interviewed in 2000 explained to me, the FARG's financial trouble at the time was due to the fact that old returnees benefited from the funds even though they were not direct victims of the genocide.[24] My informants claimed that in certain regions, notably in Umutara, Tutsi returnees bribed local representatives of genocide survivors' organizations to get the necessary signatures.

During my research I met genocide survivors who had difficulty accessing FARG funds. In one case I spoke to a Tutsi girl whose parents had been killed in 1994 and who had been adopted by her godmother, a Hutu. The local representatives of the genocide survivors' association refused to sign the girl's FARG form. They said that her godmother had the means to support her without any assistance from the FARG funds, but based on my knowledge of other families in the community who benefited from FARG assistance, this reasoning rang hollow. It was apparent to me that the root of the problem was the godmother's ethnicity. In another case, the children of an ethnically mixed marriage (a Hutu father and a Tutsi mother) could not secure the necessary signatures from the genocide survivors' organization. The family was surviving on the mother's small salary as a primary school teacher in a rural community because the father was wrongly imprisoned on charges of genocide. (He was later acquitted.) While the oldest son had found a scholarship to a Catholic secondary school, the children's mother did not know how she would manage to send the younger children to secondary school. When she tried to complete the children's FARG registration, she encountered a bureaucratic runaround from FARG leaders in the community. In one instance I witnessed a FARG representative refuse to sign the papers by insisting that she no longer represented the FARG. The next day, I saw the same FARG representative sign another applicant's papers.

Whether rightly or wrongly, many poor, rural Hutu families viewed the availability of FARG funding to Tutsi genocide survivors as a form of institutionalized ethnic preference (interviews by author 1999, 2000, 2001).[25] While they acknowledged that many orphans of the genocide deserved financial assistance with education, they pointed out specific cases of genocide survivors who were not "needy" but who benefited from FARG money anyway. Many poor Hutu argued that it would be "more just" if the Rwandan government set aside money for "needy children" without distinguishing between genocide survivors and others.

Since the first commemoration in 1995, the RPF regime has commemorated the genocide each April through the Month of National Mourning. During this time national radio and television dedicate their programming to commemorating the genocide by playing "appropriate" music, broadcasting testimonials from genocide survivors, and sponsoring town meetings to discuss national unity and reconciliation. During the first week of the month, bars and nightclubs remain closed under official orders of the government. The week culminates with a national genocide memorial ceremony, which is held each year at a different site on April 7, the first day of the genocide in 1994.[26] Through this nationalized mourning the RPF regime promotes a particular version of national history and a narrative about the genocide that promotes the polarizing ethnicized discourse and symbolic pairing of victim and perpetrator. This dichotomous ethnic division erases Hutu victims of the genocide, as well as victims of RPF-perpetrated violence (whether Hutu or Tutsi), from the national imagination. The national genocide memorial ceremonies are extremely dense sites for social production and nation-building.

A key feature of the ceremony each year is the presidential address, comparable in some ways to the State of the Union address in the United States because the president takes the opportunity to offer commentary on the situation in the country, on recent events, and on the administration's policy agenda for the coming months. A theme repeated in the annual address during the ceremonies is that of the indictment of the international community—represented every year by ambassadors (and occasionally heads of state or ministers), UN representatives, representatives of international NGOs, and other special envoys—for its tacit complicity with and inaction during the genocide.

The first ceremony in 1995 was well attended by representatives of the international media, but not a single minister or head of state from Western nations attended; only diplomats based in Kigali came (Vidal 2001:6–7). To Rwandans this absence served to underline the lack of interest of the West in the Rwandan tragedy and replicated the complete lack of intervention by the international community to stop the genocide a year earlier. In this first ceremony the multiethnic leaders of the new government each indicted the international community for its culpability in the genocide.[27]

As Pottier recounts, Kagame "reminded the world of its guilt, of how it had failed to stop the genocide, and said that this moral failure now needed converting into a moral commitment to help rebuild Rwanda. 'Everything we see here today is symptomatic of a serious sickness which had eaten our society for a very long time unchecked. . . . Despite all the speeches made here there is not a single person who has effectively answered for his involvement,' [Kagame] said" (Pottier 2002:158).

This theme of international complicity in the genocide played a central role in the annual ceremonies over the years. At the national ceremony held in 2001 in Kibungo prefecture, Kagame mobilized the bodies of victims as part of his indictment of the international community. The president's indictment had an added air of indignation as the contents of a UN report on the illegal exploitation of Congo resources, to be officially released a few days later, had already been leaked to the international media (Ekoko et al. 2001). Although the president's speech focused on the national mourning, its subtext addressed allegations that he, along with others in the upper echelons of power, had enriched themselves through the war in the Democratic Republic of Congo.

As state power became increasingly concentrated in the hands of RPF members of the cabinet and the ministries, the RPF began to "instrumentalize the genocide" to justify its rule by fiat (Brauman, Smith, and Vidal 2000:7). The regime used the genocide as a political weapon against anyone in the international community who critiqued its policies (Pottier 2002:151–178). While this instrumentalization constituted a standard political tool throughout the year, in the annual address the president took the opportunity to seal the international community's complicity in the genocide as part of the RPF's "mythico-history."[28] A second symbolic technique used in the ceremonies was the mobilization of "the compelling reality of the injured bodies" of genocide victims (both living and dead) as part of the party's nation-building project (Scarry 1985:21).

In the 2001 speech Kagame first invoked the dead bodies as evidence of the genocide: "All these bodies that we just interred testify to what happened here and elsewhere all over the country." Later in the speech he offered the bodies as evidence of the international community's complicity in the genocide: "This world has no pity. Those who lie to you, those you call benefactors, they have no pity. If they had pity, all this [pointing at the bodies] would not have happened. This happened on their watch." Through this condemnation of the international community's role in producing the injured bodies, Kagame evoked the moral superiority of the New Rwanda, whose leaders had stopped the genocide. Kagame referred to the bodies in his speech a third time, this time as symbols of the government's moral correctness in its actions: "People cannot accept that what happened in 1994 can happen again [motioning toward the bodies], that is why the Government of National Unity or the state in general has supported certain actions to keep it from happening again." Later in the speech he made clear that "certain actions" referred to the RPA's participation in the war in Congo and in killing Rwandans, inside and outside the country, presumed to be interested in committing genocide again.

While the indictment of the international community remained a constant theme of the national commemoration ceremonies between 1995 and 2005, beginning with the ceremony on April 7, 1996, in Murambi commune in southern Rwanda, the symbolic use of the dead took a dramatic departure from the first annual ceremony in which Hutu and Tutsi victims were honored and buried side by side. Rather than honoring both Tutsi and Hutu as victims of genocide, the 1996 ceremony shifted its emphasis to distinguishing between genocide "victims" (understood as Tutsi) and "perpetrators" (understood as Hutu).

In preparation for the 1996 ceremony held at the École Technique in Murambi, which had been the site of an enormous massacre of Tutsi and Hutu opposed to the genocide in 1994, 27,000 bodies were exhumed for reburial (Vidal 2001:24). Between August and October 1994, United Nations Assistance Mission for Rwanda (UNAMIR) troops based at the school had buried the thousands of bodies strewn throughout the buildings and around the surrounding area. Many Tutsi genocide survivors in the area had perceived UNAMIR's burial of the bodies as part of an effort to cover up the genocide. Indicative of this perspective was testimony given me by a Tutsi survivor when I visited the site in 2000. He explained that the UNAMIR troops had hastily buried the bodies in a mass grave and then built a basketball court overtop "to amuse themselves." Whether or not this survivor's story is accurate, it gives a good impression of the negativity many survivors held toward the UNAMIR troops who had stood by as Rwandans were massacred.

During the 1996 memorial ceremony the majority of the bodies were re-interred in consecrated mass graves. But over 1,800 bodies remained on display in the classrooms of the school (Vidal 2001:24). When I visited Murambi in 2000, in 2001, and again in 2007, they were still there. Over the years I had visited numerous other sites displaying the remains of victims, but the presentation at Murambi differed completely since the bodies had been mummified through the application of lye. Thus they appeared not as collections of bones as at many other genocide memorial sites, but rather as bodies, many still contorted in death poses, with hands covering the face or arms shielding an infant. When I asked the staff on the site, as well as people living in the surrounding area, I received various conflicting stories as to when, why, and by whom the bodies had been prepared in this way. Whether or not the regime had made an explicit decision to mummify the bodies, they mobilized the bodies as part of the mythico-history of the genocide. The bodies regularly appeared on the nightly national television news as a feature in the official diplomatic visits of international dignitaries. This display of genocide victims was controversial and opposed by many genocide survivors and survivors' organizations on the grounds that it dishonored the dead (Schotsman 2000). As Uli Linke writes in this volume, the symbolic violence of bodies on display ties into genocidal ideologies.

By tradition Rwandans are horrified by cadavers. In precolonial times, Rwandans wrapped the dead in mats and left them in the woods; no attention was paid to the bodies, and no marked graves were left. Despite this inattention to the body, Rwandans perceived the ancestors' spirits (*abazimu*) as social agents in the world of the living. Unhappy spirits could cause trouble for the living, so they were honored through regular offerings, consulted for advice through ancestor cults (*guterakera*), and provided shelter in the family compound in the form of a miniature house (*indaro*, an ancestor shrine). Since colonial times Rwandan traditional practices have been synthesized with (or in the case of more highly educated, Westernized Rwandans, supplanted by) colonial religions (principally Roman Catholicism). While many families, especially rural ones, have maintained the traditional ancestor cults (albeit discreetly so as to avoid excommunication from the Catholic Church), they began to bury cadavers according to the imported idiom of European Christianity.

In this historical context, putting the mummified remains of the dead on display "put participants in a situation that excluded the possibility of giving the dead a human signification" (Vidal 2001:24). Adding to this dehumanization are the memories of Interahamwe militiamen torturing and mutilating Tutsi bodies during the genocide.[29] Thus the display of bodies, bodies with no living descendants to honor them either through Christian burial or through traditional ancestor cults, in a context that signifies them as Tutsi, perpetuates the symbolism of the genocide.

Another important symbolic difference between the 1995 and 1996 ceremonies indicative of the shift in the regime's ideological position vis-à-vis the genocide and its commemoration was that the graves were not consecrated ecumenically in 1996. For many Rwandans the absence of religious consecration constituted further violence against the dead. As Vidal notes, "In the African context, it is unthinkable to honor the dead without religion" (2001:26). In my own experience, mourning rituals among educated (and thus more Westernized) Rwandans require a funeral Mass (if the family has the financial means) and a sacred burial, followed about 30 days later by a "lifting of mourning" marked by another Mass and a visit to the grave where prayers are made and consecrated, if possible, by a member of the clergy.

As in 1995 the multiethnic government leadership presided over the ceremony. Yet unlike in the 1995 ceremony, in 1996 attention focused on Tutsi victims of the genocide. During the ceremony a Tutsi genocide survivor gave testimony about how Tutsi had been assembled at the school and massacred. Then he began to accuse people in the crowd, by pointing at them with his finger, of participating in the killing (Vidal 2001:25). The crowd applauded as he continued his accusations and finally turned to the dais where the guests of honor were seated and pointed at the Roman Catholic bishop of Gikongoro, Monsignor Augustin Misago (Vidal 2001:25).[30] These accusations against Hutu crowd members became a new feature repeated annually at subsequent national commemoration ceremonies.

Beyond the explicit shifts in symbolism and the emphasis placed on the distinction between victim and perpetrator in the ceremonies, the nationalized mourning eclipses community-level or family-level commemorations and precludes entirely the public mourning of victims of RPA-perpetrated killings (see Burnet 2005; Vidal 2001). As Vidal (2001) argues, the nationalized mourning ceremonies operate under a substantially different symbolic system than community-level mourning. Community-level and family-level ceremonies focus on the mourning of loved ones lost in the violence and on fulfilling traditional and imported religious obligations toward the dead. In the national ceremonies, the emphasis on national mythico-histories, many of which conflict with individual Rwandans' heterogeneous experiences of violence during the civil war, genocide, and insurgency, precludes individual, familial, and communal mourning (Burnet 2005:123–176). The community-level ceremonies, first conducted in early 1994 under the direction of local Catholic parishes, better served the needs of psychological healing and social reconciliation than the national ceremonies (Burnet 2005; Vidal 2001). Given the prominence of the national ceremonies and the tendency to model local-level ceremonies after them, Rwandan citizens have little public space left to mourn in the fashion that best suits their needs.

AMPLIFIED SILENCE

The 1994 genocide was readily recognized as "ethnic violence" by the diplomatic corps, the United Nations, international human rights organizations, and social scientists, among others. However, few people recognize the current hegemony in Rwanda as an institutionalized form of ethnic violence. By suppressing open discussions about ethnicity through the national unity policy and by politicizing victimhood, the RPF regime has disguised its own *ethnisme*. While it is the state's legitimate authority to sort out who is innocent and who is guilty—punishing the perpetrators and assisting the victims—the slow movement of justice in Rwanda, as well as the Rwandan population's doubts over its legitimacy, have relegated this sorting out to the symbolic realm.

Through the nationalization of mourning and control over representations of national history and the 1994 genocide, the RPF regime symbolically claims the genocide for its own uses. Hutu opposed to the genocide and Rwandans in ethnically mixed families are erased from the national imagination. The public silence about these victims, as well as about victims of RPF-perpetrated violence, is amplified through the symbolism of the national ceremonies. As Linda Green (1999) has documented among Mayan widows in Guatemala, fear has become a way of life for Rwandans whose individual and familial experiences of violence do not fit into the nationalized mythico-histories about the genocide. While respecting the public silence about their victimization constitutes a means of coping with the complexities and risks in postgenocide Rwanda, this amplified silence also prolongs their trauma.

NOTES

I would like to acknowledge the many institutions that have supported this research. I received a Jennings Randolph Peace fellowship from the United States Institute for Peace, a Fulbright-Hays Dissertation Research fellowship and Foreign Language and Area Studies funding from the U.S. Department of Education, a grant from the Institute for the Study of World Politics, a Patrick Stewart fellowship from Amnesty International, and numerous grants and fellowships from the University of North Carolina, Chapel Hill.

1. Estimates of how many people died in the 1994 genocide vary widely. While genocide is not a question of numbers, it is important to substantiate the number I use in the text, especially for regional specialists for whom the choice may be indicative of a particular point of view. The most conservative estimate of "at least a half a million" comes from Human Rights Watch (Des Forges 1999:15) and is based on a study conducted by the demographer William Seltzer. A UN expert (Degni-Segui 1996:38) estimated that 800,000 Rwandans had died between April and July 1994, but this number included those who died from causes other than genocide. In 1995 Gérard Prunier (1997:265) estimated that around 800,000 Tutsi lost their lives between April and July 1994, along with 10,000 to 30,000 Hutu. In 2001 the Rwandan government's Ministry of Local Affairs conducted a census of genocide victims and arrived at an estimate of over one million "killed in massacres and genocide between 1 October 1991 and 31 December 1994" (UN IRIN 2001). The same report estimated that 97.3 percent of these victims were Tutsi, or about 1.04 million. Although the government report included all Rwandans who died due to massacres and genocide from 1991 through 1994, it is likely that these estimates are high given that the 1991 census estimated the Tutsi population within the country at 700,000. Although there are three ethnic classifications in Rwanda (Hutu, Tutsi, and Twa), I do not discuss the Twa at all in this chapter. As an extremely marginalized class of citizens that comprises an estimated less than 1 percent of the population, the Twa are frequently ignored in Rwandan politics. While I do not intend to endorse this practice by leaving them out of the discussion here, the Twa's place in the national imagination is too complicated to explain here. As a Bantu language, Kinyarwanda uses prefixes to indicate the part of speech of a word and whether it is singular or plural (*uMuhutu/aBahutu, uMututsi/aBatutsi, uMutwa/aBatwa*). Here I have removed the prefixes, but I do not further anglicize the terms *Hutu, Tutsi,* or *Twa* when using them as nouns by adding an *s* in the plural. This practice reflects Rwandans' own usage of these terms in English or French and attempts to undermine the (mistaken) notion that these labels apply to corporate collections of individuals.

2. Uli Linke's (2002, this volume) work on public memory and symbolic violence in Germany after 1945 is relevant to the themes I consider in this essay.

3. The research was conducted over a series of brief and long field stays in Rwanda. In 1997 and 1998 I made brief field trips (four months and three months) to Rwanda. From 1999 to 2001 I lived in a rural community in southern Rwanda for 12 months

and in a middle-class neighborhood in Kigali for another 12 months. During that time I made numerous trips to other regions of the country to gather data. In 2002 I made two additional trips to Rwanda of six weeks each. A final trip of two weeks was made in 2003. I gathered data through focus groups, formal interviews, conversations, questionnaires, participant observation, and documentary research, among other means.

4. For more on this period, see Chrétien 1995, 1997; Prunier 1997; Reyntjens 1994; C. Newbury 1995, 1998; Lemarchand 1995; D. Newbury 1998; Newbury and Newbury 2000; Longman 1995, 1997, 1998, 1999; Des Forges 1999; de Lame 1996; Jefremovas 2002; Umutesi 2000.

5. Habyarimana was killed when his plane was shot down on approach for landing at the Kayibanda International Airport on the outskirts of Kigali on the evening of April 6, 1994. He was returning from peace talks in Arusha, Tanzania.

6. In April and May 1995 two large-scale killings occurred at camps of internally displaced persons (IDPs) when soldiers opened fire on people in the camps without discriminating between armed Interahamwe or FAR soldiers and unarmed civilians including women, children, and the elderly. Smaller-scale killings of civilians and extrajudicial executions took place in late 1994 and throughout 1995 and during the massive return of refugees from eastern Zaire (now Democratic Republic of Congo) and western Tanzania in late 1996 and early 1997.

7. The Interahamwe began as the youth wing of Habyarimana's Mouvement Révolutionnaire National pour le Développement (MRND) political party in the early 1990s. Along with the Impuzamugambi (the youth wing of the extremist Hutu political party, the Coalition pour la Défense de la République [CDR]), the Interahamwe received military training beginning in 1992 and became militias in local communities throughout the country. During the genocide in 1994, the Interahamwe and Impuzamugambi militias were key elements in the genocide plan. They manned most of the roadblocks in Kigali and throughout the country and led many of the massacres. In most communities, Interahamwe and Impuzamugambi members were recognized as the biggest killers in the genocide. The FAR was the national military under President Habyarimana. The FAR soldiers participated widely in the genocide by providing tactical support to the Interahamwe militias and other civilians in attacks on large gatherings of Tutsi. Tutsi members of the FAR were executed very early in the genocide. During the genocide the FAR was simultaneously fighting a war against the RPF-RPA, who were attempting to seize the country.

8. As early as 1990, when the RPF first attacked Rwanda, thousands of Rwandan refugees in Uganda flooded to the border to return home (Prunier 1997:94). The Rwandan government estimated that by the end of 1997 approximately eight hundred thousand old caseload refugees had returned (HRW 2001:65; Kumar et al. 1996:91). In a 1996 report survey the UN Population Fund and the Rwandan government concluded that their study data "would corroborate the view" that some overestimation in the numbers of old caseload refugees had occurred (HRW 2001:65).

9. Over six hundred thousand refugees began crossing the border back into Rwanda almost immediately (UNHCHR 1997:13) Within a month of the forcible closings of the refugee camps in eastern Zaire, the Tanzanian government announced that all of the Rwandan refugees in Tanzania must return to Rwanda. Tanzanian security forces helped ensure that virtually all five hundred thousand refugees in the Ngara region returned to Rwanda (AI 1997).

10. The RPF eventually extended the transitional period by four years. National elections to elect members of parliament and a president were held in 2003.

11. Other examples include creating the cabinet-level National Unity and Reconciliation Commission, developing new national symbols (e.g., flag, state seal, and national anthem), and instituting solidarity camps (*ingando*) for new returnees, government officials, university students, released prisoners, and demobilized insurgents or rebel combatants.

12. *Nyumbakumi*, meaning "ten houses" in Swahili, is the local official responsible for ten households. Similar to birthplace on U.S. birth certificates, the commune of origin is the commune (or district) office where an individual has been officially registered, either by getting a national identity card or being inscribed on a parent's national identity card in the case of minors. By default a person's commune of origin is the same as his or her father's unless he or she officially requests for it to be transferred to another place.

13. Following the RPF victory in July 1994, the military wing of the RPF became the new national army, replacing the FAR, under the name the Rwandan Patriotic Army (RPA).

14. For example, Prime Minister Agathe Uwilingiyimana, who was killed along with ten Belgian UN peacekeepers in the first few days of the genocide (Pottier 2002:158; Vidal 2001:6).

15. Unless otherwise indicated, all translations are by the author.

16. Seth Sendashonga, a prominent Hutu member of the RPF, Colonel Alexis Kanyarengwe, a prominent Hutu member of the RPA, and Faustin Twagiramungu, a Hutu and the leader of the Mouvement Démocratique Républicain (MDR) political party, began to criticize the RPA soldiers' "excesses," both inside the government and publicly.

17. In November and December 1994 the MDR party headquarters in Kigali and the Parti Social Démocrate (PSD) party office in Brussels critiqued the actions of the new regime. Party leaders still inside the country subsequently faced great pressure and were eventually silenced. In May 1995 the national prosecutor and three other highly placed officials announced in Brussels that they had fled Rwanda and resigned their positions. In August 1995 Twagiramungu, then the prime minister, and Sendashonga, the interior minister, both fled Rwanda and resigned their positions in protest over the RPA's continued disregard for the rights of all Rwandan citizens. Both men claimed that they feared for their lives (Dialogue 1995a). Sendashonga was eventually assassinated in Nairobi in 1998 after several failed attempts on his life. Although several Kenyan men were eventually arrested and tried for the crime,

it is widely believed that Sendashonga's assassination was orchestrated by the RPA's Department of Military Intelligence (DMI).

18. This taboo against discussing ethnicity created great difficulties in asking questions about coexistence and reconciliation. As a researcher arriving in the country in April 1997, I had to learn the new vernacular for discussing these questions. The Twa constitute less than 1 percent of the population. As the consequences of the genocide and of state policies for Twa have varied widely, I do not discuss them in this essay. The phrase *politically incorrect* has become so trivialized in the United States that it is inadequate to express the level of emotional and political peril discussions of ethnicity and the genocide entail in Rwanda. Nonetheless, I use the phrase because it succinctly communicates the actual situation.

19. The Kinyarwanda term *abicanyi* literally means "killers," but in post-genocide Rwanda the word has become synonymous with "perpetrators." The Kinyarwanda term *abacengezi* literally means "infiltrators." Ironically, the same term was used by the Habyarimana regime and especially the Hutu Power extremists to label the RPF and their "accomplices." In interviews, expatriates who worked in Rwanda in 1994 and 1995 told me that in their discussions with coworkers who were old caseload refugees, they would employ the metaphorical term *tree* for Tutsi and *bush* for Hutu because according to the physical stereotypes, Tutsi were tall and slender while Hutu were shorter and stockier. Yet, I never encountered this type of discourse in my own research. The term *abatingitingi* (literally, "the Tingi Tingi people") comes from the site of an infamous refugee camp deep in the rainforest of eastern Zaire where Hutu refugees congregated following their flight from the RPA's attacks on the refugee camps closer to the Rwandan border in late 1996. These attacks were designed to force the refugees to return to Rwanda or flee further into Zaire. In 1997 the International Committee of the Red Cross and the UNHCR repatriated thousands of refugees from Tingi Tingi with air lifts.

20. The names of all informants, unless otherwise noted, have been changed. In addition, certain details of their narratives have been modified to protect their anonymity.

21. The implication of the word *entertained* was that Seraphine willingly engaged in sexual relations with the officer. In Rwanda a man does not visit a woman's home in her husband's absence without being accompanied by his own wife, girlfriend, fiancée, or other female chaperone unless the unmarried man and woman are engaged in a sexual relationship.

22. The second article of the 1948 UN convention defines genocide as follows, "In the present Convention, genocide means any of the following acts committed with intent to destroy, in whole or in part, a national, ethnical, racial or religious group, as such (a) Killing members of the group; (b) Causing serious bodily or mental harm to members of the group; (c) Deliberately inflicting on the group conditions of life calculated to bring about its physical destruction in whole or in part; (d) Imposing measures intended to prevent births within the group; (e) Forcibly transferring children of the group to another group." As Alexander Laban Hinton (2002:3) notes, the

preliminary resolution passed in 1946 included "political and other groups" in its definition. In the end, these groups were removed from the final resolution passed in 1948 because a number of countries, notably the Soviet Union, argued that they did not fit the "etymology of genocide, were mutable categories, and lacked the distinguishing characteristics necessary for definition" (Hinton 2002:3).

23. The term *Hutu Power* was used to designate the coalition of extremist Hutu politicians and political parties who supported the genocide, including the Mouvement Révolutionnaire National pour le Développement (et la Démocratie) (MRND) state party, the Coalition pour la Défense de la République (CDR), and the Mouvement Démocratique Républicain-Power (MDR-Power). The latter, led by Frodauld Karamira, broke off from the moderate opposition MDR led by Twagiramungu (Des Forges 1999:202).

24. By "direct victims" they meant that the old caseload refugees did not face the threat of being killed, although they may have lost their entire extended families living inside the country.

25. Informants used the French term *ethnisme*, analogous to *racism* in English.

26. In approximately 2002 or 2003, the government, in response to calls from genocide survivors' organizations, moved the initial week of the mourning period from April 1–7 to April 7–13. During research conducted between 1997 and 2001, many genocide survivors had complained that the original dates of the first week of national mourning were not appropriate since they preceded the genocide and killings.

27. These leaders included President Pasteur Bizimungu (a Hutu member of the RPF), Vice President Paul Kagame (a Tutsi member of the RPF), and Prime Minister Faustin Twagiramungu (a Hutu member of the MDR), among others.

28. I borrow the term *mythico-history* from Malkki 1995.

29. For more on the symbolism and treatment of bodies during the genocide, see Taylor 1999, 2002.

30. Accusations against Bishop Misago would continue in the Rwandan state media and in rumors until 1999, when President Bizimungu accused the bishop, again seated on the dais among honored guests, during the national commemoration ceremony held at Kibeho in southern Rwanda. Shortly after that ceremony Misago was arrested and put on trial for genocide. He was eventually found not guilty. For a more complete exploration of the complex layering of mythico-histories and memory in the 1996 ceremonies and at the Kibeho site in Gikongoro, see Burnet 2005.

REFERENCES

Amnesty International (AI)
1997   In Search of Safety: The Forcibly Displaced and Human Rights in Africa. London: Amnesty International.

Anderson, Benedict
1991   Imagined Communities: Reflections on the Origins and Spread of Nationalism. Rev. and ext. 2nd edition. New York: Verso.

Brauman, Rony, Stephen Smith, and Claudine Vidal

2000   Rwanda: Politique de terreur, privilège d'impunité. Esprit 267
            (August-September):147–161.

Burnet, Jennie E.

2005   Genocide Lives in Us: Amplified Silence and the Politics of Memory in
            Rwanda. Ph.D. dissertation, University of North Carolina, Chapel Hill.

Chrétien, Jean-Pierre

1995   Rwanda: Les médias du génocide. Paris: Éditions Karthala.
1997   Le défi de l'ethnisme: Rwanda et Burundi, 1990–1996. Paris: Éditions
            Karthala.

Degni-Segui, René

1996   Report on the Human Rights Situation in Rwanda. Geneva: United
            Nations Human Rights Commission.

de Lame, Danielle

1996   Une colline entre mille, ou, Le calme avant la tempête: Transformations
            et blocages du Rwanda rural. Tervuren, Belgium: Musée Royale
            de L'Afrique Centrale.
2005   (Im)possible Belgian Mourning for Rwanda. African Studies Review
            48(2):33–43.

Des Forges, Alison

1999   Leave None to Tell the Story: Genocide in Rwanda. New York: Human
            Rights Watch.

Dialogue

1995a   Carnet du 1er août au 31 septembre 1995. Dialogue 186:137–148.
1995b   Carnet du 1er mai au 31 mai 1995. Dialogue 184:99–110.

Ekoko, François, Mel Holt, Henri Maire, and Moustapha Tallet

2001   Report of the Panel of Experts on the Illegal Exploitation of Natural
            Resources and Other Forms of Wealth of the Democratic Republic of the
            Congo. New York: United Nations Security Council.

Eltringham, Nigel, and Saskia Van Hoyweghen

2000   Power and Identity in Post-Genocide Rwanda. In Politics of Identity and
            Economics of Conflict in the Great Lakes Region. Ruddy Doom and Jan
            Gorus, eds. Pp. 215–42. Brussels: VUB University Press.

Fein, Helen

1990   Genocide: A Sociological Perspective. Current Sociology 38(1):v–126.

Green, Linda

1999   Fear as a Way of Life: Mayan Widows in Rural Guatemala. New York:
            Columbia University Press.

Harff, Barbara, and Ted Robert Gurr

1998   Systematic Early Warning of Humanitarian Emergencies. Journal of
            Peace Research 35(5):551–579.

Hinton, Alexander Laban

2002   The Dark Side of Modernity: Toward an Anthropology of Genocide.
            In Annihilating Difference: The Anthropology of Genocide. Alexander
            Laban Hinton, ed. Pp. 1–42. Berkeley: University of California Press.

Human Rights Watch (HRW)

1995   World Report 1995. New York: Human Rights Watch.
1996   World Report 1996. New York: Human Rights Watch.
1997   What Kabila Is Hiding: Civilian Killings and Impunity in Congo. New
            York: Human Rights Watch.
2000   Rwanda: The Search for Security and Human Rights Abuses. New York:
            Human Rights Watch.
2001   Uprooting the Rural Poor in Rwanda. New York: Human Rights Watch.
2003   Preparing for Elections: Tightening Control in the Name of Unity. May 8.
            New York: Human Rights Watch. Available at http://hrw.org/doc/
            ?t=backgrounder.
2004   Parliament Seeks to Abolish Rights Group. Press release. New York:
            Human Rights Watch.

Jefremovas, Villia

1995   The Rwandan State and Local Level Response: Class and Region in the
            Rwandan Genocide, the Refugee Crisis, Repatriation, and the "New
            Rwanda." Paper presented at the American Anthropological Association,
            Washington, D.C., Nov. 16.
2000   Treacherous Waters: The Politics of History and the Politics of Genocide
            in Rwanda and Burundi. Africa 70(2):298–308.
2002   Brickyards to Graveyards: From Production to Genocide in Rwanda.
            Albany: State University of New York Press.

Kumar, Krishna, and David Tardif-Douglin

1996   Rebuilding Postwar Rwanda: The Role of the International Committee.
            Washington: Center for Development Information and Evaluation, U.S.
            Agency for International Development.

Kumar, Krishna, David Tardif-Douglin, Kim Maynard, Peter Manikas, Annette
            Sheckler, and Carolyn Knappet

1996   Rebuilding Post-War Rwanda (Study 4). *In* The International Response
            to Conflict and Genocide: Lessons from the Rwanda Experience. Co-
            penhagen: Joint Evaluation of Emergency Assistance to Rwanda. Report
            available at www.grandslacs.net/doc/0744.pdf.

Kuper, Leo

1981   Genocide: Its Political Use in the Twentieth Century. New Haven: Yale
            University Press.

Lemarchand, René

1995   Rwanda: The Rationality of Genocide. Issue: A Journal of Opinion
            23(2):8–11.

Linke, Uli

2002   Archives of Violence: The Holocaust and the German Politics of
            Memory. *In* Annihilating Difference: The Anthropology of Genocide.
            Alexander Laban Hinton, ed. Pp. 229–270. Berkeley: University of
            California Press.

Longman, Timothy

1995   Genocide and Socio-Political Change: Massacres in Two Rwandan
            Villages. Issue: A Journal of Opinion 23(2):18–21.

1997   Rwanda: Democratization and Disorder; Political Transformation and
            Social Deterioration. *In* Political Reform in Francophone Africa. John F.
            Clark and David E. Gardinier, eds. Pp. 287–306. Boulder, CO: Westview.

1998   Rwanda: Chaos from Above. *In* The African State at a Critical Juncture:
            Between Disintegration and Reconfiguration. Leonard A. Villalon and
            Phillip A. Huxtable, eds. Pp. 75–92. Boulder, CO: Lynne Rienner.

1999   State, Civil Society, and Genocide in Rwanda. *In* State, Conflict, and
            Democracy in Africa. Richard Joseph, ed. Pp. 339–358. Boulder, CO:
            Lynne Rienner.

Lorch, Donatella

1995   Rwandan Killings Set Back Effort to Provide Foreign Aid. New York
            Times, April 26: A3.

Malkki, Liisa H.

1995   Purity and Exile: Violence, Memory, and National Cosmology among
            Hutu Refugees in Tanzania. Chicago: University of Chicago Press.

Médecins sans Frontières (MSF)

1995   Report on Events in Kibeho Camp, April 1995. Paris: Médecins sans
            Frontières.

National Unity and Reconciliation Commission (NURC)

2000   Annual Report: February 1999–June 2000. Kigali: National Unity and
            Reconciliation Commission.

Newbury, Catharine

1995   Background to Genocide: Rwanda. Issue: A Journal of Opinion
            23(2):12–17.

1998   Ethnicity and the Politics of History in Rwanda. Africa Today 45(1):7–24.

Newbury, Catharine, and David Newbury
1999   A Catholic Mass in Kigali: Contested Views of the Genocide in Rwanda.
            Canadian Journal of African Studies 33(2–3):292–328.

Newbury, David
1997   Irredentist Rwanda: Ethnic and Territorial Frontiers in Central Africa.
            Africa Today 44(2):211–222.
1998   Understanding Genocide. African Studies Review 41(1):73–97.

Newbury, David, and Catharine Newbury
2000   Bringing the Peasants Back In: Agrarian Themes in the Construction
            and Corrosion of Statist Historiography in Rwanda. American Historical
            Review 105(3):832–877.

Pottier, Johan
1996   Relief and Repatriation: Views by Rwandan Refugees; Lessons for
            Humanitarian Aid Workers. African Affairs 95:403–429.
1997   Social Dynamics of Land and Land Reform in Rwanda: Past, Present,
            and Future. Paper presented at the Understanding the Crisis in Central
            Africa's Great Lakes Region conference, Queen Elizabeth House, Oxford,
            UK, February 1.
2002   Re-Imagining Rwanda: Conflict, Survival and Disinformation in the Late
            Twentieth Century. New York: Cambridge University Press.

Prunier, Gérard
1997   The Rwanda Crisis: History of a Genocide. New York: Columbia
            University Press.

Reyntjens, Filip
1994   L'Afrique des grands lacs en crise: Rwanda, Burundi 1988–1994. Paris:
            Éditions Karthala.
1995   La crise gouvernementale de fin août 1995 au regard du droit constitu-
            tionnel. Dialogue 186:20–23.
2004   Rwanda, Ten Years On: From Genocide to Dictatorship. African Affairs
            103(411):177–210.

Scarry, Elaine
1985   The Body in Pain: The Making and Unmaking of the World. Oxford:
            Oxford University Press.

Schotsman, Martien
2000   A l'écoute des rescapés: Recherche sur la perception par les rescapés de
            leur situation actuelle (Report). Kigali: Deutsche Gesellschaft für Techni-
            sche Zusammenarbeit (GTZ).

Taylor, Christopher C.
1999   Sacrifice as Terror: The Rwandan Genocide of 1994. London: Berg.

2002   The Cultural Face of Terror in the Rwandan Genocide of 1994. *In* An-
              nihilating Difference: The Anthropology of Genocide. Alexander Laban
              Hinton, ed. Pp. 137–178. Berkeley: University of California Press.

Umutesi, Marie Béatrice
2000   Fuir ou mourir au Zaïre: Le vécu d'une réfugiée rwandaise. Paris:
              L'Harmattan.

United Nations Department of Humanitarian Affairs (UNDHA)
1995   Humanitarian Situation in Rwanda No. 9: Update on the April 21/22
              Killings in Rwanda. Kigali: United Nations Rwanda Emergency Office.

United Nations High Commissioner for Human Rights (UNHCHR)
1997   Report of the Joint Mission Charged with Investigating Allegations of
              Massacres and Other Human Rights Violations Occurring in Eastern
              Zaire (Now Democratic Republic of Congo) since September 1996.
              Geneva: Office of the United Nations High Commissioner for Human
              Rights.

United Nations High Commissioner for Human Rights Field Operation in Rwanda
(UNHRFOR)
1997a   Killings and Other Attacks against Genocide Survivors and Persons
              Associated with Them from January through December 1996. Kigali:
              United Nations High Commissioner for Human Rights Field Operation
              in Rwanda.
1997b   Killings and Other Attacks against Genocide Survivors and Persons As-
              sociated with Them from January to Mid-February 1997. Kigali: United
              Nations High Commissioner for Human Rights Field Operation in
              Rwanda.

United Nations Integrated Regional Information Network (UN IRIN)
1996   Weekly Round-Up of Main Events in Great Lakes Region. Elec-
              tronic document, www.reliefweb.int/rw/rwb.nsf/db900sID/ACOS-
              64CP4Q?OpenDocument, accessed March 7, 2005.
2001   Rwanda: Government Puts Genocide Victims at 1.07 Million. Electronic
              document, www.reliefweb.int/w/rwb.nsf/s/FCE80E93F7905C6785256B270
              07979AF, accessed December 19, 2001.

Vidal, Claudine
1998   Questions sur le rôle des paysans durant le génocide des Rwandais tutsi.
              Cahiers d'études africaines 38(2–4):331–345.
2001   Les commémorations du génocide au Rwanda. Les temps modernes
              613:1–46.

2   TRUTH/**MEMORY**/REPRESENTATION

4   A POLITICS OF SILENCES

Violence, Memory, and Treacherous Speech in Post-1965 Bali

One of the first questions motivating my research on the violence of 1965–66 in Bali, Indonesia, was that of silence. It was 1998, almost 35 years after the state-sponsored massacres of alleged communists had left some one million Indonesians dead and hundreds of thousands of others deprived of basic civil rights. Yet these events, and their deep repercussions, remained relatively unreferenced outside the communities they had devastated.[1] In Bali, where some 80,000 to 100,000 people (or 5 to 8 percent of the population)[2] had lost their lives over a span of less than six months, stories of the violence were rarely found in the guidebooks carried by the two million–plus tourists who by the turn of the 21st century were visiting the "Island of the Gods" each year. Neither did the substantial scholarly literature on Bali offer much insight into what had happened or what the continuing implications might be.[3] Despite its domination by anthropologists, whose in-depth engagements with Balinese lives would seem likely to have turned up traces of violence, Balinese studies tended to echo official Indonesian histories by circumscribing and distancing the massacres as an extraordinary "incident" located safely in the past. Those few scholars who did mention 1965–66 tended to conclude that Balinese no longer wished to speak about this troubled time, having either forgotten, forgiven, worked through, or moved on from the past.[4] Even among Balinese themselves there seemed to be little public acknowledgment of the massacres. Reference to them was missing from the national history textbooks,[5] the Balinese media, and the pronouncements of public officials. Granted, when I began my research Indonesia was just emerging from over three decades of repressive rule, during which utterances perceived to be political risked harsh responses from the state. Yet by December 2002, four years after the fall of Suharto's dictatorship and two months after terrorist bombs exploded in a crowded nightclub in one of Bali's tourist districts, the 202 fatalities, mostly tourists, could be termed by the governor of Bali "the worst tragedy the island has experienced," with few voices in the domestic or international media to contradict him.[6] Similar settings of mass violence around the world had— if not immediately, then in the years and decades that followed—come to serve the public imagination as shorthand for human brutality: Armenia, Nazi Europe, Cambodia, Argentina, Guatemala, Bosnia, Rwanda, Sudan. Why, then, did 1965–66 seem to have disappeared not only from so-called expert attention but also from the lives of Balinese themselves? Were these silences indicative of an absence of interest or meaning? Or were they spaces of cultural and political signification with their own complex and contested genealogies? Starting from these questions, this essay—part of a larger collaborative research project on the aftermath of 1965–66 in Bali— explores some of the troubled terrain of postmassacre Bali, focusing on the processes of remembering and forgetting, and of speech and silence, that have marked it.

One of my earliest encounters with the violence in fact took the form of questioning an absence. It was July of 1998, two months after Suharto's resignation from the helm of the country he had ruled for 32 years, and I was in Bali conducting research on women's participation in the political activism that had ushered in the end of his New Order (Orde Baru) regime. A Balinese colleague, Degung Santikarma—who would soon become my research partner and husband—invited me to his family compound, a warren of alleyways, pavilions, sleeping quarters, and shrines where some 150 people lived in tight proximity. It was close to dusk, and the compound was busy with a familiar Balinese bustle of children being bathed, food being shared, and ritual offerings being prepared to the soundtrack of the evening soap operas. But something struck me, my attention so recently trained on gender, as unusual about the scene. While there were women of all ages visible, there were no men older than around 50 to be seen. I commented on this to my colleague, who gave me a look of surprise, saying that no one had ever pointed this out to him before. Later, away from those who could overhear us, he told me how his father, several uncles, and other relatives had been killed in late 1965 and early 1966, and how the few men who had survived had chosen to leave the family compound to escape the memories it held and the scrutiny of the state it enabled. "Many people are now talking about the end of the New Order," he warned me. "But it's still hard to talk about how it began."

At the time it was difficult for me to imagine that I was indeed the first person to comment on what appeared to me as a striking absence. My colleague had a large international network of fellow scholars and friends, some of whom must surely have known about the massacres. Yet as I learned more about what had happened in Bali during and after the violence, I began to see how the production, maintenance, and negotiation of silences had become a crucial feature of the everyday lives of Balinese and of their self-presentations on a global stage. Popular belief often holds that exposing genocidal violence to international scrutiny is among the most effective ways of halting it. Violence, in such framings, is something done in the dark, on the isolated edges of a civilized international community whose attention promises to spotlight and thus banish injustice. In Bali, however, an increasing incorporation into transnational flows of power, profit, and knowledge in the form of tourism, scholarship, and various modes of state-mediated modernity has served overwhelmingly to strengthen rather than slacken the force of silence. While I was undoubtedly far from being the first person to have noticed one of the many traces of violence marking my colleague's family—indeed, as I came to know them better, I began to see just how visible this history was to those in their community—I was, however, among those naive enough to think that verbalizing my notice, both as an American scholar and as someone being pulled closer into the dense social politics of survivors' worlds, was a simple matter.

As I began to work collaboratively with my colleague to try to understand the political and cultural aftermath of 1965–66 in Bali, I realized that such silences are not simply blank spots on a communicative landscape; rather, they constitute social products with particular genealogies. In large part the silences surrounding 1965–66, and the enduring resonance of violence that they often signal, can be traced to the cultural work of the state. Suharto's New Order regime (1966–98) engaged in persistent attempts to characterize the *Peristiwa '65*, or "1965 Incident," to contain a diverse range of terrifying experiences within a singular and minimizing frame ("the Incident") while at the same time expanding it into a flexibly evocative symbol (communism) that could authorize ongoing political oppression. The state's strategies for discursive management included not only the repressive imposition of silence on survivors but also an enthusiastic program of commemoration and the symbolic control of history. Suharto's regime created an official account of what happened in 1965–66, focusing on an alleged violent coup attempt claimed to have been masterminded by the Indonesian Communist Party (Partai Komunis Indonesia, or PKI) on September 30, 1965. According to this "history," the coup was put down by an army officer named Suharto, who took control of Indonesia's military and directed its "defense" against Indonesia's left before relieving Indonesia's first president, Sukarno, of his duties in March 1966.[7] The killings of suspected leftists, when they were acknowledged, were characterized as a rational response to a communist threat to national security—the legitimacy of these actions ensured by both covert and open Western support for the annihilation of the PKI (Robinson 1995; Roosa 2006).[8] Until the fall of Suharto, public debate of the events of 1965–66 was banned, and alternative analyses of both the alleged coup and the violence that followed it were censored. Borrowing from modern biomedical imagery, the state stigmatized and socially alienated those accused of being "infected" by the dangerous virus of communism—people once known as neighbors, relatives, and friends. Official portrayals painted "communists" as shadowy, sadistic figures lying in wait for a chance to contaminate the beloved nation, which in turn needed the protection of a vigilant military and a powerful system of state surveillance. For a new generation of Indonesians, the halting tales their parents might have told of their experiences—or the deep silences they may have affected to preserve their safety—were drowned out by the insistent rhetoric of the New Order. Under Suharto the state staged regular "remembrances" of the alleged September 30 coup and the military's victory over communism and spread images of communist evil and bloodthirstiness through the school curriculum, public monuments, and propaganda pieces such as the state-produced film *Pengkhianat G/30/S* (The September 30th Movement traitors), which was screened on public television and in classrooms each September 30 until 1999. Up until the last days of the New Order—and even after—state officials continued to animate the specter of communism, dismissing most social or political protest as the work of "formless organizations" (*organisasi tanpa bentuk*) of communist sympathizers or as the result of provocation by "remnants" of the PKI. Warnings to remain on guard against communism were typically expressed in the command "awas bahaya laten PKI/komunisme" (beware of the latent danger of the PKI/communism), rendering communism less a matter of party affiliation or intellectual position than an invisible but inevitable aspect of virtually any challenge to Suharto or his military regime.[9] While many Indonesians were skeptical of such claims, the latter's power often lay not in their perceived truth value or in their ability to persuasively represent communism, but in their evocation of the terror—both remembered and anticipated—accompanying the articulation of such words. To hold silence, in such a context, was a far more fraught position than a simple forgetting.

This shadowing of speech about violence has also been encouraged by certain works of Western scholars, whose descriptions of Bali have often shown a striking kinship to the framings of state history. Classic anthropological representations of Bali—the reports of Dutch colonial ethnologists who saw Bali as a series of protodemocratic "village republics" based on consensus and custom;[10] the writings of Gregory Bateson on Balinese culture as a homeostatic "steady state"; the essays of Margaret Mead on a gentle, graceful "Balinese Character"; Clifford Geertz's famous "Deep Play: Notes on the Balinese Cockfight," in which social hierarchy is made meaningful not through human bloodshed but through the mesmerizing cultural text of chickens hacking each other to bits—have overwhelmingly tended to dismiss (human) violence as external or incidental to the "real" Bali (see Bateson 1970; Bateson and Mead 1942; C. Geertz 1973).[11] Where violence has been acknowledged, it has most often been explained as a matter of cultural contamination wrought by conniving colonists or bumbling tourists, as the by-product of wrenching social change or relentless globalization, or as the result of Bali's integration into the modern Republic of Indonesia in all its military might: in Clifford Geertz's essay, it is not the cockfight that signals violence but the Javanese policemen, armed with machine guns, who interrupt the proceedings and send the audience scattering in fear. Viewed through this aperture, violence in Bali has tended to appear as an anomaly, as a spot of dust that contaminates the lens, having little to do with the real landscape at hand. To the extent that violence has been seen as atypical of or external to Bali, even contemporary scholars have been able to presume the existence of orderly, stable, and consensual symbolic systems in both pre-1965 and post-1965 Bali, bracketing the violence as optional to either historical scholarship or cultural analysis.[12] To take but one recent example, the anthropologist Michele Stephen (2006), in an essay for an edited volume entitled *Terror and Violence: Imagination and the Unimaginable*, offers a brilliant analysis, drawing on the work of the psychoanalyst Melanie Klein, of "imaginary violence," sorcery, and the figure of the "terrible mother" in Bali—without once acknowledging that in 1965–66 tens of thousands of Balinese in fact experienced horrific violence that continues to haunt personal and social imaginations.

By highlighting how scholarship on Bali has persistently failed to give sustained attention to the massacres, I am not just suggesting that anthropologists have lost opportunities for a more complete or complex understanding of Bali, or that they have refused a politically responsible engagement with their interlocutors' suffering—that they have been "missing the revolution," as Orin Starn (1991) described anthropologists' similar failure to see social tensions in 1980s Peru. Although these scholarly representations of Bali are rarely consumed as original texts by those other than upper-class, educated Balinese, they do not exist in some ivory tower far removed from everyday life, but have filtered into popular Balinese culture via the mass media and, especially, via the tourism industry. Tourist ignorance is, of course, often glibly dismissed as irrelevant to the real matters of scholarly pursuit. Jokes abound in Bali (often told by other tourists) about the holidaymaker who arrives at the airport immigration counter only to exclaim furiously that the plane was not supposed to have been going to Indonesia. But it becomes harder to ignore the place of tourism in the aftermath of massacre if one recognizes that an estimated 80 percent of Balinese depend, directly or indirectly, on the industry for their livelihoods. Tourism has simplified and commodified scholarly representations of a harmonious Bali, turning them into spectacular commercial displays used to advertise the island as an outpost of peaceful, premodern culture where life revolves around ancient, apolitical Hindu-Balinese ritual and where social relations are based on consensus.[13] In their roles as tour guides, drivers, wait staff, vendors, and performing artists, Balinese are expected to reproduce such images for tourist consumption, with the articulation of alternative views seen as not only politically dangerous but economically irrational. Balinese themselves have also become subjects of a representational regime that defines appropriate touristic subjectivity through campaigns such as the New Order–era *Sapta Pesona*, "The Seven Charms/Seductions," which exhorted Balinese to be clean (*bersih*), friendly (*ramah*), orderly (*tertib*), beautiful (*indah*), safe (*aman*), preservationist (*lestari*), and memorable (*kenangan*) to maintain their ability to attract tourists.[14] Through such discourses tourism became an instrument of state control, with Balinese admonished not to protest against injustices nor to call public attention to histories of violence because a fickle tourist audience might be watching, ready to depart for a more peaceful paradise island. Tourism has attempted to cover up violence with layers of alluring images, at the same time as it often literally covers up traumatic history, as in the case of one five-star, 500-dollar-a-night beachfront resort in Seminyak, South Bali, whose lushly landscaped grounds are known by the local community (but not, of course, by the vast majority of its guests) to cover a mass grave containing victims of 1965–66.[15] Indeed, one of the many ironies of 1965–66 is that survivors of the violence who were marked as linked to communism and thus were barred from obtaining the official "letter of good behavior" (*surat kelakuan baik*) and "letter of noninvolvement in the PKI's September 30th Movement" (*surat keterangan bebas G-30-S-PKI*) required for most salaried employment were often forced into the informal economic sector. Many survivors who began by selling trinkets to tourists or by offering them massages on the beach in the early 1970s when mass tourism began have ended up deeply invested in the industry and thus have a serious economic incentive to censor their own memories. While anthropologists often position themselves as external to or critical of this tourist economy of images, ethnographic representations of Bali that disregard its legacies of violence often fit all too comfortably with tourist and state visions of peaceful, apolitical, "well-behaved" Balinese. Ethnographic representations taken up and used to authorize the economic and political projects of tourism help to shape the limits and possibilities of what can be said in and about Bali.

The failure of the majority of the extensive area studies literature on Bali to address the violence and its aftermath has not, however, simply resulted from a willful uncaring about Balinese suffering or a theoretical and ethnographic gaze that rests more comfortably elsewhere. Indeed, if it did, it might be far more straightforward to challenge. Scholarly inattention has no doubt worked to strengthen the Indonesian state's long-standing resolve to remain silent on its own implication in the violence and on the continuing pain it has engendered, but it has been motivated by a complex set of causes. Foreign scholars' concerns have ranged from the pragmatic fear of losing hard-won government permission to conduct important research to encompassment by the habitual ways of understanding Bali that have built up over a century of academic production. Silences have been rendered easier—even "locally sensitive"—by the fact that under the New Order regime, a "clean environment" letter certifying one's lack of leftist family ties was required of Indonesian university scholars, who often served as research sponsors and assistants for foreign anthropologists and steered them away from matters considered dangerously political. A reluctance to engage with matters of violence has also, ironically, been supported by narratives of concern for the tenuous and troubling situation of victims of violence in the years following 1965–66, in which scholarly silence is presumed the most appropriate way of protecting the communities with which one works. Commonplace anthropological practices of offering pseudonyms to one's informants or of disguising place names and identifiable incidents here shade into a more general hesitancy to speak of dangerous matters or to see the powers that may take strength from such silences. Even those willing to acknowledge the place of violence face a more general challenge in that anthropology, as a rule, has found it difficult to engage with what seem to be absences, rather than easily accessible and narratable presences. In part, this is a methodological issue: it is much easier, and seems to make much more common sense, to ask people about what they remember of the past than about what they have come—or decided, or been forced—to forget. Yet this approach has implications both theoretical and ethical: a failure to think through the politics of silence has meant that the anthropological literature offers far more sophisticated understandings of how people enact practices of history making, memory, or commemoration than of how they engage in forgetting and silence. In the case of 1965–66, it means that scholarship has often elided its own reluctance to speak about violence or its own privileging of familiar narrative forms of history telling, with the conclusion that Balinese also do not concern themselves with such things.

While acknowledging that many Balinese have spoken—generally in contexts they deem nonpublic and "safe"—about the violence, my primary focus in this essay is on how terror has been articulated less through direct speech than through non-narrative practices including ritual, magic, community politics, and gender relations. I argue that far from being definitively past, the events of 1965–66 continue to channel and block possibilities for speech, social action, and political agency in Bali. Yet at the same time as I highlight how 1965–66 still saturates the island's social, cultural, and political landscape, I also explore the theoretical, methodological, and political challenges of including ethnographies of silence and forgetting in our approaches to the aftermath of violence. Posing anthropology's desire to locate and excavate sites of memory—often assumed to be staging grounds for liberatory challenges to official histories and repressive silences—against Balinese practices of concealment, suppression, and redirection, I show how a dialectic of social remembering and forgetting reworks relations of power and provides a means of ensuring a continuing coexistence in communities in which the lines dividing "perpetrators" from "victims" have been highly blurred and in which particular versions of the past have become commodities of touristic value. I conclude with a brief consideration of concepts of reconciliation, arguing that a reliance on models that privilege truth telling, confession, and linear historical narrative may fail to account for local experiences of living in the wake of mass violence and genocide.

POWERS OF SPEECH AND SILENCE

To express something of the ways in which 1965–66 shifted the discursive topography of Bali, I first tell a story. Although I present it in the form of a narrative, it is a story marked with silences, one that refers to the powers of the unsaid and to memory's ambivalent relationship to discourse. As the story of one of the women I noticed the first time I entered my colleague's family compound, it speaks to both the visibility and the concealment of violent history in everyday Balinese relations. Parts of this story were told to me by its subject, Ibu Ari, and parts I pieced together from other people's tales and from what I have seen and heard of how people speak and stay silent. Although it shows how people are not simply silenced by the state or by the pain of the past, this story does not exist spoken in the form I write it here, as a concise oral history, a point that is crucial to understanding both its power and its limits. By focusing here on one woman's experiences during and after 1965–66, I do not claim to portray a representative victim of the violence. Indeed, one of the key insights I gleaned from this and other Balinese stories is that violence does not necessarily lead to solidarity, a collective memory, or a shared subjectivity or political position among those it affects (Das 2000). Instead, violence often fragments communities and casts social interactions into tense configurations. What Ibu Ari's story offers, however, is a detailed account of the complexities and ambiguities that constitute much of what it means in Bali to live after attempts to annihilate life.

Ibu Ari was a new bride in December 1965 when a group of nationalist paramilitaries entered her family home and took her husband and her younger brother away, never to return. Soon after these two men disappeared, another one came to see her: Bli Made, a neighbor and village leader of the anticommunist Indonesian Nationalist Party (Partai Nasionalis Indonesia, or PNI), who was rumored to have had his eye on Ibu Ari for years. No one in the family compound dared deny Bli Made entrance that afternoon when he marched in wearing the heavy boots of a soldier, accompanied by half a dozen of his thugs and saying he was there to carry out an "inspection" (*periksa*), searching for proof of the family's communist allegiances. That afternoon, the "proof" they were searching for was a hammer and sickle tattoo, said to have been drawn by women sympathetic to the communist cause on their vaginas, thighs, or lower abdomens. When he ordered Ibu Ari to climb up the ladder to her family's rice barn, followed her up, and closed the door behind them, no one, they now say, could move or speak or see anything but their feet for the hour until the door opened again. And when Ibu Ari came down from the rice barn clutching her batik cloth across her breasts, she said nothing, and her family never asked. "We knew that she couldn't tell us what happened," says one of her cousins, a woman a few years younger than Ibu Ari. "How could we speak of it? Death we could speak of; death was different. Even if we were afraid, death was something ordinary. But 'inspecting' women, who could speak of it? We were afraid of the words themselves."

Ibu Ari still says nothing about that afternoon, only shakes like a tree in a storm if someone mentions Bli Made, who now appears regularly on television after having become a member of Bali's provincial legislature in 1999. Ibu Ari does not speak about it, but many in the family remember what no one knows happened or not, so they say nothing when suddenly, in the midst of the daily women's work of weaving ritual offerings, Ibu Ari will sometimes start speaking to no one they can see or hear, gripping her hands together in front of her chest, closing her eyes and rocking back and forth with the motions often used by women in trance to welcome deities into their bodies. Behind her back, though, they say that Ibu Ari is crazy, the kind of crazy, maybe, that happens when an unquiet history returns to inhabit the present.

"But what else could have been done?" Ibu Ari asks. Two years after her brother and husband disappeared she went with a group of women relatives to consult a *balian peluasan*, or spirit medium, who she hoped could tell her where the bodies had been buried. She could not, she felt, tell the medium that the men had certainly been killed—that would have immediately and openly identified her as coming from a family of alleged communists—so she said that their deaths had been *salahpati*, "wrongful deaths" that arise from suicide or accident, the kinds of deaths that might result in a missing body. She knew it was wrong to say this: It is no suicide when you have no power to resist, is it? And is it an accident, she asks, when someone—someone who has had their eye on you for a long time—comes one day and takes you away from your family, showing less mercy than one might show a dog? The medium told Ibu Ari where to look for the bodies, but she never found them; she speculates that maybe the medium guessed the truth behind her lie and lied to her "for politics," or maybe that her own diverted speech detoured the medium on her path to the truth. Whatever the case, she recounts how with no bodies to cremate, she and the other widows in the family went to their village graveyard one quiet night in 1968 and took some earth home to shape into effigies of bodies (*adegan*), which they then wrapped in white cloth. Standing in front of the gates to the family compound, they called out softly to the spirits of their family members to come home and inhabit the effigies, which they then cremated secretly, without the usual acknowledgment and assistance of the hamlet (*banjar*) association. These were proper cremation ceremonies, she insists, with seven kinds of holy water and a complete set of offerings, but she admits that after they were over, she still did not feel "satisfied" (*puas*) in her heart. She had done everything she could, but were the *pedanda* (Brahmana priests) from the Parisadha Hindu Dharma Indonesia, the official Hindu body of the state Department of Religious Affairs, right about what they were saying in the years following the violence, that it was the purification of the soul that made a cremation real, not the material body? Now, she says, she believes that the priests' pronouncements were political, part of the state's attempt to hide what really happened by denying the importance of the bodies of the missing. But back then, when the world was so confused, how could she know? After all, she was no Brahmana who might know such things. And who could she trust to answer her doubts about a ritual that had been carried out in secret, for men who were now said by the government, in its official comments on 1965, to have been atheists out to destroy religion and raise up the gods of Marx and Lenin?

There was so much in those days that was not spoken, she says. People used to talk about 1965 as the time when "ulian raos abuku matemahing pati" (you could die just because of a word). Spoken words are said in Bali to evoke actions, like the holy mantras of priests or the stories of shadow puppeteers that resonate across the visible (*sekala*) and the invisible (*niskala*) worlds, temporarily binding and directing energies, channeling the impersonal potency known as *sakti* that imbues the organic and inorganic universe. The word of a curse, spoken by the powerful, can bring illness or even death, and words can invest the inanimate—a mask, a jar of holy water—with *taksu*, or charisma. But in 1965 words became new kinds of triggers. Improperly articulated words—an insult never quite forgotten, coarse low Balinese language spoken to someone who thought they should have been addressed in refined high Balinese, flirting exchanges with someone else's wife—could return from the past to provoke horrifically exaggerated responses. A 15-year-old neighbor of Ibu Ari's who "talked too much" for some people's liking was corralled in a wicker cage used to transport pigs and then thrown into the river to drown. A man who witnessed his neighbor helping burn down someone's house called out in protest and the next day was dead. A woman food stall vendor whose welcoming small talk was heard as a promise saw her husband killed by her would-be suitor. And one word above all, *communist*, held the power to determine who lived and who died, a power no one word had ever been known to have before. Uttering the word *communist*, speakers shifted social assumptions: no longer did the powerful alone speak words of power, but the word itself, for those who dared to speak it in accusation, was imagined capable of saving one's own life and determining others' destinies. Heady, extraordinary, horrific: language became an unstable weapon in terror's fantastic arsenal, like a mythical *keris*-dagger blade loose in the hilt, which could slip and wound its bearer should the flow of battle turn backward. For as the word *communist* was wielded, it came to mean far more than one who had pledged to party membership or felt sympathy for the PKI's aims. As the ambitions of those who spoke it extended beyond the military mandate of "uprooting the PKI" to staking social claims, exacting revenge, or protecting themselves and their families in a treacherously shifting landscape, *communist* transmuted from a symbol of political affiliation in the narrow sense to an indexical sign marking the instability of knowledge and language themselves, and the impossibility of accurately reading another's signs in an opaque field of highly charged power relations. As another of Ibu Ari's cousins expressed it: "Today you call me a communist, tomorrow someone calls you a communist. Anyone could be a communist as long as someone was willing to name them as one."

Not only were words imbued with dangerous new potential but they also became disarticulated from the things they had been thought to represent: *sentimen*, an Indonesianized English word, was popularized in 1965 by army propagandists to refer to local affective ties, with people urged to sever their emotional bonds to root out communist evil in their families and villages. *Jatah*, an Indonesian word meaning an allotment or quota, was used prior to 1965 to refer to the rations of kerosene, rice, and sugar given by the government to supplement civil servants' wages, or to the share of the rice earned by a hamlet harvesting society (*sekehe manyi*) that was distributed to each member. But as the killings got underway a *jatah* became the number of men a paramilitary group aimed to execute in a particular night—a gift from the state to those who served it, the fruit of one's cooperative labors, became one's gift to the state's vision of a new order through the violent dismemberment of the social body. And a *periksa*, or "inspection,"[16] an Indonesian word reeking of state authority and of efficient, top-down bureaucracy, could enter the intimate space of one's family home or enact its control on a woman's body, bringing the state and its subjects into a terrifying new embrace as men like Bli Made claimed to be guarding the nation against what might be written—literally—on a woman's vagina. Even words like *sibling* or *neighbor* or *friend* turned slippery and treacherous, transformed into new hazards like informers, collaborators, and provocateurs. And the emotions this speech engendered—the fear Ibu Ari's cousin speaks of as being "afraid of the words themselves"—grew so strong as to choke off streams of language and to channel meaning into silent forms.

This sense of the dangerous ambiguity inherent in everyday social inter-action, and of the ability of words to conceal as well as to reveal intentions, was not new to Balinese. I interpret it as having drawn on and strengthened Balinese notions of fundamental social uncertainty that coalesce around the figure of the *leak*, a shape-changing sorcerer capable of causing illness or death. Although people may whisper their suspicion that a certain per-son is a *leak*—whispering so as not to anger the sorcerer—*leak* are not always identifiable, even to their most intimate relations. Among Ibu Ari's family it is often said that the most effective sorcerers are in fact those who prey on the people who worship at the same *merajan* temple as they do,[17] a *merajan*'s congregation comprising those who share patrilineal descent from a common ancestor. The closeness of social relationships, which promises comfort and communication, thus also enables the possibility of treachery and harm. This understanding that relationships between neigh-bors like Bli Made and Ibu Ari, or even among members of the same fam-ily, could be shot through with suspicion and unknown intentions, was heightened by the military's propaganda in 1965, which called on people to uncover the hidden "enemy within the blanket" (*musuh dalam selimut*) in the service of destroying communism "down to its roots" (*sampai ke akar-akarnya*).

This newly forceful semiotics of terror perhaps explains why when Bli Made came back every few months after his "inspection" to ask Ibu Ari for money, she did not say anything, just sold what jewelry she had to keep up the payments. As a widow marked as "politically unclean" (*tidak bersih lingkungan*),[18] with no brother or husband to protect her, she was acutely vulnerable, painfully conscious of what actions a word of hers could evoke from him or what unwanted words from him any action of hers could set loose. But Ibu Ari's payments to Bli Made were part of an exchange that never quite managed to substitute money for memory—the memories of either party to the transaction or the memories of those who witnessed something, no one quite sure what, change hands. In the months and years that followed the inspection, Bli Made would sometimes see Ibu Ari at vil-lage temple ceremonies or in the nearby market, making her way through the crowd. Once she was within shouting distance, he would yell out to her, "Oh, you want that money I borrowed from you, don't you?" As the years passed, however, and new young toughs and political party configurations emerged to eclipse Bli Made's standing in the neighborhood,[19] and as the rumors multiplied about the number of women—and not only PKI-linked women—he had sexually harassed, abused, and threatened, his public calls to Ibu Ari began to sound, people said, more and more like the desperate pleas of a debtor and less like the boasts of an invulnerable assailant. Uttering words that reduced what had transpired between them to a loan of money, Bli Made was met by silence. Ibu Ari never responded with the language of a true woman trader, with marketplace banter, or with aggressive coaxing, and with that absence of language sent out signs that grew all too easy for others to interpret. Ibu Ari took on silence as a barricade, protecting herself from the pain of memory and from the possibility of inciting more violence on her. But even as she erected this wall she opened another door to memory, her own memory of just what karmic debt had been incurred in the rice barn, and the memories of her family and neighbors, which were elaborated from an image of a closed door into an imagination of what lay beyond it during that hour when no one dared to see. Her silence did not preclude semeiosis, involving as it did an awareness of relations of signification on the part of she who does not speak and an interpretation on the part of those who do not hear (see Daniel 1996:122). She was "muted," yet her muteness spoke memory.

Nor did Ibu Ari forget other things. She thought sometimes about her husband, whom she had never had a chance to grow close to after their arranged marriage, but she thought more often about her younger brother. "He was the one person in the world I could really talk with," she remembers. "We could tell each other everything, even if we didn't always agree." Ibu Ari had not, for instance, agreed with her brother's insistence that Balinese ritual should be simplified to take account of one's economic condition. This "Hindu rationalist" movement had grown popular in the early 1960s among the young leftist men of her family, who were high caste but poor in land and the hard currency that came with it. Their thinking had led to conflict among the family, especially after 1964, when Ibu Ari's uncle died and his PKI-member son and some other young leftist men, including Ibu Ari's brother, insisted that the family hold a simple cremation ceremony for him, arguing that the essence of the ritual, its practical effects of purifying the dead so that they may take their place among the divine ancestors and later reincarnate into the family, did not require the trappings of social hierarchy represented by a vast and expensive variety of ritual offerings. Most of the women of the family, including Ibu Ari, who were used to devoting their days to making offerings and organizing their use for family rituals, were uncomfortable, feeling that such a cremation would not only undermine the value of women's ritual expertise but would also surely evoke curses from their ancestors and shame the family socially. It was a measure of Ibu Ari's closeness with her brother that they could openly debate such matters of great importance to the family, with no need to gloss their disagreement with the careful language and etiquette indicative of a woman's deference to her male relatives. Indeed, it was the language they used—the coarse Balinese *ci/ciang* for "you/me"—that Ibu Ari references to remember their intimacy.

This relationship with her beloved brother was cut short by his disappearance, but even then, the tie was not completely severed:

> We were so close, so very close. So close that when he died that afternoon, when he was killed, who knows where, nobody knew the place, that same night he came looking for me. He called out to me three times. I had already fallen asleep over there, next to that small coconut tree. Already he was looking for me. We were so close. He would tell me everything. If he spoke to our older brother once a day, he would speak to me ten times. He had left his watch behind. The day he died, his first son was just 42 days old, it was the day of his *dedinan* [infancy] ceremony. He said to me [about the child], "Later, when he's grown, don't forget about him. It doesn't matter if you have nothing to eat, you must give him the food from your own mouth, for this child who still lives." He told me to sell the watch to pay for the *dedinan* ceremony. Three times he came to me, coming back and forth, telling me, "Remember, remember, remember." I was so shocked. I didn't know that he was dead until the next day, when someone came to tell us he had been killed. They never told us where the place was where he had died, just that he was dead. He told me to remember.

As the years passed and Suharto's New Order continued its project of history making, characterizing the men who died in 1965 as communists willing to undermine family, religion, and state in pursuit of evil aims and erasing from national discourse the sexual assaults on women said to be wanton destroyers of society itself, Ibu Ari continued to receive visits from her brother. Often he would just greet her and then depart, but sometimes he would give her instructions about family ritual matters. These instructions had little to do with his former stance in favor of simplifying and rationalizing religious ritual—a stance later glossed by the state as communist atheism—but instead directed Ibu Ari to make additions to the offerings she was preparing to make them more complete. That her brother, who had exhibited little interest while alive in the women's work of offering making, was now instructing her in ritual procedure did not appear odd to Ibu Ari; she was aware that once a spirit entered the realms of the dead he or she could change in character. Indeed, in the early 1970s, when Ibu Ari was among a group of women visiting a spirit medium to inquire as to who had reincarnated in a child of the family, it was she who was addressed by name through the medium with the voice of her PKI cousin, who before his death in 1965 had caused so much controversy in the family by arguing that his own father should be cremated simply. This cousin, Ibu Ari said, told her that he had changed, that he was now a woman, and exhorted her, as her brother had, to "remember."

Perhaps it was the strength of Ibu Ari's nostalgia for an imagined time before the violence when she believed language could serve as a means of intimacy, rather than as an implement of social fragmentation, that kept the door open between her and her brother. Perhaps it was Ibu Ari's desire to be free of the stain of communism with which the state had smeared her family that led her to hear her brother as having been religiously rehabilitated, worthy of a return to history. Perhaps it was her vulnerability as a widow that left her prey to people like Bli Made that evoked in her a desire for protection from her own patriline in the spirit of her brother or, conversely, her struggle to maintain women's centrality to ritual practice that caused her to voice her brother's instructions as authoritative. But these are all anthropological attempts to come to terms with the uncanny, to strip it of its mystery. Ibu Ari herself is not interested in such explanations. Whatever the reason—and how, she asks, could the living ever really know what goes on in the realms of the dead?—even after the secret ceremony that should have freed Ibu Ari's brother from his worldly ties and allowed him to move toward reincarnation, he still visited Ibu Ari. The last visit she described took place in 2003, when she went with her family to a major ceremony at the Pura Dalem Puri, a temple associated with death rituals near the Besakih temple complex. In the midst of a crowd of hundreds, Ibu Ari felt a pair of hands descend on her shoulders. Not knowing who had touched her, she called out questioningly, "Bapak?"—the formal

Indonesian term of address for a man, the word one might use to speak to a government bureaucrat, a soldier, or a stranger. She heard a voice chide her in low Balinese: "Who are you calling 'Bapak'? Don't you [ci] know me [ciang]? Have you forgotten already?" No, Ibu Ari replied, she still remembered.

MADNESS AND UNCONSCRIPTED MEMORY

Listening closely to the story of Ibu Ari—and to the silences that are so much a part of it—we can, if we are so inclined, identify elements of the heroic. By refusing to speak with Bli Made, Ibu Ari refused to occupy the space that his talk of borrowing and paying back allotted her: the space of one owed a debt that could be satisfied, a space from which closure on past losses is possible. In her silences and their significations Ibu Ari expresses the persistence of memory, its ability, despite the pain and terror it evokes, to circumvent the treacherous realm of language and to find a social existence, no matter how tenuous and fragmentary. Speaking with her dead brother, and in the maintenance of memory she pledges to him, Ibu Ari recasts official state narratives of 1965 that would silence the dead and their families and preclude mourning for those disappeared and exiled from national belonging. By articulating her positions through ritual practice, rather than by attempting to express her suffering through a more straightforwardly referential speech, she bypasses some of the potential dangers of language in the aftermath of terror, rooting herself in a realm of religion that can also protect her from accusations of "atheist communism." But these moments of potential defiance, when she will not accept dominant narratives of truth ("what really happened") or of memory (as subordinate to state history or the erasures attempted by the perpetrators of violence), are precisely when Ibu Ari finds herself most marginalized. Even as her silences and her speech position themselves against power, they deprive her of a stable place within a community of victims—showing up the fragile fictions on which such a notion of social coherence rests in post-1965 Bali. Her own family cannot break down the door of her silence to incorporate her pain into a collective narrative of suffering, and in her speech they find signs of madness.

Ibu Ari knows that there are those who think she is crazy, but she shrugs it off with a dismissive laugh. "Let them think I'm crazy. They don't hear my brother speak; I do," she explains. But if Ibu Ari holds on to her experience as its own truth, incommensurable in its phenomenological and historical uniqueness, it is this specificity that others critically engage as they characterize her as mad. Her family insists that her madness could not be located in any particulars of her history, in any painful experiences that she alone underwent, which might have transformed her into someone who could speak with one who died violently. We were all victims, they say, each with our own impossible tale, each with our own unspeakable losses. All victims, but no one else they know speaks with the dead of 1965 in their waking hours, even if many hear the whisperings (*pawisik*) of deified ancestors, or even unnamed gods, in their dreams, and many more are possessed in trance by gods, who may themselves be long-ago ancestors, at temple ceremonies when the gods and the ancestors are called down to earth. All victims, but only Ibu Ari gives voice to a victim whose death has not yet congealed into history, who is neither a vilified enemy of the state nor a divine ancestor but someone far more complexly present in everyday life. All victims, but only one woman whose weighted silences and uncanny speech carve cracks into the family consciousness. All victims, but Ibu Ari is the one who is crazy.

But if her family doubts Ibu Ari's sanity, they do not doubt that what she experiences is real. In their eyes, hers is not a madness of delusion, a madness of failing to grasp the reality of the world around her. Ibu Ari is mad, they say, but it is not a madness that falls into any established categories. Indeed, one of the most striking aspects of the talk concerning Ibu Ari's supposed madness is its resistance to conscription. There seems to be no term in Balinese—a language not lacking in descriptions of mental illnesses or in speculations as to their various causes—that can comfortably encompass it. Asked to describe her madness, her family members sift through and reject a series of typical Balinese diagnoses: it is not the madness that afflicts victims of black magic or sorcery; it is not the madness that may occur when some ritual responsibility is overlooked and one is cursed by one's ancestors; it is not the madness that is risked when someone unwittingly disturbs one of the spirits inhabiting one's environment. Nor do they describe Ibu Ari using the lexicon of modern psychology that has filtered into popular Balinese culture through the Indonesian-language media: *skizofrenia, depresi, stres, trauma*. Most often they describe her simply as *gila*, an Indonesian word meaning "crazy" that is equally applicable to persons, mad dogs, or bizarre situations, or as *sinting*, an Indonesian word that might best be translated as "not quite all there." By using their second language, the formal national language of Indonesian, the members of Ibu Ari's family distance not only Ibu Ari but also her madness itself, placing it in a register that, if not exactly alien, remains far from intimate family speech. Yet even as they call her mad, they do not treat her as if she were suffering from a pathological illness. No one has ever suggested she seek a cure from a psychic healer or from a modern psychiatrist, as they have with a number of other family members afflicted with more easily classifiable mental illnesses. In fact, the reverse holds true: when Ibu Ari says that her brother has told her that the family must add specific offerings to the preparations for the family temple anniversary, or that they must seek out holy water from a particular temple to make a ceremony complete, her word is followed without question. For who knows what happens to those who have passed on through death, disappeared from a time when fundamental social certainties wavered and splintered? Even as it is excluded, Ibu Ari's madness returns to family practice—not quite all there, but not all elsewhere either.

Some members of the family who have witnessed Ibu Ari speaking to her brother in what appears to them as a state of trance have attempted to push her into a more familiar cultural framework, suggesting that she could perhaps herself become a spirit medium, claiming social significance as a conduit through which the living can speak to the dead. They warn that someone who has received the gift of the medium and refuses to accept it as a social role risks being cursed by the gods with madness, as can a psychic who shows arrogance in his or her personal power at the expense of acknowledging that this gift comes from the divine. Yet Ibu Ari insists that her experience is not the trance of a medium, but rather normal waking consciousness. She denies any agency in initiating this communication: her brother enters her everyday world; she does not purposely try to open a door to the unseen realm where he dwells. She rejects the idea of playing the public role of a medium, saying she has no desire for such power. She speaks with her brother, the only person she could ever really speak with, and she has no interest in speaking with others or their dead. Ibu Ari knows that many psychics repeatedly refuse to take up a social role before finally acquiescing to the unceasing demands of the divine, but she claims that there is no possibility of changing her mind. After all, she adds, who would consult a psychic who was known to have communist ties?

And were her ability to speak with the dead made public, would people start talking again about what she wished them to forget: that she was the widow and the sister of men who had been marked as communist? And would they try to force open the closed door of the rice barn, to put into language what had become for her and her family a silence weighted with ambiguous memory and ambivalent forgetting? The politics of speaking, even with the dead, are, Ibu Ari knows, treacherous indeed.

It is here, at the nexus of one woman's experience and the traumatic history her family members imagine themselves to share—to share, especially, after the fact, as they all, young and old, men and women, sympathetic or disinterested in the aims of the PKI, were marked by the state as sharing an "unclean environment"—that madness is identified. Ibu Ari is considered mad not because her behavior or the state of mind that people attribute to her can be fit into what they know of madness, but precisely because it cannot be clearly diagnosed. Although Ibu Ari is considered by her family to be one of a community of victims who have experienced similar suffering, her madness refuses a place in shared knowledge or practice, as it unsettles awareness about what can be shared. Private speech challenges collective memory, violent disappearance evokes an uncanny presence, and language grows alien and inexact as it flows through the figure of the woman searched for signs of communism. Ibu Ari's speech engages an absence familiar to all members of her family, each of whom acknowledges the deaths of loved ones during 1965, but it does not become an allegory of communal loss, a public lament of mourning, memory, and recovery.

THINKING WITH SILENCES

Models that hold silence to be simply the absence of speech, or forgetting the absence of memory, promise a relatively straightforward engagement with the aftereffects of mass violence. Operating within such frameworks, the scholar has only to wield questions about the past as tools in an excavatory process in which speech is recovered from silence and memory is released from forgetting, these absences left to the side like earth that has given up its buried artifacts. The work may be slow and painful, touching as it does on the fragments of terror still embedded in selves and society, but the main challenges are technical ones: reaching truths, recognizing references, and placing responses within a cultural and political context that can render the unthinkable subject to sense. Yet in reflecting on the silences that obtain in the wake of 1965–66, such models seem insufficient. Keeping the experiences of Ibu Ari and other survivors of 1965–66 in mind, I offer a brief consideration of some of the complexities of the engagement with silences, touching on several key concerns that may resonate across other contexts of genocide and mass violence.

One of the most pressing questions many scholars of violence face is that of the ineffability of terror, its presumed inability to be fully expressed and understood through the limited medium of language. While a number of artists, theorists, and memoirists have noted their own inability to capture extreme violence in words, Scarry has perhaps gone furthest in asserting the generic nature of pain's resistance to language, arguing that the experience of torture, rather than provoking a confessional flood of truth, in fact blocks its narration, reverting the tortured to a primordial, prelinguistic state of inarticulate embodiment (1985). In a similar vein—albeit one far more attuned to the specificities of sociopolitical location—E. Valentine Daniel describes how Sri Lankan torture victims may find it impossible not only to voice their own suffering but to hear the truth of pain in the words of others (1996). Such phenomena, Michael Taussig suggests, demand that the engaged scholar "write against terror" in a way that combats the oppressive power of silence without reproducing the reductive rationality of didactic speech that claims to have encompassed the causes and effects of extreme violence; or, as he phrases it, in a way that can "penetrate the veil while retaining its hallucinatory quality" (1987:10).

Writing in the aftermath of terror in Bali, such concerns about the relations of silence and speech to violence are highly relevant. The violence of 1965–66 has produced silences both among Balinese and among those who author representations of them, and the events spoken of often seem to exceed language's ability to capture their chilling experiential reality. Neither Ibu Ari nor her cousin—"afraid of the words themselves"—could turn Bli Made's act of terror into narrative. Yet I argue that silence is neither a natural response to physical or psychic pain nor a blunt barrier blocking the analyst—or those people who share a social space in the wake of terror—from full description and comprehension. Silence, like speech, is a cultural and political creation that takes place in particularly contoured settings, with certain interlocutors—or eavesdroppers, or informants—in earshot or mind. As Rosalind Shaw reminds us, "there are different kinds of silence" (2006:89), and each may perform particular cultural and political tasks. The interplay of silence and speech may sketch spaces of fear, secrecy, and suspicion, with the urgency of such mapping intensified in settings of violence. Speech, like silence, can conceal, accuse, and redirect, while silence, like speech, can have semiotic effects, making silences never purely monochrome, any more than speech can be strictly monologic. Ibu Ari could not tell me (likely because she could not be certain how her words would then be transmitted), but I heard it whispered by others in the family that perhaps the reason 1965 sparked a strange kind of madness in her was that it was one of her own cousins who informed on her brother as part of a plan to claim his rice land. Her own silence about this matter—and her relatives' ability to send tendrils of gossip about it through their local networks in a way they could not about her experience in the rice barn—marked a different kind of political claim than that staked by her silence at Bli Made's offer of "compensation."

Fieldwork, of course, participates in such contexts, often without realizing it. This makes it crucial not to mistake a reluctance to speak to the anthropologist for a more general absence of memory or voice, an issue that cannot be resolved by reference to such notions as rapport. Given this, I suspect that "penetration" is not the most apt of metaphors for engaging with the silences that have emerged in the wake of violence in Bali. Even if we ignore its masculinist and militarist presumptions, silence is not an even fog barricading events and emotions from view, but a variegated landscape that Balinese navigate with what knowledge and caution they can muster, sometimes drawing on local notions of how speech is channeled and dammed and sometimes moving blindly, the certainty that one can find direction on a shifting social topography undermined in the experience of terror. By describing some of the shapes, textures, and motions of Balinese silences, and the cultural and political relations in which they are enmeshed, I hope to question analytic binaries that hold speech and silence, memory and forgetting, expression and its repression, in rigid opposition, pointing toward the more complex and politically fraught processes of semiosis that have emerged in the aftermath of 1965.

Another question raised by placing forgetting and silence within one's analytic purview is that of the relationships between what took place during 1965–66 and contemporary Balinese lives. How does one know, in the frequent absence of explicit statements to that effect, that phenomena are connected, that what emerges in the present can be traced back to violence in the past? To take but one example of what I mean, I remember being struck by the intensity of a debate over another elderly woman, a cousin of Ibu Ari's. The discussion flared up around whether her foot, which was to be amputated due to an infection exacerbated by uncontrolled diabetes, should be saved to later be cremated with the rest of her body on her death. Family members educated in a modernist Balinese Hindu theology that sees the coarse material body (*awak*) as separate from and subordinate to the soul (*atma*) argued that this was not only unnecessary but disgustingly unhygienic and backward. She and others less influenced by contemporary theological claims insisted that a body lacking wholeness would follow her into her next incarnation. This debate was, I thought, "about" a number of things: competition among divergent religious interpretations and resistance by an older generation to a state-sponsored, rationalist Hinduism; the pain and stress felt by a woman whose poverty and thus lack of access to decent medical care in part derived from her family's supposed association with the Communist Party; and an attempt by a woman known as a respected ritual expert to claim authority both over religious practice and over what little—her body, her death, her movement through cycles of reincarnation—she could, at least partially, call her own. Yet the anxiety surrounding this topic also seemed to me to parallel the feeling with which that same woman had told me stories of nationalist paramilitaries dismembering alleged communists and placing their body parts about her village; entrails on the victim's doorstep and limbs marking the village's boundaries. Such stories in turn seemed to evoke, in grotesque parody, the manipulation of a Balinese ritual animal sacrifice (*caru*), in which the parts of a chicken or of another animal are ordered in space according to the Balinese compass points. And all this seemed to fit with tales I heard spoken in the intimate whispers of family gossip about the karmic consequences of violence said to work through the body, including that of the former paramilitary member known for hacking his victims apart whose child was later born with stumps as arms and legs.

To me such connections seemed reasonable, and I took them both as indications of the hold the events of 1965–66 continued to have on Balinese lives and as a reminder to look for violence not simply in purposeful physical harm or in straightforward recollections of it. Yet I also wanted to understand how the connections I was drawing differed from those this woman and her family articulated, and how all our historical diagnoses took place within a power-charged field in which making links to the violence is often perceived as a dangerous endeavor. In such settings, the challenge for the analyst becomes placing people's utterances about a violent past within frameworks both of sense making and of silence, neither reducing the present to mere reproductions of the past nor engaging in a shallow neofunctionalism that locates the past's meaning, power, and relevance solely in present concerns (Shaw 2002; Trouillot 1995). Such analyses run interpretive risk, but it is only by attempting to trace links between the past and the present, by attending to how silence blocks the emergence of certain conclusions and enables the articulation of others, that we can avoid the ahistoric and apolitical stance taken by many observers of Bali, who see "Balinese culture" as an unproblematic category, with the violence standing as an aberrant occurrence, reassuringly enclosed by historical remove.

Yet perhaps the most important question surrounding silence in Bali is that of its ethics and politics. The questions of why not only outside observers of Bali but Balinese themselves have frequently remained silent on the matter of 1965–66, and what is the continuing relevance of the violence for Balinese life, are closely entangled with the question of what it means for me—or anyone else concerned with these issues—to probe into the shapes and textures that silences take. Clearly, an analysis of, say, a Balinese temple ritual that sought to debunk its assumptions and expose it as mere mystification or trickery would be received in most quarters as highly problematic. Yet anthropology's long tradition of relativistic neutrality on matters of belief, which has often complicated activist positions, has rarely extended to silences, which are often assumed, following the convergent models of psychoanalysis, juridical witnessing, and Christian confessionalism, to result from powerful structures of repression whose dismantling promises empowerment: "But only say the word and you shall be healed." That silence itself may offer certain forms of agency that are not simply the absence of speech, that it may be striated with a more complex politics than merely a cowed acquiescence to power, has remained an underexplored possibility. If, however, we understand something of the specific social and political relations that give rise to silences—which in Bali include not only engagements with a repressive state, an overwhelmingly ignorant or indifferent international community, and a tourism industry that commodifies the erasure of violence from images of Bali but also everyday practices of living within families and communities fractured by betrayals, complicities, or suspicions—it is not at all clear that breaking the silence constitutes a sure route to liberation. Certainly Ibu Ari does not see it as such. Here I caution not simply that asking people to speak risks exposing them to the psychic pain of memory—although that is an issue for which anthropologists have often been unprepared. Indeed, such concerns must be weighed against the patronism they often imply and against the way in which they tend to paint survivors of violence as uniformly delicate victims to be approached with clinical care.[20] Ibu Ari is willing to speak of pieces of her past, and to let that speech evoke accusations of madness, to keep her commitments to memory and truth. I do, however, wish to stress that to the extent that silence arises as a response to political risk, as a tactic to ensure that new violence does not erupt within families and communities among whom memory remains poignantly present, or simply as a way to attract desired tourist dollars, attempts to excavate the remains of violence in the service of social healing or activist truth telling cannot constitute a straightforward endeavor. If I began this essay with an anecdote of questioning absence that risks being read as a classically heroic ethnographic tale of discovery, insight, and exposure, I hope to end it by urging a more complex consideration of the ethics of speech and silence and of the ramifications of how we write about them.

Rethinking our approaches to silence, and questioning analytic binaries that pose it in sharp opposition to speech, has much more than academic significance. Since the fall of Suharto's dictatorship Indonesians have wrestled with concepts of reconciliation and have begun a process—slowly, and hampered by a reluctant state—to put a National Truth and Reconciliation Commission in place (see Agung Putri 2003; Zurbuchen 2001). Most calls for reconciliation at the national level have advocated models laid out in South Africa, whose Truth and Reconciliation Commission encouraged victims of human rights abuses to speak publicly of their experiences in the service of national "healing." Yet stories like Ibu Ari's offer caution that such processes may be less than straightforward in Bali. Speaking memories of violence does not simply place one in relation to a distant past but also engages with a complex politics of the present and its articulation and concealment in social practice. A truth commission's work in Bali could not be expected to bring closure to the past—to the extent that such a possibility ever exists—but rather will open new challenges as Balinese rethink what it means to speak of and to power.

NOTES

My research in Bali has been carried out in collaboration with the Balinese anthropologist Degung Santikarma. I gratefully acknowledge the support I have received from a John D. and Catherine T. MacArthur Foundation Research and Writing grant (2000–2001), an H. F. Guggenheim Foundation grant (2003–4), a grant from the Haverford College Faculty Research Fund (2005), and a grant from the United States Institute of Peace (2005–7). For intellectual inspiration and support as I worked through the ideas in this essay, I thank Degung Santikarma, Alex Hinton, John Roosa, Gung Ayu Ratih, Hildred Geertz, Anita Isaacs, Rob Lemelson, Diyah Larasati, and Dag Yngvesson. I also thank the anonymous reviewers for Duke University Press for their comments.

1. The exact number of Indonesians killed is unknown and will likely remain so, despite recent efforts at fact-finding by victims' advocacy groups such as the Yayasan Penelitian Korban Pembantaian (Foundation for Research on the Victims of Massacre). Estimates have ranged from around three hundred thousand deaths to as many as three million, with a figure of one million frequently cited in academic and journalistic accounts of the violence. The politics of numbering the dead is, of course, far from straightforward, speaking both to the state's desire to block access to nonofficial historical research and to activists' desires to ground calls for attention to the violence in statistical claims of its significance. It is important to note, however, that while the extent of the suffering wrought by the violence of 1965–66 should be undeniable, survivors often locate its import not in its scope but in its intimacy, not in its manageable facticity but in its destabilizing incomprehensibility, not in its right to a place in the annals of the 20th century's greatest tragedies but in its continuing power to inflect possibilities for living in the present. Gyanendra Pandey discusses a comparable politics of enumerating the deaths that occurred during the partition of British India in 1947, suggesting that such "extravagant, expandable, unverifiable but credible" (2001:91) statistics function to obscure the social production of history and its qualities of rumor. For more on the challenges of estimating the death toll in 1965–66, see Cribb 2001.

2. Robinson 1995, based on research carried out while Suharto was still in power, gives an estimate of 80,000 deaths in Bali. Activists conducting fact-finding projects after Suharto's resignation have estimated the figure to be closer to 100,000.

3. The major—and until recently, only—exception is Geoffrey Robinson's (1995) important work on 20th-century Balinese politics, which includes a substantial discussion of the events leading up to the violence of 1965–66 and an analysis of the patterns it took. Since then a handful of works discussing 1965–66 in Bali have been published, including Darma Putra 2003 on the politics of Balinese literature

in the years prior to the violence; Parker 2003, chapter 4, on memories of 1965–66; Dwyer 2004 on the gender politics of the violence and its aftermath; and Dwyer and Santikarma 2003, 2007 on the cultural and political landscape of post-1965 Bali. For an overview of recent work on 1965–66 elsewhere in Indonesia, see Zurbuchen 2002.

4. In his popular history of Bali, Adrian Vickers writes: "Understandably, few Balinese want to relive this time in conversation and most, like survivors of other conflicts, prefer to block it out of their memories" (1989:172). Graeme MacRae echoes this characterization: "Most people in Ubud [Bali] who remember this era prefer not to think or, at least, not to talk about it" (2003:44).

5. The national high school and junior high school textbooks were revised in 1999 after the fall of Suharto's dictatorship to include a brief statement that the history of 1965 is debated by historians. The high school textbooks also include a new section presenting differing theories about the alleged coup and about whether it really was carried out by the PKI. The textbooks still do not make mention of the violence against alleged communists.

6. From Berata 2002. On the contrast between the Indonesian state and international media's responses to the Bali bombings and to the violence of 1965–66, see Santikarma 2004.

7. For more on the events of September 30, 1965, see Anderson and McVey 1971; Cribb 1990; Crouch 1978. For an overview of the events in Bali, see Robinson 1995. For an examination of the cultural and political repercussions of the violence in Bali, see Dwyer 2004; and Dwyer and Santikarma 2003, 2007. For discussions of the important place that 1965 as history, imaginary, and threat has held in state discourse and in public culture, see Anderson 1994; Pemberton 1994; Siegel 1998; Steedly 1993; Shiraishi 1997; Heryanto 1999.

8. While the international media at the time tended to describe the killings as an irrational outburst of primitive emotion, describing "orgies" of bloodshed and a "frenzy" of anticommunist fervor (the Pulitzer Prize winner John Hughes's book on 1965, *Indonesian Upheaval*, recently reissued as *The End of Sukarno: A Coup That Misfired; A Purge That Ran Wild* (2003[1967])), offers perhaps the best example of this sensationalist genre), state accounts instead stressed the savage excess of the left, framing military and civilian violence against alleged communists as the careful, calculated, and justified enactment of bureaucratic rationality on those who had forfeited claims to citizenship.

9. Honna 2001 details how Indonesian military ideology framed and reframed the notion of communism from 1966 to 1998 to address changing "threats" to its power, ranging from pro-democracy activism to globalization. Heryanto 1999 discusses the deployment of and resistances to the term *communist* under the New Order. Despite the fall of Suharto's dictatorship, anticommunist rhetoric continues to be used in Indonesia in attempts to effect various political ends. To take only a few examples: In Java, some Islamist groups have gained support for their agendas by

evoking an "atheist" communist genealogy to contemporary secularist movements; in Bali, a labor strike against a tourist facility was followed by the "mysterious" appearance of posters tacked to walls and trees warning against a potential resurgence of communism; in Jakarta, in preparation for an interview for a permanent resident visa at the U.S. embassy, my husband was required to be interviewed by the local police, who interrogated him from a standard set of questions that referred, among other matters, to his family's political affiliations in 1965—a new level of surveillance made possible by U.S. funds for the Indonesian police to enlist in the so-called war on terror.

10. For a discussion of romantic conceptions of the Balinese *desa adat*, or customary law village, see Warren 1993.

11. One notable exception to the tendency of this earlier generation of anthropologists to bracket violence is H. Geertz 1991, in which the author discusses a "ritual drama" performed in 1947 that involved the communal beating and torture of a group of men arrested for their participation in the anticolonial movement and for their rejection of the political authority of the traditional Kingdom of Gianyar, which had allied itself with the Dutch. Geertz argues that rather than reproducing or enacting harmony among Balinese and between humans and the unseen world, as so many other observers of Balinese ritual have argued, Balinese ritual drama has "agonistic violence at its core" (1991:180).

12. Robinson 1995 makes a similar critique of classical scholarship in Bali.

13. For a discussion of how related concepts of tourism and politics operate in Ubud, the Balinese village that reinvented itself in the 1950s as Bali's "center of art and culture," see MacRae 2003.

14. For a discussion of how tourism and state developmentalism have shaped discourses of Balinese culture in the service of state control, see Santikarma 2001.

15. Much of the work of the small group of advocates for the rights of victims of 1965–66 in Bali has consisted of trying to identify mass graves from 1965–66. Hopes for exhuming the bodies they contain are slim, however. Such land is considered by Balinese to be *tenget*—spiritually "hot" or "contaminated"—and thus unfit for Balinese to inhabit or cultivate. Much of this land was therefore sold to non-Balinese or, in South Bali, used to build tourism facilities, meaning that any attempt to find what lies beneath the ground would most likely face serious opposition from the owners of what now lies above the ground. As one activist reminded us: "Tourism is big business, big money. If you take on tourism, the next thing you know you're a communist, and the corrupt *aparat* ["security apparatus," military and police] make sure that you're buried as well."

16. Scholars of Indonesia reading my work have pointed out that the Indonesian noun for inspection should be *pemeriksaan*, not *periksa*. This is true; however, Balinese do not always speak Indonesian as they "should." Grammatically proper or not, Balinese identify *periksa*—both the word and the events—as emanating from the central Indonesian state.

17. *Merajan* is the term used by Bali's *triwangsa* ("three peoples") or upper-caste nobles. A non-*triwangsa* family would use the term *sanggah*.

18. The New Order's infamous "clean environment" (*bersih lingkungan*) policy claimed that spouses, parents, siblings, children, and even grandchildren of those marked as communists were contaminated by "political uncleanliness" and thus to be barred from participation in government or civil society. Officially the policy applied only to those who were over 12 years old at the time of the violence, with the exception of younger children of those considered to be leaders of the PKI. In practice, however, entire families, especially if they lived together in family compounds, were often considered unclean for local political purposes. Relatives of alleged communists who themselves had never been charged with crimes were barred from obtaining the *surat keterangan bebas* G-30-S-PKI, or letter of noninvolvement in the PKI's September 30th Movement, a document necessary to obtain permission to join the vast government bureaucracy, to work in the media or in social welfare, or to obtain a university teaching position or scholarship.

19. By 1972 the New Order state had grown uneasy with the power that the PNI had gained as a result of its participation in the massacres of the PKI, and it began a process of reconfiguring the political party landscape in which the PNI was banned and the government "functional group" Golkar was ensured dominance through the mandatory membership of the military, government officials, and vast national civil service.

20. I thank Gung Ayu Ratih for stressing this point in conversation, as well as in an unpublished paper authored with John Roosa on how we might rethink methodologies of oral history on 1965–66 in Indonesia.

REFERENCES

Agung Putri

2003   Evading the Truth: Will a Truth and Reconciliation Commission Ever Be Formed? Inside Indonesia 73. http://insideindonesia.org.

Anderson, Benedict

1994   Language and Power: Exploring Political Cultures in Indonesia. Ithaca: Cornell University Press.

Anderson, Benedict R., and Ruth T. McVey, with Frederick P. Bunnell

1971   A Preliminary Analysis of the October 1, 1965, Coup in Indonesia. Ithaca: Modern Indonesia Project, Cornell University.

Bateson, Gregory

1970   Bali: The Value System of a Steady State. *In* Traditional Balinese Culture. Jane Belo, ed. Pp. 384–401. New York: Columbia University Press.

Bateson, Gregory, and Margaret Mead

1942   Balinese Character: A Photographic Analysis. New York: New York Academy of Sciences.

Berata, Dewa

2002   The Kuta Tragedy and the Present-Day Bali (A Report by the Governor of Bali). Paper presented at the ASEAN +3 NTO meeting, Denpasar, Bali, December 11–12.

Cribb, Robert

2001   How Many Deaths? Problems in the Statistics of Massacre in Indonesia (1965–1966) and East Timor (1975–1980). *In* Violence in Indonesia. Ingrid Wessel and Georgia Wimhöfer, eds. Pp. 82–98. Hamburg: Abera.

Cribb, Robert, ed.

1990   The Indonesian Killings of 1965–66: Studies from Java and Bali. Clayton, Victoria: Centre of Southeast Asian Studies, Monash University.

Crouch, Harold

1978   The Army and Politics in Indonesia. Ithaca: Cornell University Press.

Daniel, E. Valentine

1996   Charred Lullabies: Chapters in an Anthropography of Violence. Princeton: Princeton University Press.

Darma Putra, I Nyoman

2003   Reflections on Literature and Politics in Bali: The Development of Lekra, 1950–1966. *In* Inequality, Crisis, and Social Change in Indonesia: The Muted Worlds of Bali. Thomas Reuter, ed. Pp. 54–85. New York: Routledge Curzon.

Das, Veena

2000   The Act of Witnessing: Violence, Poisonous Knowledge, and Subjectivity. *In* Violence and Subjectivity. Veena Das, Arthur Kleinman, Mamphela Ramphele, and Pamela Reynolds, eds. Pp. 205–225. Berkeley: University of California Press.

Dwyer, Leslie

2004   The Intimacy of Terror: Gender and the Violence of 1965–66 in Bali. Intersections: Gender, History, and Culture in the Asian Context (10)2. http://intersections.anu.edu.au.

Dwyer, Leslie, and Degung Santikarma

2003   "When the World Turned to Chaos": 1965 and Its Aftermath in Bali, Indonesia. *In* The Specter of Genocide: Mass Murder in Historical Perspective. Ben Kiernan and Robert Gellately, eds. Pp. 289–306. New York: Cambridge University Press.

2007   Speaking from the Shadows: Memories of Massacre in Bali. *In* Mass Crime and Post-Conflict Peacebuilding. Beatrice Pouligny, Simon Chesterman, and Albrecht Schnabel, eds. Pp. 190–215. Tokyo: United Nations University Press.

Geertz, Clifford
1973   The Interpretation of Cultures: Selected Essays. New York: Basic Books.

Geertz, Hildred
1991   A Theatre of Cruelty: The Contexts of a Topeng Performance. *In* State
            and Society in Bali: Historical, Textual, and Anthropological Approaches.
            Hildred Geertz, ed. Pp. 165–197. Leiden: KITLV Press.

Heryanto, Ariel
1999   Where Communism Never Dies: Violence, Trauma, and Narration in
            the Last Cold War Capitalist Authoritarian State. International Journal of
            Cultural Studies 2(2):147–177.

Hinton, Alexander Laban
2005   Why Did They Kill? Cambodia in the Shadow of Genocide. California:
            University of California Press.

Honna, Jun
2001   Military Ideology in Response to Democratic Pressures during the Late
            Soeharto Era: Political and Institutional Contexts. *In* Violence and the
            State in Suharto's Indonesia. Benedict R. O'G. Anderson, ed. Ithaca: Cor-
            nell Southeast Asia Program Publications.

Hughes, John
2003[1967] The End of Sukarno: A Coup That Misfired; A Purge That Ran Wild.
            Singapore: Archipelago. [Originally published as *Indonesian
            Upheaval.*]

MacRae, Graeme
2003   Art and Peace in the Safest Place in the World: A Culture of Apoliticism
            in Bali. *In* Inequality, Crisis, and Social Change in Indonesia: The
            Muted Worlds of Bali. T. Reuter, ed. Pp. 30–53. New York: Routledge
            Curzon.

Pandey, Gyanendra
2001   Remembering Partition: Violence, Nationalism, and History in India.
            Cambridge: Cambridge University Press.

Parker, Lyn
2003   From Subjects to Citizens: Balinese Villagers in the Indonesian Nation-
            State. Copenhagen: Nordic Institute of Asian Studies.

Pemberton, John
1994   On the Subject of "Java." Ithaca: Cornell University Press.

Robinson, Geoffrey
1995   The Dark Side of Paradise: Political Violence in Bali. Ithaca: Cornell
            University Press.

Roosa, John

2006   Pretext for Mass Murder: The September 30th Movement and Suharto's
            Coup D'État in Indonesia. Madison: University of Wisconsin Press.

Santikarma, Degung

2001   The Power of "Balinese Culture." *In* Bali: Living in Two Worlds. Urs
            Ramsayer, ed. Pp. 23–36. Basel: Museum der Kulturen and Verlag
            Schwabe.
2004   Monument, Document, and Mass Grave. *In* Beginning to Remember:
            The Past in the Indonesian Present. M. Zurbuchen, ed. Pp. 312–323.
            Seattle: University of Washington Press.

Scarry, Elaine

1987   The Body in Pain: The Making and Unmaking of the World. Oxford:
            Oxford University Press.

Shaw, Rosalind

2002   Memories of the Slave Trade: Ritual and the Historical Imagination in
            Sierra Leone. Chicago: University of Chicago Press.
2006   Displacing Violence: Making Pentecostal Memory in Postwar Sierra
            Leone. Cultural Anthropology 22(1):66–93.

Shiraishi, Saya S.

1997   Young Heroes: The Indonesian Family in Politics. Ithaca: Cornell
            University Southeast Asia Program.

Siegel, James T.

1998   A New Criminal Type in Jakarta: Counter-Revolution Today. Durham,
            NC: Duke University Press.

Starn, Orin

1991   Missing the Revolution: Anthropologists and the War in Peru. Cultural
            Anthropology 6(1):63–91.

Steedly, Mary Margaret

1993   Hanging without a Rope: Narrative Experience in Colonial and Postcolo-
            nial Karoland. Princeton: Princeton University Press.

Stephen, Michele

2006   Imaginary Violence and the Terrible Mother: The Imagery of Balinese
            Witchcraft. *In* Terror and Violence: Imagination and the Unimaginable.
            Andrew Strathern, Pamela J. Stewart, and Neil L. Whitehead, eds.
            Pp. 192–230. London: Pluto.

Taussig, Michael

1987   Shamanism, Colonialism, and the Wild Man: A Study in Terror and
            Healing. Chicago: University of Chicago Press.

Trouillot, Michel-Rolph

1995   Silencing the Past: Power and the Production of History. Boston: Beacon.

Vickers, Adrian

1989   Bali: A Paradise Created. Hong Kong: Periplus.

Warren, Carol

1993   Adat and Dinas: Balinese Communities in the Indonesian State. Kuala
            Lumpur: Oxford University Press.

Zurbuchen, Mary

2001   Looking Back to Move Forward: A Truth Commission Could Bring
            Healing for a Tragic Past. Inside Indonesia 65. http://insideindonesia.org.
2002   History, Memory, and the "1965 Incident" in Indonesia. Asian Survey
            42(4):564–581.

5   THE LIMITS OF EMPATHY

Emotional Anesthesia and the Museum
of Corpses in Post-Holocaust Germany

Inhumanity, techno-rational regimes of death, and the "banality
of evil," as Hannah Arendt (1963) termed it, succinctly capture
the governing principles of the modus operandi of modernity
in the twentieth century, and, moreover, reveal the formation of
a new kind of subjectivity: the increasing atrophy of empathy.
Emotional anesthesia or the devolution of feelings, as I suggest,
is integral to a cultural apparatus that feeds on the labor of the
negative: the abrogation of humanity. While societal practices
of affect negation may indeed be symptomatic of a capitalist
modernity, they are simultaneously embedded in specific histories, discourses, and meanings. With a focus on Germany, the
historian Helmut Lethen (1994) traces the initial formation of
the "unfeeling" subject to World War I, where he locates the
beginnings of a "phenomenology of coldness": the routinization of "techniques of emotional distance," the negation of pain,
and the training of the "fortified, reserved self" are among the
affective practices that take form at this historical moment, an
era marked by war and defeat. The emergent lack of "feeling for
others" and the subsequent construction of the "cold persona,"
as Lethen documents, was further amplified by Nazi culture
and persisted after 1945.

In contemporary Germany, emotional regimes are inevitably
part of post-Holocaust culture, shaped by conflicted memories
of a "catastrophic nationalism" (Geyer 2002). By the 1950s, in

the immediate aftermath of war and genocide, the social fabric came to be marked by an emotional void. Its symptomatology was evident in "the inability to mourn," as Alexander Mitscherlich and Margarete Mitscherlich observed (1967), that is, a notable lack of empathy with the victims of violent history: the millions murdered by the Nazi regime. Such an "absence of any sense of grief or sadness following a national catastrophe" is integral to a "psychic economy" that labors toward the unmaking of feelings—the "resistance against any emotional partaking in the events of a now rejected historical past" (Mitscherlich and Mitscherlich 1967:9). In Germany the introduction of a National Day of Mourning in 1952 marked a further closure of emotionality by a shift toward public rituals of commemoration: a move toward the symbolic and temporal incarceration of feelings (Kaiser 2004; Herzog 2001; Liebsch and Rüsen 2001). During this period of economic reconstruction the aim was to create rational agents of modernization. Emotions were perceived as an impediment to this project.

In describing the resultant paucity of emphatic abilities, the sociologist Niklas Luhmann (2000) points to a curious simultaneity of contradictory emotions in this historically traumatized society: in Germany rampant racial antipathies coexist with excessively ritualized protests on behalf of the elsewhere-victims of injustices—a "cult of concern," as Cora Stephan (1993) has called it. The work of national mourning is likewise fragmented or disjointed, scattered across a temporal landscape. But expressions of collective grief are not merely confined to commemorative ritual: they are also anchored to specific places of memory (Young 2000; Jacobeit 2002; Schmoll 2002). A poignant example is Berlin's controversial Memorial to the Murdered Jews of Europe, which, as James E. Young asserts, is a monumental site "forever inflected by the memory of having mourned . . . here" (2005). Mourning has been historicized. Grieving has been displaced into the past, entombed in a memorial's remembrance of the dead.

In Germany the work of memory is thus intimately enmeshed with "the fragility of empathy," as the historian Carolyn J. Dean (2005) shows in her probing study about the failure of compassion in the specific case of the Holocaust: in post-Holocaust Germany, she argues, the remembrance of the victims of mass murder has been ritualized, trivialized, commercialized, and rendered indifferent. Building on these schematic observations, my essay is focused on the cultural techniques that contribute to the perpetual unmaking of empathy in present-day Germany. I trace the intersections of emotion and memory to a concrete ethnographic site, specifically to reveal the productive labor of affect negation. The German "museum of corpses" offers a succinct example of this form of productivity. In the following I examine the dramatic staging of "Body Worlds" ("Körperwelten"), an exhibit on human anatomy designed by Gunther von Hagens, a German anatomist from Heidelberg. The installation was first launched under the auspices of the Japanese Society for Anatomy in 1995 in Tokyo and Osaka, where it was endorsed as a scientific exhibit on the art of preserving human remains. The display opened its doors to the German public in 1997 in Mannheim, where it was sponsored by the State Museum for Technology and Labor.[1] After its German debut in Mannheim (1997–1998), the exhibit toured through Germany and traveled to the world's capital cities, including Vienna, Brussels, Berlin, London, Seoul, Singapore, and Taipei. Most recently it was shown in North America: in Los Angeles, Chicago, Cleveland, Toronto, Philadelphia, and Boston. Although a German production, it is an exhibit with global resonance.

According to media reports from Germany, the exhibit's "dead body specimens" became "a peak attraction for the general public" at the end of the twentieth century (Roth 1998:50). In Germany and Austria the exhibition "was kept open twenty-four hours a day, seven days a week, to accommodate all visitors" (Dijck 2005:43). Indeed, the commercial success of Hagens's installation has led to "a proliferation of anatomy exhibits in Europe," prompting the creation of similarly titled "aesthetic spectacles" (Seremetakis 2001:118) that have traveled around the globe.[2] The immense popularity of these exhibits points to a new global market for the commoditization and optical consumption of human remains. My aim is to interrogate this fascination with corpses that, I suggest, succeeds by an unmaking of empathy and memory. Here I am specifically concerned with the German cultural dimensions of "Body Worlds," but I do not ignore its global significance. In contrast to previous studies (Csordas 2000; van Dijck 2001; Dijck 2005; Seremetakis 2001; Walter 2004a, 2004b) my analytic gaze is focused on the problematic of exhibiting human cadavers in Germany, a country in which public culture, despite its affinities to a global modernity, is succinctly framed by issues of genocide and conflicted memories of a violent history.

My goal is to analyze "Body Worlds" as both medical spectacle and popular entertainment in a society that continues to struggle with the aftermath of genocide. The exhibit uncannily plays out a multiplicity of themes as-sociated with the atrocities of the Nazi regime: the negation of humanity, the dehumanization of bodies, medical experimentation, anatomy as a site of anthropological truth, the mortification of flesh (historically linked to various concentration camps and killing centers), depersonalization as a formative category of identity, judicial decisions leading to dehumaniza-tion, the sexualized appropriation of bodies, the public complicity in in-stitutional violence through spectatorship, and the indifference and lack of empathy by bystanders. Although my analysis situates these regimes of violence in the context of Germany's history, specifically the Holocaust and national socialism, such practices and discourses are also relevant for our understanding of other histories of genocide. Comparative studies, look-ing beyond the German case, reveal that dehumanization and empathic failure are integral to the industrial, military, and political apparatuses of mass murder in other parts of the world (see Hinton 2002a, 2002b, 2005). An additional theme that emerges from such comparative works concerns the social labor of forgetting: in the aftermath of trauma and genocide, the zones of collective memory tend to become constricted by an imposition of silence. In Germany after 1945, the prolonged attempts to silence and forget the truth of history have been linked to denial and shame (Linke 2002).

These observations are crucial for my analysis of what I term the "mu-seum of corpses," an installation I examine through the voids of memory and empathy in a post-Holocaust society. Although Hagens's exhibit of human bodies was deemed controversial and received enormous public attention, German public discourse remained curiously silent on the per-tinent connections between genocide, memory, and representation. As C. Nadia Seremetakis points out, in Germany, "church and cultural crit-ics have criticized this usage of the dead [in the exhibit] as exploitative and disrespectful" (2001:119). Such criticisms, however, avoided engage-ment with the specters of historical violence. Thus, for almost ten years, critics and supporters were content to reiterate the curator's comforting reassurances that the bodies on display had been legitimately harvested from deceased German donors. But, as I suggest here, a multilayered re-membrance of violence, with attention to the humanity and life histories of the dead, would have soon uncovered the exhibit's link to a global traf-fic in corpses and the requisition of bodies from the third world. I aim to penetrate these zones of silence by inquiring how emotional anesthesia, in the context of a popular fascination with mutilated bodies, is produced by discourse, image, and representation.

CORPSES IN THE MUSEUM

The objects on display in Hagens's exhibit, unlike most specimens at a conventional science museum, are real human corpses: cadavers. The bodies are arranged in various stages of dissection, though without showing any signs of decomposition. The corporal remains have undergone a process of preservation, a procedure called "plastination."[3] This method of preservation is a "technique [that] involves dehydrating the dissected cadavers in an intermediate solvent of freezing acetone, replacing all body fluids and fats with reactive polymers, and curing the polymerized tissues in the final step" (Herscovitch 2003:828). Subsequently the plasticized corpses "do not rot or smell, and they maintain the structure, color, and texture of the original tissue and organs down to the microscopic level" (Herscovitch 2003:828). Salvaged from decay with an "unprecedented measure of realism" (Clewing 1998b:16), the dead are forever preserved in corporal forms that bear the mark of deep anatomical intrusions (see Figures 1–4). The bodies have been skinned, cut open, dismembered, and sectioned to expose the interior world of human physiology: muscles, bones, nerve strands, blood vessels, organs, and reproductive regions including fetuses, wombs, and penises. In short, the installation "consists of hardened plastic corpses that, while standing upright . . . render specific aspects of their anatomy graphically visible" (Ziegler 1998:1). "The preserved bodies show themselves standing up, held upright. . . . These are no longer undamaged bodies, but anatomical specimens, cut open and opened up, without skin, without organs, depending on what part of the body is to be specifically accentuated. [They are shown] composed of muscles and tendons, reduced to a filigree of nerves, or as a congealed web of blood vessels. It is a true *'theatrum anatomicum'*" (Budde 1997:11).

This anatomical theater, which consists of entire human corpses and body parts, is globally staged at almost identical sites. In Europe, Asia, and North America, the traveling exhibit is typically housed in a public archive, a museum. The dissected bodies, which have been preserved by plastination, a chemical treatment that arrests organic time, are displayed

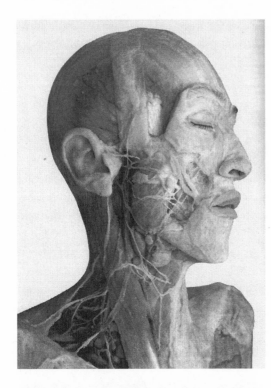

FIGURE 1 *Plastinated Woman's Head.* This female head has been partially skinned to expose nerves, muscles, and vessels, but the ear and face have been left intact. The lips are enhanced by a skin graft to accentuate this woman's femininity and sensual aura. From Landesmuseum 1997:218. Copyright by Gunther von Hagens, Institut für Plastination, Heidelberg, Germany. www.bodyworlds .com.

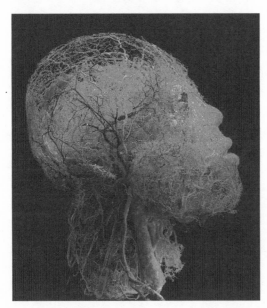

FIGURE 2 *Arterial Head.* In this display, the bones and tissues have been completely removed to show the lacy system of blood vessels: the head's arterial physiognomy. From Hagens and Whalley 2004a:202. Copyright by Gunther von Hagens, Institut für Plastination, Heidelberg, Germany. www.bodyworlds .com.

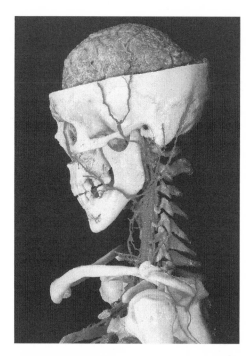

FIGURE 3 *Skeletal-Vascular Head with Exposed Brain.* From Hagens and Whalley 2004b:82. Copyright by Gunther von Hagens, Institut für Plastination, Heidelberg, Germany. www.bodyworlds.com.

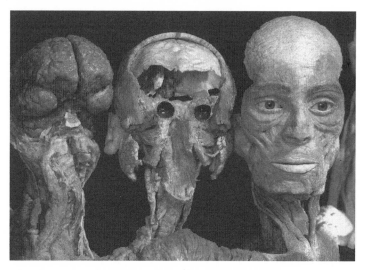

FIGURE 4 *Dissected Male Head.* This three-dimensional head has been dissected sagitally to permit a synchronic view of the expressive facial exterior, the skull anchored to the spine, and the nervous system connected to the brain. The humanity of the corpse comes into view solely as a mimetic surface. From Hagens and Whalley 2004a:172. Copyright by Gunther von Hagens, Institut für Plastination, Heidelberg, Germany. www.bodyworlds.com.

in places that likewise aim to preserve and incarcerate social time, namely, history and memory. Yet while the anatomical installations incorporate a medical grammar that proclaims scientific realism and anthropological truth by emptying the dead bodies of historical markers, the museum by contrast constitutes a highly symbolic site that narrates and commodifies memory. Anchored in such a prosthetic space, the exhibition of corpses safely travels in a world of global consumption of spectacle and entertainment. The transnational appeal of seeing mutilated bodies out of time and out of history is in part facilitated by these "new consumption experiences, new experiences of space/time compression" (Seremetakis 2001:120) that take place in this museum of corpses, a site that negates the discrete somatic fates of the dead and in turn conceals their concrete biographies of violence. Despite this turn against memory, "Body Worlds" has been able to forge a symbiotic relation with the museum, a relationship that has turned into a lucrative collaboration in the context of global consumer practices and desires. What sorts of longings and imaginaries sustain this symbiotic collaboration on a transnational scale?

The modern museum has been described as a memory site, a location of commemorative record and practice where society anchors the past (see Halbwachs 1980; Nora 1976; Le Goff 1992). Unlike other institutions of preservation, the museum not only collects but also displays the material artifacts of a people's cultural heritage: it exhibits history through objects and stages tangible encounters with the past by recourse to the sensually concrete. In the late twentieth century, this materiality or "thingness" of museum exhibits has taken on special significance (Korff 2002). For under the impact of global capitalism, in an era marked by the transient, the fugitive, and the contingent, the sensual proximity of objects in the museum conveys a heightened sense of anchorage and truth (Baudrillard 1991). Moreover, in the context of globalization, where the performance of national identity is brought onstage, the logic of time and the meaning of memory have been radically transposed. In the global arena the production of historical consciousness has become increasingly entangled with the commodity form. Encoded by temporal longings, the museum furnishes the common stock for a global memory market. As Andreas Huyssen suggests, by transforming historical pasts—such as the Holocaust—into commodity products, the museum participates in the "marketing of memory" on a transnational scale; by operating as a cultural memory industry, the museum bears the deep imprint of those globalizing forces whereby people's historical remembrances are commodified, circulated and consumed (2003:15). The modern museum is in this sense more than a mere repository for historical artifacts. It is, as Michel de Certeau phrased it, a site for the "colonization of time by a discourse of power" (1988:1). Museums not only manufacture new historical archives of peoples, places, and identities but they also participate in a global exchange of memory.

This global circulation of cultural and symbolic forms, this "traffic in memory," has been identified as a key issue during periods of transnational crisis and restructuring (Linke 2001:2222). But under globalization, with its destabilizing tendencies, we also encounter a new kind of memory market: historical memory as consumer product is increasingly centered on violence and on the body (Linke 2003). News and entertainment industries have begun to realize their profit interest by documenting genocide, war, and human rights abuses. The global media rapidly appropriate and circulate images of people's suffering: the memories of victimhood are commoditized; the remembrance of pain is commercialized (Kleinman and Kleinman 1997). Beyond this global consumption of atrocities, the public interest in and the market value of bodies has moved to the forefront of many museum exhibits. This new prominence of the body museum attests to the formation of a "physiomanic era," as Robert Schenda (1998) phrased it, which emerged "on the threshold of epochal transformations" (Clewing 1998b:16). Under the impact of deterritorialization, simulation, and cyberspace, the very proximity of bodies in the museum appeals to an intense desire for realism and authenticity among a global consumer public haunted by the contemporary struggles with memory, history, and temporality. In this context it is not surprising that the public access to mutilated human cadavers has enjoyed immense publicity and media attention worldwide. But what are the effects of this mass marketing of bodies, suffering, and death? As Michael Meng (2005) asks: "Does our exposure to the images and memories of mass murder . . . numb our ability to empathize with the victims of persecution? Has our consciousness of genocide become so ever present that mass violence seems almost banal, an ordinary, albeit tragic, part of human existence that fails to capture our attention or even our compassion? . . . A surfeit of memory and images has dulled our capacity to empathize with the victims of genocide."

Such a thinning of empathic capacities and emotional engagement cannot, however, be attributed solely to the mass mediation of atrocities. Rather, it is the virtuality and optical distance of such image-marketing techniques that produce a sense of the surreal and, in turn, enable affective detachment among consumers. Fictional violence and nonfictional images of death on television are difficult to disentangle: both are transmitted as virtual, mimetic, and visual modes of entertainment. The German exhibit of mutilated corpses makes use of similar representational techniques, although, by contrast, it strives to negate the media effect of fictional mimesis. In the exhibition surreal visuality and hyperrealism work in tandem to promote the relentless consumption of the dead. Thus while "Body Worlds" does rely on optics and visuality to annihilate compassion, it simultaneously endows its displays with a tangible, sensuous, even tactile quality that proffers an unmediated realism and an authentic facticity as a sensationalist allure. The global attraction of the unmitigated contact with bodies rests on machinations of authenticity commodified by the museum.

THE CULT OF THE AUTHENTIC

In this late modern era, governed by the perpetual *simulation of the sensual* through new media and communication technologies, the materiality of dead bodies clearly takes on new meanings. For under the impact of global capitalism, the nonvirtual presence of corpses in the museum seems to accommodate a yearning for the thingness of things—for the permanent, the tangible, the concrete (see Baudrillard 1991; Korff 2002). As such, the sensorial access to musealized corpses might nourish a late modern longing for an authentic reality, for a perceptual realism without simulation, without simulacra, or without copies. From this perspective, it is understandable why "Body Worlds" "implores the cult of the 'authentic' . . . with a perfidious turn to the genuine and real" (Roth 1998:51, 52). The display of dead bodies is promoted by a language that foregrounds the physical realism of the cadavers. As Hagens asserts: "The realism of the specimens contributes enormously to the fascination and power of the exhibit. Particularly in today's media-dominated world . . . people have retained an acute awareness of the fact that a copy is always already a mental representation, and therefore a mimetic interpretation. In this sense the exhibition satiates the tremendous desire for unadulterated realism" (1997:214).

German exhibit reviews likewise emphasize that the displays are stocked with "genuine human specimens," "real bodies," and "actual corpses" whose "naked reality" and "authenticity is fascinating" (Becker 1999:15; Nissen 1998:36; Vorpahl 1997:8), for the exhibited objects are "not artificial anatomy models, but real dead people" (Budde 1997:11), "not instructional models, but genuine corpses, presented to the museum visitors openly, in public, and in closest proximity, without the protective glass of the show case" (Schmitz 1997:8). But the titillating charge that emanates from dead bodies, this fascinating allure of the authentic, needs to be understood in terms of a more general social dynamic. For, as Gottfried Korff points out, "the gaze," or the perspective of the seeing eye, "is also always an expression of a societal self-understanding" (1999:269–270). In this era of global capitalism, with its destabilizing tendencies, the quest for anchorage and authenticity is intimately connected to the currency of the corporal turn. Such a reading is in part confirmed by the exhibit's visitor statistics. More than twenty million people have attended the exhibit worldwide, including eight million in Europe and of these six million in Germany. Journalists have hailed a "German record for a museum exhibit" with "up to 20,000 people per day" (Nissen 1998:36; Frankfurter Rundschau 1998b:33). The body museum deploys the semiotics of the corpse to appeal to a global consumer public, while at the same time signifying, explaining, and representing the dead in a culturally specific manner. The exhibit utilizes an aesthetic that not only disguises the brutality of death and dismemberment but also negates German memories of historical violence.

THE LIVING CORPSE

The public display of the corpse, which inspires both morbid curiosity and scientific interest, initially appears to be part of a more general history of human exhibitions, displays in which the themes of death, violence, and medicine are closely intertwined. As Barbara Kirshenblatt-Gimblett elaborates: "This history includes the exhibition of dead bodies . . . , the public dissection of cadavers in anatomy lessons, the vivisection of torture victims using such anatomical techniques as flaying, public executions by guillotine or gibbet, heads of criminals impaled on stakes, public extractions of teeth, and displays of body parts and fetuses in anatomical and other museums, whether in flesh, in wax, or in plaster cast" (1998:35). Earlier ethnographic or anatomical displays, built around articulated skeletons, taxidermy, wax models, or live specimens, forged a "conceptual link between anatomy and death in what might be considered museums of mortality" (Kirshenblatt-Gimblett 1998:36).[4] In these museums human suffering, biographical history, and the horror of death should become interrelated motifs. The German "Body Worlds" exhibit presents something quite different: it explicitly distances itself from this trajectory of the human museum by an emphasis on unemotional and dispassionate anatomical displays. Its galleries of plastinated corpses are not intended to inspire fear or revulsion by dramatizing death. On the contrary, this collection of dead bodies, which contains more than two hundred specimens, wants to create the illusion of life after death. According to the curator, the preservation of the corpse with silicon and plastic makes possible "a new form of postmortal existence," namely "the 'resurrection' of the enfleshed body" (Hagens 1997:214; Roth 1998:52). What are we to make of such statements? And what sorts of images are thereby invoked?

This exhibit stages human anatomy by means of dramatic visions of the normal, ordinary, and everyday body. The exhibitors strive for "an aesthetic that strips the dead of their estranging rigidity and instead emphasizes their affinity with the living" (Spiegel 1997:214). Many of the life-sized figures, these plastinated corpses, are posed to simulate familiar activities: running, standing, walking, and sitting (see Figures 5–9).

> The man appears to be running: he stands there—as if moving in a fast stride. He is naked, and moreover: he has been stripped of his skin, the muscle tissue detached from the bone. Shreds of flesh trail down. (Clewing 1998b:16)

> The *Runner* is frozen in the loping gait of a marathoner, stripped of almost everything except bones and muscles. His outer muscles fly backward off his bones, as if the muscles were being blown by the wind rushing past. The *Muscleman* is a bare skeleton that holds up its entire system of muscles. . . . The *Figure with Skin* retains all its muscles and organs, but its skin is draped like a coat over one arm. The *Expanded Body* resembles a human telescope, its skeleton pulled apart so people can see what lies beneath the skull and the rib cage. (Andrews 1998:1)

[We see] a basketball player caught mid-dribble with filleted muscles trailing behind . . . ; a human rider mounted nobly on a plastinated horse . . . ; a seated chess player concentrating intently on his game. . . . A pregnant woman reclining. (Herscovitch 2003:828)

The bodies on display are staged to perform activities from the mundane world—sports, play, and other forms of recreation. This menagerie of corpses presents human remains as a dancer, a runner, a horse rider, a chess player, a weight lifter, a swimmer, and a cyclist. These dissected and cut-open bodies, posed in typified representations with a "proximate realism" to "give the impression that they are forever alive" (Zoschke 1994:12), are depicted as skillfully crafted installations: "the 'living corpses'" (Roth 1998:52). The exhibitors describe their galleries of dead bodies as works of "living anatomy"; thereby they do not mean "stiff corpses lying prostrate on the dissecting table," but "entire bodies positioned upright . . . standing in lifelike poses" that "create anatomical individuality" and replicate "a living being" (Hagens 1997:203–4).

In this context, however, we might wonder what this persistent invocation of authenticity actually signifies. For the presumed works "of authenticity, of living realism in death" (Schmitz 1997:8), are synthetically produced artifacts, mimetic objects. They are designed to *simulate* the anatomy of live human beings. And this vital anatomy is the end product of a series of machinations: reconstructed, fabricated, aestheticized, and mimetically staged. Nonetheless the exhibitors emphatically insist on the authentic realism of their displays. By circumventing the use of conventional media such as stone, plaster, or wax, they claim to have fashioned human figures directly from organic substances: tissue, muscle, and bone. In this regard the exhibited objects are deemed "authentic anatomical specimens" (Hagens 2004b:260). But "the plastinated cadaver," as José van Dijck points out, "is as much an organic artifact as it is the result of technological tooling. . . . The cadavers are manipulated with chemicals to such an extent that that they can hardly be regarded as real bodies" (2005:47). Moreover, in the process of manufacture, human corpses are clearly instrumentalized as mere raw material: "Even a body saturated with silicone rubber must be shaped into the desired pose before the preservatives can polymerize" (Roth 1998:50–51). The human raw material, the dead flesh, is treated, transfigured, and sculpted: "The corpses are worked on without

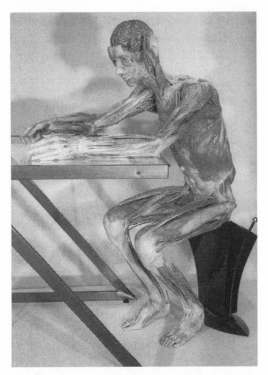

FIGURE 5 *Sitting Male Figure*. The sitting man, whose body has been skinned and partially dissected, appears to be self-content while gazing at his hands resting on a table. From Landesmuseum 1997:172. Copyright by Gunther von Hagens, Institut für Plastination, Heidelberg, Germany. www .bodyworlds.com.

FIGURE 6 *The Runner*. The body of the runner has been stripped of his skin. His muscles, which are partially detached from the bones, have been folded back or stretched laterally to simulate movement. From Hagens and Whalley 2004a:152. Copyright by Gunther von Hagens, Institut für Plastination, Heidelberg, Germany. www .bodyworlds.com.

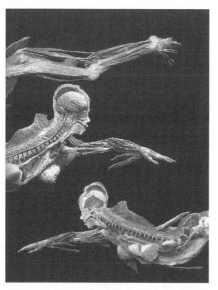

FIGURE 7 *Female Swimmer.* The body of the female swimmer has been sliced into two lateral halves to show anatomy in motion, through the play of her muscles, the curvature of her spine, and the location of her abdominal organs, specifically, as the exhibitors point out, of her uterus with ovaries and fallopian tubes. From Hagens and Whalley 2004a:175. Copyright by Gunther von Hagens, Institut für Plastination, Heidelberg, Germany. www.bodyworlds .com.

FIGURE 8 *Horse Rider.* The rearing horse holds a male rider, whose body has been dissected into three adjoining parts to reveal the deportment of his muscles, organs, and skeletal system. From Hagens and Whalley 2004a:180. Copyright by Gunther von Hagens, Institut für Plastination, Heidelberg, Germany. www.bodyworlds.com.

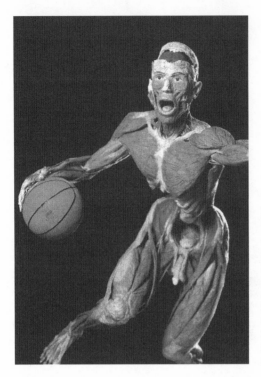

FIGURE 9 *Basketball Player*.
The basketball player, the corpse
of a man whose skull has been
cut open and whose intestines
have been removed, provides
a snapshot of the muscular
apparatus in action. From:
Hagens and Whalley 2004a:160.
Copyright by Gunther von
Hagens, Institut für Plastination,
Heidelberg, Germany. www
.bodyworlds.com.

restraint and set in poses" (Becker 1999:15). It is an assembly of "human-flesh sculptures" (Spiegel 1998:184; Frankfurter Rundschau 1998c).

These sculptures or artifactual corpses transcend any markers of death. The bodies assume lifelike postures, perform everyday activities, and display facial expressions that convey pleasure and contentment or concentrated attention. These machinations of vitality are representational strategies that divert the spectators' attention from the domains of terror and death: the lively appearance of the dead negates any awareness of the circumstances of their death, of the prolonged procedures of medical intervention, and the cruelty of dissection, as I will elaborate. The installations create a world of "living" corpses that is devoid of trauma and historicity. This anatomical realism works to annul memory: historical consciousness recedes into a blind zone. With this dissociative strategy, the plastinated figures are presented and come into view as sites of transparent scientific truth, as surfaces for the inscription of unmediated natural anatomy, which in turn "eradicat[es] all mediation between object and representation" and "render[s] all subjective intervention—inherent to representation—obsolete" (Dijck 2005:56). The exhibition of supposedly living corpses incarcerates the spectators' interpretative capacity within the self-referential field of anatomical realism. This erasure of critical perception, which is encoded into the displays, is further enhanced by the erotic appeal of the artifacts.

SEXING THE CORPSE

The bodies are preserved in such a way that "they endure, like any marble statue, far beyond the lifetime of their makers" (Hagens 1997:216). Although plastination does preserve the corpse, the curator's primary objective is not to immortalize the dead, but to restore the cadavers' anatomy to a lifelike state. The installations embody an ideology of nonalienated flesh, a mythopoeia of corporal authenticity, which in turn seeks to preserve the figures' sexual characteristics. The German body museum, however, not only articulates the naked sexuality of the corpse: it renders sex iconographically hypervisible.

With few exceptions the exhibited whole-body specimens are male. And every male figure, regardless of its anatomical disarray, has been equipped with an intact penis, emphasizing its sex, its manhood (see Figures 10–12). Even the deep-body specimens, which have been pared down to their muscular or skeletal system, show an accentuated display of unharmed male genitalia: enlarged, engorged, and oversized. The exhibits of female corpses likewise show sexualized poses: "The pregnant figure shields the genital area with her arm, while at the same time framing the fetus in her womb" (Hagens 1997:214). This woman's curved breasts are prominently accentuated: although her body has been stripped of all its skin, her nipples are placed erectly on prosthetic tissue plates (Figure 13).[5] Indeed, following the exhibition in Mannheim in 1997, this figure was replaced by another female specimen: although staged in an identical pose, her breasts are conspicuously enlarged (Figure 14). The exhibition of corpses or anatomical "object-bodies," as Max Horkheimer and Theodor W. Adorno phrased it, requires sexualization, a libidinal charge, in order "to be at once desired as that which is forbidden" (1981:277). The showing of corpses operates with an eroticization of vision: a sexualized optical regime. For in the center of these visual productions stands the voyeuristic exposure of naked corpses—of "the body's anatomical nudity" (Whalley 1997:161). But this nakedness of the corpse is accentuated by an ideographic sexualization, for the flayed bodies are endowed with either an enormous penis or voluptuous breasts.

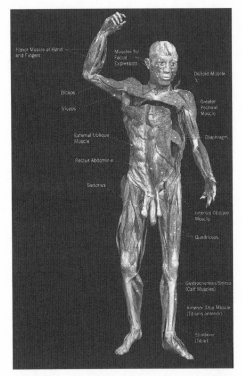

Labels on figure (clockwise from upper left):
Flexor Muscle of Hand and Fingers
Muscles for Facial Expression
Deltoid Muscle
Greater Pectoral Muscle
Diaphragm
Internal Oblique Muscle
Quadriceps
Gastrocnemius/Soleus (Calf Muscles)
Anterior Shin Muscle (Tibialis anterior)
Shinbone (Tibia)
Sartorius
Rectus Abdominis
External Oblique Muscle
Triceps
Biceps

FIGURE 10 *Muscle Man.* This man displays his body's superficial musculature. The anterior walls of his chest and abdomen have been opened on the side, and his internal organs have been removed to permit a view into the large body cavity. From a frontal perspective, as shown here, the body's masculinity is visually inscribed by the size of his genitalia. From Hagens and Whalley 2004a:132. Copyright by Gunther von Hagens, Institut für Plastination, Heidelberg, Germany. www.bodyworlds.com.

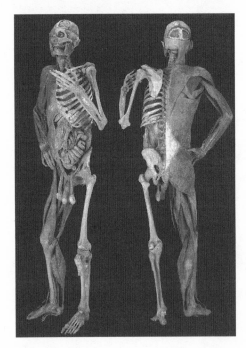

FIGURE 11 *Skeletal-Muscular Man.* The man's body has been dissected to show both his skeletal structure and muscular system. Although partially stripped to his bones, his elongated penis and testicles have been left intact. From Hagens and Whalley 2004b:144. Copyright by Gunther von Hagens, Institut für Plastination, Heidelberg, Germany. www.bodyworlds.com.

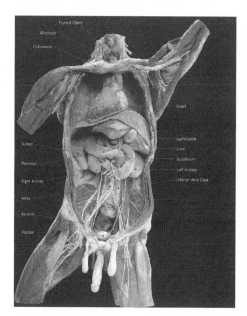

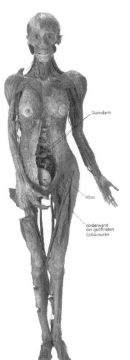

FIGURE 12 *Male Torso*. This man's torso has been sagittally opened to show the organs of the chest and the abdominal cavities (with *situs inversus*). His genitals are enlarged and elongated. From Hagens and Whalley 2004a:167. Copyright by Gunther von Hagens, Institut für Plastination, Heidelberg, Germany. www.bodyworlds.com.

FIGURE 13 *Pregnant Woman*. The upright pregnant woman has been posed with arm and hand gestures that seem to beckon us to gaze into her open abdomen, where we see her placenta with a five-month-old fetus. From Landesmuseum 1997:140. Copyright by Gunther von Hagens, Institut für Plastination, Heidelberg, Germany. www.bodyworlds.com.

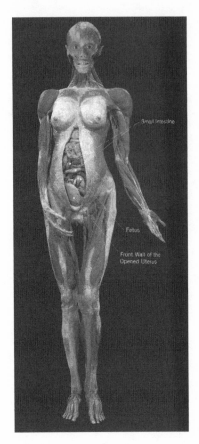

Small Intestine

Fetus

Front Wall of the
Opened Uterus

FIGURE 14 *Pregnant Woman with Enhanced Breasts.* From Hagens and Whalley 2004a:130. Copyright by Gunther von Hagens, Institut für Plastination, Heidelberg, Germany. www .bodyworlds.com.

This ideographic sexualization is perhaps most pronounced in the *Male Corpse with Skin*, an installation of exposed penile or phallic masculinity (Figure 15). The male figure shown here, the flayed body of a man who is gazing at his own skin, attempts to convey something about the importance of the human dermis—of which this particular corpse has been robbed in its entirety. The installation is captioned by the following text: "The plastinated figure . . . shows, among other things, how defenseless a human being looks without skin, and also how the skin, when no longer inhabited by the body, can be regarded as a distinct organ. Only after the skin has been painstakingly removed can the body's anatomical nudity be exposed: [We see] the bones and muscles, which in turn envelope the innermost organs" (Whalley 1997:161). The installation wants to reveal what lies beneath the skin: but the lifeless skin, which is draped over the man's arm, is a mere heuristic device in the design of an erotic optical regime. For in the center of this visual production stands the exposure of naked masculinity: the flayed corpse exhibits a large penis, framed by two equally oversized testicles. The display's visual focus on the figure's muscular body and genital masculinity reveals a preoccupation with corporal integrity, that is, with the reproductive functioning and sexual potency of the anatomical male. This same optical eroticism, focused on exaggerated penile exposition, runs through the gallery of male bodies, including the *Organ Man*, the *Male Torso*, the various "skeletal-muscular" specimens, the *Swordsman*, the *Fragmented Man*, and the *Sliced Male Body*. Even in death the body is shown to be visually seductive.

In Germany the transfiguration of human cadavers into sexual objects received nationwide attention when the exhibit moved to Hamburg's Erotic Art Museum in 2003. The choice of this site not only points to an enhanced appetite for libidinal signs but also reveals the installation's pornographic appeal. German media headlines celebrated the "striptease of corpses," the "well-endowed bodies" shown "ultranude and uncensored" (Assheuer 2003). Unsurprisingly, the Erotic Art Museum exhibit was synchronized with the curator's decision to expand the installation's section on sex and reproduction and to move pertinent specimens, including "the erect penis of one of the dead, a clitoris, and a fetus in the mother's womb" (Assheuer 2003), into the center of the exhibit (Figure 16). In Germany death and sex—corpses with sex appeal—have market value.

This optical regime, which emphasizes the hypersexuality of the dead, is clearly strategic: voyeuristic and pornographic, it aims to capture the spectators' attention within the narrow visual field of the anatomical exhibit. The corpses, shown lively, naked, and sexed, inhibit contemplation about issues that lie beyond the immediacy of perception: terror, death, victimhood, and history. But such a scopic regime, which celebrates the "striptease of corpses," is also an act of violence: the visual consumption of the naked bodies of the dead and dying forms part of German history. It surfaced as a tactic in the mortification of bodies at various Nazi concentration camps and military killing fields. As captured by detailed photographic records, the victims of genocide were not only stripped of their humanity but typically also robbed of the last vestiges of their personal

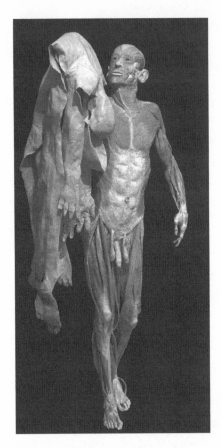

FIGURE 15 *Man Holding His Skin.*
From Hagens and Whalley 2004a:147.
Copyright by Gunther von Hagens, Institut
für Plastination, Heidelberg, Germany.
www.bodyworlds.com.

identities—their clothing. Such images of naked victims are often displayed in German museums. In a critical commentary titled *The Field of Forgetting*, Ingrid Strobl (1993) takes us to the opening of the Wannsee museum in Berlin. Designed as a permanent showcase, the photographic collage attempts to chronicle the final stages of the Holocaust. Although intended as "a site for teaching history," as Strobl points out, "mass murder is chronologically depicted without murderers" (1993:83). Shown are naked human beings as visualized through the eyes of the perpetrators:

> Seven photographs of women, who are driven naked to the pit or who are in the process of undressing, are exhibited in this room. Seven. The women, panicked by fear and shame, are pressing their arms against their breasts to cover them, and as a result their pubic hair is left ex-

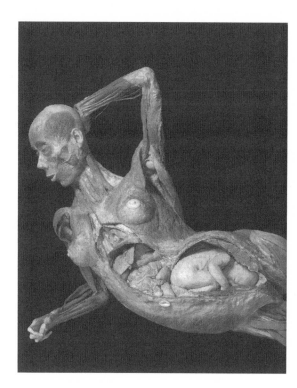

FIGURE 16 *Reclining Pregnant Woman.* The reclining pregnant woman casually stretches backward to permit a look into the interior of her cut-open abdomen, which contains the corpse of her eight-month-old baby. From Hagens and Whalley 2004a:176. Copyright by Gunther von Hagens, Institut für Plastination, Heidelberg, Germany. www .bodyworlds.com.

posed. . . . This is the final and ultimate act of humiliation before they are driven into the pit. These human beings—two million of them Soviet Jews—who were slaughtered by the troops, were often required to undress in plain view of their murderers, and then they had to place their clothes, neatly folded, into a heap. . . . Members of these execution units . . . found the time to photograph their victims during these moments of debasement and complete vulnerability. (Strobl 1993:83)

These unforgiving archives reveal that the eye of the camera, much like the aim of the gun, operates as a weapon of bodily invasion. In this panoptic theater of violence, as Allen Feldman has argued, subjugation, nakedness, and compulsory visibility are practices of ocular aggression: "Seeing and killing" and "being seen and being killed" define the zones of political terror (1997:29). As a strategic form of humiliation and debasement, the visual appropriation of the victims' nakedness is an act of violence. Moreover, within the scopic regime of Nazi racial terror, the visual penetration

FIGURE 17 *Autopsy Corpse.*
The standing man has been
preserved in a lively gesticular
pose. The body has been rendered
sensually appealing by accentuating
his masculine features: his
musculature and penis. From:
Hagens and Whalley 2004a:297.
Copyright by Gunther von
Hagens, Institut für Plastination,
Heidelberg, Germany. www
.bodyworlds.com.

of the body "establishe[d] truth claims and typicality" by negating personhood (Feldman 1997:30). Through the optics of race, nakedness reified the
victim's abject identity by a focus on the physical body (Linke 1999:51–54).
When in remembrance of the catastrophe Jewish victims are represented
or seen as individuals, it is usually in the period between life and death:
"Between the ramp and the oven, as starved, naked . . . men and women,
whose physical extremity . . . makes us stop before the photographs and
consider them one by one. By that time, however, these people were already gone: they were just not yet dead" (Wieseltier 1994:177).

These images from the past should serve to remind us of the violence
of vision that unfolds in the exhibition of bodies. Hagens's museum of
corpses clearly operates with such a modus of ocular aggression. The nudity of the corpses erases personhood by reducing individual subjects to
generic anatomical artifacts. Presented as libidinous objects, encoded by
nakedness and sex, the optical consumption of the dead distracts attention
from the body as a site of suffering (see Figure 17). The eroticism of the displays mutes awareness of the violence of visual penetration. As in the case

of political terror, as Feldman has suggested, "the circuit formed by vision and violence" in these sexual depictions of the corpses is "circumscribed by zones of blindness and inattention" (1997:29). In the following my aim is to examine these zones of blindness further.

MISOGYNOUS CORPOREALITY

The exhibit's collection of body parts contains numerous healthy organs, including nearly a dozen male genitalia. These plastinated and often elongated or erect penises, complete with scrota, are displayed in separate show cases. By contrast, women's reproductive organs, that is, the vagina and uterus with ovaries, are shown with malignancies, tumors, deformities, and cysts. The Mannheim exhibit in 1997 contained only two female figures; both were pregnant women. In one woman's corpse, the stomach and uterus had been cut open to reveal a five-month-old fetus (see Landesmuseum 1997:136, 138, 140–41). In the exhibit's catalog, this female body is mapped by textual markers that, much like pornographic techniques of accentuating erogenous zones, highlight specific regions of the body (see Figure 13). Here, however, the voyeuristic gaze is directed to the female interior—the intestines, the organs of elimination, the uterus, and the fetus—an iconographic imprint that is suggestive of a preoccupation with female secretions and bodily by-products: excrement, urine, placental tissue, and fetal substances. In the exhibit, as in the accompanying catalog, the pregnant women are grouped with an assortment of pathologies—malformed embryos, miscarriages, and aborted pregnancies: "In a glass case at the center of [this] room, visitors encounter a row of plasticized infant corpses, including a pair of conjoined twins" (Andrews 1998:4). The subsequent exhibit in Basel, Switzerland, likewise "shows Siamese twins or brain-damaged [infants] together with embryos, fetuses, and a pregnant woman's body that has been cut open" (Becker 1999:15). In London, the visitor's gaze is similarly directed toward "a pregnant woman reclining demurely in a room lined with deformed fetuses" and other "pregnancy complications" (Herscovitch 2003:828). Such an iconographic emphasis on female reproduction gone awry—the female body as pathology—belongs to and is symptomatic of a misogynist conception of womanhood. This type of imagination, focused on reproductive health and abnormality, seems particularly disturbing in the context of Germany's anatomical tradition, which, as Dijck points out, has become tainted by Nazism's medical history "involving scientific experiments on living and dead human bodies and the Nazi ideology of eugenics" (2005:60).

In this German exhibition about human anatomy, a national body politic is commemorated in musealized memory and inscribed and implanted into corpses by a medical gaze preoccupied with reproduction and sex. By way of these biological phantasms, culturally specific notions of sexuality are reified as natural or authentic anatomy. This fabrication of biomedical truth is furthermore obfuscated by the aestheticized figuration of the exhibited objects, which undercuts the possibility of critical reflection.

CORPSE ART

The exhibit of human bodies is driven by an aesthetic that seeks to commodify corpses as sculptures, as artistic figures (Figure 18). What visitors supposedly see is the "art of anatomy: the aesthetically instructive presentation of the body's interior" (Hagens 1997:214, 217). In Germany the plastinated specimens were praised as "an intellectual and creative achievement" by an "anatomy artist" who works on bodies "just like a sculptor" (Roth 1998:51). According to media reports, the "remarkable success of the current *Body Worlds* exhibition" is linked to the fact that "dissected human cadavers are ... presented as works of art" (Smith 2003:829): "Visitors could see . . . strangely disfigured corpses as art" (Frankfurter Rundschau 1998a, 1998c; see also Roth 1998:52; Spiegel 1997:214). In the curator's opinion, artistic intervention is a critical aspect of the presentations. As Hagens notes: "The corpse must be displayed artistically; otherwise it becomes an object of revulsion and obstructs the unemotional gaze" (Fonseca 1999:50); "the aesthetic pose helps to dispel disgust" (Hagens 1997:205). According to Liselotte Hermes da Fonseca (1999:50), the aesthetic dimension enables viewers to "see" the corpse as a "natural" object: the installations are supposed to instruct without eliciting any emotions. The dead, who are "here shown in a highly artistic form of preservation," are "beautiful and educational ... artistic and instructive" (Kriz 1997:9, 10). As one visitor remarked: "Some of the displays were undeniably beautiful, especially the lacy circulatory system of a rabbit, a hand, an adult, and a child" (Herscovitch 2003:828). Moreover, "no offensive odors disturb the viewing," because plastination stops the lifeless bodies from entering decomposition (Hagens 1997:216, 205). The corpses on display are "dry, hard, and scent free," "clean," and "noninfectious," and "one can touch them . . .

FIGURE 18 *Longitudinally Exploded Body*. Posed in a sitting position, with his penis dangling down to his knees, a man's torso and head have been vertically stretched to create fissures and interspaces that bring the interior of the body into visibility. From Hagens and Whalley 2004a:22. Copyright by Gunther von Hagens, Institut für Plastination, Heidelberg, Germany. www .bodyworlds.com.

with one's own hands . . . as often as one likes," "even without gloves" (Vorpahl 1997:8; Roth 1998:50, Clewing 1998a:3, and Zoschke 1994:12; Rothschild 1998:3). Indeed, the exhibition explicitly extends "an invitation to touch and to look into the bodily interior" (Schmitz 1997:8). Since the individual exhibits are strategically "placed in the very center of the walkway, the tactile contact with the artful dead is in fact palpably provoked" (Roth 1998:51).

Such a fabricated proximity to the corpse is suggestive of a "democratization of anatomy," for the exhibited objects—being "resilient, enduring, and realistic"—offer the visiting public "seemingly direct access" to the cadavers (Frankfurter Rundschau 1998b:33; Zoschke 1994:12; Becker 1999:15). The museum display is designed to facilitate "a sensory awareness of the world of the body through the immediacy of visual contact by the eye and the comprehending touch of the hand" (Bauer 1997:199). Such a sensualized exhibit undoubtedly reinforces the feeling of a material presence of real and authentic corpses—a presumed intimacy with death. Of course, this contact with death is a staged illusion, a museum effect, because the displayed objects are not stinking corpses, but synthetically sanitized bodies: "dry and odorless," "graspable," lacking "decomposition and desiccation so completely that the bodily interior ceases to be an object of revulsion" (Hagens 1997:204). The show is supposed "to diminish the horror of death" (Kriz 1997:9). But the installations retreat precisely from this reality insofar as they exhibit supposedly *living* corpses: normalized and eroticized. The prominent characteristics through which death might be experienced, the sensually apprehensible signs of decay, have been intentionally amputated from the exhibited objects. These staged encounters with dead bodies thus simultaneously furnish the necessary emotional distance.

Central to this museum exhibit is "the aestheticization of corpses. By means of the plastination technique, the exhibited objects become in large part unrecognizable as real bodies; this art form promotes a forgetting of the fact that these are indeed dead human beings" (Emmrich 1998:6). One "has to repeatedly remind oneself that this is not an artificial panopticon, but true anatomy. There are absolutely no detectable odors either. . . . the dissected bodies look . . . so deceptively lifelike that they indeed appear to be works of art" (Schmitz 1997:8). These observations are important, for they suggest that the installation-effect intentionally negates the propagated proximity to death. By means of the "aesthetic dimension of showing" (Clewing 1998c:30), the cadavers are presented in such a way that they appear un-dead. The figure of the *Muscle Man*, for instance, is described as "skillfully perform[ing] weight-lifting experiments" (Roth 1998:51). The anatomical exhibit of corpses is "lively, active, and posed" (Hagens 1997:204). The "beauty [of these corporal forms] displaces our revulsion," and "aesthetics becomes a means for pushing away disgust" (Eggebrecht 1998:1; see Reimer 1998). Out of the raw material of human remains new bodies have been fashioned: beautified, durable, and sensually accessible.

Plastination remakes the corpse into an aesthetic object: with his flesh preserved and rendered immortal, *Man with Skin* stands transfixed, focused only on himself (Figure 19). A set of motifs that typify the transfiguration of this corpse—white skin, classic facial features, a muscular body, and a heroic pose—reveal a return to an uncanny fascination with fascist

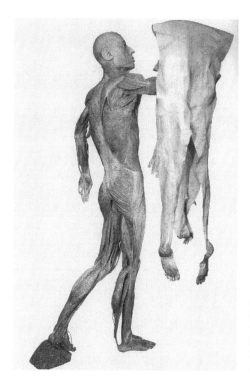

masculinity. And presented without reference to the deceased subjects' personal biography, life history, or cause of death, the plastinated specimens perform an inverse symbolic function. For the corpses are aestheticized in such a way as to suppress any evocations of violence, victimhood, or history: the performative success of the specimens is inscribed in the amputation of feelings and the erasure of memory. Plastination renders the dead bodies "timeless and thereby removes the potential of forgetting or remembering" (Fonseca 1999:58). The displayed objects, which are repeatedly described as "anatomical art works," "praiseworthy" "art objects," "artistic representations," and "skillfully" crafted "statues" or "sculptures" (Andrews 1998:1; Eberhardt 1998a:32; Roth 1998:51), successfully evade the memory work of history: they possess neither an autobiographical memory nor a historical remembrance. The installation suppresses the commemoration of the dead subjects' life histories as much as Germany's problematic history: medical experiments, eugenics, and racial hygiene under national socialism. Indeed, the refurbished corpses are crafted in the tradition of the classic white German body: they are "eternal human monuments" in a "museum without forgetting, therefore without remembrance, which means, without loss, without mourning, and, as such, without empathy" (Fonseca 1999:56, 60).

NEGATIONS OF HUMANITY

The practice of corpse art is grounded in a series of negations, in a negative dialectic that facilitates the public showing of corpses. The bodies are estranged, depersonalized, and reified. Dead bodies are morphologically transformed into living corpses. Cadavers are turned into artistic sculptures. The motionless flesh is made to stand upright. Lifeless matter is sculpted into lifelike poses. Mortality is denied by an emphasis on the resurrection of the dead body. Temporality is negated by means of synthetic preservatives. The inevitable deterioration of the body is preempted: the corpses remain forever "frozen" somewhere "between death and decay" (Hagens 1997:201); and in this manner, they come into view as eternally enduring, monumental body architecture.

But this kind of monumentalism uncannily consumes death in the same manner that "fascism feeds on bodies" (Wolbert 1982:7). While claiming to uncover forensic truth beneath the human surface, the exhibit "offers up the interior of the body as a commodity-object and use-item": the panoptic penetration of the cadavers is at once also an "anatomical cannibalism" (Seremetakis 2001:120). As in Germany's Nazi past, where the propagation of racial ideals was synchronized with a total apparatus of destruction and mass death, the exhibit's aestheticism, with its manufacture of beautified anatomical figures, is coordinated with the unscrupulous debasement of human remains. In this sense the "eviscerated bodies are themselves expressions of a post-Holocaust embodiment" (Seremetakis 2001:128). The use of the dead as artistic raw material rests on dehumanization, which is, moreover, enabled by the state's collusion in this enterprise, as I will show in the remainder of this essay.

In the exhibit, the processed corpses have been rendered anonymous. The dead subject, the very identity of this formerly living human being, has been erased from the displays: "The historical-biographical construct of the person of the deceased [is] excised from the plastinated objects" (Bauer 1997:197). Moreover, the "age and cause of death are generally withheld to avoid a 'personification' of the specimens" (Hagens 1997:201). Every remnant of subjectivity is destroyed, for the dead bodies have been "transfigured" beyond recognition (Clewing 1998b:16). "We do not know how these human beings lived, who they were, or how they died. We do not know their names, their age, their life story. Even their facial features, which have been altered by the dissection process, can no longer tell us very much" (Budde 1997:11). The exhibit shows "peeled, perforated, opened, and halved . . . dissected bodies, a 'corpse inside the corpse,' as it were" (Roth 1998:51, 52), which stands there, frozen in time, without personal identity and life history, robbed of its humanity.

But these dead bodies, through the negative labor of medical intrusions, are not merely estranged and transfigured but also objectified. The "cut-up, dismembered, and recombined three-dimensional 'living corpses'" (Roth 1998:52) are no longer recognizable as human subjects. "As soon as the dissection process begins, the corpse . . . becomes an anonymous specimen that no longer reminds us of the individuality of the deceased in any aspect" (Spiegel 1997:212). This process of dehumanization has concrete legal implications, for these subjectivity-deprived bodies can be stripped of their civil rights. The insistence on anonymity, the abrogation of identity, scientific objectification, and aesthetic figuration collude to neutralize any potential judicial concerns. In most German states, like Baden-Wurttemberg, "burial regulations generally prohibit the public display of corpses. . . . But the Mannheim judiciary determined that plastinated bodies are not 'corpses in the eyes of the law'" (Eberhardt 1997:18). From a juridical perspective the exhibited specimens are not human bodies, but lifeless matter, material objects. In a legal sense, "an anatomy-corpse becomes a 'thing' that is no longer entitled to a peaceful death if it remains anonymous, lacks any emotional attachment, and is no longer the object of commemoration" (Spiegel 1997:214). Thus defined as a thing by the German judicial system, the plastinated corpse loses its humanity. Affect and empathy are severed from the exhibited object: "It is indeed not the lifeless body or even the plastinated body saturated with synthetics that is the object of our compassionate remembrance" (Bauer 1997:197). The corpses are empty, uninhabited figures, exhibited in a human museum that negates all signs of humanity. The dead bodies are dehistoricized and thereby also without remembrance. According to the curator, "corpses . . . are after a certain point merely 'specimens.' . . . 'An anatomical specimen ceases to be the object of reverence and human compassion'" (Vorpahl 1997:8): "The lasting effect of dignity accorded to the deceased by the work of mourning is thereby extinguished. . . . The sense of emotional attachment to the deceased" has "come to an end" (Hagens 1997:207). On display are dehumanized "subjectless bodies" (Fonseca 1999:66) that are denied any affective attention. Thus rendered emotionless, the German body museum, in Helmut Lethen's words, "takes its leave from the culture of conscience" and from the "drama of the culture of shame" (1994:6–7).[6]

RECYCLING DEATH

The dead are redesigned to become lifeless matter: they are described as medical plastinates, anatomical specimens, museum objects, and juridical things—as thinglike figures. Legally dispossessed of the rights of personhood, they are not human subjects and thus not even corpses. By means of this negation of human subjectivity, the exhibit realizes "phantasms of disposition about the biomass," which "reduces the human subject . . . to a functioning apparatus" (Becker 1999:15): the human being "becomes a body . . . a physical device for study" (Budde 1997:11). Thus at the same time that the dead are emptied of their individual subjectivities and rendered bare of empathic appeal, they are constructed as forensic types. Eviscerated and opened up for inspection, human beings are exhibited as categorical biological specimens: the *Body Slice*, the *Skeletal-Muscular Man*, the *Organ Presenter*, the *Autopsy Body*, the *Exploded Body*, the *Ligament Man*, and the *Female Arterial Bone Body*. Legally dehumanized, though displayed as sexually enhanced icons of human activity, the plastinated figures have been equipped with phantasmatic identities "through a fusion of aesthetics and medical diagnostics" (Seremetakis 2001:127). The anatomically bared bodies are variously dissected to reveal specific biological functions: the nervous system, the digestive tract, the circulatory system, and the respiratory apparatus. What is shown is the "human being as a construct" (Budde 1997:11). Instrumentalized and objectified, these "nameless figures," as Hagens asserts, come on stage with "a decisive purpose" as "objects of knowledge" (Fonseca 1999:44; Hagens 1997:207, 214). Within this operational scheme, in which the body is only recognizable as an apparatus, a system, or a tract, the dead are posed as task-oriented action figures: as swordsman, spear thrower, swimmer, runner, dancer, chess player, rider, and basketball player. The installations attempt to create a functional death.

Hagens "wants to extract as much 'didactic profit' from the dead as possible" to make the dead "serve an instrumental purpose" (Frankfurter

Rundschau 1997:22; Eberhardt 1997:18). In this anatomical museum, he asserts, the dead can be "disposed of" in "a meaningful way" because they are "used for educational ends" (Vorpahl 1997:8; Hagens 1997:207): by a "productive utilization" of the deceased some additional benefit can be extracted from their bodies (Eberhardt 1998b:40). But this "postmortem exhibitionism," as the media called it (Rothschild 1998:3), operates rather more like a postmortem recycling procedure, a commercial enterprise that one recognizes on principle from the Nazi era, which in its horrifying dimensions should have been burned into German historical memory: the attempts to profit from corpses, the recycling of the dead and their body parts, and the medical exploits with racialized human material. According to Hagens, "the plastinated specimens . . . are no longer objects of mourning, but instructional objects—with the intended purpose to educate . . . 'and to serve a useful function after death' . . . to remain useful even beyond death" (Eberhardt 1997:18). Through medical intervention, he asserts, the dead body undergoes "a shift in value from a useless corpse to a useful, aesthetically instructive . . . specimen" (Hagens 1997:215). This rational economy, which simultaneously devalues and reclaims value by recycling, and which wants to harvest surplus value from the dead, is rarely acknowledged in German public discussions. And yet it is part of a cultural logic, of a capitalist mode of thinking, whereby historical consciousness is repressed in favor of an instrumental rationality: not only the living but also the dead must be usefully productive. According to Hagens emotions are an "intrusive" factor, a "digressive" obstacle in this enterprise: "mourning would interfere with learning" (Hagens 1997:203–207, 214).

In this world of purposive rationality, anatomy, and pedagogy, economy and medical science, pathology and human rights are closely intertwined. But in Germany these linkages have been ignored for a long time. It took nearly a decade from the exhibit's first showing to uncover the origin of the plastinated specimens: the corpses, contrary to the exhibitor's claims, were not bequeathed by German donors. According to investigative reports the bodies are procured from Russia, Kyrgyzstan, and China (Spiegel 2004a; Schmidt 2004). "The dead," as Michael Sappol (2005) points out, who are "conscripted to perform for the amusement of the living," are obtained "from places where human rights are precariously non-existent and bioethical standards are not enforced—such as China and the central Asian former republics of the Soviet Union—and who therefore cannot honestly meet any ethical standard of informed consent." An inspection of the exhibitor's body factory in Dalian, China, where corpses are skinned and prepared for later use, reveals the inhumanity of this enterprise: "A truck unloads 27 dead men and 4 women, still fully clothed"; there are "647 corpses," "blood-drenched . . . stacked in piles," "some with bullet holes in their heads," and, moreover, "3,909 body parts like legs, hands, or penises, and 182 fetuses, embryos, and newborns, all cataloged with serial numbers by size, age, and sex" (Spiegel 2004a, 2004b:8; Seniorentreff 2005). According to the inquiry's findings, some of the bodies derive from the purchase of executed Chinese prisoners (Spiegel 2004b, 2004c). This business with corpses, a multimillion-dollar enterprise, calls into question the exhibit's legitimacy: the purported "art of anatomy," with its sanitized installations, is in reality founded on a violent capitalism with human victims whose bodies are sold and bought for profit.[7] Not surprisingly, the exhibit stages a dehistoricized morphological landscape in which corpses are shown without historical memory and without compassion.

Such optical regimes that amputate emotions and remembrance in favor of recycling death are characteristic of attempts to purge a violent history from memory. Human anatomy is exhibited without shame. In Germany we find several analogous cases. Until the late 1990s the preserved body parts of murdered Jews, and of other victims of the Holocaust, were used as ordinary instructional material in German medical schools. Emptied of affect, such visual regimes seem to be selectively blind: for in each instance, the victim's remains had been cataloged with a notation of the place of death—a concentration camp (Komission zur Überprüfung der Präparatesammlung 1989). This regime of selective blindness might explain why present-day German medical practitioners continue to rely on a "standard anatomy textbook" authored by a Nazi physician who used concentration camp victims as models for his anatomical illustrations (Piotrowski 1997). This popular text circulates in ever new editions, even though the swastikas below the photographically reproduced illustrations are plainly evident.

Given this context, it is not surprising that the German exhibit of corpses has remained silent about the historical trajectories of Nazi anatomy lessons. The curator defines his work by detour to Renaissance art rather than via fascist aesthetics (see Linke 2006a). Yet his plastinated figures seem to capture the disposition of similar Nazi exhibits, among them the *Man of Glass*, an anatomical construct shown in the Museum of Hygiene in Leipzig in the early 1930s (Beier and Roth 1990). This transparent sculpture is part of the genealogy of plastinated human bodies. The man of glass was manufactured in an era in which the visible penetration into the corporal interior was congruent with Nazi racial ideologies: the desired transparency of bodies belonged to the optical regime of genocide. Of relevance to my analysis here, however, is the continuous return of this installation: the recycling of body objects by amputating the past. In post-Holocaust Germany, precisely at the moment of unification—in 1990 in Berlin—the glass body was retrieved from the Leipzig museum archives to become a centerpiece in an exhibit about Germany's problematic history (Beier and Roth 1990). A reunified nation required historical introspection. But twelve years later—in 2002 in Berlin—we encounter the *Man of Glass* once again: he is displayed in the foyer of an exhibit called "The (Im-)Perfect Human Being" (Raulff 2001). Hailed as an "icon of the twentieth century," the anatomical glass body has now been stripped of its Nazi origins. Described as a "functional, well-constructed, visually penetrable, and optimizable machine," the body is shown with the following caption: "The *Man of Glass*—who embodies modernity's image of humanity with its futuristic belief in the connection between science, transparency, and rationality" (Raulff 2001:7, 24). The German medical-pathological gaze, which also structures "Body Worlds," moves in a seemingly timeless realm: ultimately, it strives to negate both historicity and violence.

Unlike the mummy, the embalmed body, or the venerated relic, the exhibit's plastinated corpses are supposed to be self-referential or auto-iconic: emptied of meaning, emptied of symbolic content, and devoid of emotions. The German musealogical management of the corpse presents an antithesis to the performative efficacy of "the political life of dead bodies," as Katherine Verdery (1999) has phrased it: it is voided of representational, evocative power with regard to memory and history—it becomes a death without emotional significance or political cosmology.[8] Indeed, by annulling the humanity of the corpses, the German state distances itself from the exhibit and thereby denies moral accountability. In this human museum, contrary to Verdery's argument, dead bodies are *not* "a site of political profit" (1999:33). The corporeal displays have been invested with different meanings. Sanitized of death and violence, they conceal a history of victimization.

THE LIMITS OF EMPATHY

What do we make of these dead-body politics in unified Germany? The parade of corpses, exhibited in a museum that brings them "into the realm of the timeless or sacred, like an icon" (Verdery 1999:5), links a transformed nation to a seemingly frozen corporal landscape. As such, death may be a metaphor for the end of an era, but plastinated corpses—as symbolic vehicles overtly devoid of historical memory—also point to a renewed resistance to reevaluate the past. "What is it about a corpse," asks Verdery, "that seems to invite its use in politics, especially in moments of major transformation?" (1999:27). The body's materiality, confirmed by sight and touch, is critical to its symbolic efficacy. Localized in a strategic place such as a museum, a conventional memory site, the plastinated corpses speak to the cultural practices of unmaking remembrance. In this museum of immortality German visitors see death without mourning. It is a corporal landscape staged without historical reflexivity and thereby also without the engagement of feelings. The dead, robbed of their humanity, display their seemingly un-dead bodies with a scientific objectivity that undoes and negates the museum's task of memory production. In Germany the public intimacy with corpses is indicative of a psychic economy that, with the return of the repressed, simultaneously moves in an eroticized void of remembering and forgetting. The German contact with mutilated corpses, previously evocative of war and genocide, has been rendered safe in the cocooned space of the anatomical museum.

NOTES

Previous versions of this essay were presented at various conferences: the Annual Meetings of the American Anthropological Association in Atlanta (2004) and Washington (2005), the American Ethnological Society meeting in San Diego (2005), and the Sixth Biannual Conference of the International Association of Genocide Scholars in Boca Raton, Florida (2005). I am grateful to Kevin O'Neill and Alexander Laban Hinton for organizing various panel sessions and for their insightful commentary on earlier drafts of this essay. A first version of this project was crafted in German and appeared in 2006 under the title "*Theatrum anatomicum*." A much shorter English version of this essay was published in 2005 as "Touching the Corpse" in *Anthropology Today* 21(5): 15–19 (copyright: The Royal Anthropological Institute, London). I am indebted to the editor, Gustaaf Houtman, for his careful attention to my work. I also thank the anonymous reviewers for Duke University Press, whose critical reading greatly helped me rewrite this article. Unless otherwise noted, all translations are my own.

1. For further reference, see the accompanying exhibit catalog (*Landesmuseum* 1997). Curiously, there exist but a few scattered reports about the exhibit's reception in Japan. In these brief write-ups, which appeared in the context of the opening of the installation in Mannheim, emphasis was given to the public success of the exhibit in Japan, where close to three million people had seen the displays.

2. Such derivative exhibits include "Bodies," "Body Exploration," "Bodies Revealed," "Mysteries of the Human Body," and "The Universe Within."

3. See Hagens 2004b for a detailed description of the curator's invention and development of plastination as a method for preserving human bodies. Hagens invented this procedure while a resident at the medical school at the University of Heidelberg. After refining the technique for large-scale commercial production, he created the Institute for Plastination in Heidelberg, a privately funded anatomical body factory. At this location the bodies are treated and prepared for future use by medical schools and in Hagens's anatomical exhibits. After being implicated in the controversial enterprise with plastinated bodies in 2004, the University of Heidelberg has distanced itself from the anatomist and revoked his professorial title and faculty privileges. Hagens operates a second body factory in Dalian, China, where he now lives as a permanent resident. His recent plans for a third body factory in Poland await approval by local officials and state government.

4. A comparative analysis of the many German anthropological exhibits with living and embalmed bodies from the late 1800s through the early 1900s exceeds the scope of this essay. For exemplary references, see Thode-Arora 1989 and Matyssek 2002.

5. Interestingly, none of the male bodies has been equipped with plastinated nipples. Thus not just the female breast but the generic human nipple is here used as a strategic marker of sex.

6. For a further discussion of the German culture of shame and the struggle with memory as post-Holocaust embodiment, see Linke 2002, 2004.

7. For comparative studies on the global commodification of body parts and bioethics, see Scheper-Hughes and Wacquant 2002; Sappol 2002; and Scheper-Hughes 2005.

8. Here also consider the different symbolic investments in embalmed political bodies like that of Mao Tse-tung in China or that of Lenin in Russia.

REFERENCES

Andrews, Edmund L.
1998   Anatomy on Display. New York Times, January 7: 1, 4.

Arendt, Hannah
1963   Eichmann in Jerusalem: A Report on the Banality of Evil. New York:
            Viking.

Assheuer, Thomas
2003   Die Olympiade der Leichen. Die Zeit 35: Feuilleton, August 21. Electronic
            document, http://www.zeit.de/2003/35/K_9arperwelten, accessed
            February 9, 2007.

Baudrillard, Jean
1991   Die fatalen Strategien. Ulrike Boskopf and Ronald Vouillé, trans.
            Munich: Matthes und Seitz.

Bauer, Axel W.
1997   Anatomie und Öffentlichkeit—ein bioethischer Problemfall? In
            Körperwelten: Einblicke in den menschlichen Körper. Landesmuseum
            für Technik und Arbeit in Mannheim and Institut für Plastination,
            eds. Pp. 195–200. Mannheim: Landesmuseum für Technik und
            Arbeit.

Becker, Jürgen
1999   Zugriff auf die Biomasse. tageszeitung, October 11: 15.

Beier, Rosmarie, and Martin Roth, eds.
1990   Der gläserne Mensch—eine Sensation: Zur Kulturgeschichte eines
            Ausstellungsobjekts. Stuttgart: Hatje Cantz.

Budde, Kai
1997   Der sezierte Tote—ein schreckliches Bild? In Körperwelten: Einblicke
            in den menschlichen Körper. Landesmuseum für Technik und Arbeit
            in Mannheim and Institut für Plastination, eds. Pp. 11–28. Mannheim:
            Landesmuseum für Technik und Arbeit.

Certeau, Michel de
1988   The Writing of History. Tom Conley, trans. New York: Columbia
            University Press.

Clewing, Ulrich
1998a   Hohe Kunst oder "Ärgernis." tageszeitung, October 8: 3.
1998b   Schneller Altern im Ideenkorsett. tageszeitung, September 7: 16.
1998c   Vier gegen Keinen. tageszeitung, October 10: 30.

Csordas, Thomas J.
2000   Computerized Cadavers. In Biotechnology, Culture, and the Body. Paul
            Brodwin, ed. Pp. 173–192. Bloomington: Indiana University Press.

Dean, Carolyn J.
2005   The Fragility of Empathy after the Holocaust. Ithaca: Cornell University
            Press.

Dijck, José van

2005   The Transparent Body: A Cultural Analysis of Medical Imaging. Seattle: University of Washington Press.

Eberhardt, Johanna

1997   Leichen im Sinne des Gesetzes? Frankfurter Rundschau, December 17: 18.

1998a   "Körperwelten" sind Magnet. Frankfurter Rundschau, July 21: 32.

1998b   Sie wollen nicht unsterblich, sondern nur nützlich sein. Frankfurter Rundschau, February 18: 40.

Eggebrecht, Harald

1998   Mehr als nur Haut und Knochen. Süddeutsche Zeitung, January 17: 1.

Emmrich, Michael

1998   Sich selbst begreifen. Frankfurter Rundschau, February 28: 6.

Feldman, Allen

1997   Violence and Vision: The Prosthetics and Aesthetics of Violence. Public Culture 10(1): 24–60.

Fonseca, Liselotte Hermes da

1999   Wachsfigur—Mensch—Plastinat. Deutsche Vierteljahresschrift für Literaturwissenschaft und Geistesgeschichte 73(1): 43–68.

Frankfurter Rundschau

1997   Über das Sterben. Frankfurter Rundschau, November 22: 22.

1998a   Ausstellung. Frankfurter Rundschau, November 3: 25.

1998b   "Körperwelten" waren Magnet fürs Publikum. Frankfurter Rundschau, March 3: 33.

1998c   Die Leichenshow: Bericht über eine umstrittene Ausstellung in Mannheim. Frankfurter Rundschau, April 16: 8.

Geyer, Michael

2002   "There Is a Land Where Everything Is Pure: Its Name Is Land of Death": Some Observations on Catastrophic Nationalism. In Sacrifice and National Belonging. Greg Eghigian and Matthew P. Berg, eds. Pp. 118–147. Arlington: Texas A&M University Press.

Hagens, Gunther von

1997   Der plastinierte Mensch. In Körperwelten: Einblicke in den menschlichen Körper. Landesmuseum für Technik und Arbeit in Mannheim and Institut für Plastination Heidelberg, eds. Pp. 201–216. Mannheim: Landesmuseum für Technik und Arbeit.

2004a   Anatomy and Plastination. In Body Worlds: The Anatomical Exhibition of Real Human Bodies. Gunther von Hagens and Angelina Whalley, eds. Pp. 9–36. Heidelberg: Institut für Plastination.

2004b   On Gruesome Corpses, Gestalt Plastinates, and Mandatory Interment. In Body Worlds: The Anatomical Exhibition of Real Human Bodies.

Gunther von Hagens and Angelina Whalley, eds. Pp. 260–282.
Heidelberg: Institut für Plastination.

Hagens, Gunther von, and Angelina Whalley, eds.
2004a   Body Worlds: The Anatomical Exhibition of Real Human Bodies.
Heidelberg: Institut für Plastination.
2004b   Körperwelten—Die Faszination des Echten. Heidelberg: Institut für
Plastination.

Halbwachs, Maurice
1980   The Collective Memory. Francis J. Ditter Jr. and Viola Yazdi Ditter, trans.
New York: Harper and Row.

Herscovitch, Penny
2003   Rest in Plastic. Science, February 7: 828.

Herzog, Markwart, ed.
2001   Totengedenken und Trauerkultur. Berlin: Kohlhammer.

Hinton, Alexander Laban
2005   Why Did They Kill? Cambodia in the Shadow of Genocide. Berkeley:
University of California Press.

Hinton, Alexander Laban, ed.
2002a   Annihilating Difference: The Anthropology of Genocide. Berkeley:
University of California Press.
2002b   Genocide: An Anthropological Reader. Malden, MA: Blackwell.

Horkheimer, Max, and Theodor W. Adorno
1981   Interesse am Körper. In Dialektik der Aufklärung. Pp. 276–281.
Frankfurt/Main: Suhrkamp.

Huyssen, Andreas
2003   Present Pasts: Urban Palimpsests and the Politics of Memory. Stanford,
CA: Stanford University Press.

Jacobeit, Sigrid
2002   kz-Gedenkstätten als nationale Erinnerungsorte: Zwischen
Ritualisierung und Musealisierung. Berlin: Humboldt University.

Kaiser, Alexandra
2004   Der Volkstrauertag als rituell-performatives Medium der Bewältigung
von Kriegserfahrung und des Gedenkens an die Gefallenen und Krieg-
stoten. Paper presented at the Doctoral Colloquium of the Ludwig-
Uhland-Institut, Inzigkofen, February 6.

Kirshenblatt-Gimblett, Barbara
1998   Destination Culture: Tourism, Museums, and Heritage. Berkeley:
University of California Press.

Kleinman, Arthur, and Joan Kleinman
1997   The Appeal of Experience, the Dismay of Images. *In* Social Suffering.
        Arthur Kleinman, Veena Das, and Margaret Lock, eds. Pp. 1–24.
        Berkeley: University of California Press.

Kommission der Überprüfung der Präparatesammlungen
1989   Abschlussbericht der Kommission zur Überprüfung der Präparatesam-
        mlungen in den medizinischen Einrichtungen der Universität Tübingen
        im Hinblick auf die Opfer des Nationalsozialismus. Archived material,
        Academic Senate, Senatsakte, Drucksache Nr. 87 ss 1989, July 13, 1989,
        University of Tübingen, Germany.

Korff, Gottfried
1999   Reflections on the Museum. Journal of Folklore Research
        36(2–3):267–270.
2002   Museums-Dinge. Cologne: Böhlau.

Kriz, Wilhelm
1997   Einführung. *In* Körperwelten: Einblicke in den menschlichen Körper.
        Landesmuseum für Technik und Arbeit in Mannheim and Institut für
        Plastination, eds. Pp. 9–10. Mannheim: Landesmuseum für Technik und
        Arbeit.

Landesmuseum für Technik und Arbeit in Mannheim and Institut für Plastination,
eds.
1997   Körperwelten: Einblicke in den menschlichen Körper. Mannheim: Lan-
        desmuseum für Technik und Arbeit.

Le Goff, Jacques
1992   History and Memory. Steven Rendall and Elizabeth Claman, trans. New
        York: Columbia University Press.

Lethen, Helmut
1994   Verhaltenslehren der Kälte: Lebensversuche zwischen den Kriegen.
        Frankfurt/Main: Suhrkamp.

Liebsch, Burkhard, and Jörn Rüsen, eds.
2001   Trauer und Geschichte. Cologne: Böhlau.

Linke, Uli
1999   German Bodies: Race and Representation after Hitler. New York:
        Routledge.
2001   The Anthropology of Collective Memory. International Encyclopedia of
        the Behavioral and Social Sciences 3(1): 2219–2223.
2002   Archives of Violence: The Holocaust and the Politics of German Memory.
        In Annihilating Difference: The Anthropology of Genocide. Alexander
        Laban Hinton, ed. Pp. 229–271. Berkeley: University of California Press.

2003   Volks-Körper-Kunde: Überlegungen zu einer wissenschaftlichen Amnese. *In* Unterwelten der Kultur. Kaspar Maase and Bernd Jürgen Warneken, eds. Pp. 65–94. Cologne: Böhlau.

2004   Shame on the Skin: Post-Holocaust Memory and the German Aesthetics of Whiteness. *In* Colors 1800/1900/2000: Signs of Ethnic Difference. Birgit Tautz, ed. Pp. 183–211. Amsterdam: Rodopi.

2006a   Art for Art's Sake? Anthropology Today 22(6):23.

2006b   *Theatrum anatomicum. In* Verführerische Leichen—Verbotener Verfall: "Körperwelten" als gesellschaftliches Schlüsselereignis. Liselotte Hermes da Fonseca and Thomas Kliche, eds. Pp. 140–182. Berlin: Pabst Science.

Luhmann, Niklas
2000   Borniert und Einfühlsam zugleich. *In* Short Cuts. Pp. 113–119. Frankfurt/Main: Zweitausendeins.

Matyssek Angela
2002   Rudolf Virchow: Das Pathologische Museum. Darmstadt: Steinkopff.

Meng, Michael L.
2005   Empathy after the Holocaust. *Review of* The Fragility of Empathy after the Holocaust. *In* H-German, H-Net Reviews, August 2005. Electronic document, http://www.h-net.org/reviews/showrev.cgi?path=59351154543528, accessed February 9, 2006.

Mitscherlich, Alexander, und Margarete Mitscherlich
1967   Die Unfähigkeit zu Trauern. Munich: C. H. Beck.

Nissen, Klaus
1998   Anatomie nach Mitternacht. Frankfurter Rundschau, February 27: 36.

Nora, Pierre
1976   Les lieux de mémoire. 3 vols. Paris: Gallimard.

Piotrwoski, Christa
1997   Ein Anatomie-Klassiker mit Hakenkreuzen: NS-Opfer als Modelle für Zeichnungen? Frankfurter Rundschau, May 17: 8.

Raulff, Helga, ed.
2001   Der (im-)perfekte Mensch: Vom Recht auf Unvollkommenheit. Ostfildern-Ruit: Hatje Cantz.

Reimer, Ulf
1998   Nächtliche Wallfahrt zu den Toten. Süddeutsche Zeitung, March 2: 1, 2.

Roth, Jürgen
1998   Body Counts. Konkret 4:50–52.

Rothschild, Markus
1998   Das nennt man "postmortalen Exhibitionismus." tageszeitung, October 8: 3.

Sappol, Michael

2002   A Traffic of Dead Bodies: Anatomy and Embodied Social Identity in Nineteenth-Century America. Princeton: Princeton University Press.

2005   Why the Dead Are a Killer Act. Los Angeles Times, June 12. Electronic document, http://www.latimes.com, accessed June 20, 2005.

Schenda, Rudolf

1998   Gut bei Leibe: Hundert wahre Geschichten vom menschlichen Körper. Munich: C. H. Beck.

Scheper-Hughes, Nancy

2005   The Global Traffic in Human Organs. In The Body: A Reader. Miriam Fraser and Monica Greco, eds. Pp. 208–215. New York: Routledge.

Scheper-Hughes, Nancy, and Loïc J. D. Wacquant, eds.

2002   Commodifying Bodies. London: Sage.

Scheytt, Stefan

1997   In Silikon und Ewigkeit. Die Zeit, August 14: 1–3.

Schmidt, Thomas E.

2004   Party der Plastinate. Die Zeit, January 22. Electronic document, http://zeus.zeit.de/text/2004/05/Spitze_5, accessed February 9, 2006.

Schmitz, Helmut

1997   . . . was die Welt im Innersten zusammenhält. Frankfurter Rundschau, November 12: 8.

Schmoll, Friedemann

2002   Erinnerungskulturen: Zukunft der Erinnerung. Constance: Volksbund Deutscher Kriegsgräberfürsorge.

Seniorentreff

2005   Woher bekommt er die Leichen? In Seniorentreff.de, January 19. Electronic document, http://www.seniorentreff.de/koeln/Koerperwelten/hago2.htm, accessed February 9, 2007.

Seremetakis, C. Nadia

2001   Toxic Beauties: Medicine, Information, and Body Consumption in Transnational Europe. Social Text 68:115–129.

Smith, Orla

2003   Nota Bene: Anatomy. Science, February 7: 829.

Der Spiegel

1997   Ausstellungen: Stachel im Fleisch. Der Spiegel, October 6: 212–214.

1998   Mut zur Todesnähe. Der Spiegel, August 31: 182–85.

2004a   Dr. Tod: Die horrenden Geschäfte des Leichen-Schaustellers Gunther von Hagens. Stefan Aust, ed. Theme issue, Der Spiegel, January 19.

2004b   Leichenhandel: Neue Vorwürfe gegen Leichen-Plastinator. Der Spiegel, January 24: 8.

2004c   Leichen ohne Totenschein. Der Spiegel, March 1: 56.

Stephan, Cora

1993   Der Betroffenheitskult: Eine politische Sittengeschichte. Berlin: Rowohlt.

Strobl, Ingrid

1993   Das Feld des Vergessens. Berlin: Edition ID Archiv.

Thode-Arora, Hilke

1989   Für fünfzig Pfennig um die Welt. Die Hagenbeckschen Völkerschauen. Frankfurt/Main: Campus.

van Dijck, Jahn

2001   Bodyworlds. Configurations 91:189–216.

Verdery, Katherine

1999   The Political Lives of Dead Bodies. New York: Columbia University Press.

Vorpahl, Annette

1997   Der Tank für den Elefanten steht bereit. Frankfurter Rundschau, October 25: 8.

Walter, Tony

2004a   Body Worlds. Sociology of Health and Illness 26:464–488.

2004b   Plastination for Display. Journal of the Royal Anthropological Institute 10:603–27.

Whalley, Angelina

1997   Der menschliche Körper—Anatomie und Funktion. In Körperwelten: Einblicke in den menschlichen Körper. Landesmuseum für Technik und Arbeit in Mannheim and Institut für Plastination, eds. Pp. 49–194. Mannheim: Landesmuseum für Technik und Arbeit.

Wieseltier, Leon

1994   After Memory. In The New Republic. D. Wickenden, ed. Pp. 169–183. New York: Basic Books.

Wolbert, Klaus

1982   Die Nackten und die Toten des "Dritten Reiches": Folgen einer politischen Geschichte des Körpers in der Plastik des deutschen Faschismus. Giessen: Anabas.

Young, James E.

2000   At Memory's Edge: After-Images of the Holocaust in Contemporary Art and Architecture. New Haven: Yale University Press.

2005   The Memorial's Return to History. In H-German Discussion Logs: Messages from Germany (MFG 7), June 1, 2005. Electronic document, http://h-net.msu.edu/cgi-bin/logbrowse.pl, accessed February 9, 2007.

Ziegler, Erdmann
1998   Kommentar: Gruselpräparate. tageszeitung, October 8: 1.

Zoschke, Barbara
1994   Qual des letzten Willens. tageszeitung, April 13: 12.

6   FORGOTTEN GUATEMALA

Genocide, Truth, and Denial in Guatemala's Oriente

GRINGO TOURIST: Have you heard about the atrocities, political problems in this area?
DOCTOR FUENTES: No. Those things only happen in other countries, not here.
—*Men with Guns*

In the celebrated John Sayles film, *Men with Guns*, the protagonist, Dr. Humberto Fuentes, a premier surgeon in an unnamed Latin American city, tries to locate his former students who were sent out years earlier to serve the underprivileged in the country's mountain villages. As a man of medicine on the eve of his retirement, Fuentes yearns to validate his own legacy through his students' charitable work for the poor. As he searches for his students, he finds that each one has been killed or has disappeared. Sheltered in the capital city, and thus protected from the ongoing military conflict in the rural areas, Fuentes is largely unaware of the atrocities that have become a fact of life for those who live outside the city. His dawning awareness of this cycle of violence—and his accompanying incredulousness—is the prominent theme of the film.

As he continues on his journey, he encounters Indian peasants, a repentant priest, gringo tourists, and an AWOL soldier, all of whom remind him that violence and atrocities simply form a part of life. These characters' aloofness illustrates violence and "fear as a way of life" (Green 1994):[1] a shrug of the shoulder over the murder of a student, the matter-of-fact retelling of village massacres, the commonplace rapes of young women by soldiers. Sayles uses Fuentes's ignorance of the violence—and of the indigenous peoples' attitudes toward it—to represent the ignorance of the audience, and as the doctor gradually accepts the mounting evidence of genocide, viewers of the film are forced to recognize the desperate resignation of the indigenous peasants. In Guatemala, the unnamed Central American country the film is based on, Fuentes's character is not an anomaly.

For researchers in Guatemala, the resigned acceptance of violence as a way of life constitutes a manifest reality. I entered the field with my accrued knowledge—from books, newspapers, and articles; from Amnesty International and human rights reports—but I was unaware of the political realities. In the early 1990s, when the peace accords were still years away, I visited Guatemala as a young student. I stayed in the tourist town of Antigua, taking Spanish classes among the young German and Australian travelers and visiting the "quaint" Maya villages to buy silver half-moon earrings and vibrant cloth. I also met young American activists who whispered to me about the ongoing civil war, the frequent massacres and disappearances, the armed teenaged soldiers who lined the streets around the central plaza. Later, as a young Ph.D. student arriving in the field after the accords, I looked up to the anthropologists and activists who were there working amid the tragedy, collecting the testimonies of survival and resilience among the Highland Maya.

Though I work with a Highland Maya group, my experience in Guatemala differed from that of many activists and academics because the atrocities did not occur in or even near my field site. This situation of relative peace lent a distinct slant to my research because I dealt primarily with a population that was not directly affected by the genocide and which thus perceives the civil war differently than many academics and Westerners.

Although Guatemalans who have lived outside the centers of genocide—from the onset of the civil war in 1960 to the present—consider violence a commonplace occurrence, some frequently deny the concept of a civil war. Likewise, they either profess ignorance of the massacres associated with the war or claim that stories recounting these massacres are exaggerated, even though the findings of Guatemala's truth commission

(Comisión de Esclarecimiento Histórico, CEH) have been published and are broadly known. Despite evidence that implicates them in criminal acts, those involved in the counterinsurgency during the conflict maintain impunity. Likewise, successful implementation of the peace accords remains distant.

While the war may be over, a network of elected and nonelected individuals (many former military) continues to control the state, exerting much of its influence via connections to drug trafficking and organized crime, and some researchers link this cartel to the attacks on defenders of human rights (Peacock and Beltran 2003). Similarly, since the end of the internal conflict, gang activity has risen sharply, and incidents of random violence and violent death have increased (Moser and McIlwaine 2001). The rise in these types of crimes may be related to Guatemala's "culture of silence,"[2] since the underreporting of politically motivated murders is symptomatic of the type of fear of persecution that promotes genocide denial.

This essay addresses how Ladino and Maya peoples in the eastern portion of Guatemala, an area considered outside the war zone, continue to deny genocide. Even though eastern Guatemala (also known as El Oriente) was supposedly unaffected by *La Violencia* (the period of heightened violence of the 1980s), this region was directly involved in the early years of the conflict and later through the military's recruitment policies, which included the recruitment of elite Ladinos as military officers and the coerced conscription of indigenous and poor Ladinos as foot soldiers. While genocide denial in this region is related to the role played by the Oriente in the development and propagation of the conflict, it is perpetuated both by a continuous military presence that enforces a culture of silence and by a state-sponsored discourse that refutes the notion of a political motivation for supposedly commonplace acts of violence. Witnesses of crimes may perceive the justifiability of a crime differently depending on their relationship to the perpetrators and victims, and their stake in the outcome (Stewart and Strathern 2002). The Oriente as a witness to genocide has varied actors, many directly or indirectly involved in the conflict, as Ladinos and Maya from the region served in the military and all others grew up in a bastion of Ladino identity and power. As a collective witness to genocide, eastern Guatemala legitimizes state action and supports Ladino hegemonic rule through persistent denial.

Guatemala is figuratively, geographically, and ethnically constructed as an Indian West and a Ladino East (MacLeod 1973). Ladinos are the peoples of European and Maya descent who tend to emphasize their Hispanic heritage to separate themselves from Guatemala's large Maya population. This geographical distinction has remained a valid construct as it continues to predict cultural, political, and economic processes in Guatemala. The locations of violence during the civil war also followed from East to West, or from the Ladino regions to the Maya regions, as the early period of the civil war was concentrated in the East—led and supported by a mostly Ladino following—and later spread to the West to ferret out a suspected Maya-supported insurgency.

The period of genocide during Guatemala's 36-year civil war was aimed at the Maya population in the West, even though many Ladinos were also killed during the violence.[3] Regardless, many believe the conflict was an expression of hundreds of years of suppression of the Maya people.[4] The height of the genocidal activity occurred from 1977 to 1986 and was concentrated in the departments of Huehuetenango, El Quiche, Baja Verapaz, and Chimaltenango, regions that have large concentrations of Maya (Gulden 2001). Racism and the struggle to maintain power over Guatemala's indigenous population culminated at the height of the civil war in the 1980s in a scorched-earth campaign and the consequential population resettlements aimed at Maya communities (Valentino 2004).

The Oriente is considered the epicenter of Ladino power. The colonial Spanish preferred the Oriente to the Western Highlands for its superior land and thus occupied the region in higher numbers than the West (Macleod 1973). Some claim that the Eastern Maya may have been subject to greater suppression than the western Maya because they were forced into labor as the Spanish expanded into the East and thus subjected to a higher degree of incorporation into Ladino society (Metz 1998). These assertions are supported by higher rates of bilingualism and low rates of monolingualism among the eastern Maya. Nonetheless, the eastern Maya have survived even though they are surrounded by large Ladino populations and are isolated from other Maya groups (Adams and Bastos 2003).

From early on, the Oriente was dominated by the Spanish, which resulted in a population of peoples of mixed ancestry. The prominence of the term *Ladino*—and the group's accompanying cultural and political dominance—did not occur until after the regime of Raphael Carrera in the mid-1800s. A Ladino from the Eastern Highlands, Carrera led a conservative counterrevolution that was crucial to Guatemala's nation-building and that secured Ladino power from the white elites of Guatemala City (Carlsen 1997; Sullivan-Gonzalez 1998). *Mulatto, mestizo,* and *criollo* were some of the terms that described the great and diverse populations of the Central American republic that descended from the colonial power structures that brought indigenous, black, and European blood together. Before this time ethnic categories were much more diverse than the Ladino-Maya duality that informs ethnic identity in Guatemala today.[5]

The East-West divide in Guatemala illustrates the rift between the mostly Maya population in the West and the Ladino population of the East. Guatemala is split into several regions, the Western Highlands (El Occidente), the East (El Oriente), the lowland Pacific Plain (La Costa), and the jungles of Peten and the Caribbean coast. Despite a geographical diversity that transcends West versus East, this construct dominates the popular conception of the country. In the imagined Guatemala, the East is considered the Ladino domain, a dry desert region and a "Wild West" of sorts, where tall Ladino men informed by a machismo culture carry guns in their holsters and fight drunken battles. In contrast, the West is considered the Indian domain, a land of impenetrable chains of volcanoes and hidden, fog-enveloped villages where the mysterious Maya still practice their ancient ways and speak unintelligible indigenous languages. In truth, these regions are much more diverse, with small populations of Ladinos living side by side with Maya in the West and also very large yet isolated Maya populations in the East.

These regional and ethnic constructions added to the reaffirmation of racism during and after the civil war, as the Maya West was targeted for genocide and the supposed superiority of the Ladino East was used to support that genocide. While racism may not have been the main reason behind the bloodshed, as thousands of Ladinos were also killed during the insurgency of the 1960s and throughout the conflict (Valentino 2004), the genocide of the Maya was no mere coincidence; state-sponsored terror was hardly indiscriminate. The construction of East versus West in Guatemala is essential to understanding how local Guatemalans and the military perceive how the war played out in each region.

My research is based on fieldwork in the municipality of San Pedro Pinula, in the department of Jalapa in eastern Guatemala, as well as on several months of fieldwork in Boston and Atlanta among various communities of migrants from San Pedro Pinula. Located in the Eastern Highlands, San Pedro Pinula is a municipality of over 55,000 and contains one of the Oriente's most populous Maya groups, with over 98 percent considered to be Eastern Pokomam Maya. As mentioned before, even though the Oriente is considered Ladino, it does contain various large populations of indigenous peoples, the two largest being the Chorti and the Eastern Pokomam. In spite of several ethnographies on the Chorti (Wisdom 1940; Metz 1995) and the Eastern Pokomam (Tumin 1952; Gillen 1951), the Maya of the Oriente remain outside the usual focus of Maya studies.[6]

Ladinos make up the remaining 2 percent of the population in San Pedro Pinula, and they wield political as well as economic power (Dary 2003; Rodman 2006). The town center serves as a general gathering point, supply depot, and bureaucratic center for the predominantly rural population of the municipality. The Eastern Pokomam Maya live in 46 villages and hamlets nestled in the mountains surrounding the town. Ladinos raise cattle, make cheese, run the formal businesses, own most of the land in and around Pinula, and traditionally depend on Maya labor to maintain their lifestyle. Ladinos rent land to the Pokomam Maya in exchange for labor and a share of the maize and bean harvest. Most Ladinos reside in the pueblo, yet they make up only about 10 percent of the town's population.

My research in San Pedro Pinula and in the United States concentrates on how transnational migration is changing the historical, economic, and social relationships between the Maya and the Ladinos and has created opportunities for migrants to gain economic and social capital confronting race, class, and gender divides. I document how ethnic relations between the dominant landholding Ladinos and the Eastern Pokomam Maya are transformed as Maya migration to the United States upsets the social structure and as the Maya break from their historical dependency. How migration impacts ethnic relations reveals the discourse on the construction of race, as well as the history of ethnic tension and conflict in the region, betraying how violence and fear often pervade people's lives.

The 1950s and 1960s were important periods in the development of state-sponsored oversight of guerrilla activity in the East. This control led to an eastern involvement in genocidal activity in the West and consequently contributed to the development of military tactics used in the genocide of the 1980s. The roots of Guatemala's civil war actually lie the period following the overthrow of Jacobo Arbenz Guzmán in 1954, when the Castillo Armas regime cracked down on labor organizations to weed out "communists" and rural organizers who supported Arbenz's political and agrarian reforms (May 2001). During the days of the liberation (from Arbenz's rule) and for weeks afterward, local vigilante groups rounded up labor organizers and their followers, sending many to local jails and, in some cases, assassinating them on the spot (Grandin 1997). In the eastern city of Chiquimula, rural labor organizers were killed by firing squad and many others held in jail without charge (May 2001). In Jalapa vigilante groups were headed by Ladino landowners who felt threatened by lower-class Ladinos and local Maya who had supposedly supported agrarian reform. As the word of the liberation movement's success spread, men swept through the town of San Pedro Pinula, burning down houses, arresting local Maya, and shooting and killing men in the local cemetery after they were told to dig their own mass grave (personal communication 2001). The *hoyo* (hole) in the cemetery has remained the town's shameful secret. Spoken of only in whispers, it has come to symbolize to the local Maya the possible repercussions of organizing against the Ladinos. As one Ladino, 51, put it, "ever since the liberation, the Indians have remained ever more cautious of the Ladinos. They remember the bloodbath that took place after the liberation" (personal communication 2001). A local Maya in his late 80s, who remembers being sent to jail in Jalapa after the liberation, explained the bloodshed as follows:

> Quietly the Ladinos knew that there was a movement coming in from Honduras through Esquipulas. After the movement came through Esquipulas the Ladinos formed cleaning groups and went and found all

the Indians who had been measuring land (during the agrarian reform) and started killing them. They went to the *campo santo* [cemetery], and there is a big hole where they shot everyone. Some Indians survived the massacre because they begged their patrons to save them. Let's say you are my *mozo*,[7] and I was in the cleaning group—I could vouch for him and say, he's a good guy, don't kill him. En ese tiempo los mozos estaban llorando debajo de la cama de sus patrones [At this time, the workers were crying underneath the beds of their patrons]. (personal communication 2001)

The violence that characterized this period is attributed to the forced submission by the Ladinos of "a vibrant organized rural labor force" (May 2001:7) throughout Guatemala, which in the Oriente was an important marker in a long line of violent events in the indigenous communities' collective memory of a history of repression.

The rate of state-sponsored killing is measured by "corpses found," a phrase that affirms that a corpse has been found in a public place, a customary way to warn and terrorize the communities during the early years of the conflict, from the 1960s to the 1970s (Morrison and May 1994:123). Though the number of documented executions during this period does not compare to the mass killings of the war's later stages, the period set the tenor of the conflict, as the state set up over nine thousand rural military commissioners and began to receive massive military assistance from the U.S. government. Using the justification of "sporadic" guerrilla activity in the East to militarize the region and to test its scorched-earth campaigns (the forced expulsion of indigenous peoples and the destruction of villages suspected of providing guerrilla support), the state effectively sponsored the development of death squads. Commissioners worked with local landowners to form armed vigilante groups in the East, suppressing both Ladino and Maya peasants (Handy 1984). In the Maya Oriente this meant that Ladino landowners reasserted their power over the mostly landless Maya in an attempt to secure control over lands they almost lost during the agrarian reform of the Juan José Arévelo / Jacobo Arbenz Guzmán period. Accordingly, the conflict was not neatly split along ethnic lines, which contributed to widespread fear and repression, not only among those oppressed but also among the oppressors themselves (Green 1994). Such pervasive mistrust perpetuated existing tensions throughout the communities.

In San Pedro Pinula some recount this era as a time of militarization, with commonplace fear of oppression from soldiers and local *orejas* (spies). Many Pinultecos recount that the military set up a post in the center of town, and the presence of soldiers became a normal part of town life. The government claimed that the soldiers were needed to protect the population from an increasing number of thieves and other delinquents in the countryside, but before this era, many Ladino families spent the rainy winter season living out in their *majadas*, rural farmsteads just outside of town, without fear of becoming victims of such malfeasance. Living on the farm during the rainy season was an economical decision since it allowed the landowner to be close to the cattle when their production of milk and cheese was at its highest. Today locals generally report that, since the 1960s, it has become too dangerous to take the family out to the *majada*, although they cannot quite seem to agree on the explanations for the end of this practice, as some confirm the government contention of a rise in delinquency or thievery, while others attribute it to fear of guerrillas or the military.

DENIAL OR FEAR AS A WAY OF LIFE

This section reviews Ladino and Maya conceptualizations and constructions of the civil war, the denial of mass killings, as well as that of a guerrilla movement and of the notion of genocide in general. In her article, "Fear as a Way of Life," Linda Green says that "routinization allows people to live in a chronic state of fear with a facade of normalcy" (1994:231). Her work explains how people become accustomed to violence as they adapt it to the routines of their everyday lives. In time, claims Green, they become almost immune to violence as they integrate into their lives a continual mistrust of neighbors and family.

My experience in the field was similar to Green's, as I found it difficult to separate my everyday life from the lived experience of fear. Although it may seem paradoxical, living in an environment in which violence is acceptable actually supports the notion that the stories of civil war and mass killings are simply fiction, an invention of the army used to intimidate the rural population. Many Pinultecos were simply unable to acknowledge the reality of the violence occurring around them. In large measure this avoidance-denial mechanism is attributable to living in a constant state of fear, because such a state of events allows one to rationalize the extraordinary as ordinary: common occurrences—regardless of their nature—cannot be directly attributed to a phenomenon as extraordinary as war; they are, rather, as Green ascertains, simply a way of life. The notion that violence is connected to a larger and discrete event (such as a 36-year civil war) that began at a certain time (1960) and ended at another (1996) is not commonly accepted by locals. Violence is something that happens and has happened since anyone can remember: memories of horrific events are not informed by events specific to a war, but are instead part of a larger continuum of ethnic tensions and inevitable historical conflicts.

Though Green claims that only upper-class Ladinos deny the massacres in the rural areas, I found that this denial permeated the Oriente, and my experiences with Ladinos and Maya in the East were similar to my experiences with middle- and upper-class Ladinos in the capital. When people learned I was an anthropologist, for example, they were fearful (for me), as they connected anthropology to Myrna Mack, the Guatemalan anthropologist assassinated by the Guatemalan government in 1990 due to her investigations into the mass killings. Breaching the subject of Mack did not validate the truth of the actual occurrence of massacres as one would expect, but reconfirmed the notion that Mack was generally too nosy for her own good. While logic would explain that Mack was following through on some valid leads (and thus confirming the truth about the massacres), most eastern Maya and Ladinos instead emphasize Mack's culpability in her own death. This position substantiates the idea of violence as an individual matter; violence occurs when one gets involved in issues that are not one's business. Even the murder of Bishop Juan José Geradi Conedera and the subsequent highly publicized trial did nothing to improve the validity of the truth commission to locals, as they still question whether the massacres in the West really occurred. Although the stories all made the national news, many Pinultecos refuse to believe them to this day, claiming that they were attributable to delinquency, invented by the military, or concocted by the newspapers.[8]

Among both Ladinos and Maya, many continue to deny the war as well as the massacres, albeit for different reasons. Local Ladinos do not accept the concept of a civil war, choosing to believe instead that the army invented the guerrillas to maintain control of the Maya and eliminate the Maya population, a policy that some Ladinos see as legitimate. The idea of fictive guerrillas fits with the logic that no one in their right mind would attempt such an insurrection. One male Ladino in his early 30s expressed this belief: "The army made up that there were ever any guerrillas. I often traveled and got stopped at military checkpoints. The soldiers were always saying they were looking for guerrillas and they were somewhere out there, but I never saw any. They just made it up. No one would fight against an army when you know you are going to lose" (personal communication 2001).

Another male Ladino, 37, spoke of the military and the misuse of the term *civil war*: "How can you call it a civil war when no one was fighting anyone? A civil war is when you have two groups, two enemies fighting one another—there was no enemy. The army just does it to make money. Guatemala doesn't need a big army. The military has all tanks and helicopters, and it's just so they can make more money—like a big cycle—they pretend there are guerrillas and they fight and the officers get to wear their fancy medals and for what? Medals for nothing. There is no war, no guerrillas" (personal communication 1999).

Ladinos in the region also tend to accept the state-sponsored belief that that the violence was not political but a result of "delinquency," a term used to describe crime and to characterize people reportedly involved in any type of criminal activity.[9] When interviewed, a retired Ladino military officer, 84, who worked in the secret police from the 1950s to the 1980s, consistently referred to his "assignments" (during which he was given the names of people to track down and arrest) as "delinquents" who were involved in "delinquent" behavior (personal communication 2002). This individual completely denied that his targets were involved in political subversion or were wanted by the state for their political involvement or beliefs. Delinquents were simply people engaging in violent acts and crimes, something that required punishment by the state. As an officer who took orders from above, he made no connection between political subversion and his assignments to apprehend the supposed delinquents. This attitude that violence is a separate, individual act not connected to the state continues to persist among Ladinos in the region.

Further, violence and murders in the region are often attributed to feuds between Ladino families. While this idea is consistent with research showing that some families have used the military presence and their own participation in Civil Defense Patrols (paramilitary civilian militias) to settle long-standing land and debt disputes (Green 1984; Paul and Demarest

1988; Stoll 1999), it does not touch on the role the military presence played in exacerbating these disputes. Moreover, the idea of these feuds contributes to the denial of the military's role in unexplained disappearances and murders. It is accordingly quite difficult to distinguish between political violence and this kind of intercommunity violence (Stoll 1999).

Family feuds have also been used to aggravate ethnic tensions in the community. Recently a prominent Ladino landowner was gunned down on his land, and the town's rumor mill characterized it as a revenge killing performed by the relative of an Indian man murdered by the Ladino for cattle theft, as many Ladinos still believe they have the right to kill an Indian for any infraction. One male Ladino landowner, 44, explained: "Before, when Indians stole firewood from your land, you could go kill them, and the cops would ask why you killed this person, and you could have said 'he was stealing this from me,' and they would just take him to the morgue and not say anything, but now with the human rights everything is *jodido* [screwed up]" (personal communication 2004).

While it is possible that the Ladino landowner had indeed committed murder, the nature of the event was distorted in a way that emphasized ethnic conflict rather than call attention to a feud that began years ago and involved two prominent Ladino families. Regardless of the truth of the event, acts of violence occur consistently throughout the community, and the majority of inhabitants make no distinction between violence from years past and violence occurring after the military occupation. Conversely, it is important to emphasize how ethnicity is used to manipulate and reconfirm the power structure between Ladinos and Indians, and how it validates Ladino impunity.

The Maya, on the other hand, blame the violence on consistent Ladino and foreign oppression. Maya in the region pass along accounts of this oppression, and though many of the Maya I interviewed cited specific incidents of violence perpetrated by the army, they invariably connected these to a larger history of oppression involving the Spanish, the army, local Ladinos, and gringos.[10] Elder Maya recount stories of planes dropping bombs on villages and the gringos passing through the East on their way to the capital during the time of liberation. Some elder women recount seeing demonstrations on their way to Esquipulas, a holy site that was formerly the destination of a yearly pilgrimage for both local Maya and Ladinos. One Ladina woman and one of the few standing female *patronas* (landowners), in her early 60s, recounted how local Maya remained silent due to fear of Ladino repression: "The *naturales* [Maya] here used to own the land; there were very few Ladinos, maybe ten families, and they bought the best land for themselves, but then the *naturales* got it back, and within three months the government came and took the land for the Ladinos, and this is what has made people so afraid. People heard from their grandparents what happened and even the *naturales* who worked for us never spoke because their parents told them not to talk about anything, to stay silent" (personal communication 2001).

Maya elders warn their grandchildren not to trust Ladinos, attributing past oppression not only to local Ladinos who stole Maya lands but also to the gringo compatriots who helped them in their endeavors. While the high number of Maya in the military would seem to increase Maya awareness of civil conflict and genocides that have occurred outside their communities, their participation in the military has not affected the general conceptualization that violence forms a part of their existence and has done so since the arrival of the Spanish.

Local Ladino and Maya still struggle to accept that massacres occurred in their own country. While some deny the mass killings completely, others believe the military and the newspapers invented these rumors. Others waver on the subject, arguing that there is no evidence to support genocide, yet recent news reports showing exhumations on TV have begun to affect these perceptions. Even so, the majority of the community does not believe that large-scale massacres occurred. Different terms to characterize periods of violence, *La Situación* and *La Violencia*, have been used alternately to contrasting effect, with *La Situación* describing the belief in periodic violence as a fact of history, and *La Violencia* recognizing the role of the state in establishing and executing a campaign of terror (Sanford 2003).

I concur with Victoria Sanford that the term *La Violencia* appears to be a neutral one that does not fully acknowledge the severity of the violence, but when used by Guatemalans in reference to and in the context of the civil conflict, the term nevertheless proves extremely powerful. The extent to which the community members examined in this study continue to deny the genocidal aspects of the civil conflict is evidenced by the rare usage of that term and the common usage of *La Situación* to describe both their past and present environment. Local Maya and Ladinos thus continue to ignore the evidence of state-sponsored killings as they accept the consistent threat of violence, neither recognizing the origins of its presence nor contesting its claims to legitimacy.

FEEDING GUATEMALA'S MILITARY MACHINE: LADINO OFFICERS AND MAYA FOOT SOLDIERS

The East versus West/Ladino versus Maya regional and ethnic construction was evident in certain of the processes of the Guatemalan civil war. For example, the West was targeted for genocide, while the East largely supported that genocide. The Oriente fed Guatemala's military machine by providing Ladino officers and Maya foot soldiers for the civil conflict in the West. The purposeful conscription of Oriente Ladinos as officers reaffirms racist notions of Ladino superiority and Maya inferiority. As ex-military Ladinos explained, since the dictatorship of Jorge Ubico in the 1940s and throughout the military history of Guatemala, the army has purposefully recruited officers from the Oriente, looking especially for men considered *bien Ladino*, or of principally Spanish ancestry, and thus embodying the characteristics of an ideal officer: tall, strong, fair-skinned, smart, and capable. One Ladino ex-officer, now in his late 70s, explained why he did not end up high in the officer ranks. Even though he is Ladino, he ended up serving for one of the less prestigious officer camps because he was not tall enough to be selected for the upper army division. He further detailed recruitment policies in towns known for their Ladino men of "purer" Spanish ancestry: "Since the times of Ubico they looked for tall white men, like Ladinos from Chapparon, Monjas, and Mita. I was in Monjas, but I wasn't tall enough for them, so I ended up in the lower corps. In fact, you know that President [Alfonso] Portillo's father was born in this town—we have many famous *militares* and people in high places in the city and government" (personal communication 2001).

Some Ladino men remember being forced to join the army as mere foot soldiers during the regime of Ubico. They describe how the military organized dances for the sole purpose of rounding up young men to join the army. As the years passed this form of forced conscription evolved to target young Maya men throughout rural towns in the Oriente, as well as throughout Guatemala in general. It appears that only rural Maya men were rounded up in the later years of the war (Green 1984). While policies of forced military conscription appear to have been executed without specific regard to ethnicity, officer recruitment certainly paid attention to ethnicity, and foot soldiers during the civil war were principally Maya. Ladinos were also able to use financial or social power to avoid mandatory military service by paying off military officers, using family connections, or migrating to the United States.

While the Ladinos fled to the United States to avoid military service, Eastern Pokomam Maya, lacking the resources to migrate, remained, falling victim to military roundups and having to endure military service. Some Maya saw military jobs as a better option than working for Ladinos in town, so many Maya men left their villages in San Pedro Pinula to serve in the army, often in the Policía Militar Ambulante (Mobile Military Police), alongside indigenous peoples from other regions of Guatemala. In contrast, many Maya groups from the Western Highlands fled to the United States during the height of the civil war in the 1980s and 1990s.

Maya men from San Pedro Pinula fought in the worst battle zones such as Ixcán, the Ixil triangle, and Playa Grande. After their time in the military, Maya ex-soldiers depended on promises of work as congressional bodyguards in Guatemala City, but they were frustrated to find this impossible after the signing of the peace accords. A combination of a lack of opportunities in and outside the army, as well as the opening up of the once Ladino-dominated migration to the United States, encouraged many Maya to migrate to the north in the 1990s. I met one young Maya man as he was leaving for the United States after six years in the army working for the Mobile Military Police on a military base and training as a Kaibil (in the specialized forces) in Poptun for over 45 days. His thin physique attested to his claims of scant provisions, and he recounted having to kill his own dog with his two hands and eat it to survive. He left the Kaibiles very traumatized and would often wake up in the night screaming from nightmares. The ex-soldier, 26, described why he left to work in the United States and how his time in the army proved a fruitless endeavor: "I really wasted my time in the army. I thought I would receive training or learn some skills. Before, you could get work in the city as a congressional bodyguard, but since the peace accords there is no work for ex-soldiers. I spent all that time for nothing. I am going to the States because there is nothing here for me" (personal communication 2001).

In villages heavily affected by forced and voluntary army conscription, the return of ex-soldiers serves as a reminder of the violence and of the fear that has always been a part of the community psyche (Green 1984).

Some ex-soldiers in San Pedro Pinula use their experience in the army as a weapon to intimidate local Ladinos, which helps support their positions in Ladino-Maya business exchanges or aids them in entering Ladino-dominated occupations such as cattle ranching. Many Ladinos fear the Maya ex-soldiers for the combination of their knowledge of weaponry and the supposed savagery of the Indian. Even so, local Ladinos often take advantage of the ex-soldiers, using their experience in warfare as a pretext for recruiting them as hired guns. On several occasions ex-soldiers were hired by Ladinos to settle local Ladino family feuds. As one Ladino aptly put it, "Su vida vale el precio del balazo y los centavos para el indio" [your life is worth only the price of a bullet and the couple of cents it takes to pay an Indian to kill you] (personal communication 1999).

While I was doing research in one village, local Ladinos warned me against working with certain families, as they were known as dangerous assassins. One local Ladino, who was also known to be able to acquire handguns, told me that a family had come to him in the night asking to buy a gun. As the story goes, the Ladino warned the obviously enraged and drunken Maya not to do anything rash and wait until the sun came up to settle their anger ("deja que la sopa enfríe"—let the soup get cold). Yet in spite of his ostensibly pacifistic counsel, the Ladino sold them the weapon anyway and was not surprised to hear about a shooting in the village the following day. Most Ladinos find this sort of behavior surprising, disturbing, and, most important, threatening to their own well-being, as Indians used to settle their intravillage disputes with machetes rather than guns. Moving from the use of machetes to guns in the Indian villages reminds local Ladinos of the changes that have taken place since the peace accords.

Human rights (*derechos humanos*) is one of the only phrases used among Ladinos in the community that allude to the peace accords. While some workshops funded by MINUGUA (United Nations Verification Mission in Guatemala), which has been monitoring the implementation of the peace agreements, have reached the departmental capital of Jalapa, there has been very little participation in them. Human rights reports confirm the surge in crime that has followed the conflict and the state's inadequate response to the escalating violence (MINUGUA 2002). Some Ladinos feel this increase in crime coincides with the implementation of the peace accords. When discussing changes in the community, Ladinos complain that their once compliant Maya workers now hear what Indians in other parts of the country are making and thus want higher pay and fewer hours, claiming that if they do not get what they want, they will use this new tool, human rights, to their advantage.

Ladinos also complain that these human rights have made the Indians less respectful and lazier. Some Ladinos no longer feel they have the right to do whatever they want with the local Maya population, fearing there will be repercussions where formerly there were none, even for crimes such as murder and rape. The biggest fear of Ladino landowners regarding human rights concerns the long-standing belief that local Maya will try to re-acquire untitled lands currently under the control of local Ladinos. This confirms evidence that Ladinos feel a reverse discrimination with the increasing credibility of the truth commission and the belief that the peace accords will only benefit the Maya. Diane N. Nelson has also documented Ladino resentment and fear of an impending "race war" (2003:133). The fear re-ignites memories of the local Indian rebellion during the Arevelo period, the subsequent Ladino submission, and fuels beliefs of the re-emergence of ethnic conflict in an already ethnically charged region. For Ladinos the denial of the civil war and an emphasis on the supposedly pro-Maya (and conversely, anti-Ladino) discourse occurring in postconflict Guatemala may be a way to cope with the possible loss of their hegemonic power and sublimates the possibility of continued violence (i.e., in the form of ethnic conflict).

MAYA AND GENOCIDE AWARENESS
IN THE UNITED STATES

Transnational migration has provided a venue for San Pedro Pinula's Pokomam Maya migrants to find out about Guatemala's civil war in the United States. The presence of different Maya ethnic groups in the same U.S. communities has created an avenue for intercultural exchange among these groups, which results in the transmission of information regarding genocide in Guatemala. In Boston the Eastern Pokomam Maya migrants live and work alongside Quiche and Mam Maya from the Western Highlands, whose sense of indigenousness is vastly different from and stronger than that of the Pokomam. Moreover, they have formed contacts with North Americans, including members of local church organizations, who openly discuss the history of Guatemala's civil conflict. One male Pokomam migrant, 23, in Boston reported his transformation in the United States, as he learned and began to accept stories about the civil war, the atrocities, ethnic conflict, and most important, began to achieve a sense of pride as a Maya. Having met Maya migrants from the West who had experienced or at least knew about the genocide, this migrant began to collect books in Spanish on the subject. On several occasions he sought my help in locating these books and questioned me on what I knew about genocide. He looked up to the Maya from the Western Highlands who had grown up in an environment perceived by him to be better than his own: "I wonder what my life would have been like if I had been born in the Occidente. I wish I had been born there, and it wouldn't have taken me this long to be proud of who I am" (personal communication 2002).

This migrant had never experienced a sense of Maya solidarity or ethnic pride, or even ever used the word *Maya* in reference to himself. As second-class citizens in San Pedro Pinula, Maya are referred to as *indígena* (indigenous), *natural* (natural), *pobre* (poor), *campesino* (peasant), and (most commonly) *indio* (Indian), which is the most derogatory. Though the Pokomam Maya had suffered under an intense military occupation since the 1960s, they did not experience the atrocities of large-scale massacres, as did the Maya of the Western Highlands. Contact with these Western Highland Maya has been enlightening since it has exposed the easterners to oral testimonies and literature on the Maya movement and the civil war, a history that has long remained inaccessible to them.

The presence in the United States of Maya ex-soldiers has proven more problematic since postwar trauma has followed them in their quest for a new life. Many soldiers, especially those who were stationed in the conflict zones during the war, are feared by noncombatant migrants. Stories abound concerning ex-soldiers in the United States who take to drinking to absolve their post-traumatic stress disorder and who often have violent confrontations with their *paisanos* (compatriots), many of whom come from the same town or village. I received a phone call recently from a Ladino about his new roommate, a Maya from one of San Pedro Pinula's outlying villages. The Ladino was fearful and confided that the newcomer's past history as a soldier was the cause of his fear. One positive aspect of the migration experience for Ladino-Maya relations is the interethnic friendships that develop in the United States as Maya and Ladino are forced to live and work in the same environment outside of the constraints of

Guatemala's rigid social structure (Taylor, Moran-Taylor, and Rodman Ruiz 2006). Unfortunately, the formation of such friendships has remained scant among several ex-soldiers whose violent behavior has created fear within the migrant community. In 2006 there was a stabbing in Boston's Dorchester neighborhood that resulted in the death of a Guatemalan man from this region. Witnesses claim that the fight was a drunken brawl between an ex-soldier and his upstairs neighbor. Even if these claims are unsubstantiated, the rumors have created and confirmed migrants' fear and animosity toward Maya ex-soldiers.

CONCLUSION

As the country tries to come to terms with its recent past and still tenuous future, inhabitants who flatly refuse to perceive violence as more than background noise struggle with confirming and accepting the past genocide. Guatemalans, Maya and Ladino alike, who live outside the regions directly affected by mass killings do not always readily perceive, much less accept, the fact of genocide as it occurred in other regions of their country. Instead, they conceive of violence as a relatively mundane aspect of an apathetic existence, rather than as a product of a political event that began in the 1960s and did not end until the signing of the peace accords in 1996. In some communities outside the zones directly affected by mass killings, and in the current case the Ladino-dominated Maya municipality of San Pedro Pinula, the inhabitants deny the salient fact of genocide, much as they deny the historical periods of armed resistance against the state. While local constructions of the civil war may be at odds with how Guatemalan history is recorded, the importance of the Oriente's role in Guatemalan history is not. Though long considered to be politically inconsequential during the last decades of the civil war, this region was directly involved in greasing the country's military machine through the recruitment of Ladino officers and the conscription of Maya soldiers. Even given the Oriente's express involvement in the war, many of its people strive to maintain an atmosphere in which the denial of mass killings is commonplace and through which the status quo is upheld. The migration of Maya and Ladinos (both ex-soldiers and noncombatants) from the region to the United States has opened up the possibility for a transnational exchange of information on the civil war, though the pace of change initiated by such exchanges is slow, since it is tempered by centuries of ethnic divisions and apathetic attitudes.

Various obstacles within these populations interfere with the objectives of the peace process, and long-standing ethnic divides have already created resistance to the goals of the peace accords. Ladinos perceive the changes wrought by the initiatives for peace, such as the widespread awareness of the idea of human rights, as a threat to their power and positions as landowners and patrons. They also see the implementation of the peace accords as beneficial only to the Maya population. Ladino perceptions of the ultimate effects of the peace process are just one difficulty among many in a region in which the construction of the civil conflict is at odds with recorded history. Yet a better understanding of the ethnic divides that perpetuate these beliefs may work toward achieving the goal of a more peaceful Guatemala.

NOTES

1. Linda Green (1994) discusses how everyday violence becomes an accepted worldview for many Maya and forms part of "social memory." This article uses Green's concept to explain how a repressive state has created a widespread consciousness for the Ladino and the Maya populations and affected attitudes about life and living throughout the Guatemalan state.

2. Green (1984) discusses the culture of fear and refers to Guatemalan "self-censorship," and specifically to Maya silence and secrecy in response to Ladino racism. My experience with Guatemalans includes every level of society. Ladino children are taught from a young age not to confide in strangers and are taught to be secretive about their comings and goings. Although strangers will comfortably chat on a local bus, no one reveals where one is from or where one is going. While in the United States knowledge is power, in Guatemala knowledge can be a death sentence.

3. Guatemala's civil war is considered to have lasted for about 36 years starting in 1960 after a failed coup by reformist army officers in response to the corruption of the Ydigoras government. The signing of the peace accords in 1996 is generally considered the civil war's end (see Handy 1984; Booth 1980).

4. While the last two decades of the conflict were concentrated in the Western Highlands and targeted Maya villages, many Ladinos were also killed throughout the conflict as state repression aimed at them throughout the country. See Stoll 1999 and Nelson 2003 for a further discussion of the civil conflict as "race wars."

5. While this essay employs the Ladino-Maya ethnic dichotomy, I do recognize that there exists great diversity among these populations in class as well as degree of ethnicity, especially in the Eastern Highlands. See Little-Siebold 2001 and Taylor, Moran-Taylor, and Rodman Ruiz 2006 for more information on ethnic identity construction in the Eastern Highlands.

6. For more on Ladino and Maya identity in Eastern Guatemala, see Moran-Taylor 2003; Rodman 2006; Little-Siebold 2001. Census data identifies Guatemalans as

"Ladino," "Indian," or "other" and does not clearly reflect regional variations in the construction of ethnicity. Census data does reflect larger patterns but varies over time for various reasons (who is administering the census, what economic or social implications a certain ethnic identity has at the time), but generally Maya and Ladino identity is associated with language use, dress, and social customs. In the Jalapa region, while many Pokomam Maya no longer speak the Pokomam language or even consider themselves Maya, others consider them Indian. They often self-identify as poor, peasants, or simply in opposition to local Ladinos. Local Ladinos have varying levels of Ladinoness based on their ancestry, skin color, and other perceived ethnic markers. In general, the Pokomam Maya of Jalapa are considered a cohesive ethnic group due to their historically sustained and persistent existence in opposition to local Ladino power. Richard Adams and Santiago Bastos (2003) call indigenous peoples in Eastern Guatemala who have no specific claim to a Maya group or Maya language *indios locales* (local Indians).

7. *Mozo* literally means "peon" or "worker," but in the context of ethnic relations in Jalapa, it refers to the Ladino's Maya worker. In this region the Maya and Ladino maintain a codependent patron-client relation that goes beyond that of a typical paid worker to his or her boss. Maya are usually bound to the Ladino patron by debt service and/or a sharecropping relationship. Social obligations for both sides also define the relationship, but they usually benefit the Ladino landowner more.

8. Pinultecos's suspicious nature is common throughout Guatemala. In a country where impunity reigns and political crimes are made to look common, and where varying versions of the truth are in constant conflict, all crimes are suspect. During the Gerardi trials, a multitude of conspiracy theories were concocted by the military and supported by the media (see Goldman 2007). The theories were varied, from a crime of passion twisted with homosexuality to gang involvement, perpetuating stereotypes of those targeted as undesirables. In San Pedro Pinula, intrafamilial feuds are made to look like interethnic community conflicts, validating Ladinos as extrajudicial enforcers of law and order while simultaneously perpetuating stereotypes of local Maya as animalistic and uncontrollable.

9. Green (1994) also found that the state described atrocities as crimes committed by delinquents. Delinquency seems to take on a new meaning in the Guatemalan context to explain crimes associated with state repression or guerrilla activity.

10. Gringos in this case are not only North Americans but also any light-skinned person who is a stranger to the community.

REFERENCES

Adams, Richard, and Santiago Bastos
2003   Las relaciones étnicas en Guatemala 1944–2000. Guatemala City: Cirma.

Booth, John A.
1980   A Guatemalan Nightmare: Levels of Political Violence, 1966–1972. Journal of Interamerican Studies and World Affairs 22(2):195–225.

Carlsen, Robert
1997   The War for the Heart and Soul of a Highland Maya Town. Austin: University of Texas Press.

Dary, Claudia
2003   Identidades étnicos y tierras comunales en Jalapa. Guatemala City: Instituto de Estudies Interétnicos.

Gillen, John Philip
1951   The Culture of Security in San Carlos: A Study of a Guatemalan Community of Indians and Ladinos. New Orleans: Tulane University of Louisiana, Middle American Research Institute.

Goldman, Francisco
2007   The Art of Political Murder: Who Killed the Bishop? New York: Grove Press.

Grandin, Greg
1997   To End with All these Evils: Ethnic Transformation and Community Mobilization in Guatemala's Western Highlands, 1954–1980. Latin American Perspectives 24 (2):7–34.

Green, Linda
1994   Fear as a Way of Life. Cultural Anthropology 9(2):227–256.

Gulden, Timothy R.
2001   Spatial and Temporal Patterns in Civil Violence: Guatemala 1977–1986. Working Paper, 26. College Park: Bookings Center on Social and Economic Dynamics, University of Maryland School of Public Affairs.

Handy, Jim
1984   Gift of the Devil: A History of Guatemala. City: South End.

Little-Siebold, Christa
2001   Beyond the Indian-Ladino Dichotomy: Contested Identities in an Eastern Guatemalan Town. Journal of Latin American Anthropology 6(2):176–197.

MacLeod, Murdo J.
1973   Spanish Central America: A Socioeconomic History, 1520–1720. Berkeley: California University Press.

May, Rachel A.
2001   Terror in the Countryside: Campesino Responses to Political Violence in Guatemala, 1954–1985. Athens: Ohio University Center for International Studies.

Metz, Brent
1995   Experiencing Conquest: The Political and Economic Roots and Cultural Expression of Maya-Chorti Ethos. Ph.D. dissertation, State University of New York, Albany.

1998   Without Nation, without Community: The Growth of Maya National-
            ism among Chortis of Eastern Guatemala. Journal of Anthropological
            Research 54:325–349.

Moran-Taylor, Michelle J.
2003   International Migration and Culture Change in Guatemala's Maya *Oc-
            cidente* and Ladino *Oriente*. Ph.D. dissertation, Arizona State University.

Morrison, Andrew, and Rachel May
1994   Escape from Terror: Violence and Migration in Post-Revolutionary Gua-
            temala. Latin American Research Review 29(2):111–132.

Moser, Caroline, and Cathy McIlwaine
2001   Violence in a Post-Conflict Context: Urban Poor from Guatemala. Wash-
            ington: World Bank.

Nelson, Diane N.
2003   The More You Kill the More You Will Live: The Maya, "Race," and Biopo-
            litical Hopes for Peace in Guatemala. *In* Race, Nature, and the Politics of
            Difference. Donald S. Moore, Jake Kosek, and Anand Pandian, eds. Pp.
            122–146. Durham, NC: Duke University Press.

Paul, Benjamin, and William Demarest
1988   The Operation of Death Squads in San Pedro La Leguna. *In* Harvest of
            Violence: The Maya Indians and the Guatemalan Crisis. Robert M.
            Carmack, ed. Pp.119–154. Norman: University of Oklahoma Press.

Peacock, Susan C., and Adrian Beltran
2003   Hidden Powers in Post-Conflict Guatemala: Illegal Armed Groups
            and the Forces behind Them. Washington: Washington Office on Latin
            America.

Rodman, Debra H.
2006   Gender, Migration, and Transnational Identities: Maya and Ladino Rela-
            tions in Eastern Guatemala. Ph.D. dissertation, University of Florida.

Sanford, Victoria.
2003   Buried Secrets: Truth and Human Rights in Guatemala. New York: Pal-
            grave Macmillan.

Sayles, John, dir.
1997   Men with Guns. Los Angeles: Anarchist's Convention Films. DVD.

Stewart, Pamela J., and Andrew Strathern
2002   Violence: Theory and Ethnography. New York: Continuum.

Stoll, David
1999   Rigoberta Menchú and the Story of All Poor Guatemalans. Boulder, CO:
            Westview.

Sullivan-Gonzalez, Douglass
1998   Piety, Power, and Politics: Religion and Nation Formation in Guatemala, 1821–1871. Pittsburgh: University of Pittsburgh Press.

Taylor, Matthew J., Michelle J. Moran-Taylor, and Debra H. Rodman Ruiz
2006   Migra Landscapes: The Impacts of International Migration on Guatemalan Culture and Land. Geoforum 37:41–61.

Tumin, Melvin M.
1952   Caste in a Peasant Society: A Case Study in the Dynamics of Caste. Princeton: Princeton University Press.

United Nations Verification Mission in Guatemala (MINUGUA)
2002   Human Rights Report 13: July 2001–July 2002. Guatemala City: United Nations.

Valentino, Benjamin A.
2004   Final Solutions: Mass Killing and Genocide in the Twentieth Century. Ithaca: Cornell University Press.

Wisdom, Charles
1940   The Chorti Indians of Guatemala. Chicago: University of Chicago Press.

3   TRUTH/MEMORY/**REPRESENTATION**

Elizabeth F. Drexler

7 ADDRESSING THE LEGACIES OF

MASS VIOLENCE AND GENOCIDE IN

INDONESIA AND EAST TIMOR

Trials, especially international tribunals, as well as truth commissions have been put forth by the international community as ways of working through traumatic pasts of mass violence and genocide to establish stable futures governed by the rule of law.[1] Transitional institutions and postconflict reconstruction initiatives are often premised on the idea that speaking about past violence will lead to individual and social healing.[2] In recognition of the haunting presence of historical grievances, trials, no less than truth commissions, attempt to rewrite competing historical narratives, both to settle accounts and to fill in missing pieces of particular narratives.[3] In and after situations of mass violence and genocide the truth never simply awaits discovery. Similarly, the memories are never unmediated.[4] Institutions of truth and memory contribute to the production of the very truth they appear to discover at the same time that they shape and are shaped by the memories they appear to confirm or contradict.

Institutional forms and processes shape narratives of past violence: certain institutional truths are prioritized as collective identities are narrated through transitional institutions in the aftermath of mass violence. I conducted fieldwork in East

Timor and in Indonesia to explore the dense interconnections between transitional institutions and representations. Three different transitional institutions addressed the violence perpetrated during the 1999 referendum for independence in East Timor: an ad hoc tribunal in Jakarta; an internationalized, UN-supported tribunal, the Special Panels for Serious Crimes in East Timor; and a truth commission in East Timor, the Commission for Reception, Truth and Reconciliation (CAVR). Despite these multiple institutional responses, legacies of past violence persist, generating further institutional responses but failing to mitigate distrust and fueling new conflicts. In this essay, I suggest that these legacies persist because of the failure to examine the complex logics of collaboration and betrayal.

During more than two decades of Indonesian occupation, human rights organizations and other advocates exposed the "secret war," genocidal state violence, and heroic Timorese resistance they witnessed.[5] In contrast, the postindependence transitional institutions have emphasized violent acts between Timorese attributed to conditions of war and chaos necessary to secure independence. The transitional institutions have failed not only to demonstrate how conditions of civil war could develop but also to hold the Indonesian military accountable for the violence it perpetrated.[6]

International advocates and Timorese activists reject the civil war narrative and instead demand an international tribunal to hold the Indonesian military accountable. Many Timorese I interviewed, however, were equally concerned about injustices in independent Timor: some new elites were rumored to have betrayed the struggle for independence in the past, while figures who sacrificed much for independence found themselves marginalized in the new government. In struggling to tell the past as they remember it, people with whom I spoke frequently touched on the themes of betrayal and collaboration. Their comments inspired me to consider not only stories of the past but also the conditions of possibility for remembering and representing the past inside and outside official institutions.

I agree with many advocates and analysts that Indonesian violence must be addressed.[7] Yet based on my research on state violence in Indonesia and on transitional institutions in East Timor, I argue that it is important to address the complex role of betrayal and collaboration between and within forces in conflict. Refocusing attention on conflict between Timorese might at first glance appear to constitute yet another betrayal of the Timorese that supports the Indonesian civil war narrative. But I suggest that examining collaborations and betrayals may instead prove essential both to considering representational strategies after mass violence and to holding the Indonesian military accountable for systematic repression, social polarization, and the creation of conditions for mass violence. This approach offers possibilities for rethinking advocacy strategies based on the representation of violence and genocide.

FROM THE SECRET WAR TO THE REFERENDUM

The history of the Indonesian occupation of East Timor is inseparable from struggles over the representation and documentation of violence. During the occupation a number of individuals and organizations reported both the Indonesian campaigns of terror and repression and the armed resistance.

Prior to independence the half-island nation of East Timor was a Portuguese colony for over three hundred years.[8] The other half of the island was colonized by the Dutch as part of the Netherlands East Indies, which became modern Indonesia in 1945. East Timor remained a colony until Portugal's 1974 revolution initiated an abrupt decolonization process with limited opportunities for the creation of political parties and self-governance. The three parties that ultimately took shape advocated different visions for Timor's future. Initially, the larger parties formed a coalition to oppose the smaller party, which favored integration with Indonesia. Through the manipulations of Indonesian intelligence, the coalition fell apart resulting in a coup, a countercoup, and a brief civil war (Jardine 1999). In December 1975, after the social democratic party had declared Timor's independence and in the midst of the Cold War, the Indonesian president Soeharto launched a dramatic invasion and sustained occupation to forcibly annex the territory.[9] In July 1976, Indonesia declared East Timor its twenty-seventh province. Between 1975 and 1979, an estimated two hundred thousand Timorese pro-independence figures and ordinary civilians—about one-third of the population—were killed as a direct or indirect result of the Indonesian invasion and occupation. Although Indonesia formalized its annexation of East Timor in July 1976, the United Nations never formally recognized Indonesian claims to sovereignty over the territory (Robinson 2002; Taylor 1999; Anderson 1995). In the context of the Cold

War, countries such as the United States that were well poised to act on and enforce UN Security Council resolutions on Timor instead officially and unofficially supported Soeharto.[10]

Extensive military operations continued until the 1999 UN-supported referendum; human rights workers and journalists continued to testify to their severity and brutality. Five international journalists were killed as they reported on the "integration" of East Timor into Indonesia.[11] Throughout the 1980s Soeharto's authoritarian rule kept the province almost completely closed to outsiders. Members of the resistance smuggled documentation of the abuses perpetrated by Indonesian soldiers out of the territory, and Timorese in exile testified to what they had witnessed. Despite the severe controls, journalists and others continued to find ways into Timor, publishing accounts of repression authenticated by firsthand encounters with danger and secrecy.

In 1989 the Indonesian government began to allow journalists and visitors into East Timor to demonstrate that conditions were "normal." In November 1991 a memorial procession for a pro-independence youth left two hundred Timorese dead and many others missing.[12] The international media broadcast both the banners celebrating the pro-independence leader Xanana and the brutal beatings and killings of Timorese by the Indonesian armed forces. This event, which became known as the Santa Cruz massacre,[13] is widely believed to have been a turning point in international advocacy for Timor. The video footage and other graphic images of state violence galvanized international outrage, which helped create global support networks for East Timor.

After Santa Cruz Indonesia faced international criticism for the violence it perpetrated. In response the country held internal military trials in which several low-ranking officers were lightly punished for their participation in the Santa Cruz killings (Amnesty International 1991, 1992). Timorese in exile and global advocacy networks continued to circulate testimony and evidence of military repression and human rights violations, as well as to document histories of the resistance movement's persistent struggle (Aditjondro 1994; Budiardjo 1984; Jardine 1999; Carey 1995; Gunn 1997). In 1996 two Timorese, Bishop Carlos Belo and José Ramos-Horta (the current president), shared the Nobel Prize for Peace, highlighting Timor's international profile.

The Asian financial crisis of 1997 and its aftermath, especially the end of Soeharto's thirty-two-year authoritarian rule in 1998, rendered Indonesia more susceptible to international pressure as it sought economic assistance. In January 1999, without the support of the powerful Indonesian armed forces, Soeharto's successor, B. J. Habibie, announced a referendum to accept or reject the offer of "special autonomy" within Indonesia. Following the announcement the Indonesian military (TNI) and militia groups initiated relentless campaigns of terror and intimidation.[14] Both civilians and military personnel holding positions in the regional government used state funds for pro-integration and militia activities.

In May 1999, despite a series of well-documented incidents that evidenced the collaboration between the TNI and the militia groups in creating turmoil, intimidation, and terror that threatened the referendum process, Portugal, Indonesia, and the UN agreed that Indonesian troops would be responsible for maintaining security during the referendum ballot.[15] At the same time the TNI continued to train pro-Indonesian militias to intimidate voters and demonstrate that choosing independence would result in total destruction (Robinson 2002). Militia groups did not limit their violence to Timorese; when the unarmed UN Mission in East Timor (UNAMET) personnel arrived later in May to prepare for the referendum, its members became targets of, as well as witnesses to, violence and intimidation.

Despite these campaigns of terror, 98 percent of registered Timorese voted, 78 percent of them to reject the Indonesian autonomy proposal in favor of independence, on August 30, 1999.[16] On September 4, when the results were announced, the TNI deployed Timorese militias to create the appearance of a civil war.[17] As part of a "scorched earth" campaign, members of the TNI and of the pro-Indonesia militias intensified their killings, rapes, torture, destruction, and involuntary deportation of large numbers of citizens of the newly independent East Timor to Indonesian West Timor, a district of Indonesia. An estimated six hundred thousand Timorese were forcibly relocated to Indonesian West Timor.[18] Over thirteen hundred civilians were killed.[19] The complicity of the Indonesian military in campaigns to disrupt the referendum process was obvious to most observers in Timor, but UNAMET was unable to convince the international community to send peacekeeping forces to Timor until after the referendum (Robinson 2002; Nevins 2002). The situation remained violent until the International

Force in East Timor (INTERFET) restored security in late September. A UN Transitional Authority for East Timor (UNTAET) was established by UN Security Council Resolution 1272/99 in October 1999 with the mandate to "exercise all legislative and executive authority, including the administration of justice."

INSTITUTIONS OF TRUTH AND JUSTICE: CIVIL WAR

In January 2000, UN Secretary General Kofi Anan received reports from both the UN Commission of Inquiry on East Timor (ICIET) and the Indonesian Commission for the Investigation of Human Rights Violations in East Timor (KPP-HAM) that documented the involvement of high-ranking Indonesian military personnel in the 1999 violence.[20] Nevertheless, the UN did not commit the political and economic resources necessary for an international tribunal. Despite the failed promise of the TNI to secure the referendum, the UN accepted Indonesian government promises that military perpetrators would be tried by the Ad Hoc Human Rights Tribunal in Jakarta.

In a strategy celebrated at the time for its potential to maintain individual criminal accountability without overburdening the court system (Stahn 2001), UNTAET established institutions both for trials and for a truth commission. A hybrid tribunal, the Special Panels for Serious Crimes, was created in Dili with the dual goals of holding perpetrators of serious crimes in 1999 accountable and of contributing to the development of a functional and legitimate justice system for the new nation. The truth commission (CAVR) was designed both to seek the truth about past violence (importantly, from 1974 through 1999) and to facilitate the resettlement of displaced persons and the reconciliation of divided communities.

As the mandates of these organizations ended, two more institutions were established. The UN Commission of Experts considered the results of the justice processes for East Timor, reviewing the work of both the Special Panels for Serious Crimes in Dili and the Ad Hoc Human Rights Tribunal in Jakarta. Pointing to the failure of both these tribunals to bring high-ranking Indonesian military officers to justice, an alliance of Timorese NGOs and others have demanded that the UN establish an international tribunal. Ramos-Horta, then the foreign minister, opposed an international tribunal, prioritizing instead good relations with Timor's largest neighbor. In 2005, Indonesian and Timorese authorities agreed to establish the

Commission for Truth and Friendship to resolve the legacies of 1999. Officials both in Timor-Leste and in Indonesia stated that this commission renders any international tribunal unnecessary. In the following sections I describe these three institutions in greater detail to consider how they shape narratives about past violence.

Ad Hoc Human Rights Tribunal, Jakarta

Political conditions had shifted by the time the ad hoc court began its investigations, significantly diminishing the tribunal's ability to bring the suspects named by the KPP-HAM to trial (Mizuno 2003). The legal basis of the court was unclear, further complicating investigations, indictments, and trials.[21] When the ad hoc tribunal for Timor was established, its jurisdiction was limited both temporally and geographically by political negotiations. Initially, the court was permitted to investigate only crimes occurring after the referendum, supporting the idea promulgated by military figures that the violence in Timor spontaneously erupted between Timorese when the results were announced. In contrast to the KPP-HAM mandate to investigate crimes in all districts of Timor between January 1 and October 25, 1999, the court's jurisdiction was ultimately limited to events that had taken place in April and September in three districts.[22] Such limited temporal and geographic jurisdiction made it more difficult to establish patterns of violence and of continuing relationships between the TNI and the militia groups.

Once the trials commenced in February 2002, they became a theater of military impunity.[23] Many of the accused did not attend their hearings. Judges critical of the military faced intimidation. The court was unable to safeguard the rights of victims who might have appeared as witnesses; many Timorese refused to testify. Several victims in the Liquisa Church massacre, one of the priority cases tried by both the ad hoc tribunal and the Special Panels for Serious Crimes, told me that they had wanted to attend the Jakarta tribunal and give their testimony, but that they did not participate because they received no guarantees for their safety. In the Jakarta courtroom, victims and other witnesses were often questioned in a way that benefited the accused. Indicted military members remained in active-duty positions; many witnesses called were their subordinates, compromising their ability to provide accurate information. Members of the military, in full uniform, were bussed to the courthouse to fill the audience, often intimidating witnesses or other spectators. Though the court did convict some defendants, they all remained free pending appeal cases; most were ultimately acquitted.[24]

The narrative produced by the Jakarta ad hoc tribunal attributes the 1999 violence to a civil conflict resulting from tensions within East Timorese society over the results of the referendum for independence. The indictments establish this pattern by their failure to distinguish militia groups and to point out their relationship with the TNI; they generalize violence to factions for and against independence. Consistently substituting the word *clash* for *attack* supported the idea of "horizontal" violence (ELSAM 2003). In this narrative the TNI failed to prevent the violence or commanders failed to prevent their subordinates from committing human rights violations. Indonesian military and militia leaders have written numerous biographies and memoirs about their operations in Timor (Suratman 2002; Wiranto 2003; Jasmi 2002; Makarim et al. 2002). These accounts extend the civil war narrative to introduce an international conspiracy in which the UN manipulated the referendum ballot (Somomoelijono 2001). The TNI has consistently prioritized narratives that emphasize threats to Indonesian national integrity and to state sovereignty.

Special Panels for Serious Crimes, Dili

The special panels represented a new hybrid or internationalized tribunal designed to incorporate international expertise and staff without the expense and political ramifications of setting up an international tribunal. A team of one Timorese and two international judges tried cases at the Dili District Court. The special panels were granted exclusive jurisdiction over war crimes, crimes against humanity, and genocide in addition to murder, sexual offenses, and torture occurring between January 1 and October 25, 1999 (UNTAET Regulation 2000/15). High-ranking Indonesian military members were indicted for designing, financing, and coordinating the crimes against humanity implemented by militia groups. Yet these suspects were not extradited to Timor for trial, nor were Timorese militia leaders and government officials who chose to remain in Indonesia. The absence of these figures not only compromised justice efforts but also limited the court's ability to provide critical evidence and testimony about crimes. Although some indictments stated that particular militia groups were linked to state-organized civil defense groups, neither the indictments nor the hearings captured the genealogy of militia groups in prior security operations. Systematic violence that had occurred during the Indonesian occupation was disqualified from judicial examination, as was earlier violence between the Timorese parties. Systematic discrimination that might have been examined under a genocide indictment was not incorporated into crimes against humanity indictments.

The Serious Crimes Unit (SCU), which was established to investigate and prosecute serious offenses, and the special panels concluded their operations in May 2005. Almost all of those accused in the ten priority cases of crimes against humanity remain at large in Indonesia.[25] The unit filed a significant number of other indictments, but most of those accused also remain at large in Indonesia.[26] Many cases could not be brought to trial because the accused resided outside East Timor. Arrest warrants have been filed with Interpol; however, there is no indication that these will produce results. My interviews with SCU staff, judges, and other investigators revealed that an enormous amount of material related to these cases had been collected, although almost none of it has been brought to public attention or discussion. The unit very belatedly initiated a program of public forums to discuss indictments, often traveling to different regions. In preparation for closing the operations, another round of public sessions was held. These sessions were criticized for failing to effectively address questions and to involve communities in the justice process.

The panels were rife with technical problems related to transcription, translation, due process, appeal, and a number of other significant legal issues. The first trial, the Los Palos case, was extensively analyzed from legal perspectives.[27] The importance of evaluating the Timor case against international legal and human rights standards cannot be underestimated as the efficiency and cost-effectiveness of this hybrid model is likely to make it increasingly appealing to the international community (Cohen, 2002); however, my concern lies with how legal and technical issues affect the process of producing truth about the past.

In the East Timor model, justice has been prioritized as a necessary step for reconciliation and nation-building. Most Timorese say that justice is important, and yet the serious crimes investigations and prosecutions inspired very little public interest. The new courthouse most often remained empty. Hearings were dull. Frequent translation issues slowed down questioning, and judges' vacations and other scheduling issues further interrupted the trial and the flow of any story that might be uncovered.

Many Timorese expressed frustration that the architects and primary perpetrators of the systematic violence were not brought to justice. Many called the hybrid tribunals a charade. They noted that the families of low-ranking militia members convicted and serving jail time became a burden to the community. Others criticized the courts for not considering cases that occurred prior to 1999. Communities that provided evidence in hopes that the bones of their loved ones would be discovered or that justice would be served were disappointed when their cases were not tried. Defense lawyers criticized their counterparts for attributing acts to their clients—whom they described as poor, illiterate farmers swept up into circumstances beyond their control—that lay beyond their capabilities.

The picture that emerged from the trials was one of individuals complicit in and aware of systematic plans to commit crimes against humanity. Sometimes the acts tried were the same as those processed through the community reconciliation hearings, which I will describe below. Even though the scu indicted Indonesia's commander in chief, the trials reinforced the idea that the powerful remained beyond the law and thus extended patterns in which the law was corrupt and arbitrary. The failure of both tribunals to hold the TNI accountable for its role in designing and orchestrating the violence has fueled demands for an international tribunal, but in 2003, Timor's foreign minister, Ramos-Horta, stated that the new nation would not pursue an international tribunal and that the nation's energies were best spent burying the past and rebuilding a relationship with Indonesia. In addition to noting that Indonesia had changed since 1999, Ramos-Horta also pointed to the fact that Timorese were victims not just of Indonesians but also of other Timorese (Sydney Morning Herald November 7, 2003). This emphasis on the Timorese role in perpetrating violence aligns with the Indonesian civil war narrative.

Commission for Reception, Truth, and Reconciliation in East Timor (CAVR)

The CAVR had a much more comprehensive mandate than the other institutions, investigating human rights violations that occurred between April 25, 1974, and October 25, 1999.[28] The CAVR conducted public and closed hearings nationwide, took statements from both victims and perpetrators, carried out criminal investigations and historical research, and obtained international documentation.[29] The commission produced a two thousand–page report attempting to establish the truth about all past violations and to make recommendations to the government of Timor-Leste for the future.[30]

The community reconciliation program (PRK) has been celebrated as a major innovation. Individuals wishing to be reconciled with particular communities (deponents) submitted statements of nonserious crimes. These statements were reviewed by the deputy general prosecutor for serious crimes to establish that the deponent applying for reconciliation was not sought on other charges of more serious crimes.[31] In the community hearings deponents testified to their actions, often emphasizing their lack of power or control in an overall system of intimidation and forced participation in the campaign of terror orchestrated by infamous militia leaders who remained just over the border in Indonesia. Community members in attendance had the opportunity to question what happened, often producing responses that attributed culpability to other militia members who remain in West Timor. Community-level discussions I attended did not focus on larger patterns of violence but on specific acts. Most communities agreed to accept the deponent and promised to no longer ostracize him or her after the symbolic act of reconciliation was fulfilled (e.g., cleaning the church).[32] Thus in community reconciliation hearings, testimony had immediate effects, and the community was bound to act as if the narrative given were true.

In terms of legitimacy the community reconciliation hearings were difficult to separate from the credibility of the regional and national commissioners who sat on the panel that moderated the hearings. In addition, the actual hearings were framed by an invocation of customary (*adat*) practices, the significance of which varies among different communities and could influence the community response to the event. Some victims I interviewed criticized the process because they felt pressured to accept statements from the perpetrator that were not as complete or as remorseful as they had hoped. Often these victims expressed their dissatisfaction with the process by departing from the hearing.

The picture that emerged from the community reconciliation hearings that I attended was of a number of individuals forced by circumstance to commit regrettable acts. I heard deponents refer to a situation of war and to a time that was "hot." They said that they were forced to do these things; had they not acted they themselves might have been killed. Different versions of this story, which always pointed to masterminds elsewhere, pervaded discussions. The masterminds or strategists were often named, but with the note that they remained in West Timor. Justice and truth in these contexts were often deferred promises: deponents pledged their testimony for a future opportunity to hold higher-ranking militia members responsible when they returned. There is no longer an institutional mechanism to hold returning perpetrators accountable or to hear the promised testimony.

Some militia members who committed nonserious crimes during 1999 cleared their names and reconciled with their communities through the PRK hearings; many communities learned new information about the crimes committed. Many people complained, however, that the PRK hearings rarely addressed violence prior to the referendum process; thus acts perpetrated in 1999 were taken out of a longer history of violence and betrayal. Likewise, many people complained that acts of violence perpetrated by Falintil, the resistance movement, were rarely discussed in any of the institutions.

One of the only official contexts for discussing political parties and violence was the CAVR national hearing in which political party leaders publicly apologized and acknowledged mistakes they had made in 1974–75. This hearing amazed most Timorese and other observers. One person complained to me that the leaders had reconciled with each other but had failed to reconcile with the ordinary people who had fought for their parties. This hearing proved extremely important symbolically. It was not intended to elaborate on the connections between political party conflict and the implementation of Indonesian operations.[33] And yet a focus on the 1974–75 conflict without an examination of the transformation of political party differences during the occupation might suggest that there were deep-rooted differences between Timorese that erupted in violence after the referendum results.

Despite their different agendas and the constraints facing them, the three institutions have all publicly enacted a version of events that emphasizes violence between Timorese in a time of war. At the same time, the conditions of possibility for such violence and the process through which it was subtly and systematically developed over two decades remain invisible in official institutions and representations of historical and legal truth.

BETRAYAL AND COLLABORATION

Violence during the Indonesian occupation of East Timor has been represented in a range of forms: human rights reports, personal testimonies, journalistic accounts, fiction, photographs, and films, as well as UN and government investigations, resolutions, and reports (see Ajidarma 1994, 1996; Shackleton 1995; Aditjondro 1994; Budiardjo 1984; Jardine 1999; Carey 1995, as well as Amnesty International and Human Rights Watch reports produced throughout the occupation). Most of them claim to reveal a truer account of the events based on personal experience and witness. Similarly, anthropological fieldwork and methods often disclose untold stories that contradict official accounts. My analysis is inspired by comments I heard from individuals whose memories, experiences, and visions of justice did not always correspond to official versions of the past produced by the transitional institutions. Most often these individuals did not participate in official institutional events. Many conversations began when I asked why these Timorese did not involve themselves or what aspects of the past they thought were not discussed in official contexts. The resulting stories proved compelling, but rather than writing an alternative version of the past based on these silenced accounts, I have chosen to consider how representations about violence in Timor have been produced at different times. Exploring the conditions of possibility for producing "the truth" about campaigns of violence challenges official accounts by pointing to how silences and exclusions corrupt institutions.

A woman who worked for the armed resistance movement, Falintil, both in the forest and in the city was describing her interactions with the Indonesian Special Forces (Kopassus) when she said: "If he [Kopassus contact] wants to kill someone, he has a friend make a photo or a video for us. He has all the authority; he can do anything. If the army brings three women to rape, they have to photograph them. Our strategy was like this, I said to him, if you want to kill someone, make a photograph for me. That was the photo that I sent out. I sent out all the photos that I got." I was struck by her matter-of-fact tone and puzzled as to why Kopassus would give her these photographs. I asked her if the victim was recognizable in the photo, and she responded: "No, the face has to be covered, it cannot be sent out if the victim can be recognized." I asked what the photos were used for, and she explained: "It's for the diplomatic struggle. They [the outside world] would say 'what war?' if there was no proof. Ramos-Horta talks outside, so we have to work here to get proof, so that the outside can be strong." She gave several examples of smuggling the photos out. For example, she wrapped the photos and put them underneath cookies in a tin that she stowed with her small bag of clothes on the night bus to West Timor. Food was not inspected; she told me she had used cookies three times. In West Timor, she handed the package to a tourist in a meeting arranged by the "outside" network and conveyed in various code terms. Before considering why Kopassus might surrender photographic evidence of their crimes to their enemies, I first consider the efforts of international advocates to document violence and resistance during the occupation.

Much as Falintil members wanted to demonstrate beyond a doubt that torture, rape, and extrajudicial killings were occurring in Timor, some Western supporters were determined to document the Falintil soldiers. In a recent book Irena Cristalis (2002) details her attempt to film the Falintil soldiers with Jill Joliffe during the occupation. She recalls from her initial meeting that the Falintil messengers were concerned "that the international media adopted the line of Indonesian propaganda: that Falintil was no more than a group of fifty or so cranky, poorly armed old men. . . . Falintil was eager to show the world that it was still a force to be reckoned with" (2002:7). She describes the long journey from meeting these representatives in Jakarta to East Timor, traveling overland for more than two weeks. The trip into the mountains to meet Falintil members ended in a drainage ditch facing the automatic weapons of Kopassus soldiers. Cristalis's account of their arrest provides a personalized glimpse into security operations in Timor during the occupation. Yet the tale concludes with a surprising analysis: "It was hard not to agree with Jill's [Joliffe] suspicion that we were victims of a set-up, and betrayal from within the Timorese resistance. . . . Like other such movements around the world, East Timor's was beset by factionalism. Jill had been involved so long that she had become a part of it" (2002:17). In this case, the betrayal may initially have been invisible. They viscerally experienced the conditions of terror and abuse that structured daily life for most Timorese during the Indonesian occupation. What they may not have experienced (at that time) was that their arrest and detention resulted from a betrayal within the resistance.

This synopsis emphasizes the importance of representing violence and the power to perpetrate violence in the international arena. It also suggests critical elements in the conditions of possibility for the representation of systematic mass violence. Protocols of human rights reporting have established violations and evidentiary procedures: their language, lack of context, and corporate author signal objectivity. Photographs and film perform a similar function; they allow audiences to witness firsthand violence perpetrated in secret conditions. The photographs' content typically overwhelmed any reflection on the conditions of their production. Support networks disseminated images and testimony to an audience prepared to make sense of them. Campaign materials provided a context and particular meaning for images, as well as suggesting follow-up actions.

Clearly distinguished protagonists—the repressive state forces, the heroic resistance, and the innocent victims—structured the conflict discourse. In this context certain images would not make sense: a smiling soldier handing over evidence to a member of the resistance; or members of the resistance setting up filmmakers who have taken great risks to document their struggle. What made the representation of violence possible in these instances simultaneously produced violence. Collaboration and betrayal animated state operations to eradicate the resistance.[34]

Transitional institutions did not address collaboration and betrayal between and within the two forces. A cell system structured the resistance throughout the occupation. It was hard to know who was doing what for the cause. Postindependence institutions have not clarified this matter. The constantly repeated refrain "it was a time of war" implies spontaneous, emotional actions, not calculated decisions, secret acts, and established networks of information and resources. During the occupation the TNI relied on its informants, as well as on festering resentments initiated by political conflicts and extended by betrayal, to implement its operations and to translate state violence into so-called horizontal violence. The statement "Timorese were victims of other Timorese" fails to address how this dynamic created conditions in which mass violence became possible and was perpetrated. This official statement also fails to account for or resolve this complicated dynamic. While such a statement may have been intended to encourage forgetting certain aspects of the past, especially by constricting the social space available for recalling them, I learned in my interviews that issues of betrayal remained prominent in people's recollections of the past and interpretations of independence.

Betrayal and collaboration both occur through the figure of the *mohu*, a kind of informer. A series of interviews revealed the doubleness of the *mohu* and emphasized how difficult it was for individual experiences to match the narratives prioritized by governments, officials, and others charged with creating a successful transition.

I met one woman at a mutual friend's workplace. She had come from her office dressed in a gray two-piece suit, shiny silver along the seams where it had been repeatedly ironed. She sat on the edge of her chair, self-consciously pulling the hem of her skirt to her knees and sliding her feet further into her leather shoes. She told me she had only finished elementary school and had spent much of the Indonesian occupation in the forest working with the resistance. I asked her about her family and her experiences with the resistance. She mentioned that her husband worked for Indonesian intelligence. Many other people had indicated that relatives had worked for the Indonesians to protect their families, so I was surprised when she subsequently commented that he had ordered her torture. Our conversation drifted through other topics. The next day we met again. I asked her if she could tell me more about her husband's work as an intelligence agent and if he was a *mohu*. She sighed and said many people said her husband had helped them in 1999 in the refugee camps. Her husband had at one time worked for the resistance, but he was arrested, spared by a relative who worked with the Indonesian forces, and trained as an informer. Eventually she realized that he had become a "mastermind" for the Indonesian intelligence. In the course of the conversation she emphasized the complexity of the *mohu*. There were, she said, "two different kinds of *mohu*: those who tell the TNI who to kill and others who work [with them] and then tell us the Indonesian plan. [They tell us] you have to leave here or you will be arrested." In some cases survival depended on knowing the difference. "The TNI assisted the Falintil in significant ways." She emphasized: "During the 1980s we would all have died if it were not for the good-heartedness of some of the TNI who didn't see, or pretended they did not see, us." She cataloged the contributions of various military branches for several hours. "Lots of people wanted to help me from Brimob [mobile police brigade], Kopassus, and policemen, even civil servants. They all knew that at some time Timor would become independent." In her analysis the rightness of the resistance motivated non-Timorese members of the security apparatus to contribute. She was not unaware that the soldiers were betraying their government. She commented: "One [member of the] Brimob wanted to sell explosives and bullets; he wanted to meet the people in the forest because he also wanted to contribute. He is a two-headed person. He doesn't like his own government." Our conversation never considered the possibility that this assistance might have been part of a strategy, just as her interactions with the military units were mediated by complex strategies and goals. Official institutions have failed to consider these gray areas and ambiguities that animated and extended the violence.

INSTITUTIONS, MEMORY, AND CORRUPTION

The failure of transitional institutions to resolve the dynamics of collaboration and betrayal threatens to corrupt Timorese institutions and to extend a dangerous logic of the past. One person said, "Lots of people we called *mohu* before are now in the [government]." Others also noted that some members of the new Timorese armed forces (FDTL) had suspicious pasts. A famous fighter, "the bravest in battle," was now "very stressed," even mentally unstable, because of this issue. It is precisely the institutions of governance in the new nation that are supposed to guarantee the truth of who worked for, and against, the resistance. Many people I spoke to were confused that past efforts had not been rewarded with positions in the postindependence government.

Memory resides in daily practices and in everyday lived realities. Institutions structure the possibilities for individual lives and the terms of remembering the past in the present. Each repetition of a politically expedient narrative that does not align with past experiences corrupts memory at the same time that it diminishes the social legitimacy of new institutions. Transitional institutions, especially tribunals, not only judge the truth about past violence but also endeavor to make sense of traumatic events, placing facts into narratives. Institutions endorse logics that may make it impossible, or politically dangerous, to recall certain memories and to ask certain questions about what happened in the past.

Corruption was a problem in the Indonesian regime and now threatens the new regime. More attention must be paid to the relationship between institutional corruption and the corruptions of memory. Current institutions may be tainted by memories that fall outside official narrations at the same time that memories, both individual and social, may be corrupted by current institutional practices and policies. Comments on the process of representing violence in Timor disclose critical silences in transitional institutions. A TNI that cooperates with its enemy to sustain an independence struggle obviously contradicts the Indonesian civil war narrative. Holding the TNI accountable for providing assistance as well as for systematic killings lies beyond the scope of existing legal institutions, but it may be critical in preventing further campaigns to rewrite genocidal violence as civil war or as horizontal violence in other parts of Indonesia, especially in Aceh and Papua.

It is beyond the scope of this essay to consider Indonesian memories; however, an analysis of Indonesian print media, testimonial accounts about East Timor, and subsequent policy debates and decisions suggests that systematic repression and state violence were forgotten as anxieties about national disintegration were recalled. The failure of the Indonesian ad hoc tribunal to hold the TNI accountable is widely acknowledged. The legal maneuvering by which systematic state killing was rewritten as civil war has not yet been fully explored. The conditions of possibility for genocidal killing have not been accounted for either politically or judicially. Failure to understand these conditions may mean that current and future Indonesian state violence will again be rewritten as civil war. Examining the role of collaboration and betrayal in the violence does not diminish the responsibility of the Indonesian armed forces for the systematic campaigns of violence and repression they perpetrated during the decades of occupation. In fact, such an analysis may come closer to doing justice to Timor's past and to preventing future state violence in Indonesia.

CONCLUSION

Finding evidence of genocide has challenged activists since the term was coined (Power 2003). In the aftermath of the Holocaust advocates focused their efforts on demonstrating that the unimaginable had occurred and on developing legal tools to hold perpetrators accountable. In subsequent genocides, graphic images of victims and accounts of torture, repression, and systematic killing have played an important role in campaigns for intervention.

The term *genocide* performs crucial legal and political work. Indeed, in the case of East Timor, political advocacy that ultimately resulted in the deployment of peacekeeping forces likely depended on declarations that genocide was occurring in East Timor. Indonesian activists and reformers were eager to use the Timor case to end military impunity. Indonesian lawmakers included the concept of genocide in the legislation that established the human rights tribunal. The credible Indonesian investigative commission found evidence of crimes against humanity but not of genocide. International analysts have debated whether the violence in Timor in fact constituted genocide. Indonesian lawmakers excluded war crimes from the jurisdiction of the tribunal. Excluding war crimes ensured that military violence against state enemies would be exempt in future cases. The failure to establish that mass killings in Timor qualified as genocide severely limited opportunities to hold perpetrators accountable.

Declaring mass violence to be genocide can result in dramatic political action. However, the context for political and discursive struggles over what counts as genocide has shifted since the term was coined. The imperative to end deniability once meant documenting the occurrence of the unimaginable. More recently, mass killing and genocidal violence have been widely broadcast and acknowledged. The violence is no longer unimaginable or deniable, but the goal of "never again" remains unmet. Images and evidence of violence acts may be subject to renarration as shifting political contexts demand the reinterpretation of evidence, and technical arguments may be made that such acts do not constitute genocide.

The prevention of and accountability for genocide requires a nuanced understanding of the conditions in which genocide becomes possible and occurs. Anthropological methods are well suited to capturing the complex political, legal, symbolic, and social dynamics that contribute to genocidal violence and to subsequent legal and political impunity. Accounts detailing the complexity of collaboration and betrayal complicate the demands of advocacy strategies for unambiguously differentiated perpetrators and victims engaged in documented genocidal violence. Such accounts, however, offer great insight concerning the development of the conditions in which violence occurs and, therefore, opportunities for prevention and advocacy. The term *genocide* when first coined represented a legal innovation;

now, a better understanding of the conditions for genocide may contribute to more effective innovations and strategies for prevention and accountability. The successful rewriting of systematic state violence as civil war in Timor suggests that the challenge of representing genocide may now have more to do with issues of rewritability than of deniability.

NOTES

1. The literature on transitional justice and truth commissions is extensive. For further reading, see Hayner 2001; Kritz 1995; Malamud-Goti 1996; Rotberg 2000; Popkin and Roht-Arriaza 1995; Feher 1999; Neier 1999; Crocker 2000.
2. On the relationship between narration and trauma, see Caruth 1995; on the possibilities of "restorative justice" and collective narration, see Minow 1998.
3. For debates on the role of trials in writing history, see: Douglas 2001; Osiel 1997.
4. Of the extensive literature on collective memory, see, e.g., Halbwachs 1992; Sturken 1997; Antze and Lambek 1996; Bal, Crewe, and Spitzer 1999; Jellin 2003.
5. Indonesian rule over East Timor was not recognized internationally. For the documentation and analysis of the Indonesian occupation and Timorese resistance, see Aditjondro 1995; Gunn 1997; Budiardjo 1984; Carey 1995; Jardine 1999; Taylor 1999.
6. The failure of the transitional institutions was not a failure to expose Indonesia's role nor simply the failure to hold Indonesia accountable for its role in the violence; rather, it was a refusal to acknowledge or hold accountable the main actors in the face of common knowledge of the leading role the TNI played in creating and arming the anti-independence militias (even before the referendum was agreed).
7. This account, therefore, is not "neutral"; for a critique of neutrality, see Drexler, 2008.
8. The new nation refers to itself as Timor-Leste. Historical documents generated use the former name, East Timor. I have used East Timor throughout this essay when referring to events in the past and Timor-Leste for current references.
9. On the invasion, see Nevins 2005; Taylor 1999. For a discussion of Soeharto's rise to power in the Cold War context, see Roosa 2006.
10. Based on recently released documents that detail meetings between Henry Kissinger and Soeharto in Jakarta the day before Indonesia's invasion, Geoffrey Robinson has written that Gerald Ford gave his assurances to Soeharto that "the United States would 'understand' if Indonesia deemed it 'necessary to take rapid or drastic action' in East Timor" (2002:163). Robinson further notes that these transcripts reveal that the United States bypassed the complications of using U.S.-supplied weapons to attack another country, encouraging the Indonesians to construe the attack as self-defense. While U.S. support was less official, Australia granted de jure recognition to the annexation. Australia profited in the form of lucrative contracts for exploitation of oil and mineral resources. The division of this resource wealth remains problematic as Australia and Timor attempt to negotiate an equitable contract for

the Timor Gap. Joseph Nevins (2002) documents the complicity of a number of countries in the years following the occupation through the 1999 violence.

11. On October 16, 1975, five international journalists were killed in the town of Balibo as they reported on the invasion of East Timor by Indonesian forces.

12. For an excellent analysis of how this incident and patterns of violence are related to changes within the military command structure, see Kammen 1999.

13. Santa Cruz was the name of a neighborhood in Dili where a large cemetery was located. Thousands of Timorese marched from the Church to the gravesite of a pro-independence youth killed by the military. Pro-independence banners were unfurled at what was considered one of the first mass demonstrations against Jakarta. Soldiers blocked the roads and shot at the crowd, killing more than two hundred and fifty people. At the time and according to later reports, many more of the injured taken to the hospital were also killed.

14. In April 1999, the police were separated from the armed forces (Angakatan Bersenjata Republik Indonesia, ABRI) and the military was renamed TNI (Tentara Nasional Indonesia).

15. For an analysis of the role of the international community in this and other decisions, see Nevins 2005 and Robinson 2002.

16. The results were 334,580 for independence and 94,388 for special autonomy within Indonesia.

17. Tanter, van Klinken, and Ball 2006 contains the most complete documentation of various militia groups, their histories, and their relationships to specific military units.

18. The Indonesian Commission for the Investigation of Human Rights Violations in East Timor (Komisi Penyelidik Pelanggaran Hak Asasi Manusia di Timor Timur, KPP-HAM) estimates are significantly lower, only 250,000. See the KPP-HAM report, reproduced in Tanter, van Klinken, and Ball 2006.

19. Estimates of the number killed vary; most reports of and on the institutions under discussion reiterate figures between 1,300 and 1,500. The CAVR final report analyzes a range of data to determine the number of victims. In many cases quantifying mass violence is politically charged and contentious. In Timor debates over numbers have been far less significant than the problem of accounting for widely documented and acknowledged murder and destruction.

20. In the five months following the referendum, the Indonesian Commission for the Investigation of Human Rights Violations in East Timor (KPP-HAM) produced a report linking violence in Timor to the highest echelons of the TNI, including the commander in chief, General Wiranto. International audiences and human rights organizations praised the efficient and credible work of this commission. Subsequently, international criticism of Indonesia was reduced. It is likely that the military cooperated with the KPP-HAM only to ensure that there would be no international tribunal.

21. Particularly contentious issues included issues of nonretroactivity and of crimes of omission.

22. Of the 670 cases documented in the KPP-HAM report, the ad hoc tribunal investigated only 5.

23. Shoshana Felman (2002) provides an incisive analysis of two "trials of the century" as "veritable theaters of justice."

24. The court convicted only six of the eighteen people tried. Eurico Guiterres, a notorious militia leader, has remained free pending appeal. Only the former Timorese governor, Abilio Soares, has served any time in jail.

25. Of the 183 people indicted in the ten priority cases, 168 remain in Indonesia. The ten priority cases were: April 6, 1999, Massacre at the Liquisa Church complex: Armed Besi Merah Putih militia attacked refugees seeking protection in the church, leading to the death of about 30 people. Indonesian police and military removed and disposed of the victims' bodies; April 12, 1999. Murder of Cailaco villagers: The military subdistrict command and Halilintar militia kidnapped six individuals in Cailaco and brought them to the military command resort and then to Manuel Soares Gama's house where they were murdered. The same day there was retaliation, believed to be done by Falintil. Gama and two TNI members were killed and four wounded. The following day, the Halilintar militia retaliated by capturing six local citizens who were tortured and publicly executed at the subdistrict military command; April 17, 1999, attack on the home of Manuel Carrascalao: Five thousand pro-integration supporters gathered in Dili to confirm the appointment of Eurico Gutteres as the commander of the Aitarak militia. Besi Merah Putih and Aitarak militias attacked the home of Manuel Carrascalao and refugees from Liquisa, Alas, and Turiscai who had sought protection at the house. Fifteen people were killed, including Carrascalao's son. The 50 surviving refugees including National Council of Timorese Resistance (CNRT) leader Leandro Isac were taken to the police headquarters; September 5, 1999, attack on the Dili diocese: Following the referendum security in Dili had broken down. Despite the fact that TNI and POLRI (Indonesian police) were patrolling the streets, militias dressed in black with Aitarak printed on their shirts attacked refugees at the Dili diocese—25 people were killed; September 6, 1999, attack on the home of Bishop Belo: About five thousand refugees had sought protection at the bishop's complex. A TNI lieutenant colonel evacuated Belo to the police headquarters. Subsequently militia groups, including those wearing Aitarak uniforms, attacked the refugees and forced them to leave the complex, which was then burned. At least two people were killed in this incident; September 4, 1999, massive destruction and murders in Maliana: Maliana is one of the closest points in East Timor to the Indonesian border. Following the referendum vote Maliana was controlled by the military, police, and Dadurus Merah Putih and Halilintar militias; UNAMET and pro-independence supporters were harassed. Refugees attempting to flee to West Timor were stopped at checkpoints, and many were said to have been disappeared. On September 4 about 80 percent of the buildings in Maliana were destroyed; September 8, 1999, Maliana police station killings: Dadurus Merah Putih militias killed refugees in the Maliana police station with direct support from TNI

and POLRI. At least three people were killed; September 4–6, 1999, massacre in the Suai Church complex: Following the killing of a high school student by the Laksaur militia and members of the TNI in the Debos area, villagers fled to the Suai Church, which already contained other refugees. Laksaur militia and the TNI burned down residences and government buildings in Suai. On September 6 villagers were evicted from their homes. Around midday, several militias together with the TNI and POLRI attacked refugees at the church. Regional civilian (the Regent) and military commanders (Suai subdistric military commander) led the attack. Priests and refugees, at least 50 people, were killed; refugees who tried to flee the compound were shot by military personnel positioned outside the complex. Corpses were disposed under military direction. One mass grave has been exhumed; September 21, 1999, murder of the Dutch journalist Sander Thoenes: Thoenes's body was found in Becora, East Dili, on September 22. The day he had arrived in Dili he had gone to Becora on a motorcycle with a Timorese man. The motorcycle was stopped by three motorcycles, a car, and a truck. The attackers wore TNI uniforms and carried automatic weapons. This was one of many violent incidents perpetrated by the TNI Battalion 745 as it crossed from Los Palos on the far eastern end of Timor to Indonesian West Timor after the ballot results were announced; September 25, 1999, killing of religious figures in Los Palos: The Tim Alfa militia, under the direction of Joni Marques, attacked a car of journalists and clergy driving from Los Palos to Baucau. Thirteen people were killed.

26. Of the 391 individuals charged in the 95 indictments filed by the SCU, 280 of the accused remain at large in Indonesia.

27. Observers criticized the special panels for not upholding human rights standards for the accused, frequently noting that the defense remains woefully underresourced. Critical analyses inspired concrete improvements, particularly in terms of providing minimal translation and transcription facilities for the court. For a review of the panels on legal grounds, see JSMP 2002; Linton 2001; Strohmeyer 2001; Katzenstein 2003.

28. UNTAET established the CAVR with three main functions: truth seeking, community reconciliation, and recommendations to the government (Regulation 2001/10).

29. I have analyzed the CAVR because, unlike the other two institutions, its proceedings have not received widely publicized international attention.

30. While this essay was in production, the CAVR released its report *Chega!* This report provides detailed documentation of patterns of violence and makes strong demands for justice. I have analyzed this report in a subsequent talk (Drexler 2007).

31. Over one thousand deponents gave statements to participate in the PRK process. Eighty-four of them failed the prosecutor's review, but they were not indicted for crimes that the PRK process could not address.

32. If further information reveals the deponent to have been involved in more serious crimes, the latter are processed by the court system. Despite initial concerns that communities would demand unreasonable acts of reconciliation, very few did.

33. The CAVR final report explored this dynamic. It remains to be seen how information from that report will enter public discourse.

34. For discussions of the Indonesian intelligence operations during the occupation, see Taylor 1999; Tanter 2001; Moore 2001. For an excellent analysis of related political metaphors in current Timorese discourse, see Kammen 2003.

REFERENCES

Aditjondro, George J.
1994   In the Shadow of Mount Ramelau: The Impact of the Occupation of East
           Timor. Leiden: Indonesian Documentation and Information Center
           (INDOC).

Ajidarma, Seno Gumira
1994   Saksi mata. Yogyakarta, Indonesia: Bentang.
1996   Jazz: Parfum dan insiden. Yogyakarta, Indonesia: Bentang.

Amnesty International (AI)
1991   East Timor: The Santa Cruz Massacre. London: Amnesty International.
1992   Indonesia/East Timor—Santa Cruz: The Government Response. London:
           Amnesty International.

Anderson, Benedict
1995   East Timor and Indonesia: Some Implications. In East Timor at the
           Crossroads: The Forging of a Nation. Peter Carey and Carter G. Bentley,
           eds. Pp. 137–147. Honolulu: University of Hawai'i Press.

Antze, Paul, and Michael Lambek, eds.
1996   Tense Past: Cultural Essays in Trauma and Memory. New York: Routledge.

Bal, Mieke, Jonathan Crewe, and Leo Spitzer, eds.
1999   Acts of Memory: Cultural Recall in the Present. Hanover, NH: University
           Press of New England.

Budiardjo, Carmel, and Liem Soei Liong
1984   The War against East Timor. London: Zed.

Carey, Peter, and Carter G. Bentley, eds.
1995   East Timor at the Crossroads: The Forging of a Nation. Honolulu: Uni-
           versity of Hawai'i Press.

Caruth, Cathy
1995   Trauma: Explorations in Memory. Baltimore: Johns Hopkins University
           Press.

Cohen, David
2002   Seeking Justice on the Cheap: Is the East Timor Tribunal Really a Model
           for the Future? Asia Pacific Issues: Analysis from the East West Center
           61:1–8.

Cristalis, Irena

2002   Bitter Dawn: East Timor, a People's Story. London: Zed.

Crocker, David A.

2000   Truth Commissions, Transitional Justice, and Civil Society. *In* Truth v. Justice: The Morality of Truth Commissions. Robert I. Rotberg and Dennis Thompson, eds. Pp. 99–121. Princeton: Princeton University Press.

Douglas, Lawrence

2001   The Memory of Judgment: Making Law and History in the Trials of the Holocaust. New Haven: Yale University Press.

Drexler, Elizabeth F.

2007   The Failure of International Justice in Indonesia and East Timor. Paper presented at Rutgers University Workshop on Local Justice, Newark, NJ, April 19.

2008   Aceh, Indonesia: Securing the Insecure State. Philadelphia: University of Pennsylvania Press.

Feher, Michel

1999   Terms of Reconciliation. *In* Human Rights in Political Transitions: Gettysburg to Bosnia. Carla Hesse and Robert Post, eds. Pp. 325–338. New York: Zone.

Felman, Shoshana

2002   The Juridical Unconscious: Trials and Traumas in the Twentieth Century. Cambridge: Harvard University Press.

Gunn, Geoffrey C.

1997   East Timor and the United Nations: The Case for Intervention. Lawrenceville, NJ: Red Sea Press.

Halbwachs, Maurice

1992   On Collective Memory. Lewis A. Caser, ed. and trans. Chicago: University of Chicago Press.

Hayner, Priscilla B.

2001   Unspeakable Truths: Confronting State Terror and Atrocity. New York: Routledge.

Jardine, Matthew

1999   East Timor: Genocide in Paradise. Monroe, ME: Odonian.

Jasmi, Khairul

2002   Eurico Guterres: Melintas Badai Politik Indonesia. Jakarta: Sinar Harapan.

Jellin, Elizabeth

2003   State Repression and the Labors of Memory. Judy Rein and Marcial Godoy-Anativia, trans. Minneapolis: University of Minnesota Press.

Judicial System Monitoring Programme (JSMP).

2002   The General Prosecutor v. Joni Marques and Nine Others (the Los Palos
            Case). Dili: JSMP Report.

Kammen, Douglas

1999   Notes on the Transformation of the East Timor Military Command and
            Its Implications for Indonesia. Indonesia 67:61–76.

2003   Master-Slave, Traitor-Nationalist, Opportunist-Oppressed: Political
            Metaphors in East Timor. Indonesia 76:69–85.

Katzenstein, Suzanne

2003   Searching for Justice in East Timor. Harvard Human Rights Journal
            16(6):245–278.

Komisi Penyelidik Pelanggaran Hak Asasi Manusia di Timor Timur, The Commission
            for Investigation of Human Rights Violations in East Timor
            (KPP-HAM)

2000   Executive Summary Report. Jakarta: Komnas-HAM.

Kritz, Neil J., ed.

1995   Transitional Justice: How Emerging Democracies Reckon with Former
            Regimes. Washington: United States Institute of Peace Press.

LaCapra, Dominick

2001   Writing History, Writing Trauma. Baltimore: Johns Hopkins University
            Press.

Lembaga Studi dan Advokasi Masyarakat, Institute for Policy Research and Advocacy
            (ELSAM)

2003   The Failure of Leipzig Repeated in Jakarta: Final Assessment of the
            Human Rights Ad-Hoc Tribunal for East Timor. Jakarta: ELSAM Lembaga
            Studi dan Advokasi Masyarakat.

Linton, Suzannah

2001   Rising from the Ashes: The Creation of a Viable Criminal Justice System
            in East Timor. Melbourne University Law Review 5.

Makarim, Zacky Anwar, Glenny Kairupan, Andreas Sugiyanto, and Ibnu Fatah,
            eds.

2002   Hari-hari terakhir Timor Timur: Sebuah kesaksian. Jakarta: PT Sportif
            Media Informasindos.

Malamud-Goti, Jamie

1996   Game without End: State Terror and the Politics of Justice. Norman:
            University of Oklahoma Press.

Minow, Martha

1998   Between Vengeance and Forgiveness: Facing History after Genocide and
            Mass Violence. Boston: Beacon.

Mizuno, Kumiko

2003   Indonesian Politics and the Issue of Justice in East Timor. *In* Governance in Indonesia: Challenges Facing the Megawati Presidency. Hadi Soesastro, Anthony L. Smith, and Han Mui Ling, eds. Pp. 114–164. Singapore: Institute of Southeast Asian Studies.

Moore, Samuel

2001   The Indonesian Military's Last Years in East Timor: An Analysis of Secret Documents. Indonesia 72:7–44.

Neier, Aryeh

1999   Rethinking Truth, Justice, and Guilt after Bosnia and Rwanda. *In* Human Rights in Political Transitions: Gettysburg to Bosnia. Carla Hesse and Robert Post, eds. Pp. 39–52. New York: Zone.

Nevins, Joseph

2002   An Analysis of International Complicity in Indonesia's Crimes. Asian Survey: A Bimonthly Review of Contemporary Asian Affairs 42(4):623–641.

2005   A Not-So-Distant Horror: Mass Violence in East Timor. Ithaca: Cornell University Press.

Osiel, Mark

1997   Mass Atrocity, Collective Memory, and the Law. New Brunswick, NJ: Transaction.

Popkin, Margaret, and Naomi Roht-Arriaza

1995   Truth as Justice: Investigatory Commissions in Latin America. *In* Transitional Justice: How Emerging Democracies Reckon with Former Regimes. Neil J. Kritz, ed. Pp. 262–289. Washington: United States Institute of Peace Press.

Power, Samantha

2003   A Problem from Hell: America and the Age of Genocide. New York: Perennial.

Robinson, Geoffrey

2002   "If You Leave Us Here, We Will Die." *In* The New Killing Fields: Massacre and the Politics of Intervention. Nicolaus Mills and Kira Bruner, eds. Pp. 159–184. New York: Basic Books.

Roosa, John

2006   Pretext for Mass Murder: The September 30th Movement and Suharto's Coup D'État in Indonesia. Madison: University of Wisconsin Press.

Rotberg, Robert I.

2000   Truth Commissions and the Provision of Truth, Justice, and Reconciliation. *In* Truth v. Justice: The Morality of Truth Commissions. Robert I.

Rotberg and Dennis Thompson, eds. Pp. 3–21. Princeton: Princeton University Press.

Shackleton, Shirley
1995   Planting a Tree in Balibo: A Journey to East Timor. *In* East Timor at the Crossroads: The Forging of a Nation. Peter Carey and Carter G. Bentley, eds. Pp. 109–119. Honolulu: University of Hawai'i Press.

Somomoelijono, Suhardi
2001   Menguak konspirasi internasional di Timor Timur: Sebuah analisis yuridis. Jakarta: Lembaga Studi Advokasi Independensi Peradilan Indonesia.

Stahn, Carsten
2001   Accomodating Individual Criminal Responsibility and National Reconciliation: The UN-Truth Commission for East Timor. American Journal of International Law 95(4):952–966.

Strohmeyer, Hansjorg
2001   Collapse and Reconstruction of a Judicial System: The United Nations Missions in Kosovo and East Timor. American Journal of International Law 95(1):46–63.

Sturken, Marita
1997   Tangled Memories: The Vietnam War, the AIDS Epidemic, and the Politics of Remembering. Berkeley: University of California Press.

Suratman, Tono
2002   Untuk negaraku: Sebuah potret perjuangan di Timor Timur. Jakarta: Sinar Harapan.

Tanter, Richard
2001   East Timor and the Crisis of the Indonesian Intelligence State. *In* Bitter Flowers, Sweet Flowers: East Timor, Indonesia, and the World Community. Richard Tanter, Mark Selden, and Stephen R Shalom, eds. Pp. 189–208. Lanham, MD: Rowman and Littlefield.

Tanter, Richard, Gerry van Klinken, and Desmond Ball, eds.
2006   Masters of Terror: Indonesia's Military and Violence in East Timor. New York: Rowman and Littlefield.

Taylor, John G.
1999   East Timor: The Price of Freedom. London: Zed.

Wiranto
2003   Beraksi di tengah badai. Jakarta: Institute for Democracy of Indonesia.

Conerly Casey

8   MEDIATED HOSTILITY

Media, Affective Citizenship, and Genocide in Northern Nigeria

On May 11, 2004, Muslim *'yan daba* (ward gang members) and *almajirai* (Qur'anic students), living in the city of Kano, the commercial and religious center of northern Nigeria, brutally murdered their neighbors and fellow residents, referring to them as *arna* (unbelievers), *Kiristoci* (Christians), and *ba'ki* (strangers).[1] The crisis followed several months of communal violence in Plateau State that Muslim residents of Kano felt had been condoned through the inaction of the Christian governor of the state, Joshua Dariye, and the Christian president of Nigeria, Olusegun Obasanjo. Local media detailed the horrifying experiences of Muslim Hausa victims who had returned to Kano along with the bodies of their dead relatives. There were passionate and vivid international components—protests over the killing of Palestinian leaders by the Israeli army and over the brutal treatment of prisoners in Iraq by the U.S. army—that culminated in a public burning of the effigies of Ariel Sharon and George W. Bush. The language of Muslims and Christians, "indigenes" and "strangers," used to describe the identities of victims and killers, the spiritual and material power associated with them, and the spatial patterning of the violence led to a conflation of identity, morality, and security, with Nigerian Christians held responsible for the actions of Plateau residents and the Nigerian, U.S., and Israeli presidents.

National and transnational media have become the terrains on which new diasporic, micronational, and regional "affective citizenships" are forged, deployed, and contested. I use the term *affective citizenships* to denote displays of feeling about belonging to, and having agency within, the state. In northern Nigeria, CNN, the BBC (which also airs in Hausa), Nigerian Television, Al Jazeera, and a number of other Middle Eastern stations seek to authorize their stations as legitimate, central brokers of political power—the centers of democracy, of Islam, and of the Nigerian nation-state. Within Nigeria local media reflect and constitute the political sentiments of majority ethnic groups (the Hausa, Yoruba, and Igbo) and religions (Islam and Christianity), of majority/minority relations of power embedded in histories of political violence.

In this essay I consider the resonances of media and affective citizenships, which in Nigeria derive from colonial and postcolonial citizenships based on ethnicity, religion, and region, and the antagonisms between and among the killers and victims, subjects and objects of the May 11 violence. Drawing on Allen Feldman's (1991:2) concept of "historiographic surfaces" and their relations to violence, I consider media places for remembering, reenacting, producing, imitating, and reproducing power, as well as for making power an animated material force. As "historiographic surfaces," media are "sites of legitimation and authorization [that] suppress historicity through linear, teleological, eschatological, or progressive temporalities" (Feldman 1991:2). Media are also what Geoffrey White (2005) refers to as "emotive institutions," which channel and repeat affective institutional information, fracturing and instantiating the appearance of continuity—temporal, spatial, and emotional—between political centers and the *talakawa* (commoners; poor). Media insert and collapse space, so that Kano, the center of Islamic politics and religion in northern Nigeria, and Jos, the northern center of Christian politics and religion, a four-hour drive to the southeast, become distant, alien sites of human existence *and* dangerously close, locations of potentially evil others and of a located possibility of alien, migrant invasion.

I evaluate the relations of antagonism between perpetrators and their victims as mediated, historical, and social entanglements of identity, memory, emotion, and agency (Antze and Lambek 1996; Cole 2001; Hinton 2005; Huyssen 2001; Stoller 1995; Taussig 1991; Volkan 1998). To some readers acknowledging the grievances of killers may itself be immoral, even complicit in violence, a complex problem in a world in which victimized children and teenagers often become killers. While I in no way condone the violence that Muslim youths committed on May 11, it is crucial for the survival of ethnic and religious minorities to ask at what point we recognize victimhood and intervene on behalf of victims. Who has a right to protection against violence? Who should and must defend victims? How do our own sensorial memories—our "truths" of violence, remembered, reenacted, and (re)experienced via the media—amplify hostility, fueling genocidal massacres, and generational transmissions of violence?[2] In the weeks preceding the May 11 violence, what media characters and story lines dovetailed with Muslim Hausa historical perceptions of violence that, accompanied by visceral memories, intensified the polarization of Nigerian political identities? How did local, national, and global representations of violence, ideas, and enactments of visceral memory and the supposed truths of violence—via assertions of passionate political authority, legitimacy, social justice, and belonging—ignite violent forms of affective citizenship and the slaughter of thousands of innocent people?

GENOCIDE AND COLONIAL CONSCIOUSNESS

Since the 1960s, when most European colonies gained independence, there has been ongoing debate about whether to equate colonialism with genocide, a perspective most persuasively argued by Jean-Paul Sartre (1968), who considered colonial state-forming massacres, the colonial use of violence to maintain authority, and the systematic, pervasive attacks on cultures of local populations to fit the definition of genocide—to be "acts committed with intent to destroy, in whole or in part, a national, ethnical, racial or religious group" (see the United Nations Convention on the Prevention and Punishment of the Crime of Genocide, 1948, for the complete definition).

Views opposing the equation of colonialism and genocide arose in relation to the definition of genocide, particularly the problems of establishing the colonial intent to commit genocide, of defining what numbers, proportions, or sections of a population constitute a "part," and of determining international criminal jurisdiction when sovereign states are often the main perpetrators of genocide (Lemkin 2002; Kuper 2002). While Leo Kuper (2002:51), in his analysis of Sartre's perspective, suggests that Sartre overstates the uniformity of mass violence and the intention to commit genocide across colonialisms, he cites many examples of this intent in the African and Asian histories of colonialism. Kuper finds the "slaughter of the Herero by the German rulers of South West Africa in 1904 . . . among the most exterminatory and horrifying of the reprisals for rebellion," while postcolonial "struggles for power between Hutu and Tutsi in Rwanda and Burundi, and between mainland Africans and Arabs in Zanzibar . . . partition, as in India, and repression of secessionary movements, as in Bangladesh, and some would say as in Nigeria, have taken a genocidal form" (2002:52–53).

Kuper refers to the Nigerian government's massacre and systematic starvation of Biafran secessionist Igbo during the Nigerian civil war as genocide. Nigerian memories of genocidal massacres, and the historical perceptions that accompany them, however, are far more extensive and complicated. Nigerians of diverse backgrounds tend to agree with Sartre's position—that British colonial massacres of ethnic, racial, and religious groups in what is now Nigeria constituted genocide—yet there is far less consensus about other massacres such as the one of Biafran Igbo secessionists, the massacres of ethnic minorities such as Ogoni who refused to join Igbo secessionists (Bastian 2000; Saro-Wiwa 1992), or the Nigerian military slaughter of Ogoni who protested against Shell Oil (Bastian 2000; Saro-Wiwa 1992). These massacres, and other, less internationally broadcast killings, have complex political contexts that, forgotten or repressed in personal memories, or denuded in media representations, strengthen prejudices and identifications with victimhood, while reinforcing stereotypes of Africans as unruly and violent.[3]

From the fifteenth century on, guided by ethnocentric, paternalistic ideas of modern civilization, Europeans interacted with West Africans for "religious evangelization, as a source of slaves, and ultimately as a resource to be gobbled up by the aggressive imperial expansion of the late nineteenth century" (Falola 1998:50–51). British colonial administrators artificially constructed a British colonial state from politically neighboring but autonomous polities and peoples, ranging from empires to "stateless groups" (Crowder 1978; Falola 1998; Levin 1997; Tamuno 1972). In 1898 Flora Shaw suggested the name "Nigeria" for the British colonial state, though policy varied considerably from one territory to the next with the formation of administrative districts, political boundaries, and the local form of administrative rule based on "convenience and political ambition" (Levin 1997:136). The British takeover of the Royal Niger Company in 1900, indirect rule as the British governing principle in northern Nigeria, and the consolidation of British colonial power under the Sokoto Caliphate framed the regional motif of British colonial policy (Falola 1998; Last 1967; Levin 1997).

The first boundary between north and south, in 1909, separated the Tiv, grouping together Tiv south of the boundary with their political enemies under one district and native court (Levin 1997; Tamuno 1972). Debates in Nigeria arose about administrative jurisdictions, for instance, about whether territorial boundaries should be "racial boundaries," marked by kinship, ethnicity, culture, and language, or by local jurisdiction, recognizing political conquests and local exchange relations (Levin 1997:136). Colonial administrative policy fostered the consolidation of ethnic, religious, and regional identities by separating the predominantly Muslim Hausa north of the country, the Muslim and Christian Yoruba west, and the Christian Igbo east into three administrative units, lumping Nigeria's over 300 ethnic minorities with ethnic majorities in their regions. In the ethnically and religiously diverse Middle Belt, whose inhabitants were arbitrarily folded into colonial administrative units, persistent struggles to convert "pagans" to Islam and to Christianity have been a means of establishing political blocs, ethnic, religious communities with strong ties to the land and its resources (Falola 1998; Paden 1986).

British administrative policy, which Mahmood Mamdani (1996) refers to as "decentralized despotism," led to intense proselytizing and competition for political power and state resources, affectively constructing non-Muslim Hausa such as Christian Igbo as "outsiders" to the Northern Region, "strangers" to be mistrusted. According to John Paden (1971:141), "certain Ibo cultural traits seemed to take on special importance within a Hausa context, especially those traits which resisted assimilation: endogamy, maintenance of obligations in the Eastern Region, and the persistence of certain traditional religious customs among the lower classes."

The fragility of Hausa and Igbo relations persisted and worsened during the transition to independence on October 1, 1960. Nnamdi Azikiwe, the Igbo leader of the NCNC (Nigerian Council of Nigerian Citizens), a political party with widespread support in the predominantly Yoruba western region, became Nigeria's first head of state, while Abubakar Tafawa Balewa, of the NPC (Northern Peoples Congress), a Muslim Hausa, became prime minister. The political association of ethnicity and religion with political party, and the manipulation of emotive ethnic and religious symbols, emerged in the struggle for postcolonial political power (Anthony 2002;

Diamond 1983; Paden 1973). Independence brought with it, for northern Muslims, a renewed interest in world Islamic affairs, participation in grassroots Muslim brotherhoods, and efforts to reimpose shari'ah criminal codes that had been excised at independence.

On the night of January 15, 1966, Igbo and Yoruba coup leaders murdered the Hausa federal prime minister, the northern and western premiers, the federal finance minister, and senior commanding officers (Last 2000). The Nigerian military arrested the assassins but never tried them, and an Igbo, General Johnson Aguiyi-Ironsi, became military head of state. On May 24, 1966, Aguiyi-Ironsi announced plans to unify the country by abolishing existing regions, making it possible for any Nigerian to get a job, own businesses, or buy property for a house in any part of Nigeria. This opening of the predominantly Muslim Hausa north to southern Christian Igbos was particularly troubling for many northern reformist Muslims who considered Christian practices defiling. Anger and rioting erupted in northern Nigeria where Muslim Hausas, fearing increased numbers of Christian Igbos and their domination of local markets, killed hundreds of Igbos, razing their properties to the ground. In July northern military officers killed Aguiyi-Ironsi and 47 Igbo officers. Radio reports of Hausas being killed in the eastern, predominately Igbo region sparked riots and the massacre of at least seven thousand Igbos living in northern Nigeria. In 1967 Igbos began talking of the secession of the entire eastern region, Biafra, to create a safe haven for refugee Igbos that would necessarily include areas where non-Igbo minorities lived and worked (Last 2000; Paden 1973).

The Igbo succession culminating in the Nigerian civil war generated thousands of internally displaced persons, requiring state governments to manage disputes about their constitutional and pragmatic rights and protections. Under Murtala Mohammed and Obasanjo political attempts to establish a Federal Shari'ah Court of Appeal failed, but Islamic courts gained state-level appellate status, and this status was incorporated into the 1979 constitution (Williams 1997). These events, coinciding with the 1979 Iranian Revolution, emboldened reformist Muslims who considered the implementation of shari'ah criminal law a way to confront Nigeria's social, political, and economic woes. Nigeria's oil boom, in the 1970s, and the state's "petro-Capitalism" and "spoils politics," further deepened political antagonisms based on ethnic, religious, and regional interests in political power at federal and state levels (Watts 2001:99). In the 1980s and 1990s the creation of new states (Levin 1997), the convergence of religious and state politics (Falola 1998; Williams 1997), and development projects (Ocheje 1997) again displaced large numbers of Nigerians, reviving constitutional disputes over state jurisdictions and the sedimentary ethnic, religious, and regional dimensions of federal and state rights and protections.

The 1999 election and political leadership of Obasanjo, a Yoruba born-again Christian whom reformist Muslims refer to as "the U.S.'s boy," further deepened regional antagonisms between north and south, conflating identity, morality, and security with Nigerian national and world insecurities. Triggered by local and global media reports, Muslim Hausa maintain a historical record of the violence against Muslims in visceral memories of attacks on Muslims in Nigeria, in the Israeli-occupied Palestinian territories, in Afghanistan, in Iraq, and, most recently, in Lebanon. The modes of media representation that authorize and legitimate the "truths" of this violence differ among Muslims and across media forms and may validate or confront Muslim Hausa historical perceptions and feelings of hatred and hostility, leading to both consensus and fissure within Kano Muslim communities. In part, the differences between and among the majority Muslim Hausa and minority Muslim and Christian Nigerians living in Kano are related to struggles over the political and religious "truths" claimed by the Kano Muslim Hausa political elite. Elite Muslim Hausa have a strongly placed sense of time, consciousness, and origin backed by the Sokoto Caliphate and British indirect governance through Muslim Hausa elite. Their control over the political affairs of Kano State variably renders Christian and Muslim minorities as virtually invisible or as highly visible state problems. In Kano, remembered truths collide with mediated truths—media representations that legitimate and justify Muslim Hausa religion, the truth and supposedly true form of Islam, and its relation to political power, the confluence of which has significantly changed within the past two decades.

KANO, MEDIA PROPAGANDA, AND VIOLENCE

Located in the north of Nigeria toward the border with Niger, the city of Kano is the commercial and religious center of the north, serving a vast area from Burkina Faso to the west to Chad and Cameroon in the east. Kaduna is the next largest city to the south, followed by Abuja, the Nigerian capital, and then Lagos on the coast.

While the people of Kano have identified as Muslim Hausa for several centuries, aligned with one of two Sufi orders, the Qadiriyya and the Tijaniyya, Kano has incorporated large communities of Yoruba (about half of whom are Christian, the other half, Muslim) and Igbo, who are predominately Christian. It includes well-established communities of Muslim Lebanese and smaller communities of people from other parts of Nigeria and Africa, from the Middle East, Europe, and Asia.

Kano has an emir, or traditional Islamic political leader, whose ancient palace, and the Central Mosque attached to it, stands in the old city or Gari.[4] Surrounding the Gari, remnants of 20-foot-high walls built during the twelfth century create weathered hills crossed by indented walkways. Most of the 'yan daba hangouts and positions of surveillance are around the gates and walkways of their wards, points of visual power, security, and escape.

Beyond the predominately Muslim Gari lies the congested sprawl of greater Kano: more cosmopolitan by far, a maze of commercial and industrial sections interspersed between newly developed residential quarters for the rich. Two miles from the old walls is the tree-lined Government Residential Area (GRA), its colonial stone houses a contrast to newer Arabic-style residences. Unlike the Gari, this quarter boasts some ethnic, religious, and regional diversity, for it is mainly populated by the Kano middle and upper classes who work in the professions, in small business and manufacturing, and in government service. There are tensions between Muslims who live in the single-family compounds of the GRA and their extended family relatives in the Gari who complain that the Westernization and elitism associated with life in the GRA results in an unruly selfishness that separates Muslim Hausa families. No 'yan daba have historically congregated in the GRA, although in 1999–2002 the GRA became one of the main sites of political and religious protest and violence, especially violence associated with the profiling and states of emergency implemented to regulate "prostitution" and the consumption of alcohol. The other areas were neighborhoods on the outskirts of the Gari such as Doraye and Tudun Wada, whose populations are also culturally mixed but tend to be poor, and Sabon Gari (the new city), comprising a large market and residences of mainly southern Christians.

Kano is media-saturated. The most widely received television stations are the Nigerian Television Authority (NTA), CNN, the BBC, and Al Jazeera, though there are a range of African, European, and Middle Eastern stations available to Kano residents. Funded by political and religious leaders, Kano radio stations have mushroomed from one to five within the past decade, reaching even the poorest among the rural communities in Kano's metropolis. Front-page Nigerian newspaper headlines flood the streets at every major intersection, with radios blaring through the honks of unruly traffic. Wealthier Kano residents typically buy and read daily newspapers, then pass them to friends and neighbors with whom they sit to discuss major stories. I first heard about the slaughter of Muslim Hausa in Yel-wan Shendom from colleagues at Aminu Kano Teaching Hospital who had read about it in the *Daily Trust*, one of the most widely read newspapers in northern Nigeria. Because Nigerian newspapers tend to promote ethnic, religious, and regional perspectives, scholars buy three or more newspapers for a range of political positions, a practice not condoned by reformist Muslims who consider information from Christians as propaganda, publishing their own newspapers in Hausa.[5] With increased Sunni and Shia reformism in northern Nigeria, Muslim youths consider interactions with so-called outside media, international and Nigerian, as sources of knowledge *and* paths to hell. One young Muslim wrote in his personal diary:

> I don't think one can reach spiritual alrightness in this world of today. Spiritual correctness seems advisable, but unless the inner self understands this, it will be useless stopping. I am going to listen to the music I like, hoping that it will not be a source of my ruin. It seems to be a paradox, but for the meantime, it seems, I can't help it. Yes, I stopped watching TV, reading some novels. But some of these things give one more experience in life. There is no point in stopping these when the inner self yearns for them. Yes, I will watch TV to a reasonable extent. Because of *zuhudu gudun duniya* [running from unnecessary materialism] by the false self, I became apparently disconnected from my surroundings—externally. I did not realize what was happening around me. I don't care what is happening in the country, who is who, or where is where. Yes, I should at least know what is happening around me. I must unveil my ignorance and open my eyes and learn things about this world to some extent. I must overcome my identity problem. My relations have to be truthful and not casual and deceptive. No one is an enemy.[6]

The media impact on personal and group identities—group memories that sediment into *the* memory and *our* collective consciousness of the truth of violence, of citizenship and of belonging—is critical to analyses of many forms of conflict and violence. While post-Vietnam researchers sought to understand the impact of media violence by counting instances of specific forms of violence displayed in the media, more recent studies suggest that youths respond to story lines, to genres of media (Barker and Petley 2001) and to personalities of characters (Caughey 1994) rather than to images of violence. Scholarship about media in the third world addresses the roles of media in Western forms of development and in cultural imperialisms (Foster 1996–97; Kulick and Wilson 1992), but people in places like northern Nigeria watch media from India, China, and the Middle East far more frequently (Larkin 1997).

In the 1980s one of the most notorious gang leaders in northern Nigeria, Change, took his name and fashioned his personality, dress, walk, and the way he held his sword around Chiang Kai-shek, the leader of the Nationalist Army of China, who Change asserted expelled Sun Yat-sen, establishing himself in Taiwan in 1949 ('dan Asabe 1991). Change had become familiar with Chiang Kai-shek through widely circulating Chinese videotapes. In colonized societies such as Nigeria, colonial power, not rights, arbitrarily defined citizenship, a legacy that riddles contemporary efforts to define jurisdictions, citizenship, and rights in the postcolonies (Comaroff and Comaroff 2004; Mbembe 2001). Interactions with mass media, such as Change's identification with Chiang Kai-shek, constitute sites of personal and social struggle (Ginsburg 1994; Larkin 1997; Mankekar 1993; Spitulnik 1993), in Change's case, to define masculinity, power, and other personal attributes of leadership and political authority. Media are not the only vehicles of political legitimacy and authority, but they have particular relevance for Kano Muslim youths who value age grades, watch media with their peers, and want to respect their elders but have no trust in Nigerian political or religious leaders. Youths such as Change look to the media for ideas about democracy, citizenship, and social justice, variably seeking an Islamic democracy based on individual human rights, masculine power, and majority rules (Casey 2007).

In 2004 a group of armed young Muslims calling themselves the Taliban killed policemen in Borno State who they claimed had killed members of their group who were protesting anti-Islamic politics, elitism, and corruption in Nigeria and in the United States. Such examples of the mimetic appropriation of or the identification with media characters and story lines are numerous. Yet to what extent does the role modeling of people like Chiang Kai-shek or of the Taliban reflect internalizations of a culture of the state, cultural imperialisms, or identifications with ethnic, religious, and regional political communities? What is the state military-masculinist iconography in Nigeria, and how does this compare or contrast with the Muslim iconography associated with 19th-century jihadists such as Shehu Usman 'dan Fodio, Nigerian former military political leaders such as Obasanjo, or Islamic martyrs and revolutionaries such as Osama bin Laden? How might such identifications alter group memories and consciousness so as to fuel relations of antagonism among Kano residents?

A HISTORY OF POLITICAL SELF AND OTHER

Most sociocultural studies explain collective violence as anxiety about failing or blurred social or political identities and the desire to purify them (Douglas 1966; Bauman 1991; Daniel 1996; Malkki 1995) or as constitutive of social and political identities and solidarity (Durkheim 1995; Feldman 1991; Hinton 2005). Implicit in such explanations is the importance of basic trust, which may define and flame political identifications prior to collective violence and is critical to post-trauma healing and to the reconstruction of trust in oneself and in the institutional and cultural practices that structure daily experience (Ewing 2000; Luhrmann 2000; Robben 2000). The mourning and social channeling of collective trauma—the ways in which people collectively remember and forget trauma—are powerful aspects of group identification and recovery that impact the likelihood of future violence (Taussig 1987; Volkan 1998; White 2005).

It is difficult to understand the ways in which political antagonisms in northern Nigeria grew leading to the violence of May 11 without acknowledging the sediment of political identifications in the country and of the collective traumas of the 19th-century Islamic jihad, colonialism, the Nigerian civil war, and the recent implementation of shari'ah criminal law as state law, alongside the Bush administration's war on terror and war in Iraq. The founder of the Sokoto Caliphate in northern Nigeria, the reformist Shehu Usman 'dan Fodio (1754–1817), sought to purify Islam, distilling the words and deeds of the Prophet Muhammad, according to the Maliki school of law and the Sunni tradition, as the basis for a unified spiritual *ulama* (community) (Last 1967; Paden 1986). Shehu Usman was considered revolutionary because he called for jihad against Muslims he perceived to be infidels (Hunwick 1997).

Shehu Usman's reformers, concerned with establishing "a just society as defined in the classical Islamic state, were fearless in criticizing and later attacking the entrenched establishment," predominantly Sufi (Paden 1986:39). Debate arose among Muslims about whether Shehu Usman, through his writings on Sufism and the brotherhoods, had sanctioned or participated in the Sufi order Qadiriyya.[7] Further complicating the spiritual and political unity that Shehu Usman sought was the existence of several anti-Caliphate, antijihad states including Argungu (Kebbi), Gobir (Tsibiri), Maradi, Damagaram, Gumel, Borno, Ningi, Abuja, and Daura (Baure) (personal communication with Phillip Shea, Kano, July 19, 2004). The idealisms and violence of caliphate-forming unification, the establishment of personal integrity, austerity, and scholarship among the *talakawa* (commoners; poor), including women, *and* its conflicted, at times violent enforcement made the jihad serve as an inspiration for Islamic revitalization and for the aggressive return to shari'ah criminal law in twelve states of northern Nigeria in 1999 and 2000.

While jihadist violence was theoretically based on the politics of unification and on positive social transformation, the violence itself destroyed such unity, establishing hierarchical relationships between Muslims of various sects, factions, and states, the legacy of which continues today (Jalingo 1980; Paden 1973). Colonial state-forming violence generated additional fractures of identification and power by introducing the race-based political identities of "settler" and "native," further complicated by the British administrative "difficulty in deciding whether it was 'ruling,' or advising in accordance with 'native custom'" (Paden 1986:72). Indirect rule through the three major ethnic groups—the Hausa, Igbo, and Yoruba—and the contradictions and tensions between colonial rule and the pre-existing caliphal system, smoldered, to some extent transmuting the settler-native dialectic by fracturing what Mamdani refers to as "the race consciousness of natives into multiple and separate ethnic consciousnesses" (2001:23).

Within the past three decades the relations between ethnic and religious groups in Nigeria have reached boiling points with hundreds of youths fighting bloody street battles, burning mosques and churches, homes and businesses (Casey 1998, 2007, 2008a, 2008b). Among Muslims persistent conflicts about whether to sanction religious history and mystical traditions that predate the 19th-century jihad have become the norm. Litigation between adherents of *bori* has become increasingly common, focusing on the "genuineness" and "originality" of *bori* and their capacity to represent Hausa "traditional culture."[8] There are complex patterns of conflict, for *bori* as traditional culture is tolerated and protected by the Sufi emirate yet condemned by Muslims who lay claim to Sunni orthodoxy.

In the late 1970s a burgeoning media industry and increased access to media coincided with a powerful Sunni orthodox movement, Jama'atu Izalat Al-Bidah Wa Iqamat Al-Sunnah (the Society for the Eradication of Innovation and the Establishment of the Sunna), led by Sheik Abubakar Gumi, the former grand kadi (paramount Islamic judge), and Mallam Isma'il Idris, a former military imam. Popularly known as Izala, this movement had a stated purpose of *tajdid* (reform and rejuvenation), inspired by Shehu Usman's achievements and Saudi Wahhabism yet realized through the day-to-day struggle against what they perceived as the *bida* (religious innovation) of *bori* and the Sufi brotherhoods (Barkindo 1993; Hunwick 1997; Ibrahim 1991; Loimeier 1997; Umar 1993). Conflicts among reformist Sunnis and Shias, nonreformist Sufis of the Tijaniyya and Qadiriyya orders, and adherents of *bori* emerged in response to the sensory structures associated with Sufi and *bori* ritual uses of music, dance, perfumes, and amulets, the visiting of the tombs of Sufi saints, and excessive feasting and celebrations, practices that draw spirits to humans. Reformist Sunni Muslims considered such practices forms of *shirk* (polytheism, or the forbidden association of partners such as humans, the jinn, or witches with Allah), *bida*, or *sabo* (blasphemy) *and* thought them economically excessive, contributing to high levels of anxiety about communal security and salvation. The intellectualism of the Izala leadership, along with vast funding from Wahhabis in Saudi Arabia, contributed to a rapid explosion of Izala publications, radio and television programs, and cassettes, which competed with media from other parts of Nigeria and the world.

During the 1990s conflicts between and among Muslims and Christians intensified. In October of 1991 *'yan daba* killed hundreds of people during demonstrations against the Kano crusade of the Christian evangelist Reinhard Bonnke (Casey 1998; Falola 1998). On December 26, 1994, Gideon Akaluka, a Christian Igbo, was arrested and charged with using the Qur'an as toilet paper. A few days later three Muslim Hausa who claimed to be part of a faction of the Muslim Brotherhood broke into his jail cell, decapitated him, and paraded his head in front of the judge's home, a death sentence they considered just. Months later, on May 30, 1995, an argument between two men, one Muslim Hausa and one Christian Igbo, erupted into violence that swept the city and left several hundred people dead and thousands injured, rekindling memories of the violence in Kano that preceded the Biafran Igbo succession and the Nigerian civil war (Casey 1998). In July of 1995 southern Christians who lived in the Sabon Gari area of Kano found postings on their doorways that read, "Leave immediately or the Islamic Army will force you out." As the Sabon Gari became increasingly fortified, Muslim Hausa news reporters attempted to reassure Muslims that Christian Igbos were not preparing for war.

An increase in the speed and density of media, telecommunications, and travel, and thus an amplification in the intercultural accountings of Nigeria's worsening "realities," tied to traumatic memories of killing and victimhood, cojoined a split within the Muslim Student Society reformers. Some reformers who had previous Izala affiliations found the pro-Saudi, Salafi-inspired Dawa, or missionary movement. Others joined the pro-Iranian Umma (Hunwick 1997; Ibrahim 1991), which took a firmer position on the implementation of shari'ah and the need to establish an Islamic state (Hunwick 1997:39). The Umma split again into the Hodaybiya, which favored some accommodation with the secular state, and the 'yan Shia, which, inspired by the mujahideen struggle in Afghanistan, preached no compromise with a secular state (Hunwick 1997:39).

In March of 2001 'yan daba killed Muslim Yoruba living in Kano following the mass killing of Muslim Hausa in the predominately Yoruba town of Sagamu in Nigeria's southwest (Casey 2008a, 2008b). Local media reinforced talk of "marginal Muslims," described by 'yan daba and reformist Muslim Hausa as "Muslim saboteurs," who they said killed, associated with kafirai (unbelievers), and failed to support the implementation of shari'ah law as Nigerian state law (Ado-Kurawa 2000). Seven months later 'yan daba killed over a hundred people in three days of protests over the U.S. bombardment of Afghanistan, violence that returned during a mid-December protest against the U.S. government.

Nigerians describe cycling violence between so-called natives and settlers, Muslims and Christians, and monotheists and polytheists living in northern Nigeria as a result of clashes between cultural, religious, or ethnic, market-based groups, particularly Muslim Hausa and Christian Igbo, along with the minority groups that associate with them. It is important to remember, however, that such identities are political ones that toughened during the jihad and colonialism, hardened through the violence of Nigeria's civil war, and crystallized further during the violent implementation of shari'ah criminal law that literally divided the city of Kaduna just south of Kano into a Muslim north and Christian south. These identities continue to polarize with attacks on Palestinians, the war on terror, and the war in Iraq. The stated motives and justifications for violence in Plateau and Kano States are tied to a politics of affective citizenry of self- and other definitions of native and settler, Muslim and Christian, monotheist and polytheist, through the violence of self- and other-policing and through the historical and legal polarizations of such political identities.

MEDIATED HOSTILITY AND VIOLENCE

In the weeks before the May 11 crisis, Muslim Hausa residents of Kano were paying close attention to reports of terrorism in Nigeria, as well as to violence in Plateau State, in the Palestinian territories, and in Iraq. Muslims quickly dismissed as ploys by the United States to keep a firm grip on the political affairs of Nigeria reports of the U.S. State Department's alleged concern with an Afghani-associated Taliban in Yobe and Bornu States, of the existence of al-Qaeda in Plateau State, and of the salafist group in Kano State. Abdullahi Bego wrote a cover story, "Who Are Nigeria's Terrorists?" for the popular *Weekly Trust*: "The war [on terror], launched by U.S. President Bush following the September 11th attacks, has effectively cowed most nations of the world to submission after Bush declared 'you are either with us or with the terrorists.' . . . In Nigeria, unless the alleged terrorists are clearly identified, people are likely to assume that the terror alarm is simply a bandwagon effect of this global war on terror or simply an attempt to further ridicule the Shari'ah legal system which many Northern states have opted to implement" (2004:2).

In the same issue, Sheikh Ibrahim El-Zakzaky, the leader of the Islamic Movement in Nigeria, argued that "the 'propaganda' about the existence of terrorist cells in the North [of Nigeria] may be part of a general plan by the United States to prepare the ground for coming into the country" (Gwantu 2004:1). He was voicing a popularly held concern that the Bush administration plans a war in Nigeria to "steal" the petroleum. Mohamed Wader, the dean of social science at the University of Abuja, provides a similar, though more moderate, point of view: "What they [U.S. government officials] don't understand is that people don't even agree with what bin Laden is doing. But people identify with him. That's the principal thing. Maybe the second thing is this question of Shari'ah . . . Shari'ah becomes a convenient camouflage for them. But the real thing is that Muslims allowed bin Laden to become their champion because he was able to defy the greatest powers. This made him attractive to Muslim people, even in northern Nigeria. . . . Otherwise, apart from the connection of Islam, Muslims in northern Nigeria know nothing about bin Laden" (Bego 2004:1–2).

Indeed, the polarization of Western Christian and Eastern Islamic political identities by world leaders such as Bush and bin Laden has hardened political identifications in Nigeria, not just among Muslims but across a range of political actors concerned with global justice and security. Muslim youths in northern Nigeria take bin Laden and Saddam Hussein as heroes, adorning their motorcycles and buses with stickers of these leaders' images. Rather than identify with the religious politics of these men, they identify with Islam in general, and with the military masculinity and willingness of such leaders to "stand up" to Bush, who they associate with anti-Islam, elitism, corruption, and violence.

In the week prior to the May 11 crisis, leaders from Muslim factions in the old city of Kano met to discuss holding a protest march marking the death of the Palestinian leaders Sheiks Ahmed Yassin and Abdul-Azeez Rantisi.[9] After some debate they decided that a public demonstration might become too passionate, degenerating into violence, so they asked people to dedicate prayers at their local mosques. Shortly thereafter reports of the American and British abuses of Iraqi prisoners at Abu Ghraib hit the news. Pictures of Muslim Iraqis naked and tied together, or being dragged by British and American soldiers, some of them women, made local and international news, further angering Kano Muslims. In a *Weekly Trust* article the editor, Aisha Umar Yusuf, wrote: "Many Arabs have expressed anger and disappointment that Bush did not apologise for the prisoner abuse scandal during his interview on two Arabic-language television channels on Wednesday. That anger was fuelled again on Thursday with the publication of more photos. One picture shows a U.S. soldier with a prisoner on a dog leash, while another shows a soldier giving a thumbs-up sign next to what seems to be a dead body" (2004:3).

The sexualized, animal violence depicted in the photographs of the Abu Ghraib prisoners evoked a range of emotions: *haushi* (indignation), *tashin hankali* (agitation), *fushi* (anger), and *gaba* (hostility). In response to reading about Abu Ghraib, a *'dan daba* (singular of *'yan daba*) from Kano said in an interview with me, "A Muslim is a brother of Muslims. Whenever a Christian sees a Muslim, he will humiliate him, while a Muslim will humiliate a Christian" (August 21, 2004). Such emotions mapped onto memories of the humiliating violence of colonialism, placing additional pressure on many Muslim Hausa who prefer to maintain a smooth, tranquil facial expression and consider excessive emotionality a character weakness.

On May 2, 2004, Nigerian newspapers reported attacks by Christian Torok on Muslim Hausa and Fulani living in Plateau State, particularly in Yelwan Shendam and neighboring villages. Reports estimated between 67 and 200 deaths in Yelwan Shendam alone, with women and children raped and taken as slaves for labor and sex, violent acts amplified by the Abu Graib sentiments. The news reports highlighted Governor Dariye's language and references to Muslim Hausa victims as "strangers," "settlers," and "tenants" who had no one but themselves to blame for the violence.

The victims of the violence in Yelwan Shendam and neighboring villages, many of whom had relatives in Kano, came to seek refuge in the city. Several FM radio stations aired accounts of their attacks, making people within the predominately Muslim old city of Kano feel increased *gaba* and *tashin zuchiya* (literally, a rise in the heart, angry or hot tempered). News reports entered the Kano streets where gossip, rumors, and daily talk focused on violence against Muslims and on Kano Muslims as the victims of Christian imperialists, colonizers and settlers who, already having appropriated their land and resources, were now after their lives.

During the Friday Juma'a Mosque, on May 7, *malams* (imams) around the city announced the plan to hold public prayers for the victims of Plateau State violence and a protest rally during which they would march to the governor's house to ask that he demand security for Muslims living in Plateau State, in Iraq, and in the Palestinian territories. The arrival of a truckload of victims on Sunday, May 9, again heightened tensions as survivors told Muslims in the city about their attacks, testimonials that were vividly broadcast on radio.

On May 11, at 10:30 a.m., the rally took place at the Aliyu Bin Abi Talib Mosque in the GRA. Musa Umar Kazaure of the *Weekly Trust* reported that during the rally, speeches "were delivered; special prayers were offered condemning Governor Dariye of Plateau, President Bush of America and Ariel Sharon of Israel for their atrocities and wickedness to Muslims and Islam. A seven-day ultimatum was given to President Obasanjo to intervene and stop the genocide in Plateau State or they will adopt a series of actions against the government. The portrait of Governor Dariye of Plateau State and those of President Bush of America as well as that of Arial Sharon of Israel were burnt and the protesters marched to the Kano State Government House where they were received by the governor, Malam Ibrahim Shekarau" (2004:1–2).

During the protest two large overnight buses from the southern, predominantly Christian part of Nigeria drove by the roundabout close to the mosque where the rally was taking place. Youths threw stones at the buses and then ran down Zoo Road and into the Gyadi-Gyadi area, burning shops and houses, attacking *arna, Kiristoci,* and *ba'ki.*

The next day we heard that the industrial areas of Sharada and Challewa, along with Panshekara, a town 20 minutes outside of Kano where many Christian industrial workers live, were all heavily attacked. The palace of the *Eze Ndigbo* (Igbo traditional ruler) was burned to the ground as the aged *Eze* narrowly escaped death, joining other Igbos in fortified areas such as Sabon Gari. These acts brought forth visceral memories and outrage about the Kano attacks on Igbos in 1995 and in 1966.

I witnessed armed Muslim youths smashing cars while they yelled for the security staff at Bayero University, a federal institution, to give them the *arna.* The youths killed six people on the campus, a place that during all previous violence in Kano had proven a safe haven. Thousands were killed before the Nigerian military arrived, then establishing their shoot-to-kill policy of dealing with the perpetrators.

Unlike the victims of the massacres of Christians and non-Hausa Muslims in Kano during the years 1991, 1995, and 1999, the victims of the May 11 violence gathered evidence of intentional, planned actions that they might use to support a charge of genocide against the perpetrators. Victims claimed that *'yan daba,* with the assistance of *almajirai,* some as young as five, carried lists of all Christians living in or near the industrial areas and in areas of mixed ethnicity and religion outside of the old city.[10] While the killers were almost exclusively Muslim boys and teenagers, their victims were of both sexes and ranged in age from babies to the elderly. Victims who survived, some as young as five, told me that the perpetrators had asked them to recite verses from the Qur'an before deciding whether to kill them. Prior to the day of violence, an *alhaji* in Panshekara purchased drums of petrol for the perpetrators to use as ingredients for the Molotov cocktails that burned over a hundred Christians and their homes and businesses.[11] While *'yan daba* and *almajirai* were unable to penetrate the heavily fortified Sabon Gari, victims considered their attack on the palace of the *Eze Ndigbo* deliberate and highly symbolic.

A PLAN FROM ABOVE?

A Christian police detective of the Bompai Central Intelligence Division (CID) told me that the Kano state governor, Malam Ibrahim Shekarau, knew of the impending crisis.[12] He said Bompai detectives had arrested 28 people from Brigade who were planning the May 11 violence after the ward head of Brigade had notified police of this plan. According to the detective, Shekarau called the CID to request the release of one of these prisoners, whom the detective considered the major political player of the group. The detective said that armed young men had come into the city from several neighboring towns and cities, among them Katsina, Wudil, Kura, and 'Yadda Kwari to fight on behalf of Kano Muslims. He considered the violence well planned by members of the Shekarau government. The detective said the governor delayed bringing the military into Kano, an indication of his complicity with the perpetrators. He said Malam Rabiyu Kwankwaso, the federal minister of defense, ordered the military into Kano when he heard reports of violence on CNN.

Alternatively, there were widespread rumors that Kwankwaso, the former governor of Kano State and a Sufi of the Qadiriyya sect, had planned the attacks to bring down the reformist Sunni Muslim Shekarau administration, that in other words, the planned killing of Christians in Kano formed part of a national political agenda to wreak havoc in states that had adopted shari'ah law, withdrawing from the secular federal government. The targeting of Challewa and Sharada industries and of their Christian minority employees were indicative of the political and economic dimensions of the May 11 violence. The Muslim Hausa political elite conflated ethnicity and religion in formations of political identity and victimhood, drawing parallels between the violence of colonial exploitation and the minority nepotism of today's Kano industries to generate affective citizenship among disaffected youths.

'YAN DABA AND THEIR ALMAJIRAI RECRUITS

Through hunting and warrior traditions, 'yan daba and almajirai have historical links to anticolonial Islamic religious politics ('dan Asabe 1991). These youths, highly skilled in the uses of weaponry and magic, have ambiguous roles in Muslim communities, where they have been employed by religious and political leaders to strong-arm public opinion. 'Yan daba are also part of a larger phenomenon—the emergence of ethnic and religious vigilantes across Nigeria after the 1999 democratic transition and demilitarization, most notably the Yoruba O'odua Peoples Congress in the southwest (Akinyele 2001) and the Igbo Bakassi Boys of the southeast (Baker 2002; Harnischfeger 2003; Smith 2004). Vanguards in the politics of identity and citizenship, these ethnic and religious vigilantes represent divergent political imaginings of Nigeria and believe in the use of power to enforce certain ethnic, religious, and regional interests. Given demilitarization, deregulation, and the primacy of the market, Nigerian vigilantes use violence to "control the means of coercion," gaining advantage in conflicts over state sovereignty and the appropriation of resources (Mbembe 2001:78). Violence occurs in the struggle for national and state codification of new rights and privileges, as extrajudicial challenges to the international judiciary, the Nigerian nation-state, Nigerian state governments, and against corporate elites, whom vigilantes claim turn a deaf ear to the needs of the poor (Casey 2007, 2008a).

'Yan daba identify themselves as Muslim Hausa, but they have incorporated youths from diverse ethnic backgrounds into their gangs, particularly almajirai who come to Kano from across northern Nigeria to study the Qur'an. 'Yan daba take non-Hausa words, like scorpion or pusher, or words combining Hausa with references to people elsewhere, such as kayaman (reggae man) or Takur Sahab (person who has a leader in India) as street names. They have adopted a style of dress they associate with "Westside niggers," Los Angeles–based rappers. In their sunglasses, chains, and baggy jeans, 'yan daba show a broad interest in world youth cultures, questioning me, through whirls of Indian hemp, about the impact of rappers like Tupac

Shakur and the revolutionary politics of his Black Panther mother. 'Yan daba have tenuous relations with Muslim Hausa political leaders, who they feel fail to address their needs for jobs and education. When asked what leaders they admire or who they trust for information about the social injustices they experience, 'yan daba give the names of leaders they have learned about via the media—Saddam Hussein, Osama bin Laden, Tupac Shakur, Bob Marley, and Nelson Mandela—a motley crew of heroes who either advocate a military masculinity and violent power to resolve social problems or who support peaceful resistance.

The children and young men who killed on May 11 perceive themselves as victims—victims of colonial violence, state violence, communal violence, 'yan daba violence, and of state and religious institutional exclusions. Most 'yan daba join a gang in childhood after having witnessed a brother or friend killed by a rival ward gang member. Others join for the economic opportunities of the daba-controlled black market, selling petrol, Indian hemp, and smuggled clothes, while yet others again join for "fun," for a distraction from the bored complacency of joblessness. During the years 2000–2002, 'yan daba were frequently arrested and beaten by Nigerian police for selling black market petrol, which the poorly paid policemen then confiscated to sell themselves. One 'dan daba was hung by his heels and beaten for three days, his eyes bloodshot as he recounted the trauma.

'Yan daba consider their violence a form of Muslim solidarity and belonging, yet on questioning, it is clear that they trust no one. The political and religious leaders who recruited many of them into the violence of May 11 told them that eliminating the arna, Kiristoci, and ba'ki would avenge the deaths of Kano natives who had lived in Plateau State, creating a paradise, a spiritual community of caring and belonging, a material world of ample money for education and jobs. These leaders cultivated violent forms of affective citizenship, insisting on a majority ethnic Hausa rendering of Islamic authenticity through daily talk, rumors, and media portrayals of the 19th-century jihad, of shari'ah as the rightful democratic law, of Hausa indigenity in Plateau and Kano States, of religious purity and community, and of the victimhood of world Muslims. Some young men who killed were paid for their "work" and felt "satisfied that their mission was complete" (interview with a 'dan daba from the old city of Kano, August 16, 2004). Yet, others joined in violence without pay.

A *'dan daba* described the complexities of religious affiliation as gang members mobilized for violence: "If there's a fight between Muslim Brothers and Tijaniyya, or between Tijaniyya and Qadiriyya, it's the *'yan daba* within these groups that will fight. But if there's a fight between Muslims and non-Muslims, all *'yan daba* will get involved in the fight to help their Muslim brothers, in the name of Muslim brotherhood, to fight in the name of Islam" (interview with a *'dan daba* from the old city of Kano, October 15, 2000).

Beyond intra-Muslim conflicts, a *'yan daba* told me, violence between ward gangs had given way to "fighting with other tribes [*kabilu*], like the Igbos who cheat our people who stay in the South" (interview with a *'dan daba* from the old city of Kano, July 21, 2004). Another said: "On the part of religious violence, there is something happening in Kano. The coming of Christians who say they can cure a leper, blind man, and the rest because of a certain charisma they have. Muslims believe only God can cure any disease, so no Christian can have the authority to do this kind of work in a Muslims' town" (interview with a *'dan daba* from the old city of Kano, August 21, 2004).

After May 11, *'yan daba* and their *almajirai* recruits legitimized state violence against their "enemies" via self-interpreting languages and models for social order that echo colonial violence, wherein the state regarded itself as the creator and sole power to judge its own laws. Justifying his violence against *arna*, a *'dan daba* said: "We do this violence because there isn't any authority that we can go and report to. You yourself could be your own authority. Even I, myself, I am my own authority. If you do something wrong to me, I could pass my judgment on you. . . . We know there's no authority that hears our complaints, only God. We stand firm. Anyone who touches us will not go free" (interview with a *'dan daba* from the old city of Kano, August 16, 2004).

CONCLUDING REMARKS

Among northern Nigerians, the relations of political antagonism, forged during the 19th-century Islamic jihad, British colonialism, and the Nigerian civil war and subsequent violence, intersect with media portrayals of violence against Muslims within and outside Nigeria's national borders. Such antagonisms are rooted in, reproduce, and transform the ideologies and feelings of affective citizenship, fusions of ethnic, religious, and regional citizenship based on ethnic customary law *and* religious law, *and* on the historical perceptions of enclosure and exclusion that underpin memories of belonging. This kind of citizenship is backed by law, but a law that historically has been arbitrary and violent in its application. Ethnic citizenship—with colonial and juridical ties to land and resources and supported by the language of originality and indigenity—has conjoined with substantive, borderless religious citizenship (and similar inherent notions of originality, authenticity, and purity) to create volatile forms of citizenship. In northern Nigeria affective citizens join the state, typically dominated by an ethnic, religious, and regional majority, Muslim Hausa, to "carve out autonomous material spheres of effect and affect that diverge from formal political rationalities" (Feldman 1991:4) The May 11 violence in Kano was an escalation of antagonisms and heightened polarizations of self and other, conflations of identity, morality, and security that sediment opposing colonial, religious, ethnic, and global political identities. In media-saturated places such as northern Nigeria, youths' ambivalent experiences of adult leadership and of local ethnic and religious media and global media are best understood in relation to historical ruptures of identity, memory, emotion, and agency, processes that become sedimented within the body and enacted by the body. While not the only means of legitimating authority, the media have particular relevance for Kano Muslim youths who want to belong but for whom the social histories and felt qualities of violence make trust difficult if not impossible. With no other moral authority, political or religious, at hand, the media can easily suppress historicity, channeling and repeating affective references to the historical ruptures of the 19th-century jihad, colonialism, the Nigerian civil war, and most recently, the massacre of Muslim Hausa in Yelwan Shendom, shaping the truths of violence, ideologically and viscerally, and thereby legitimating and authorizing violence as an affective form of citizenship.

NOTES

I dedicate this essay to Phillip Shea, who survived the May 11 violence, only to succumb to malaria on April 5, 2006. I am deeply grateful to have shared in Phil's warmth, strength, and extensive knowledge of northern Nigeria. I am thankful for the assistance of Aminu Sharif Bappa, Usman Aliyu, and Show Boy, and for the *'yan daba*, and their families who allowed me into their lives. For reasons of confidentiality they shall remain unnamed, but I greatly appreciate my experiences with them. I thank Abdulkarim 'dan

Asabe, Salisu Abdullahi, Murray Last, Istvan Patkai, Aminu Taura Abdullahi, Aminu Inuwa, Aisha Usman, Mike Aliyu, and Umar Sanda for their important contributions to my thinking about this project. I thank Shobana Shankar for her comments on an early draft of this article, as well as the anonymous reviewers for Duke University Press. I am grateful to faculty in the departments of psychiatry and sociology at Bayero University and in the Department of Anthropology at the University of California, Los Angeles, for research affiliations and a sense of home base. I am indebted to Allen Feldman, Uli Linke, and Alexander Hinton for their mentoring and inspiration for this project, and to Kevin O'Neill and Alexander Hinton for their thoughtful editorial comments. However, the project would have been impossible without the generous support of the Harry Frank Guggenheim Foundation (2000–2002) and the skillful guidance of Karen Colvard, as well as without a Fulbright IIE Lecturing/Research Award (2004).

1. The majority of residents living in Kano identify themselves as Muslim Hausa or Muslim Hausa-Fulani. Current use of the term *Hausa* extends beyond ethnicity to describe cultural and language communities on both sides of the Niger/Nigeria border. People commonly refer to the *ha'be*, "Aborigines; indigenous tribes" (Bargery 1993[1934]:432), as the only "pure Hausa." Following the 19th-century jihad in northern Nigeria, Muslim Fulani conquered the Hausa and established themselves as a ruling class (Paden 1986; Palmer 1914; Robinson 1896; Tremearne 1914). Marriages of Hausa and Fulani became increasingly common, though people distinguish between marriages with descendants of the Fulani ruling class and with those of "cattle Fulani," who are nomadic. People who wish to emphasize ancestral connections to the Fulani ruling class use the term *Hausa-Fulani* more often.

2. Leo Kuper (2002:61–62) "assumes that the charge of genocide would not be preferred unless there were a 'substantial' or an 'appreciable' number of victims." He uses the term *genocidal massacre* to describe the obliteration of a village or villages.

3. Many Nigerians consider the Nigerian military massacres of people living in the oil regions of the Niger Delta to be genocidal, on par with the genocide of the Ogoni during which the Nigerian military, serving as a private security force for Shell Oil, slaughtered whole villages. By contrast, military officers involved in the Ogoni crisis describe Ken Saro-Wiwa as a Nigerian national "security risk," legitimating their violence as a "state of emergency," a rationale common to the violence resulting from state-sponsored colonial and multinational extractions of oil. These are blood sacrifices of minorities to maintain state power.

4. *Gari* is both the name of the area within Kano and the Hausa word for "town" or "old city."

5. Similar dynamics are widespread. Mirroring reformist Muslims, fundamentalist Nigerian Christian communities consider Muslim news reports to be "propaganda," while in the United States, political left- and right-wing Americans likewise describe the news of their political rivals as propaganda.

6. This quote comes from an entry of August 24, 1994, in the personal diary of a young Muslim in his mid-twenties. He gave me a hundred pages of his journal to help me understand the problems of youths in northern Nigeria.

7. See Paden 1986:43, which cites unpublished works by Ahmed Mohammed Kani and by D. M. Last to support both sides of this debate.

8. *Bori* is widely regarded as animism or a spirit possession cult that predates Islam (Besmer 1983; Callaway and Creevey 1994; Greenberg 1946; Masquelier 1993; Onwuegeogwu 1969; Palmer 1973; Tremearne 1914; Wall 1988). Scholars describe the *bori* spirit possession rituals, practiced in Kano State, as standing in religious opposition to Islam (Besmer 1983; Onwuegeogwu 1969) and as articulating alternative or oppositional gender experiences (Callaway and Creevey 1994; Wall 1988). Through my work with *sarakuna bori* (kings of *bori*) and *malamai* (Qur'anic scholar-healers), I found a link between the beliefs and practices of *bori* and a sect of Islam (1400 A.D.) whose adherents followed the practices of the Prophet Sulayman. *Sarakuna bori* suggest that Allah gave Sulayman the power to "tie" or "bind" spirits to humans, thus legitimating contemporary *bori* spirit possession practices. In all writings about *bori*, the jinnou, Sulayman, is the spirit king. Here, I am not addressing the origin of *bori*, but rather the historical power and contentiousness of narrations about 'yan bori and *bori* practices. 'Yan bori describe themselves as Muslims, while Kano Sufis and reformist Sunnis and Shias refer to them as "fallen Muslims," "marginal Muslims," or "pagans."

9. Protests over the killing of Abdul-Azeez Rantisi occurred all over northern Nigeria. In an article for the *Weekly Trust* Nasir Dambatta wrote, "The just concluded Maulud celebration by Muslims in Kaduna was unprecedentedly colourful as the metropolis was dotted with big posters of martyred Ahmed Yassin and Abdul-Azeez Rantisi" (2004:4). Dambatta quoted Malam Ibrahim, a political science undergraduate at Ahmadu Bello University in Zaria, who said, "the celebration of the two Islamic beacons underscored the significance of Maulud Nabiya," which has "suffered the criticism of stooges of the Western world, wearing the garb of Muslims." He also quoted another participant, Ustaz Musa Idris Nasarawa, who said "there is a growing consciousness on the part of Muslims the world over that they have been marked for atrocities by neo-colonialists, masquerading as champions of democracy and human rights."

10. *Almajirai* bragged to the child of a Muslim professor (who will remain anonymous for reasons of his family's security) that they had helped perpetrators identify Christians living on the Bayero University campus.

11. This is an estimate based on my visual inspection of Panshekara following the May 11 violence, on interviews with seven victims of violence in Panshekara, and on those with four victims who were attacked in Challewa but live in Panshekara.

12. This man will remain anonymous for his personal safety.

REFERENCES

Ado-Kurawa, Ibrahim
2000   Shari'ah and the Press in Nigeria: Islam versus Western Christian Civilization. Kano: Kurawa Holdings.

Akinyele, R. T.

2001   Ethnic Military and National Stability in Nigeria: A Case Study of the
            Oodua People's Congress. African Affairs 100(401):623–640.

Anthony, Douglas A.

2002   Poison and Medicine: Ethnicity, Power, and Violence in a Nigerian City,
            1966 to 1986. Portsmouth, NH: Heinemann.

Antze, Paul, and Michael Lambek, eds.

1996   Tense Past: Cultural Essays in Trauma and Memory. New York:
            Routledge.

Baker, Bruce

2002   When the Bakassi Boys Came: Eastern Nigeria Confronts Vigilantism.
            Journal of Contemporary African Studies 20(2):223–244.

Bargery, G. P.

1993   A Hausa-English Dictionary and English-Hausa Vocabulary. 2nd edition.
            Zaria, Nigeria: Ahmadu Bello University Press.

Barker, Martin, and Julian Petley, eds.

2001   Ill Effects: The Media/Violence Debate. London: Routledge.

Barkindo, B.

1993   Growing Islamism in Kano City since 1970. *In* Muslim Identity and Social
            Change in Sub-Saharan Africa. Louis Brenner, ed. Pp. 91–105. Blooming-
            ton: Indiana University Press.

Bastian, Misty

2000   "Buried under Six Feet of Crude Oil": State-Sponsored Death and the
            Missing Body of Ken Saro-Wiwa. *In* Ken Saro-Wiwa: Writer and Political
            Activist. Craig W. McLuckie and Aubrey McPhail, eds. Pp. 127–152. Boul-
            der, CO: Lynne Rienner.

2006   Terror against Terror: 9/11 or "Kano War" in the Nigerian Press? *In* Terror
            and Violence: Imagination and the Unimaginable. Andrew Strathern,
            Pamela J. Stewart, and Neil L. Whitehead, eds. Pp. 40–60. London: Pluto.

Bauman, Zygmunt

1991   Modernity and the Holocaust. Ithaca: Cornell University Press.

Bego, Abdullahi

2004   Who Are Nigeria's Terrorists? Weekly Trust, May 1–7:1–2.

Besmer, Fremont

1983   Horses, Musicians and Gods: The Hausa Cult of Possession-Trance.
            Boston: Bergin and Garvey.

Callaway, Barbara, and Lucy Creevey

1994   The Heritage of Islam: Women, Religion, and Politics in West Africa.
            Boulder, CO: Lynne Rienner.

Casey, Conerly

1997   Medicines for Madness: Suffering, Disability, and the Identification of Enemies in Northern Nigeria. Ph.D. dissertation, University of California, Los Angeles.

1998   Suffering and the Identification of Enemies in Northern Nigeria. Political and Legal Anthropology Review 21(1):1–25.

2007   "Policing" through Violence: Fear, Vigilantism, and the Politics of Islam in Northern Nigeria. *In* Global Vigilantes: Anthropological Perspectives on Justice and Violence. David Pratten and Atreyee Sen, eds. Pp. 93–126. London: Hurst.

2008a   Identity and Difference in Northern Nigeria. *In* Regional and Ethnic Conflicts: Perspectives From the Front Lines. Judy Carter, Vamik Volkan, and George Irani, eds. Upper Saddle River, NJ: Pearson Prentice Hall.

2008b   "Marginal Muslims": Politics and Perceptual Bounds of Islamic Authenticity in Northern Nigeria. Theme issue, "African Muslims in the Age of Neoliberalism," Benjamin Soares and Marie Nathalie LeBlanc, eds. Africa Today 54(3):67–92.

Caughey, John L.

1994   Gina as Steven: The Social and Cultural Dimensions of a Media Relationship. Visual Anthropology Review 10(1):126–135.

Cole, Jennifer

2001   Forget Colonialism? Sacrifice and the Art of Memory in Madagascar. Berkeley: University of California Press.

Comaroff, John L., and Jean Comaroff

2004   Criminal Justice, Cultural Justice: The Limits of Liberalism and the Pragmatics of Difference in the New South Africa. American Ethnologist 31(2):188–204.

Crowder, Michael

1978   The Story of Nigeria. London: Faber and Faber.

Dambatta, Nasir

2004   Muslims Mourn Yassin, Rantisi. Weekly Trust, May 8–14: 1–4.

'dan Asabe, Abdulkarim

1991   'Yan Daba: The "Terrorists" of Kano Metropolitan? Theme issue, "Youth and Health in Kano Today," Kano Studies: 85–115.

Daniel, E. Valentine

1996   Charred Lullabies: Chapters in an Anthropology of Violence. Princeton: Princeton University Press.

Diamond, Larry

1983   Class, Ethnicity, and the Democratic State: Nigeria, 1950–1966. Comparative Studies in Society and History 25(3):457–489.

Douglas, Mary

1966   Impurity and Danger: An Analysis of Concepts of Pollution and Taboo.
            London: Routledge and Kegan Paul.

Durkheim, Émile

1995[1912] The Elementary Forms of Religious Life. Karen E. Fields, trans. New
            York: Free Press.

Ewing, Katherine Pratt

2000   The Violence of Non-Recognition: Becoming a "Conscious" Muslim
            Woman in Turkey. In Cultures under Siege: Collective Violence and
            Trauma. Antonius C. G. M. Robben and Marcelo M. Suárez-Orozco, eds.
            Pp. 248–271. Cambridge: Cambridge University Press.

Falola, Toyin

1998   Violence in Nigeria: The Crisis of Religious Politics and Secular Ideolo-
            gies. Rochester, NY: University of Rochester Press.

Fanon, Franz

1963   The Wretched of the Earth. Constance Farrington, trans. New York:
            Grove.

1967   Black Skin, White Masks. Charles Lam Markmann, trans. New York:
            Grove.

Fein, Helen

2002   Genocide: A Sociological Perspective. In Genocide: An Anthropological
            Reader. Alexander Laban Hinton, ed. Pp. 74–90. Malden, MA: Blackwell.

Feldman, Allen

1991   Formations of Violence: The Narrative of the Body and Political Terror in
            Northern Ireland. Chicago: University of Chicago Press.

1997   Violence and Vision: The Prosthetics and Aesthetics of Terror. Public
            Culture 10(1):24–60.

Foster, Robert

1996–97   Commercial Mass Media in Papua New Guinea: Notes on Agency,
            Bodies, and Commodity Consumption. Visual Anthropology Review
            12(2):1–17.

Ginsburg, Faye

1994   Some Thoughts on Culture/Media. Visual Anthropology Review
            10(1):136–141.

Gore, Charles, and David Pratten

2003   The Politics of Plunder: The Rhetorics of Order and Disorder in Southern
            Nigeria. African Affairs 102(407):211–240.

Greenberg, Joseph

1946   The Influence of Islam on a Sudanese Religion. New York: J. J. Augustin.

Gwantu, Waziri Isa
2004   America Wants to Invade Nigeria. Weekly Trust, May 1–7:1–2.

Harnischfeger, Johannes
2003   The Bakassi Boys: Fighting Crime in Nigeria. Journal of Modern African
            Studies 41(1):23–49.

Hinton, Alexander Laban
2005   Why Did They Kill? Cambodia in the Shadow of Genocide. Berkeley:
            University of California Press.

Hinton, Alexander Laban, ed.
2002   Genocide: An Anthropological Reader. Malden, MA: Blackwell.

Hunwick, John
1997   Sub-Saharan Africa and the Wider World of Islam: Historical and Con-
            temporary Perspectives. In African Islam and Islam in Africa: Encounters
            between Sufis and Islamists. Eva E. Rosander and David Westerlund, eds.
            Pp. 28–54. Athens: Ohio University Press.

Huyssen, Andreas
2001   Present Pasts: Media, Politics, Amnesia. In Globalization. Arjun
            Appadurai, ed. Pp. 57–77. Durham, NC: Duke University Press.

Ibrahim, Jibrin
1991   Religion and Political Turbulence in Nigeria. Journal of Modern African
            Studies 29(1):115–136.

Jalingo, Ahmadu Usman
1980   The Reformist Tradition in Northern Nigeria. Ph.D. dissertation, Univer-
            sity of Edinburgh.

Kazaure, Musa Umar
2004   How Plateau Crisis Spilled over to Kano. Weekly Trust, May 15–21:1–2.

Kulick, Don, and Margaret Wilson
1992   Echoing Images: The Construction of Savagery among Papua New
            Guinean Villagers. Visual Anthropology 5(2):143–152.

Kuper, Leo
2002   Genocide: Its Political Use in the Twentieth Century. In Genocide: An
            Anthropological Reader. Alexander Laban Hinton, ed. Pp. 48–73.
            Malden, MA: Blackwell.

Larkin, Brian
1997   Indian Films and Nigerian Lovers: Media and the Creation of Parallel
            Modernities. Africa 67(3):406–440.

Last, Murray
1967   The Sokoto Caliphate. Ibadan: Longman.

1991   Adolescents in a Muslim City: The Cultural Context of Danger and Risk. Theme issue, "Youth and Health in Kano Today," Kano Studies: 41–70.

2000   Reconciliation and Memory in Postwar Nigeria. *In* Violence and Subjectivity. Veena Das, Arthur Kleinman, Mamphela Ramphele, and Pamela Reynolds, eds. Pp. 315–332. Berkeley: University of California Press.

Lemkin, Raphaël

2002   Genocide. *In* Genocide: An Anthropological Reader. Alexander Laban Hinton, ed. Pp. 27–42. Malden, MA: Blackwell.

Levin, Michael D.

1997   The New Nigeria: Displacement and the Nation. Journal of African and Asian Studies 32(1–2):134–144.

Loimeier, Roland

1997   Islamic Reform and Political Change: The Examples of Abubakar Gumi and the 'Yan Izala Movement in Northern Nigeria. *In* African Islam and Islam in Africa: Encounters between Sufis and Islamists. Eva E. Rosander and David Westerlund, eds. Pp. 286–307. Athens: Ohio University Press.

Luhrmann, Tanya M.

2000   The Traumatized Social Self: The Parsi Predicament in Modern Bombay. *In* Cultures under Siege: Collective Violence and Trauma. Antonius C. G. M. Robben and Marcelo M. Suárez-Orozco, eds. Pp. 158–193. Cambridge: Cambridge University Press.

Malkki, Liisa H.

1995   Purity and Exile: Violence, Memory, and National Cosmology among Hutu Refugees in Tanzania. Chicago: University of Chicago Press.

Mamdani, Mahmood

1996   Citizen and Subject: Contemporary Africa and the Legacy of Late Colonialism. Princeton: Princeton University Press.

2001   When Victims Become Killers: Colonialism, Nativism, and the Genocide in Rwanda. Princeton: Princeton University Press.

Mankekar, Purnima

1993   National Texts and Gendered Lives: An Ethnography of Television Viewers in a North Indian City. American Ethnologist 20(3):543–563.

Masquelier, Adeline

1993   Narratives of Power, Images of Wealth: The Ritual Economy of Bori in the Market. *In* Modernity and Its Malcontents: Ritual and Power in Postcolonial Africa. John L. Comaroff and Jean Comaroff, eds. Pp. 3–33. Chicago: University of Chicago Press.

Mbembe, Achille

2001   On the Postcolony. Berkeley: University of California Press.

Ocheje, Paul D.

1997   Ethnic Minority Problems in Nigerian Politics 1960–65. Uppsala,
            Sweden: University of Uppsala Press.

Onwuegeogwu, Michael

1969   The Cult of the Bori Spirits among the Hausa. *In* Man in Africa.
            Mary Douglas and Philip Kaberry, eds. Pp. 279–306. New York:
            Tavistock.

Paden, John

1971   Communal Competition: Conflict and Violence in Kano. *In* Nigeria:
            Modernization and the Politics of Communalism. Robert Melson and
            Howard Wolpe, eds. Pp. 73–94. East Lansing: Michigan State University
            Press.

1973   Religion and Political Culture in Kano. Berkeley: University of California
            Press.

1986   Ahmadu Bello, Sardauna of Sokoto: Values and Leadership in Nigeria.
            Zaria, Nigeria: Hudahuda.

Palmer, H. R.

1973   Bori among the Hausas. Man 14:113–117.

Philips, Abu

1988   Ibn Taymeeyah's Essay on the Jinn (Demons). Riyadh: Tawheed.

Robben, Antonius C. G. M.

2000   The Assault on Basic Trust: Disappearance, Protest, and Reburial in
            Argentina. *In* Cultures under Siege: Collective Violence and Trauma.
            Antonius C. G. M. Robben and Marcelo M. Suárez-Orozco, eds.
            Pp. 70–101. Cambridge: Cambridge University Press.

Robinson, C.

1896   Hausaland. London: Sampson Low, Marston.

Saro-Wiwa, Ken

1992   Genocide in Nigeria: The Ogoni Tragedy. London: Saros International
            Publishers.

Sarte, Jean Paul, and Arlette El Kaim-Sartre

1968   On Genocide and a Summary of the Evidence and the Judgments of the
            International War Crimes Tribunal. Boston: Beacon.

Smith, Daniel J.

2004   The Bakassi Boys: Vigilantism, Violence, and Political Imagination in
            Nigeria. Cultural Anthropology 19(3):429–455.

Spitulnik, Debra

1993   Anthropology and Mass Media. Annual Review of Anthropology
            22:25–43.

Stoller, Paul

1995   Embodying Colonial Memories: Spirit Possession, Power, and the Hauka
            in West Africa. New York: Routledge.

Tamuno, T. N.

1972   The Evolution of the Nigerian State: The Southern Phase. 1895–1914. New
            York: Humanities Press.

Taussig, Michael

1987   Shamanism, Colonialism and the Wild Man: A Study in Terror and Heal-
            ing. Chicago: University of Chicago Press.
1991   The Nervous System. New York: Routledge.
1997   The Magic of the State. New York: Routledge.

Tremearne, A. J.

1914   Ban of the Bori. London: Heath, Cranton, and Ouseley.

Umar, Mohammed

1993   Changing Islamic Identity in Nigeria from the 1960s to 1980s. *In* Muslim
            Identity and Social Change in Sub-Saharan Africa. Louis Brenner, ed.
            Pp. 154–178. Bloomington: Indiana University Press.

Volkan, Vamik

1998   Bloodlines: From Ethnic Pride to Ethnic Terrorism. Boulder, CO:
            Westview.

Wall, Louis

1988   Hausa Medicine: Illness and Well-being in a West African Culture.
            Durham, NC: Duke University Press.

Watts, Michael

1996   Islamic Modernities? Citizenship, Civil Society, and Islamism in a
            Nigerian City. Public Culture 8(2):251–289.
2001   Violent Geographies: Speaking the Unspeakable and the Politics of Space.
            City and Society 13(1):85–117.

Weekly Trust

1999   Hausas Massacred in Sagamu. Weekly Trust, August 6–12: 1–2.

White, Geoffrey

2005   Emotive Institutions. *In* A Companion to Psychological Anthropology:
            Modernity and Psychocultural Change. Conerly Casey and Robert B.
            Edgerton, eds. Pp. 241–254. Malden, MA: Blackwell.

Williams, Dat Ama Tokunbo

1997   Religion, Violence and Displacement in Nigeria. Journal of Asian and
            African Studies 32(1–2):33–49.

Yusuf, Aisha Umar

2004   Bush Expresses Regrets over Iraqi Prisoners' Abuse. Weekly Trust, May
            8–14:1–3.

9   CLEANSED OF EXPERIENCE?

Genocide, Ethnic Cleansing, and the Challenges
of Anthropological Representation

In February 2007, a scholarly squabble broke out on the pages
of the journal *East European Politics and Societies* as the result
of the anthropologist Robert Hayden's critical review of the
political scientist Sabrina Ramet's (2005) book, *Thinking about
Yugoslavia: Scholarly Debates about the Yugoslav Breakup and
the Wars in Bosnia and Kosovo.* At the heart of the dispute lay
the question of how to assess what had happened in the former
Yugoslavia in the 1990s, both in terms of empirical data and of
interpretive bent. The contentious tone taken by the two scholars (with charges of "slurs" and "irresponsible self-indulgence"
flung about) reflected the high stakes of any discussion about
Yugoslavia's dissolution: these debates inevitably involve questions of blame and culpability and how to label and explain violence, particularly whether to deem certain policies and actions
in the war as genocidal. As I read Hayden's (2007) and Ramet's
(2007) charges and countercharges, I recalled my own introduction to the passions the Yugoslav breakup provoked in the
scholarly community.[1]

As a young anthropology graduate student who had just
completed a preliminary summer of fieldwork in Italy and Croatia in the summer of 1992, I attended a conference held at the
University of Kent dedicated to the wars in Yugoslavia. The war
in Bosnia had only begun two months earlier, and emotions
were raw among the scholars—foreign and "Yugoslav"—in

attendance. Discussions quickly broke down into shouting matches and emotional accusations of being pro-Serb, pro-Croat, or pro-Bosnian. I had followed the conflicts through the news but did not have full command of the issues, having just begun to investigate a different set of ethnic conflicts at the northeastern borders of the former Yugoslavia. As my fieldwork with Italians who had left Yugoslavia after World War II unfolded, however, I soon found myself in a scholarly and political terrain similarly marked by charges and countercharges of genocide, as the Yugoslav conflict occasioned a reconsideration of events that had happened fifty years earlier.

Debates about violence in the former Yugoslavia—whether the events of the 1990s or of the 1940s and 1950s—were further complicated by the appearance of a new term, *ethnic cleansing*, to describe mass killings and population transfers. In a 1993 article, "Among the New Words," John and Adele Algeo registered the appearance of the term in the lexicon of American speech. They defined *ethnic cleansing* as entailing "the removal of ethnic minorities from a society by forced migration or genocide, as in former Yugoslavia" (1993:412). Right from its introduction into the American vocabulary the term's definitional relationship to genocide, as well as to forced migration, has thus proven unclear. Is ethnic cleansing an aspect of genocidal violence, does it encompass genocide (as the Algeo definition suggests), or is it synonymous with genocide?[2] The blurring of the ethnic cleansing label with genocide has furnished the former with the moral power of the latter, even as the former lacks the legal contours of genocide (albeit often imprecise themselves and difficult to prove) that make it a tool of international law.

In this article I examine what the use of the ethnic cleansing label offers in terms of conceptual clarity (for scholars) and political capital (for groups claiming to be victims of the practice). I do so through an analysis of scholarly debates about ethnic cleansing before turning to the specific case of Italians who left the Istrian peninsula after World War II, when that area passed from Italian to Yugoslav control, and who often describe their experience as "Yugoslavia's first ethnic cleansing." In critically interrogating the use of the ethnic cleansing concept by Istrian Italian "exiles," I signal from the outset my own unease as an anthropologist in either rejecting the use of the label (and therefore appearing a "denier") or wholeheartedly embracing it (and thereby endorsing a certain political position and risking a simplified, overly ethnicized explanation).

As the Istrian Italian claim to be victims of Yugoslavia's first (and forgotten) ethnic cleansing suggests, considerable attention has been paid to the origins of both the term *ethnic cleansing* and the actual practice (whether labeled as such or not). Citing various examples of the term's usage in the media, for example, the Algeos found that sources traced the term's introduction into international consciousness to George D. Kenney, a Yugoslav desk officer at the U.S. Department of State who spotted the phrase in a cable from the American embassy in Belgrade, or, alternatively, to a July 1991 news story in which a member of the Croatian Supreme Council used the term. The sociologist Veljko Vujačić instead locates the first use of the term by Serbian nationalists in the 1980s; they feared that Albanians in Kosovo were demographically "cleansing" Serbs from the province. Dražen Petrović, of the Sarajevo University School of Law, on the other hand, relates it to Yugoslav military vocabulary in the 1990s (Mulaj 2003:695–696; see also Mazsu 2003:743). As these various claims about the etymology of the ethnic cleansing label suggest, scholars began to use as an analytic category a term that originated among the participants (both perpetrators and victims) of violence.

Though some historians claim a much earlier usage of the term, locating it in World War II or even in the Balkan Wars of the early twentieth century,[3] other observers have instead argued that *ethnic cleansing* merely offers a new name for an old practice. As a rabbi quoted in the Algeo piece put it, "We have heard it before. 'Ethnic cleansing,' the euphemistic code word for final solution and genocide" (1993:412–413). Scholars, journalists, politicians, and others have thus depicted ethnic cleansing as offering a new conceptual vocabulary, if not necessarily a new practice. But does the term actually offer a new critical framework, or should scholars be warned, as Rogers Brubaker and Frederick Cooper have urged for the notion of "identity," that the salience of ethnic cleansing "as a category of practice does not require its use as a category of analysis" (2000:5)? The ethnic cleansing tag does appear to have proven productive for describing a variety of ethnic conflicts in the contemporary world, as well as for relabeling or reinterpreting past episodes of violence. Even as the concept may direct attention to neglected histories, however, it also threatens to obscure critical aspects from view. Anthropologists interested in the experiences of those subjected to such processes need to be equally attentive to what a focus on ethnic cleansing opens up and what perspectives it may close down.

Here we may heed Alexander Laban Hinton's comments on an anthropology of genocide as equally relevant for an anthropology of ethnic cleansing (even if the conceptual status of ethnic cleansing in relation to genocide is not always clear): "Because of their experience-near understandings of the communities in which such violence takes place, anthropologists are uniquely positioned to address these questions . . . genocide is always a local process and therefore may be analyzed and understood in important ways through the ethnohistorical lens of anthropology" (2002:1, 3). In understanding empirical events from an anthropological perspective, then, what does the classification ethnic cleansing write in, and what does it write out? Given that the category of ethnic cleansing embodies what Brubaker (2004) deems "groupism,"[4] what place remains for individual experiences or other, nonethnic markers of groupism? Key aspects of women's experiences, for example, range among the elements that the ethnic cleansing interpretation has tended to downplay for the Istrian case, as I will discuss further. In reflecting on the politics of the ethnic cleansing interpretation for the specific Istrian example, I also consider the broader question of the responsibilities of anthropologists who study and interpret the violence of genocide and ethnic cleansing.

THE ETHNIC CLEANSING CONCEPT

The term *ethnic cleansing*, like the older *genocide*, has occasioned considerable debate over its definition and application, as well as its origins.[5] Though the scholarly dissection of *ethnic cleansing* and *genocide* may at times appear overly abstract or detached, behind these debates lie the impassioned questions of moral urgency that have led to the kinds of heated exchanges like those between Hayden and Ramet with which I began this essay. Indeed, the editor of *East European Politics and Societies* made the unusual move of having an author respond to a book review because of "the absence of detached reviewers" (Prizel 2007:181). Though referring specifically to the scope of Ramet's work and to the difficulty of finding appropriate reviewers whose work Ramet did not reference, Ilya Prizel might also be taken to indicate the challenges of finding specialists who could remain dispassionate about the issues of violence that marked Yugoslavia's end.

At the heart of the debate about ethnic cleansing lies the issue of what the concept *does*, that is, its analytical and political purchase. Writes Klejda

Mulaj: "Ethnic cleansing is not what lawyers call a 'term of art,' lacking a legal definition and also a body of case law. It is instead a term used by soldiers, journalists, sociologists, social scientists, and others to describe a phenomenon which is not defined by law. That said, a general agreement on a precise meaning of 'ethnic cleansing' (despite the fact that several definitions of the term have been offered) is so far lacking" (2003:696).

As does the identity concept critiqued by Brubaker and Cooper, ethnic cleansing runs the risk of meaning "too much (when understood in a strong sense), too little (when understood in a weak sense), or nothing at all (because of its sheer ambiguity)" (Rieber 2000:1). Given this indeterminacy,[6] some scholars have rejected the term out of hand, noting that "the term *ethnic cleansing* is currently widely used to characterize a variety of these phenomena [i.e., population transfer, expulsion, deportation, resettlement], but it lacks precision and has become increasingly a weapon in the propaganda wars" (Rieber 2000:3). This raises questions of scholarly responsibility in even employing the label *ethnic cleansing* given its role as "a weapon in the propaganda wars."

In an analysis of what she deems genocide in Bosnia-Herzegovina from 1992 to 1995, the anthropologist Tone Bringa (2002) argues that part of the popularity of the term *ethnic cleansing* stems from the lack of a legal imperative to intervene to stop it, in contrast to the (relatively) more clear-cut legal term of *genocide* (see also Woodward 1996:755). Bringa thus makes a forceful argument concerning what is at stake in maintaining a clear analytical distinction between the terms *ethnic cleansing* and *genocide*:

> To many policy makers in Europe and the United States it was convenient to describe what was going on as "ethnic cleansing." . . . I believe there would have been a moral obligation (pushed by public opinion) for the international community (and primarily the West) to intervene had "genocide" and not "ethnic cleansing" become the defining crime of the wars in Bosnia-Herzegovina. That is not to say, however, that "ethnic cleansing" in all cases became a euphemism for "genocide." The systematic murder of Muslim and Croat civilians that took place in Eastern and Northern Bosnia was not the pattern everywhere in Bosnia ("ethnic cleansing" does, however, entail crimes punishable as grave breaches of the Geneva Conventions and as crimes against humanity). But at least during the first half of the war the phenomenon of ethnic cleansing

exoticized the war in Bosnia, and, I believe, made it more difficult for people to engage. The concept also contributed to blurring the lines in people's minds between perpetrator and victim, between attacker and attacked. The term is vague in that what constitutes "ethnic cleansing" is often vague, so it was easier to accuse all sides in the conflict of ethnic cleansing (and thus treat them as equally guilty). (2002:203)

Noting the domestification and banalization of the ethnic cleansing label, Bringa concludes: "*Ethnic cleansing* is not a legal term, and while genocide is defined as a crime of intent in legal terms, *ethnic cleansing* was originally used to describe the expulsions of unwanted populations (in order to create an ethnically pure territory) through terror tactics such as intimidation, discrimination, rape, torture, murder, looting and burning of homes, and the destruction of religious and cultural objects. However, through overuse and politically motivated misuse, the term was watered down. It was even used about the consequences of negotiated changes of political-military borders" (2002:203).

From the opposite direction, Hayden has contended that a rhetoric of genocide was used in Bosnia-Herzegovina to describe what in reality is best deemed "ethnic cleansing," that is, an "unmixing of peoples." Too frequently in accounts of 1990s Bosnia, Hayden notes, *genocide* and *ethnic cleansing* have been treated as interchangeable terms. He suggests, "An uncomfortable conclusion follows: the depiction of the expulsion of a population depends on the political position of the party making it" (1996:742). Originally published in the *Slavic Review*, Hayden's article prompted a number of critical responses (Lilly 1996; Wallace 1996; Woodward 1996), a reaction Hayden predicted in his article. The criticism of Hayden's piece underscores the dangers of raising scholarly objections to what are quite often literally life and death issues. Does the moral urgency of the situation thus foreclose certain kinds of critical discussion of ethnic cleansing and genocide?

The divergent takes of Bringa and Hayden on what a critical discussion of the ethnic cleansing concept in Bosnia entails points to the challenges—particularly for anthropologists—of defining ethnic cleansing in relation to genocide from an analytical, legal, and "moral" point of view. John Cerone contends that the slippage between the two concepts has serious consequences: "In the recent application of Croatia to the World Court in a case against the Federal Republic of Yugoslavia alleging genocide, the two terms are used almost interchangeably. Further, this confusion is not limited to unilateral declarations, as the United Nations Security Council and General Assembly have used the phrase 'ethnic cleansing' to refer to a range of different acts" (2003:739). All such analyses of the fuzziness of the ethnic cleansing concept, however, rest on an assumption of genocide as the normative baseline, an assumption that neglects the imprecision of genocide's definition and the difficulty of proving intent, an aspect of genocide's legal definition that is usually absent from characterizations of ethnic cleansing.[7] One unintended effect of the ethnic cleansing concept thus may be the consolidation of the genocide concept, which comes to appear more clear-cut *relative* to the charge of ethnic cleansing.

Despite the indeterminacies of the ethnic cleansing concept, a large and growing body of scholarly literature explores episodes now labeled ethnic cleansing. Though much of this literature initially examined the former Yugoslavia, historians soon began to expand its usage. Nonetheless, much of the literature has remained focused on southeastern and eastern Europe (e.g., see Naimark 2001), regions historically characterized by ethnic mosaics that proved troublesome to the homogenizing nation-states that succeeded multiethnic empires. This raises the issue of whether ethnic cleansing risks becoming for southeastern Europe what Arjun Appadurai deems a "gatekeeping concept" (1986), a key trait that presumably defines (and also delimits the understanding of) a culture area.[8]

Defining the ethnic cleansing concept as distinct from (if in close relation to) genocide, however, has usefully focused or redirected attention to historical episodes of violence—in southeastern Europe and beyond—that previously fell under the radar screen of genocide scholars. In part this lack of attention to some episodes of violence reflected the enormity of genocide, and in particular of the Holocaust, which led scholars to neglect some instances of violence not easily classified. As Timothy Snyder puts it, "Ethnic cleansing hides in the shadow of the Holocaust. Even as horror of Hitler's Final Solution motivates the study of other mass atrocities, the totality of its exterminatory intention limits the value of the comparisons it elicits" (2003:197). From another direction, this general scholarly neglect followed from a definition of genocide that omitted class violence or the persecution of specifically political groups.

Yet armed with the new ethnic cleansing concept, historians have now begun to revise the picture of state socialism in twentieth-century Europe, inserting an ethnic element into a narrative that had previously been viewed largely in terms of class ideology. A subset of historical work has thus fruitfully applied the ethnic cleansing label to the ethnic reconfiguration of the Soviet Union prior to World War II and to Eastern Europe immediately after the war as the result of the expulsions and the flight of ethnic Germans, as well as other minorities deemed politically suspect or compromised by their behavior during the war (including Hungarians in Czechoslovakia and Ukrainians and Belorussians in Poland). The historian Terry Martin, for example, has offered a new vision of the Great Terror in Stalinist Russia as entailing "the culmination of a gradual shift from predominantly class-based terror to terror that targeted (among others) entire nations" (1998:852).

Martin's careful research reveals the power of the ethnic cleansing concept to extend the historical perspective and rethink former truisms, a process further aided by the post–Cold War opening up of archives. Likewise, recent collections of essays have begun to offer a new view of the so-called internationalist nationalisms that characterized many of the East European socialist regimes emerging from World War II. Whereas a growing body of work had already productively used the concept of nationalism to rethink the experience of state socialism (Connor 1984; Verdery 1991), a new focus of research looks at the ethnic cleansing of minorities that accompanied the installation of socialist regimes in post-1945 Eastern Europe. Much of the work has centered around the most massive ethnic cleansing: the expulsion en masse of an estimated 15 million ethnic Germans, population movements sanctioned by Allied agreements at Potsdam and Yalta (Zayas 2003). The expulsion of minorities helped provide these new regimes with some legitimacy independent of Soviet support (see Kersten 2001:84). Not only could governments claim to have rid the state of the "enemy within" but they also confiscated a stock of properties and goods that could be redistributed; the ethnic status of these minorities often coincided with higher economic status. Furthermore, "Many of the regions designated as new living areas for expellees, especially in Poland and eastern Germany, were at the forefront of collectivization and crash industrialization" (Kramer 2001:17). As regimes carried out economic centralization, the use of properties expropriated from expelled minorities helped mute resistance to these economic changes (Ther 2001:59). At the same time, an insistence on ethnically cleansed nation-states contributed to the destruction of what remained of prewar democratic regimes, as in Poland (Linek 2001:129).

As these conclusions suggest, research on postwar episodes of ethnic cleansing offers a productive new angle on the consolidation of power in the Eastern European communist regimes. In the Istrian case, for instance, the ethnic cleansing framework has refocused mainstream historiography on ethnic elements of the policies of the Yugoslav socialist regime in early postwar Istria that remained unacknowledged in a leftist historical tradition emphasizing ideological conflict between fascism and communism. (Work that did stress the ethno-national aspect of the Istrian exodus was often dismissed, not always unfairly, for being nationalist or pro-fascist itself.) As in the Istrian case, the ethnic cleansing framework more generally dismantles understandings of state socialism as having frozen or repressed ethnic tensions, even as scholars also take up in nuanced ways the question of "pre-socialist antecedents [that] are extremely important for understanding recent ethnic tensions" in Eastern Europe (Hann 1996:390). Chris M. Hann and others have suggested that this revised history can thus offer lessons not just about the past but also for understanding present crises.

Snyder goes as far as to argue that the lack of attention and conceptual clarity in the past to what scholars now classify as ethnic cleansing emboldened the agents of such violence: "To have forgotten the particulars of ethnic cleansing may be necessary for the creation of particular national histories. To have forgotten the prevalence of ethnic cleansing may have been necessary for the creation of European histories in which borders and nations are unproblematic categories. Throughout the twentieth century, ethnic cleansers knew that borders and nations were for the making" (2003:234).

Mark Kramer (2001:8–11) and Ana Siljak (2001) instead draw more specific lessons from historical episodes of ethnic cleansing. They contend, for example, that examining the historical experience of ethnic Germans cleansed from Eastern Europe puts into question the view—voiced by Hayden, as well as by John J. Mearsheimer and Robert A. Pape (1993) and Mearsheimer and Stephen Van Evera (1995), among others—that the partition of ethnically mixed countries and organized population transfers offer the best solution for avoiding or minimizing bloodshed. Kramer notes that research on the postwar transfers reveals the extremely high human costs of partition. "The forced migration of the 1940s was a bloody, cruel, and costly process that was feasible only in the aftermath of what had been by far the largest and deadliest war in history" (2001:10). Using ethnic cleansing as a framework can thus direct attention to the sorts of experiences—those of refugees, who bear the costs of partition—that realist approaches to international relations tend to write out or downplay (see also Ballinger 1999).

Other scholars instead use the experience of ethnic cleansing after World War II to draw more problematic conclusions about violence in the 1990s former Yugoslavia. Andrew Ludány links the expulsion of Hungarians from Vojvodina in 1944–45 to events in Bosnia in the 1990s, noting that "the method used by the Partisans [in the 1940s] was similar to what became the pattern in Bosnia-Herzegovina in 1993–95" (2003:587). He finds a connection between the two eras in the 1986 "Memorandum" by the Serbian Academy of Sciences, which Ludány treats as the "restatement and legitimization of the ideals expressed by the Serbian Culture Club for a Greater Serbia [in the 1930s and 1940s]" (2003:589). The further reduction of the percentage of ethnic Hungarians in Vojvodina as a result of the resettlement of Serbian refugees in the region between 1991–95 ("Serbianization") thus appears, in Ludány's analysis, as of a piece with earlier expulsions and massacres of ethnic Hungarians. Here, the positing of continuity of ethnic cleansing writes out the intervening years of socialism under Tito and the crucial differences between processes in 1944–45 and the 1990s.

John Schindler has made a similar argument in his study of the post–World War II destruction of Yugoslavia's ethnic Germans, the *Donauschwaben*. In addition to representing the only complete ethnic cleansing of a Yugoslav minority group (in contrast to other partially cleansed groups like Yugoslavia's ethnic Hungarians and Italians), contends Schindler, "the theoretical and practical roots of the Balkan tragedies of the past decade, the origins of what the world has come to denounce as ethnic cleansing, lie in the terrible experience of Yugoslavia's ill-fated ethnic Germans" (2003:359). More specifically, Schindler claims that "the Greater Serbian ideology and secret police techniques which formed the backbone of ethnic cleansing against Bosnian Muslims and Kosovar Albanians" in the

1990s can be traced to the cleansing of Yugoslavia's Germans (2003:371). Yet perhaps Schindler's strongest link between the actions of the 1940s and the 1990s is that Jovica Stanisic, the head of Serbia's secret police between 1991 and 1998 and the "architect of the next round of ethnic cleansing in Yugoslavia" (Schindler 2003:370) came from a Danubian town and grew up in a house built and formerly inhabited by ethnically cleansed Germans. On the one hand, then, the idea of examining earlier episodes of ethnic cleansing in Yugoslavia creates interest in and a persuasive conceptual framework for long-neglected topics, such as the fate of Yugoslavia's ethnic Germans. It also raises key questions about the role played by memories of past violence in fanning contemporary violence (for Yugoslavia, see Denich 1994; Hayden 1994; Levene 1994). On the other hand, positing continuity between this "early" ethnic cleansing and the cleansing campaigns of the 1990s risks conflating two different historical periods and downplays divergences in the domestic situations of the 1940s and the 1990s in Yugoslavia, as well as in the external international environment.

Another related historical episode that has been viewed anew through the ethnic cleansing lens involves the mass migration of ethnic Italians from the Istrian peninsula when it passed from Italian to Yugoslav control after World War II. Since Yugoslavia's dissolution this history of displacement has been rediscovered in Italy as an episode of ethnic cleansing. Though Italian *esuli* (exiles or former refugees) from Istria had long been viewed with suspicion as "fascists" or simply forgotten in Italy, the events of the Yugoslav wars of the 1990s offered exiles a powerful and persuasive framework through which to present their experiences. But what experiences are brought into view by understanding events in Istria between 1943 and 1955 in terms of ethnic cleansing? What experiences does a narrative of ethnic cleansing remove from sight? And what conceptual framework should a scholar of Istria adopt, given the charged political context of debates about whether Istria's Italians were subjected to ethnic cleansing?

Though issues of political context freight claims of genocidal violence or ethnic cleansing past and present in similar ways, the relationship between the temporal dimension and those political contexts poses other questions. What modus operandi do different ethnographic situations of violence require? Do anthropologists studying and writing on ongoing violence, like Bringa and Hayden, have different responsibilities than do anthropologists, like myself, studying episodes of violence that happened half a century ago?

ISTRIA: YUGOSLAVIA'S (OTHER) FIRST ETHNIC CLEANSING?

During the 1990s Italian journalists, politicians, and scholars uncovered a largely forgotten episode in recent history: the migration or flight of between 200,000 and 350,000 persons from the Istrian peninsula, as well as from the nearby city of Fiume/Rijeka and the Dalmatian city of Zara/Zadar, when Italy lost those territories to socialist Yugoslavia after World War II.[9] Though the majority of individuals who left Istria identified as Italians, self-identified Croats and Slovenes who did not want to live in a socialist state also numbered among the migrants.[10] Despite this, the Istrian exodus, or *l'esodo istriano*, has been figured in the Italian imagination as an Italian phenomenon, as the tragic end result of a campaign of ethnic cleansing. What had long been the dominant interpretation of events among the associations of *esuli* became, in the 1990s, the truism in Italy about what had taken place in the decade following World War II. Key to the realignment and new visibility of this history was the bloody breakup of Yugoslavia.

Once *ethnic cleansing* had become a household term during the Bosnian war, the exiles and their supporters found a receptive audience for their claim to have suffered Yugoslavia's first ethnic cleansing. "Look what they're doing to each other in Bosnia," exiles would tell me again and again during my research in Trieste, the border city where approximately one-third of the exiles resettled, "that's exactly what they did to us 50 years ago!" Such assertions draw on common stereotypes of the Balkans as a place of perpetual bloodshed. In his popular history, *A Tragedy Revealed*, the Italian journalist Arrigo Petacco trades on this assumption when he maintains, as part of his historical contextualization of the Istrian events, "Serbians and Croatians have always been divided by an ancestral hatred that has literally shed rivers of blood. . . . 'Ethnic cleansing' is not a tragic new development of modern times; it has long been a constant in the relations among the various groups in the Yugoslavian mosaic" (2005:17, 26).

Whereas Yugoslavia's dissolution provided the means for a repositioning of the exiles' story vis-à-vis national historiographies, the narrative element central to the story's reframing as one of ethnic cleansing is the series of executions carried out in the karstic pits known as the *foibe*. In Istria in

1943 and 1945 and in Trieste at war's end, the *foibe* became the sites of grisly executions by communist partisans and Yugoslav soldiers of both military and civilian personnel. Although the numbers and identities of the *foibe*'s victims remain fiercely disputed,[11] the pits have become the symbol of the tragedy of Italy's lost eastern provinces. The victims of the *foibe*, runs the popular thinking, were "killed for the sole crime of being Italian." This facile interpretation not only flattens out the complexities of who ended up in the *foibe* and why—Italian and German troops, for example, had used some of these pits as dumping grounds for bodies—but it also minimizes differences between the 1943 and 1945 episodes of violence.[12] These different moments of violence became emplotted in a seamless narrative of anti-Italian sentiment (for more on these narrative mechanisms, see Ballinger 2003). The *foibe*, in turn, are said to have motivated the exodus of Italians, further reinforcing an unbroken narrative of persecution.

The preface to the English translation of Petacco's book (2005) crystallizes this continuum of *foibe*-exodus-genocide when the translator Konrad Eisenbichler describes how a discussion of the *foibe* at an Istrian diaspora association in Toronto in 1991 initiated his interest in the project.

"Only a few individuals had the nerve, or the courage, to scream out the awful word that had come to encapsulate all their pain and anger: *foibe!*," writes Eisenbichler, who then contends: "The truth was out—Yugoslavian Communists had carried out a *genocide* and a forced evacuation of Italians from Dalmatia, Istria, and Venezia Giulia of *biblical proportions* and this tragedy reverberated deeply with recent events in Serbia and in Kosovo . . . an entire people had lost their homes, their lands, and many of them their lives *only* because they were Italian (2005:ix; emphasis added).

In remembrance of this, streets and monuments to the "martyrs of the *foibe*" have sprung up around Italy in places ranging from Trieste to Milan and Rome. This remembrance of the "martyrs" has also been tied to legal efforts to prosecute individuals responsible for the *foibe* crimes on the charge of genocide. Since the mid-1990s several legal proceedings in Italy have sought to bring *infoibatori* (those who carried out the crimes) to justice. Though the initial charge made in such trials was that of genocide, eventually the cases went forward under the accusation of "multiple homicide" (in recognition that the genocide charge is difficult to prove for the Istrian case, at least from a legal point of view). In this instance, ethnic cleansing remains a powerful and persuasive descriptive tool, precisely because it is fuzzier than genocide. At the same time, ethnic cleansing carries with it suggestions or implications (at least outside the courtroom) about genocide, as indeed has happened in the Istrian case. "The interchangeable use of the terms genocide and ethnic cleansing does not render justice to either term," asserts Mulaj; "genocide would be devalued and cheapened while the nature of ethnic cleansing would be obscured rather than explained" (2003:711).

Such a danger appears an all-too-real possibility given the slippage between the claims of genocide and ethnic cleansing for the Istrian example. The focus on genocide, and in particular on the *foibe*, draws a picture of an extinguished population and an emptied land. Yet not only did the dead in the *foibe* represent a small minority of the Italians from Istria (four thousand out of two hundred thousand, if we use conservative estimates for both) but a small but significant number of Italians also remained in socialist Yugoslavia. Though accurate numbers prove hard to come by, an estimated 30,000 Italians (those who remained and their descendants) live in contemporary Istria (divided between Slovenia and Croatia). For Italians living in Italy the focus on the *foibe* as part of a genocidal design associates Istria exclusively with images of death and suffering, neglecting the reality that life did go on there for an Italian minority, as well as for a Slavic majority.[13] Furthermore, the continued use of categories such as *esuli* and *rimasti* to describe those who left and those who stayed in Istria freezes Istrian Italians and their descendants in fixed, unchanging categories (see Sponza 2005).

Both the genocide and the ethnic cleansing concepts also diminish an attention to agency, since victims are presumably targeted on the basis of an ascribed identity. Yet in the Istrian case population flows took place over a decade and for a variety of reasons. The migration flows responded to the many twists and turns in the territorial dispute between Italy and Yugoslavia over the region. The first flight of Italians occurred in 1943, after Benito Mussolini's overthrow by the Grand Fascist Council, the Italian military collapse on September 8, and the establishment of the Kingdom of the South. In the power vacuum created by the collapse of the Italian state and before German troops moved in to secure Istria, partisans briefly gained control, and the first episodes of violence in the *foibe* took place. This prompted what some deem the "black exodus" (*l'esodo nero*), when state functionaries and those most associated with the fascist regime left

Istria. In 1944 Allied bombings and the subsequent Yugoslav occupation of the Italian city of Zara/Zadar (on the Dalmatian coast) led to most of the Italian residents abandoning that city.

Population movements out of Istria and the city of Fiume/Rijeka (part of the Carnaro or Kvarner region) resumed as the war drew to a close in May 1945. As the Yugoslav troops and the Western Allies "raced" to take Trieste, a confrontation emerged between Tito's troops—which held the city for 40 days and carried out executions in the *foibe* around Trieste— and the Anglo-Americans. Eventually the Yugoslavs withdrew and the contested territory was divided into a Zone A (administered by an Anglo-American–run Allied Military Government) and a Zone B (controlled by the Yugoslav military). Individual migrations took place during this time but soon acquired an organized form after the 1947 peace treaty with Italy awarded the southern half of Istria to Yugoslavia. Article 19 of the treaty stated that all "Italians" resident in the respective territory on or before June 10, 1940, had the legal right (though by no means the obligation) to opt for Italian citizenship.[14] Opting for Italian citizenship required relocating to Italy.

To be eligible for Italian citizenship, the principal requirements were Italian as the *lingua d'uso* (language of customary use) and *domicilio* (domicile, here usually interpreted as primary residence) in Italy. This created complications in Istria, where 20 years of fascist Italianization policies meant that most residents (including ethnic Slavs) spoke Italian. Local people's committees overseeing the option process from the Yugoslav side frequently turned down requests on the grounds that the applicants were not "really" Italians (judging either by linguistic usage or their ethnic surnames) and created other obstacles to migration ranging from police intimidation of those waiting in lines at option offices to bureaucratic headaches. The statement made by Umberto S. to the pro-Italian Comitato di Liberazione Nazionale dell'Istria (Committee for the National Liberation of Istria, CLN) in April 1948 speaks to the experience of many Istrians who found their options blocked.

The option process took place in Portole [small town in the Istrian interior] in open contradiction with the terms of the Peace Treaty in as much as all those citizens whose customary language was Italian but whose surname retained its Slavic origins could not exercise their option to opt. Such was the case of my cousin, Dr. D.S., whose language of use is Italian, but who could not exercise his right to opt because he is considered a Croatian [Yugoslav] citizen. In this way many young people, whose customary language is Italian but to whom it wasn't permitted to opt, have been called to arms [by the Yugoslav military] and sent to Susak, to Dalmatia, and to Serbia, as we know from letters they have written to their relatives. I myself, having been accused of spreading propaganda urging young people not to present themselves when called up and of carrying out espionage work for the Italian Army, had to avoid sure arrest, and thus I clandestinely fled from Portole on April 4, 1948, taking refuge in Trieste. (CLN, Dichiarazione politica n. 113)

On the other hand, the relatives and close associates of those who successfully opted for Italy often became the targets of abuse, at times being fired from places of employment or having homes requisitioned. Such actions further prompted individuals to leave. The attitude of the Yugoslav authorities toward migration was thus not always consistent or coherent. Nor was the process of migration uniformly unidirectional, as the term *ethnic cleansing* might imply. After the option processes of 1948 and 1952 many Istrians in the new Zone B, redrawn after the 1947 settlement, held out in hopes that the territorial dispute would ultimately be decided in favor of Italy. When the 1954 Memorandum of Understanding ostensibly resolved the territorial question,[15] awarding Zone A (which included Trieste) to Italy and Zone B (northern Istria) to Yugoslavia, it prompted the mass migration (*Grande Esodo*) out of Zone B.

In many cases, apart from dramatic exceptions such as the *foibe* killings and the threat of the *foibe*, individuals and families thus made *choices* (albeit anguished and difficult ones) about leaving. Indeed, many of the former exiles from Zone B I interviewed in the mid-1990s stressed that the authorities did not force them to leave, in contrast to some of the migrants of 1945. In a few instances, informants who participated in the exile associations in Trieste admitted that they or their parents had emigrated during the exodus for purely personal or family reasons. Anna*,[16] an older woman born in Umago/Umag who now lives with her adult son in Trieste, noted that in 1947 she and her husband had merely moved to Trieste from Zone B for personal reasons. They never "learned to hate the Yugoslavs," as she put it, and her husband's parents stayed in Istria. Anna's father-in-law lived to the age of 95, and in her opinion stayed in Istria because he did not want to lose his house, rather than out of any political motivation.

Certainly, though, in many other instances, families may have seen little choice but to leave. Yet after 1945 physical threats generally gave way to subtler forms of intimidation such as the nationalization and confiscation of properties, the interruption of transport services (by both land and sea) to the city of Trieste, the heavy taxation of salaries of those who worked in Zone A and lived in Zone B, the persecution of clergy and teachers, and economic hardship caused by the creation of a special border currency, the Jugolira. This returns us to the question of the limitations of the ethnic cleansing label, or even that of "forced migration" (usually considered one aspect of ethnic cleansing). Brubaker has noted the problems with forced migration as an umbrella category: "It is insufficiently differentiated, and it obscures the fact that there is almost always, even in the case of flight from immediately threatening violence, a more or less significant element of will or choice involved in the act of migration" (1998:1049). He adds that "even where fear is a central motive of the migrants, it is not always appropriate to speak of forced migrations" (1998:1049).

Yet Brubaker cautions that one should not label "ethnomigrants" as merely economic migrants, a distinction sometimes applied by Italians to Istrian Slavs who left the peninsula at the same time, as well as to Slavs who left Istria under fascism. In many cases, these Slovene and Croatian migrants after World War II may have had similar motives to the Italians leaving Istria, motives in which political, religious, and economic questions intertwined. Though most of the persons giving testimony to the CLN of Istria about their reasons for leaving Istria self-identified as Italians, some individuals of Slavic ethnicity (Slovene or Croat) also added their voices to the CLN's documentation of the Yugoslav regime's abuses. Antonia S., a resident of Isola/Izola and of (self-declared) "Slovene nationality," reported threats and intimidation toward all residents, not just Italians, who had not gone to vote in the elections of 1950 held in Zone B. Antonia's husband, like many others who recognized the election for the mockery it was, had refused to vote. "On April 16 [1950] two Titoist activists entered my house and tried to break down the door of the room where my husband was. Not having success, they left and came back a second time. . . . 'If you don't go to vote,' they told me, 'something terrible will surely happen to you.' Naturally I replied to them that I didn't feel like voting, and then I added: 'I am of

Slovene nationality, but I absolutely don't share your way of doing things.' They left after threatening reprisals. Unfortunately, the episode left me very upset: we are living the worst moments of our lives. I have to add that neither I nor my husband went to vote" (CLN, Dichiarazione politica n. 401).

When talking about the choices made by Istrians—whether of Italian, Slovene, or Croat identification—one must be careful not to overstate the degree to which some choices were voluntary. Writing of the so-called voluntary population exchange of Hungarians from Czechoslovakia and Slovaks from Hungary, Róbert Barta points to a variety of coercive factors to "illustrate the extent to which any 'voluntary' elements in this exchange of populations was purely sham" (2003:573). He adds, however, a revealing comment that reminds us of the simplifying and flattening power of the ethnic cleansing thesis: "The whole episode must be regarded as ethnic cleansing, pure and simple" (2003:573). In the Istrian case, perhaps less attention should be paid to the seemingly "pure and simple" and more to distinguishing and differentiating the specific migratory flows (see Pupo 2005:191). Terms such as *forced migration* or *ethnic cleansing* may prove more apt for describing certain moments and places in Istria during the decade following World War II than for others.

Furthermore, interpreting events in Istria between 1943 and 1955 through the ethnic cleansing framework has also entailed a kind of narrative tailoring designed to align the Istrian story with the paradigmatic cases of genocide and ethnic cleansing: the Holocaust and the Yugoslav wars, respectively. Leaders of exile associations, individuals writing memoirs, and many everyday Istrians recounting their life stories draw on imagery associated with other places and other times: cattle cars, stars of David, death marches (Ballinger 2000, 2003).[17] Istrian Italians often speak of their exodus as an event of "biblical proportions," as does Eisenbichler (the son of refugees from Lussino/Losinj) in his preface to Petacco's (2005) history. The reference to things biblical invokes, of course, the metanarrative of exodus: the flight of the Israelites out of Egypt. At the same time, exiles also draw on more concrete references to the historical persecution of the Jews in the Holocaust. Father Flaminio Rocchi, an Istrian priest who served as a spiritual leader for the community in exile, explicitly linked the history of the Istrian victims with that of those of the Holocaust. He noted that after the war some Istrian refugees in Trieste had lived in the Risiera di San Sabba, the former Nazi concentration camp that had served as a transit point for Italian Jews being sent to extermination camps deep in the Reich. "Entire families, including, in 1959, that of my sister (comprising five persons), women, the elderly, children, were amassed in the same cells, dirty, moldy, without light. . . . The walls and the beams still bore scratched names, dates, stars of David, crosses, invocations" (1990:82). Rocchi thus created an analogy between the suffering of the exiles and that of the Jews, even as he also made a claim for an actual link—the physical space of the Risiera di San Sabba—joining those two histories.

The attempt to appropriate (or at least share in) the moral power embodied in the narrative of the ultimate victimization, the Holocaust, is not unique to the Istrian exiles, of course. Analyzing discourses of victimhood in the Yugoslav wars of the 1990s, Marco Živković commented ironically on what he identified as "the wish to be a Jew" (2000) and on the ways in which analogies to the Holocaust informed understandings of ethnic cleansing in Yugoslavia. By positioning themselves as analogous to both the Jews and the victims of ethnic cleansing in 1990s Yugoslavia, the Istrian exiles thus doubly draw on the Holocaust tropes of victimhood—in their original form and as refracted through the new narratives of ethnic cleansing forged in the Yugoslav wars of succession.

This narrative framework clearly offers Istrian exiles moral and political capital, as well as a new audience for their histories. It does so, however, at the risk of obscuring experiences that complicate or write against such a powerful and persuasive account. (It also runs the danger of allowing some observers to downplay or dismiss the gravity of the Istrian exodus precisely because, in their eyes, comparisons with the Holocaust appear so exaggerated.) To this point, relatively little work has explored how experiences during the Istrian exodus differed according to gender. Women have typically been presented as undifferentiated victims alongside men or have figured as the objects of sexual violence. One notorious case of such violence occurred in 1943, when the university student Norma Cossetto was raped repeatedly by her captors before being thrown into the *foiba* (singular of *foibe*) of Surani. In the exile community Cossetto has become a martyr. Petacco's book on the exodus moves from Cossetto's experience to claim that "atrocities of the sort to which Norma Cossetto fell victim were not, unfortunately, the exception, but the rule. All the women were raped before being thrown into the *foibe*, and all men suffered unspeakable abuse" (2005:46). In claiming this, Petacco projects events in 1990s Bosnia (a war tactic of mass rapes) back onto his interpretation of Istria in 1943. The rhetoric of rape—now woven into the narrative about the *foibe* and the exodus from Istria—thus works to portray Istrian women uniformly as victims. Starting from the assumption that events in Istria fall under the rubric of ethnic cleansing means that actions considered aspects of ethnic cleansing, such as rape, are also assumed (in tautological fashion), even though such actions should in fact be considered among the kind of *evidence* scholars need to determine whether ethnic cleansing has actually occurred.

Not surprisingly, exile narratives—both written and oral—typically depict the "immorality" of the actions of the Tito regime by focusing on incidents in which the sanctity of the family and of gender norms are violated (see Ballinger 2003). Gianni*, an elderly man from Pirano/Piran, admiringly recalled the "patriarchal family" model that had prevailed in Istria under both Austria and Italy until the communist regime assaulted hearth and home. Speaking for his wife, who meekly deferred to her husband throughout the five hours that I visited them in their apartment in Trieste, this man recounted how, after having been imprisoned and tried in Capodistria/Koper on the charge of "espionage,"[18] he managed to make his way to Trieste. Telling authorities that he needed to visit his father, who worked in Trieste (Zone A) and who remained there after being blocked by the Yugoslav authorities from returning to his residence in Pirano/Piran (Zone B), Gianni never returned to Pirano/Piran. Accompanied by his wife and child to the border between Zone A and Zone B, Gianni watched helplessly as the rest of his family was denied permission to go to Trieste. Having been turned back, his wife—four months pregnant—miscarried. His wife and child did eventually follow Gianni to Trieste, where they spent eight years in cramped conditions at the Silos refugee camp before obtaining state-built housing in Borgo San Sergio.

In recounting his family's experiences Gianni emphasized how the Yugoslavs in Istria violated the "natural" unity of the family. The story of the wife's miscarriage—a detail mentioned by Gianni rather than by his wife, who looked somewhat uncomfortable with the telling of this part of the story—comes to symbolize the lack of respect for the family, the pillar of the two previous regimes.[19]

Though the experience of women was often recounted for them by men and through a framework validating traditional gender roles, it should be noted that some of my female informants also related personal histories in ways that similarly underlined the "unnatural" behavior of the Yugoslavs and their lack of respect for the family. Laura*, born in 1925 in Castagna (a village near Buie/Buje), spent much of her childhood in Ancona, where her father had been transferred through his job for the state railroad. When he retired in 1943, however, Laura's father made the unfortunate decision to return the family to Istria a mere two months before the capitulation of the Italian army on September 8. Laura spent seven years in Istria, "the worst years of my life," remaining on the peninsula with her husband and young daughter until they finally left in 1950. Laura recounted that the partisans had come to her house and taken away a male relative, who was then killed in the *foibe*.[20] About ten days later the partisan returned to the house with the jacket of the dead man. When her daughter saw the coat, she began to sob hysterically. The Yugoslav asked the little girl why she was crying, and Laura quickly interjected, "she has a toothache."

For Laura this story symbolized that under the Yugoslav regime one could not even cry, the most "natural" of impulses for a frightened young girl. For a long time afterward, Laura told me, her daughter became terrified at the sound of men shouting. In Laura's opinion, these events had done "some type of damage to the girl's nervous system." Laura's account thus reaffirms a prevailing narrative of women as victims. Yet here the victim appears to be Laura's daughter (for whom Laura speaks), in contrast to her quick-thinking and protective mother.

In contrast to Laura, many of the women I interviewed who had left Istria as children or adolescents had come to think of their migration as having created new opportunities for them, rather than as having ruined their lives. This did not prove true just for women, of course, but for many young people who left villages or small towns in Istria for cities in Italy and abroad (given that approximately one-third of the refugees emigrated to places like the United States, Canada, Australia, and Argentina). One man whose family emigrated from the town of Rovigno/Rovinj and relocated in Bari, for instance, noted the greater educational and cultural opportunities available to him once his family left. Yet for women such migration typically offered even greater freedom and excitement than it did for their male counterparts.

For some women I interviewed who originally came from small towns in Istria, living in refugee camps alongside teenage boys provided them with the opportunity for interactions that they might not have had in prewar

Istria. Contrary to the tales of suffering and indignities in the refugee camps described by many other exiles, the stories told by women who had been adolescents at the time often invoked nostalgia for their camp days, recalling jokes and flirtations, friends and rites of passage. Remembering her family's migration from Fiume/Rijeka to Italy, where they lived in a refugee camp in Trieste, the writer Marisa Madieri captures a young woman's sense of her horizons opening up even as the world around her was crashing down: "Even the tragedy of the war was for me a curious adventure: bombings, fires, alarms, flights to shelter seemed to me strange episodes that didn't endanger me but rather made my life more interesting" (1987:13).

Mirella,* a woman from Rovigno/Rovinj with whom I became quite friendly, spoke with great fondness of her family's move to Australia with the exodus. Here the young Mirella mastered English and enjoyed not only the relative freedoms of an "Anglo-Saxon" society but also the greater possibilities for female education. Mirella had planned to go to university and study English literature. A year away from high school graduation, Mirella was informed by her parents—who had not adapted to their new environment so easily and who missed their home region—that the family would be moving back to Istria. The timing of this move (in the early 1960s) was motivated by a Yugoslav deadline, after which it would be impossible to (re)gain Yugoslav citizenship. For Mirella the return to Istria, rather than the exodus from it, has proven the tragedy that marked her life. She found herself cast into a narrow, close-minded society (from her Australian perspective) in which girls were treated as objects and in which she could barely communicate with her peers. One of Mirella's contemporaries and an immediate neighbor in the days when the family returned to Rovigno/ Rovinj commented that "everyone" (referring to the other teenagers in the town) viewed Mirella as a snob and ignored her. Today Mirella has a daughter (whose father she did not marry) and a successful career, yet she remains the object of malicious gossip and harbors real bitterness toward her parents for the choice they imposed on her to return to Istria.

Mirella's unhappy story highlights the tangible sense of possibility offered to many of the young women who left Istria. Such findings do not prove especially surprising or unique, given that migrations may disrupt parental forms of authority as children master the codes of the new environment more quickly. In particular, women moving out of fairly "traditional" societies may experience migration as bringing freedom from more restrictive regimes of female conduct (on gendered memories of a Jewish migrant family from Algeria, see Bahloul 1996).

In some settings in Istria, however, strong-minded, working women were not unusual, and thus the exodus did not uniformly represent a loosening of restrictions for women. For example, Rovigno/Rovinj had (and still has today) a tobacco factory built during the Hapsburg period. The town also had a long socialist tradition born out of its labor culture, as well as a tradition of working-class humor, as I discovered on many afternoons as I drank coffee with older women now retired from the tobacco factory. (That Mirella experienced 1960s Rovigno/Rovinj as a patriarchal backwater, however, reminds us that the freedom for women in the worker culture of the town proved relative to other places in Istria.) Not surprisingly, many Italians—male and female—in Rovigno/Rovinj actively participated in the antifascist cause during the war. Here, too, women found new opportunities as partisans and, after the war, as party and Italian minority activists. Other women I interviewed there, however, insisted that they had not chosen to remain in Istria. Rather, the choice was made for them, by parents or husbands, precisely because they were women. Indeed, the marked demographic imbalance in the Italian community that remained in Istria after World War II reflects not only the loss of men in the war but also that in many families one daughter chose (or was designated) to remain with the elderly parents, while the rest of the children emigrated. The ethnic cleansing label effectively writes out these complexities of the gendered experience of migration (and nonmigration, in some cases) from Istria.

At the same time, the ethnic cleansing concept has undoubtedly and usefully refocused attention on ethnic dimensions of events in Istria, which before the 1990s were often described in terms of the conflict between fascism and communism, followed by the Cold War confrontation of democratic capitalism and state socialism. Furthermore, for those presenting themselves as victims of ethnic cleansing, the term helps generate political credibility and sympathy, which in the case of the Istrian exiles has meant allies in their pursuit of claims to property restitution and compensation. Yet I also hope to have suggested here what dimensions of experience may be lost to understanding if the Istrian events are read *exclusively* in terms of ethnic conflict and if Istrians are cast into the role of passive victims, especially if accounts assume ethnic cleansing a priori, rather than view it as something to be empirically demonstrated. What happens to questions of class conflict, which overlap but are not coterminous with ethnic issues? What about gender and generational differences in the experience of displacement? How do geographic differences—northern versus southern Istria, towns versus rural areas—impact experiences? And what about issues of choice and agency?

Whereas Carol Lilly (1996) feared that using the term *ethnic cleansing* in place of *genocide* for events in 1990s Bosnia made for "immoral obfuscation," using the term *ethnic cleansing* to describe events in Istria may make for scholarly and even political obfuscation. Or, to be more precise, describing what happened in Istria after World War II solely in terms of ethnic cleansing risks obfuscation, as does the opposite stance—the complete denial of the strong ethnic elements at work in tandem with other aspects such as gender, class, and political identification. Unlike Brubaker and Cooper, who find the notion of identity so problematic that they advocate abandoning it as an analytical (as opposed to "folk") category, I do not believe scholars should throw out the ethnic cleansing concept quite yet (though we might do so if in the future its use sees further devaluation). The term does contribute to our understanding of conflicts once read largely in terms of other causes. Nonetheless, scholars must take care to distinguish between the politics (and emotions) of ethnic cleansing claims and the difficulties of analytically untangling causality, motivations, and consequences.

REFLECTIONS ON THE SCHOLAR'S DILEMMA

Hinton has noted that while anthropologists may be uniquely placed to offer insight into the phenomenon of genocide (and, I would add, to the related phenomenon of ethnic cleansing, regardless of how exactly we define it), they have often remained oddly silent on the topic (2002:1). As the current volume demonstrates, this anthropological reticence has begun to disappear. Yet an anthropology of genocide, or an anthropology of ethnic cleansing, raises tricky questions for anthropologists. Anthropologists are particularly adept at deconstructing narratives and practices—not to prove them false, but rather to show how they reflect the sociocultural contexts that engendered them.

Deconstructing claims about genocide or ethnic cleansing, however, carries a particular risk because these discourses represent truth claims of a special sort and possess a powerful moral charge. Deconstructing such narratives, as I have done here by looking critically at the ethnic cleansing thesis in relation to the Istrian exodus, may strike some, informants and scholars alike, as deeply problematic, possibly even as offensive or immoral. I have already encountered puzzlement and even anger in the Istrian exile community in Trieste over my analyses. At the same time, the moral judgments made of the scholar's stance may vary widely, depending on the particular audience. In presentations to members of the Istrian diaspora in North America, my description of the pervasiveness of the ethnic cleansing thesis in both political and scholarly discussions in Italy has provoked a different kind of puzzlement. Many Istrians outside Italy remain unaware that their experiences are widely described in terms of ethnic cleansing, and quite a few have commented to me on what they consider the inappropriateness of this label for their personal histories.

For anthropologists working on topics that touch ongoing or recently concluded events, the ethical and moral questions become even more acute. Is it ethical to deconstruct certain claims when researching what Nancy Scheper-Hughes calls "extreme situations" (1995:415)? Hayden's critique of the use of the language of genocide in Bosnia, for example, provoked angry, even hostile, responses. Raising the question of "the scholar's responsibility to elucidate and not further obfuscate issues," Lilly charges: "Here Hayden moves beyond amoral realism to immoral obfuscation and seriously compromises his scholarly integrity" (1996:751). Yet even if one does not agree with Hayden's interpretation of events in Bosnia or with his assertion that an internationally recognized partition from the outset would have spared lives, is it necessarily unethical to inquire into the politics of the rhetoric of genocide, given that we live in an age in which the Holocaust and genocide have become the ultimate reference, analogy, and claim? The stakes of such inquiry prove high regardless of whether the violence occurred in the past or in the contemporary moment, though ongoing violence brings with it a different kind of urgency and ethical challenge for the anthropologist.

In calling for a "militant anthropology" that politically engages anthropologists with emergencies in the contemporary world, Scheper-Hughes herself uses a violent rhetoric in her proposal: "The new cadre of 'barefoot anthropologists' that I envision must become alarmists and shock troopers—the producers of politically complicated and morally demanding texts and images capable of sinking through the layers of acceptance, complicity, and bad faith that allow the suffering and the deaths to continue without even the pained cry of recognition of Conrad's [1910] evil protagonist, Kurtz: 'The horror! the horror!'" (1995:417).

In Scheper-Hughes's estimation, anthropology's trademark cultural relativism has become an excuse for political inaction in the face of suffering and violence, thereby promoting an irresponsible moral relativism. Hinton echoes this when he contends that cultural relativism has hindered anthropological work on genocide (2002:2). But accepting claims of genocide and ethnic cleansing as moral absolutes on which anthropologists must charge into action as "shock troopers" risks, in some instances, other kinds of complicity on the part of the anthropologist. Writing of identity, Brubaker and Cooper note the slippage between the term's use as "a category of practice" and "as a category of analysis" (2000:5). They astutely point out that this slippage follows not from intellectual imprecision but instead "reflects the dual orientation of many academic identitarians as both *analysts* and *protagonists* of identity politics" (2000:6), an observation that also holds true for debates about ethnic cleansing and genocide and the appropriate stance of scholars who also advocate for certain understandings and policies. Scheper-Hughes's call for a militant anthropology embodies the tension created by this dual orientation, as well as the presumption that we (scholar-activists) can always sort out in clear-cut terms who is a victim, who is a perpetrator, and what course of action we should take in adequately and appropriately responding to such violence.

Only after completing my fieldwork on memories of the Istrian exodus did I realize, for example, how informants' narratives had worked to draw me in. By various strategies these accounts rendered the ethnographer complicit not only with the judgment of Istrian events as an unproblematic episode of ethnic cleansing (an interpretation that I continue to grapple with in my own ongoing historical work on the exodus) but also with the frequent condemnation of the ostensible perpetrators of this ethnic cleansing, the "Slavs." At the same time, I was wary of accounts of Slavic victimization under fascism that suggested that the violence against Italians at war's end was somehow justified. In contemporary Trieste the history of the *foibe* and of the exodus is often invoked to delegitimize claims of an autochthonous Slovene minority, as if these 21st-century Triestine Slovenes had some responsibility for the events in the 1940s. Even more commonly the exodus comes to "justify" generalized chauvinistic attitudes toward Croats and Slovenes as former victims become victimizers (though in contemporary Trieste this victimization has usually taken the form of symbolic, rather than physical, violence).

My own sense of the web of complicities spun around me by my Istrian Italian informants, as well as my awareness of the ways in which the ethnic cleansing account has flattened out the nuances of individuals' experiences, comes from over a decade of work in Trieste and Istria in a political context in which the scholarly endorsement or refutation of the ethnic cleansing label's applicability to the Istrian Italians becomes de facto a political choice. Working in quite a different setting, that of Indonesia's indigenous peoples, Tania Murray Li has written eloquently of the dilemmas for scholars and activists posed by indigenous people who participate in the violence of ethnic cleansing. She notes that such actions not only disrupt the image of native peoples as victims but that they also force "academics and activists who have analysed and, indeed, promoted 'resistance' and 'empowerment' by indigenous peoples to confront the violently embodied outcomes which can ensue" (2002:361). Drawing on Liisa Malkki's work, Murray Li further highlights the dilemmas of "sedentarism," that is, the unquestioning valorization of the native, the autochthonous, and the rooted. In Indonesia the dark side of this sedentarism includes the sometimes violent exclusion of migrants, many of whom may be as vulnerable as the indigenous people themselves. With peoples displaced by development and environmental crises, a logic privileging claims to rootedness means that such refugees can never find a home in Indonesia that does not "belong" to a previous claimant. In raising this uncomfortable issue, Murray Li aims to break a deep silence in the scholarly community and especially in the indigenous rights movement in regard to the justification of exclusion in the name of tradition.

The conclusions drawn by Murray Li for Indonesia's indigenous peoples echo my own analysis of the exclusive and excluding nature of contemporary Istrian understandings of autochthony, although this exclusion has remained at the symbolic level (Ballinger 2004). Yet such conclusions do not necessarily hold for anthropologists working on other cases involving violence and its consequences,[21] reminding us that one of anthropology's strengths lies in its attention to specific sociocultural contexts. Some scholars of genocide, notably Scheper-Hughes and Hinton, have criticized Franz Boas's trademark cultural relativism, asking whether it proves appropriate for topics demanding moral clarity and urgency such as genocide. Indeed, in a slightly rephrased version, this dilemma lies at the heart of Hayden's critique of Ramet's analysis of the scholarship on the Yugoslav breakup and of Ramet's classification of works into two main camps:

> On the one side are those who have taken a moral universalist perspective, holding that there are universal norms in international politics, that these norms are founded in Universal Reason and expressed in international covenants such as the Universal Declaration of Human Rights, and that, in recounting the horrors of the recent War of Yugoslav Succession of 1991–5, the analyst *must* account for the disintegration of socialist Yugoslavia and the outbreak of hostilities, identifying culpable parties. . . . On the other side are authors who reject the universalist framework, with its emphasis on universal norms and universal human rights and who, in their accounts, embrace one or another version of moral relativism. (Ramet 2005:1–2)[22]

Individual anthropologists confronted with situations of evil and violence have taken different stances on this choice between moral universalism and moral relativism, stances that reflect an anthropologist's particular location in time and space to the violence, as well as anthropology's critical awareness of the dilemmas built into universalisms. Certain aspects of the contested Boasian approach, however, point to useful ways for anthropologists studying such violence to proceed. The Boasian inductive method, which rejected the use of generalizations to explain particularities and instead relied on close empirical work to generate theoretical hypotheses, represents a source of strength for an anthropological discipline seeking to contribute to the empirical and conceptual understanding of genocide and ethnic cleansing. Thus it may prove more appropriate to think of anthropolog*ies* of such violence than to propose a singular or unified anthropological approach. In so doing anthropologists may ultimately go beyond the limitations of the ethnic cleansing concept.

NOTES

The research for this article was made possible by a 1999 Summer Grant from the National Endowment for the Humanities, the NEH Post-Classical Humanistic/Modern Italian studies Fellowship at the American Academy in Rome, and multiple awards from the Fletcher Fund at Bowdoin College. Many thanks go to the Istituto Regionale per la Cultura Istriana for permitting me to consult the documentation of the Comitato di Liberazione Nazionale dell'Istria (CLN). I am grateful to Alex Hinton, Kevin O'Neill, and the anonymous reviewers for Duke University Press for their careful and critical readings of this piece. As always, I reserve my greatest thanks for the many Istrians who have shared their experiences with me.

1. The debate also brought to mind an earlier scholarly dispute between Hayden and Bette Denich, on the one hand, and Thomas Cushman, on the other, over interpreting the conflicts in the former Yugoslavia. For different perspectives on this particular debate, go to the articles by Cushman, Denich, Hayden, and others in *Anthropological Theory* (2005).

2. In his introduction to the edited volume *Redrawing Nations: Ethnic Cleansing in East-Central Europe, 1944–1948*, for example, Mark Kramer defines genocide as *one* possible aspect of the larger phenomenon of ethnic cleansing. "For analytical purposes," he contends, "ethnic cleansing can be seen as encompassing several types of repressive actions, including *deportations* (the coercive transfer of minorities to distant regions within a country), *expulsions* (the forced removal of minorities from one country to another), and *genocide* (deliberate, mass slaughter aimed at complete extermination)" (2001:1). After evaluating a variety of definitions, Klejda Mulaj proposes her own: "Ethnic cleansing is a deliberate policy designed by and pursued under the leadership of a nation or ethnic community or with its consent, with the view to removing an 'undesirable population' from a given territory on the basis of its ethnic, national, or religious origin, or a combination of these, by using systematically force or intimidation (2002:698).

3. Philipp Ther maintains, "the term 'cleansing' had been widely used before in German, French, Polish and Czech (*Säuberung, purification, oczyszczanie, ocista*) and many other languages" (2001:43; see also Kramer 2001:1). According to Philip Cohen, "cleansing" was used during the Balkan Wars (1912–13) to characterize Serbia's treatment of acquired territories (Mulaj 2003:696).

4. Brubaker has forcefully critiqued the reifying language of even much constructivist work on identity for the ways in which such scholarship often presumes that groups exist and then demonstrates how members of groups "construct" their identities along various axes. Brubaker instead lays out an approach that examines how the notion of "groupness" itself comes into being and is enacted at various moments. In the case of ethnic cleansing and genocide, the external ascription of groupness by perpetrators relies on a foundationalist notion of groups, on the one hand, and helps constitute a strong sense of groupness, on the other.

5. Article 2 of the UN Convention on the Prevention and Punishment of the Crime of Genocide (1948) states "genocide means any of the following acts committed with intent to destroy, in whole or in part, a national, ethnical, racial or religious group, as such:

   (a) Killing members of the group;
   (b) Causing serious bodily or mental harm to members of the group;

(c) Deliberately inflicting on the group conditions of life calculated to bring about its physical destruction in whole or in part;

(d) Imposing measures intended to prevent births within the group;

(e) Forcibly transferring children of the group to another group" (United Nations 2002:44; see also Lemkin's innovation of the term, 2002).

Beyond this legal definition, however, scholars have variously sought to define genocide in sociological terms (Fein 2002), in relation to modernity (Bauman 2002[1989]), and in relation to colonialism (Bodley 2002[1999]). Some have used genocide "in the strictest sense to mean the conscious, systematic attempt to exterminate physically an entire population group (ethnic, religious or national)" and thus have restricted its use to "only the Armenians during the First World War and to the Jews and Roma during the Second World War" (Rieber 2000:3). Other authors have written about the potential for genocide (Nagengast 2002) along a continuum of genocidal acts ranging from what Leo Kuper and Robert Melson call "genocidal massacres" to "total domestic genocide" (cited in Lilly 1996:749). Issues of contention include the question of intent and how to situate "ethnocide" and "cultural genocide" within the framework of genocide.

6. Argues János Mazsu, "Despite the widespread use of the term by the mass media during the new Balkan War, its exact meaning was never clearly defined. This was the reason why the expression 'ethnic cleansing' was often preceded with the prefix 'so-called'" (2003:744).

7. I thank an anonymous reviewer for Duke University Press for bringing this point to my attention. In his well-received *Fires of Hatred: Ethnic Cleansing in Twentieth-Century Europe*, a synthetic overview of ethnic cleansing in Europe, the historian Norman Naimark clearly distinguishes genocide from ethnic cleansing on the basis of intent. Naimark contends that ethnic cleansing—which operates "to remove a people and often all traces from a concrete territory" (2001:3)—is not a synonym for genocide, even though the consequences (if not the intent) of such policies may be genocidal. He asserts that the *results* of the "ethnic cleansing" of Anatolian Armenians by Turks in 1915 were genocidal, even if evidence proves unclear as to whether Turkish *intentions* were genocidal. In such situations, "both literally and figuratively, ethnic cleansing bleeds into genocide, as mass murder is committed in order to rid the land of a people" (2001:3–4). The ethnic cleansing classification in Naimark's usage thus appears to offer scholars a way around the troubling issue of proving intent, something key to definitions of genocide.

8. For a related discussion, see Ballinger 1999:89.

9. The exact number and ethnic makeup of the refugees remains debated. The standard statistical study endorsed by Istrian Italian exiles gives a figure of 350,000 ethnic Italians (Colella 1958). More recent Italian studies (Donato and Nodari 1995) have argued for a number closer to 200,000 persons.

10. Writing of the process by which some individuals in Istria could legally opt for Italian citizenship, Sandi Volk argues that at war's end there were many individuals (at least in rural areas) for whom "national identity was not yet definitely formed," de-

spite 20 years of harsh Italianization policies promoted by the Italian fascist regime. In Volk's estimation, the mass migration occasioned by the option signaled the moment at which those leaving "definitively chose also their national identity . . . the exodus was thus also a key moment of denationalization in which an imprecise number (in any case a minority) of Slovenes and Croats in Istria made the passage to Italianness" (2004:32). Yet it remains difficult to prove that choosing Italian citizenship necessarily entailed an obligatory internalization of an Italian national identity, especially as many individuals came to Italy only to emigrate abroad soon after. Raoul Pupo and Aleksander Panjek recognize this in their suggestion that the option offered a kind of safety valve for general dissatisfaction with the Yugoslav regime in Istria, leading many of uncertain identity to *declare* themselves Italian. "More or less voluntarily, more or less uncertainly, many [optants] chose a nationality, others changed it, others yet declared one for the sake of convenience" (2004:352).

11. Though figures given for *foibe* victims sometimes run as high as 50,000, scholars believe that the numbers lie closer to 4,000 or 5,000 (Stranj 1992:89; Pupo 1997:37).

12. For a discussion of the 1943 *foibe* killings as a spontaneous outburst of hatred toward those associated with the Italian fascist regime, see Pupo 1997:43–48.

13. Elsewhere I have discussed in detail the Istrian exiles' use of rhetorics of silence to negate the living actuality of Istria (Ballinger 2003). In remembering their lost homeland, these exiles often fix on material traces of the past—cemeteries, churches, crumbling buildings—that testify, as they see it, to the rootedness of Italianate culture on the peninsula. These are also frequently sites of abandonment or decay, the image of which testifies to the extinction of Italian culture in the area, which some exiles elide with the extinction of *all* culture and life. Not only does this negate the peninsula's contemporary Slavic residents but it also denies the presence of an Italian minority that sees itself as the custodian of Italian culture in Istria. For a further discussion of the rhetorics of silence in relation to genocide, see Dwyer this volume.

14. This option clause also applied to the Val d'Aosta and the Dodecanese Islands, other territories lost by Italy after World War II.

15. The agreement operated as a de facto settlement until ratified by Italy and Yugoslavia as the Treaty of Osimo in 1975. The treaty prompted widespread criticism and political protest in Trieste. When Yugoslavia dissolved in 1991, some exile association leaders argued that Osimo no longer proved valid, given that one of its signatories had ceased to exist.

16. Where indicated by an asterisk, I have used pseudonyms for my informants.

17. On this topic I have benefited from ongoing conversations with the historian Marta Verginella, who is examining such questions from a different angle.

18. The charge of espionage was frequently used by the local authorities to target individuals, likely in the hope of encouraging them to leave the territory. While espionage was a stock charge, Gianni did in fact secretly collect information for seven or

eight months for the CLN dell'Istria e di Trieste, a pro-Italian group documenting abuses of Italians in Istria and fighting to keep Istria Italian.

19. Pro-Italian propaganda and cartoons of the time often depicted the communist partisans, particularly the women, in monstrous terms. The male partisan may appear as something freakish, a hybrid of man and ape. An article in the underground pro-Italian newspaper *Il grido dell'Istria* described the female partisan as "an animal that belongs to the human species, of the female sex; as a result of special living conditions and of practices contrary to nature, it is facially, corporeally and spiritually transformed. In that transformation what was most delicately feminine becomes a monstrous being, huge and muscular, masculine" (Sluga 1994:192).

20. This episode of violence presumably took place in 1945, rather than in 1943, since Laura married and had her daughter once she returned to Istria in 1943.

21. In replying to various comments on her *Current Anthropology* article, however, Scheper-Hughes does admit "that there are many different paths to morally engaged and politically committed anthropology" (1995:438). Writing of ethnic cleansing in the problematic context of groups that are victims in one moment and perpetrators in another, Mark Levene recognizes, "Definition and demarcation are, of course, a necessary part of any scholarly discipline, even one associated with the study of mass murder" (1994:445). Yet Levene quickly adds, "In practice, however, I think one can see how fluid the above demarcation lines actually are" (1994:445). Indeed, this fluidity lies at the heart of the definitional dilemma of how to consider ethnic cleansing in relation to genocide. Levene makes a plea for flexibility in categorization and for attention to (changing) contexts. Though scholars should heed his urgings, they also must keep in mind not only the internal context of their own analyses but also the contemporary political contexts in which they produce and publish their studies, one in which easy analytical slippage along a continuum of ethnic cleansing and genocide may be taken to justify action or inaction, sympathy or condemnation. At stake is both the broader political context for such scholarship and the contextualization of violence within specific scholarly works.

22. Ramet does, however, recognize that some literature does not fall into either group, and this proves just one aspect of Ramet's complex and nuanced discussion of scholarship on various aspects of the Yugoslav conflict. Ramet (2007), in fact, charges Hayden—who focuses on the question of what he calls "moralizing discourse"—with dealing with only one chapter of her book.

REFERENCES

Algeo, John, and Adele Algeo
1993   Among the New Words. American Speech 68(4):410–419.

Appadurai, Arjun
1986   Theory in Anthropology: Center and Periphery. Comparative Studies in Society and History 28:356–361.

Bahloul, Joëlle

1996   The Architecture of Memory: A Jewish-Muslim Household in Colonial
            Algeria, 1937–1962. Catherine du Peloux Ménagé, trans. Cambridge:
            Cambridge University Press.

Ballinger, Pamela

1999   The Politics of the Past: Redefining Insecurity along the "World's Most
            Open Border." In Cultures of Insecurity: States, Communities and the
            Production of Danger. Jutta Weldes, Mark Laffey, Hugh Gusterson, and
            Raymond Duvall, eds. Pp. 63–90. Minneapolis: University of Minnesota
            Press.

2000   Who Defines and Remembers Genocide after the Cold War? Contested
            Memories of Partisan Massacre in Venezia Giulia in 1943–1945. Journal of
            Genocide Research 2(1):11–30.

2003   History in Exile: Memory and Identity at the Borders of the Balkans.
            Princeton: Princeton University Press.

2004   "Authentic Hybrids" in the Balkan Borderlands. Current Anthropology
            45(1):31–60.

Bárta, Róbert

2003   The Hungarian-Slovak Population Exchange and Forced Resettlement
            in 1947. In Ethnic Cleansing in Twentieth-Century Europe. Steven Béla
            Várdy, T. Hunt Tooley, and Agnes Huszár Várdy, eds. Pp. 565–574. Boul-
            der, CO: Social Science Monographs.

Bauman, Zygmunt

2002[1989] Modernity and the Holocaust. In Genocide: An Anthropological
            Reader. Alexander Laban Hinton, ed. Pp. 110–133. Malden, MA:
            Blackwell.

Bodley, John H.

2002[1999] Victims of Progress. In Genocide: An Anthropological Reader. Alexander
            Laban Hinton, ed. Pp. 137–163. Malden, MA: Blackwell.

Bringa, Tone

2002   Genocide in Bosnia-Herzegovina, 1992–1995. In Annihilating Differ-
            ence: The Anthropology of Genocide. Alexander Laban Hinton, ed.
            Pp. 194–225. Berkeley: University of California Press.

Brubaker, Rogers

1998   Migrations of Ethnic Unmixing in the "New Europe." International
            Migration Review 32(4):1047–1065.

2004   Ethnicity without Groups. Cambridge: Harvard University Press.

Brubaker, Rogers, and Frederick Cooper

2000   Beyond "Identity." Theory and Society 29(1):1–47.

Cerone, John

2003   Recent Developments in the Law of Genocide and Implications for
Kosovo. *In* Ethnic Cleansing in Twentieth-Century Europe. Steven Béla
Várdy, T. Hunt Tooley, and Agnes Huszár Várdy, eds. Pp. 729–741. Boulder, CO: Social Science Monographs.

Colella, Amedeo, ed.

1958   L'esodo dalle terre adriatiche: Rilevazioni statistiche. Rome: Stab. Tip. Julia.

Comitato di Liberazione Nazionale dell'Istria (CLN)

1948–1954   Dichiarazione politiche. Archived material, Istituto Regionale per la
Cultura Istriana. Trieste, Italy.

Connor, Walker

1984   The National Question in Marxist-Leninist Theory and Strategy. Princeton: Princeton University Press.

Cushman, Thomas

2005   Response to Hayden and Denich. Anthropological Theory 5(4):559–564.

Denich, Bette

1994   Dismembering Yugoslavia: Nationalist Ideologies and the Symbolic
Revival of Genocide. American Ethnologist 21(2):367–390.

2005   Debate or Defamation? Comment on the Publication of Cushman's
"Anthropology and Genocide in the Balkans." Anthropological Theory
5(4):555–558.

Donato, Carlo, and Pio Nodari

1995   L'emigrazione giuliana nel mondo: Note introduttive. Quaderni del
centro studi Ezio Vanoni, n.s. 2(3–4):1–166.

Fein, Helen

2002   Genocide: A Sociological Perspective. *In* Genocide: An Anthropological
Reader. Alexander Laban Hinton, ed. Pp. 74–90. Malden, MA: Blackwell.

Hann, Chris M.

1996   Ethnic Cleansing in Eastern Europe: Poles and Ukrainians beside the
Curzon Line. Nations and Nationalism 2(3):389–406.

Hayden, Robert M.

1994   Recounting the Dead: The Rediscovery and Redefinition of Wartime
Massacres in Late- and Post-Communist Yugoslavia. *In* Memory, History,
and Opposition under State Socialism. Rubie S. Watson, ed. Pp. 167–184.
Santa Fe: School of American Research Press.

1996   Schindler's Fate: Genocide, Ethnic Cleansing, and Population Transfers.
Slavic Review 55(4):727–748.

2005   Inaccurate Data, Spurious Issues and Editorial Failure in Cushman's
"Anthropology and Genocide in the Balkans." Anthropological Theory
5(4):545–554.

2007   Moralizing about Scholarship about Yugoslavia. East European Politics
            and Societies 21(1):182–193.

Hinton, Alexander Laban
2002   The Dark Side of Modernity: Toward an Anthropology of Genocide.
            In Annihilating Difference: The Anthropology of Genocide. Alexander
            Laban Hinton, ed. Pp. 1–40. Berkeley: University of California Press.

Kersten, Krystyna
2001   Forced Migration and the Transformation of Polish Society in the
            Postwar Period. *In* Redrawing Nations: Ethnic Cleansing in East-Central
            Europe, 1944–1948. Philipp Ther and Ana Siljak, eds. Pp. 75–86. Lanham,
            MD: Rowman and Littlefield.

Kramer, Mark
2001   Introduction. *In* Redrawing Nations: Ethnic Cleansing in East-Central
            Europe, 1944–1948. Philipp Ther and Ana Siljak, eds. Pp. 1–41. Lanham,
            MD: Rowman and Littlefield.

Lemkin, Raphaël
2002   Genocide. *In* Genocide: An Anthropological Reader. Alexander Laban
            Hinton, ed. Pp. 27–42. Malden, MA: Blackwell.

Levene, Mark
1994   Yesterday's Victims, Today's Perpetrators?: Considerations on Peoples
            and Territories of the Former Ottoman Empire. Terrorism and Political
            Violence 6(4): 444–461.

Lilly, Carol S.
1996   Amoral Realism or Immoral Obfuscation? Slavic Review 55(4):749–754.

Linek, Bernard
2001   "De-Germanization" and "Re-Polonization" in Upper Silesia, 1945–1950.
            In Redrawing Nations: Ethnic Cleansing in East-Central Europe,
            1944–1948. Philipp Ther and Ana Siljak, eds. Pp. 121–134. Lanham, MD:
            Rowman and Littlefield.

Ludányi, Andrew
2003   The Fate of Hungarians in Yugoslavia: Genocide, Ethnocide, or Ethnic
            Cleansing? *In* Ethnic Cleansing in Twentieth-Century Europe. Steven
            Béla Várdy, T. Hunt Tooley, and Agnes Huszár Várdy, eds. Pp. 575–599.
            Boulder, CO: Social Science Monographs.

Madieri, Marisa
1987   Verde acqua. Turin: Einaudi.

Martin, Terry
1998   The Origins of Soviet Ethnic Cleansing. Journal of Modern History
            70(4):813–861.

Mazsu, János

2003   The Shifting Interpretation of the Term "Ethnic Cleansing" in Central and Eastern Europe. *In* Ethnic Cleansing in Twentieth-Century Europe. Steven Béla Várdy, T. Hunt Tooley, and Agnes Huszár Várdy, eds. Pp. 743–755. Boulder, CO: Social Science Monographs.

Mearsheimer, John. J., and Robert A. Pape

1993   The Answer: A Three-Way Partition Plan for Bosnia and How the US Can Enforce It. New Republic, June 14: 22–28.

Mearsheimer, John J., and Stephen Van Evera

1995   When Peace Means War: The Partition That Dare Not Speak Its Name. New Republic, December 18: 16–21.

Mulaj, Klejda

2002   Ethnic Cleansing in the Former Yugoslavia in the 1990s: A Euphemism for Genocide? *In* Ethnic Cleansing in Twentieth-Century Europe. Steven Béla Várdy, T. Hunt Tooley, and Agnes Huszár Várdy, eds. Pp. 693–711. Boulder, CO: Social Science Monographs.

Murray Li, Tania

2002   Ethnic Cleansing, Recursive Knowledge, and the Dilemmas of Sedentarism. International Social Science Journal 173:361–371.

Nagengast, Carole

2002   Inoculations of Evil in the U.S.-Mexican Border Region. *In* Annihilating Difference: The Anthropology of Genocide. Alexander Laban Hinton, ed. Pp. 325–347. Berkeley: University of California Press.

Naimark, Norman M.

2001   Fires of Hatred: Ethnic Cleansing in Twentieth-Century Europe. Cambridge: Harvard University Press.

Petacco, Arrigo

2005   A Tragedy Revealed: The Story of the Italian Population of Istria, Dalmatia, and Venezia Giulia, 1943–1956. Konrad Eisenbichler, trans. Toronto: University of Toronto Press.

Prizel, Ilya

2007   Editor's Note. East European Politics and Society 21:181.

Pupo, Raoul

1997   Violenza politica tra guerra e dopoguerra: Il caso delle foibe giuliane, 1943–1945. *In* Foibe: Il peso del passato. Giampaolo Valdevit, ed. Pp. 33–58. Venice: Marsilio.

2005   Il lungo esodo: Istria; Le persecuzioni, le foibe, l'esilio. Milan: Rizzoli.

Pupo, Raoul, and Aleksander Panjek

2004   Riflessioni sulle migrazioni ai confini italo-jugoslavi (1918–1960). Identità, politica e metodo. *In* Oltre l'Italia e l'Europa: Beyond Italy and

Europe; Ricerche sui movimenti migratori e sullo spazio multiculturale. Carlo Donato, Pio Nodari, and Aleksander Panjek, eds. Pp. 343–360. Trieste: Edizioni Università di Trieste (EUT).

Ramet, Sabrina P.
2005   Thinking about Yugoslavia: Scholarly Debates about the Yugoslav Breakup and the Wars in Bosnia and Kosovo. Cambridge: Cambridge University Press.
2007   A Review of One Chapter: An Example of Irresponsible Self-Indulgence. East European Politics and Societies 21(1):194–203.

Rieber, Alfred J.
2000   Repressive Population Transfers in Central, Eastern, and South-Eastern Europe: A Historical Overview. In Forced Migration in Central and Eastern Europe, 1939–1950. Alfred J. Rieber, ed. Pp. 1–27. London: Frank Cass.

Rocchi, Flaminio
1990   L'esodo dei 350 mila Giuliani Fiumani e Dalmati. Rome: Difesa Adriatica.

Scheper-Hughes, Nancy
1995   The Primacy of the Ethical: Propositions for a Militant Anthropology. Current Anthropology 36(3):409–440.

Schindler, John
2003   Yugoslavia's First Ethnic Cleansing: The Expulsion of the Danubian Germans, 1944–1946. In Ethnic Cleansing in Twentieth-Century Europe. Steven Béla Várdy, T. Hunt Tooley, and Agnes Huszár Várdy, eds. Pp. 359–372. Boulder, CO: Social Science Monographs.

Siljak, Ana
2001   Conclusion. In Redrawing Nations: Ethnic Cleansing in East-Central Europe, 1944–1948. Philipp Ther and Ana Siljak, eds. Pp. 327–36. Lanham, MD: Rowman and Littlefield.

Sluga, Glenda
1994   No-Man's Land: The Gendered Boundaries of Post-War Trieste. Gender and History 6(2):184–201.

Snyder, Timothy
2003   The Causes of Ukrainian-Polish Ethnic Cleansing 1943. Past and Present 179:197–234.

Sponza, Nicolò
2005   Al di là degli Esuli e dei Rimasti: Una riflessione sul nostro futuro. La Ricerca 44–45: 1–2.

Stranj, Pavel
1992   The Submerged Community: An A to Z of the Slovenes in Italy. Mark Brady, trans. Trieste: Editorale Stampa Triestina.

Ther, Philipp

2001   A Century of Forced Migration: The Origins and Consequences of "Eth-
            nic Cleansing." *In* Redrawing Nations: Ethnic Cleansing in East-Central
            Europe, 1944–1948. Philipp Ther and Ana Siljak, eds. Pp. 43–74. Lanham,
            MD: Rowman and Littlefield.

United Nations

2002   Text of the UN Genocide Convention. *In* Genocide: An Anthropological
            Reader. Alexander Laban Hinton, ed. Pp. 43–47. Malden, MA: Blackwell.

Verdery, Katherine

1991   National Ideology under Socialism: Identity and Cultural Politics in
            Ceaușescu's Romania. Berkeley: University of California Press.

Volk, Sandi

2004   Esuli a Trieste: Bonifica nazionale e rafforzamento dell'italianità sul con-
            fine orientale. Udine: Kappa Vu.

Wallace, Paul

1996   The Costs of Partition in Europe: A South Asian Perspective. Slavic
            Review 55(4):762–766.

Woodward, Susan

1996   Genocide or Partition: Two Faces of the Same Coin? Slavic Review
            55(4):755–761.

Zayas, Alfred de

2003   Anglo-American Responsibility for the Expulsion of the Germans, 1944–
            48. *In* Ethnic Cleansing in Twentieth-Century Europe. Steven Béla Várdy,
            T. Hunt Tooley, and Agnes Huszár Várdy, eds. Pp. 239–253. Boulder, CO:
            Social Science Monographs.

Živković, Marko

2000   The Wish to Be a Jew: The Power of the Jewish Trope in the Yugoslav
            Conflict. Cahiers de l'URMIS 6:69–84.

Antonius C. G. M. Robben

EPILOGUE

The Imagination of Genocide

Men may dyen of ymaginacion So depe may impression be take.
—Geoffrey Chaucer, *Miller's Tale*

The imagination of genocide begins with a body count. Numbers are crucial in determining whether or not a group was killed "in whole or in part" to justify the term genocide (Hinton 2002:43). The numbers of genocide overwhelm us by their magnitude. Yet this visceral reaction is only the beginning, so Kevin O'Neill and Alex Hinton remark in their introduction to this volume, because genocide staggers us also with images and questions. The editors imply not only that these numbers, images, and questions are shocking and emotionally unsettling but also that they make us lose our existential bearings because they are so hard to imagine and comprehend. This sense of incomprehensibility affects all human beings, whether they are survivors, perpetrators, bystanders, witnesses, collaborators, journalists, scholars, artists, or any other person in whatever time and age who stands speechless before a genocide past or present. This incomprehensibility is layered and many sided. Just as there is never one cause of genocide, so there is not one all-encompassing representation that can dispel this uncanny sensation. The understanding of genocide requires many forms and ways of imagining because the imagination is much broader than representation and involves conceptualization, mental visualization, sublimation, contextualization, and anticipation; it runs the gamut from reality to fantasy, from memory to illusion, and from past to future.

This volume reveals several new sides of genocide, ethnic cleansing, and mass killings. The authors are particularly interested in the consequences of genocide, the radiation if you will, on the survivors and the suffering societies. There is attention to agency and denial, and to imagined communities of victims, resisters, and perpetrators. Several essays demonstrate that genocide does not end when the killing stops, but that it may echo in efforts at social mourning, repair, and reconciliation. Finally, genocide does not occur in a vacuum, but is embedded in an ambivalent international community that is quick to condemn mass killings but slow to mobilize into action. Thus this book's authors imagine genocide in indirect and inchoate ways. They look at consequences rather than killings, and at what threatens to become rather than what was. Their imagination reaches backward in time through representation, forward through anticipation, and contemplates the present through the detection of sublimations of the past. As such, their imagination of genocide approaches in a roundabout way the planning of genocide, the mental visualization of annihilation, and its subterranean survival in new cultural forms.

REPRESENTING MASS VIOLENCE

The "grey zone" is an ambiguous and morally confusing social space "where the two camps of masters and servants both diverge and converge"—so Primo Levi characterized the collaboration of privileged inmates with their captors in Nazi concentration camps (1988:42). The gray zone is also a moral trap. Entry provides temporary empowerment in life-or-death situations, but it may entail lasting feelings of guilt about having survived at the expense of others.

Gray zones are not only a consequence of degrading incarceration but they can also be military strategy. Adolescents in many different societies have been recruited into militias, guerrilla organizations, regular and private armies after having been forced to massacre their relatives. They have become victim-perpetrators who slaughter on command with contradictory emotions of rage and dispassion. Forced collaboration makes them complicit in atrocious acts. However, as Victoria Sanford demonstrates so well for Guatemala, one may kill on command but not forget on command. Agency makes incursions into emotion, but it falters when traumatic events overwhelm personal defenses. Some collapse under the psychological strain, while others recognize a shared social trauma with other survivors and unite to undertake action through testimony, trial, and exhumation to remember the dead.

Guatemala's gray zone was not that of Nazi concentration camps, Cambodian labor camps, or Argentine secret detention centers where escape was nearly impossible and where subhuman conditions and constant abuse persuaded some inmates to collaborate. The Guatemalan zone was inhabited by mostly young men who lost parents and relatives after an army massacre and then enlisted in the military or army-controlled civil patrols to escape poverty, marginalization, and powerlessness. Boot camp taught them to hate and to kill. Their hatred was mobilized from their own suffering and redirected to carry out atrocities.

The gray zone is not a uniform but a heterogeneous social space, as Elizabeth Drexler reveals in her moving essay about East Timor. It is not exclusively populated by victim-perpetrators but also by collaborators with ambiguous political motives. Some Timorese were intimidated into joining the Indonesian militias that ran a terror campaign on the island, while others became informers or acted as double spies whose loyalties shifted over time, such as Indonesian soldiers who spared the lives of independence fighters and members of the resistance who betrayed comrades. The Guatemalans and Timorese who entered the gray zone damaged themselves and their respective postwar societies by becoming enmeshed in an emotional tangle of survival and guilt, impotence and betrayal, faith and mistrust. Such conflicting emotions need to be unraveled to allow for mourning and acceptance. The unpredictable behavior of ex-combatants, due to post-traumatic stress disorders or unresolved inner conflicts, provokes fear among Guatemalans living in the United States and thus perpetuates an imaginary state of war that prevents them from coming to grips with the Guatemalan genocide.

Mourning in postconflict East Timor is handicapped by the imposition of a dichotomy of good versus evil, of Timorese independence fighters versus the Indonesian military. Tribunals and truth commissions instill a Manichaean structure that does not correspond to people's experience of differentiated gray zones, that denies their reality, and that thus makes society dismiss those interstices as illusions and as figments of a deranged imagination. The rejection of intermediate positions between good and evil denies legitimacy to people's experiences and obstructs the recovery of Timorese society.

Rwandan society is also pressured into accepting a government-induced Manichaean representation of the 1994 genocide, as Jennie Burnet shows. Victim-survivors and perpetrators are classified in the sharp ethnic categories of Tutsi and Hutu, despite the official rhetoric about a unified national identity and about ethnicity being a product of colonialism. The polarized and polarizing discourse about Tutsi victims versus Hutu perpetrators has become a political instrument to consolidate the power of the Tutsi-controlled government, but it fails to do justice to the varied experiences of the country's citizens. Hutu victim-survivors are excluded from the genocide survivor category and are denied social and financial assistance.

The Rwandan government has used national commemorations to impress its ethnicized rendition of the genocide on the national and international community. Prominent officials blame the Western world and the United Nations for their unwillingness to interfere in the slaughter of eight hundred thousand Tutsi, while praising the Tutsi army in exile for stopping the genocide after a successful military campaign against Rwanda's national army. Such attempts to achieve a hegemonic version of the past run the danger of backfiring, as I have demonstrated for the case of Argentina's struggle with its past (Robben 2005b). Commemorations, memorials, and monuments do not always displace traumatic memories or transform memory and lived experiences into history, as Pierre Nora (1978, 1984) has argued. In Argentina the ritualization of the past continues to be condemned by certain human rights groups and has increased division within the country. There is not one collective Argentine memory about the 1976–83 so-called dirty war, but there exist different social memories based on diverse experiences and conflicting political interests (Robben 2005a, 2005b).

The Manichaean discourses in Rwanda and in East Timor perpetuate the social and psychic traumas of large portions of resident populations and obstruct the process of mourning by excluding those social groups that do not fit in the hegemonic dichotomy. Burnet illustrates with much sensitivity how the suffering of Tutsi victim-survivors is officially sanctioned while Hutu victim-survivors are denied mourning and are even stigmatized as members of a murderous ethnic group. The official denial of their suffering deprives Hutu widows of a historical narrative for their mourning and makes it harder for Rwandan society to achieve the national reconciliation so desired by its government.

Guatemalans have hardly been able to mourn their dead because of a hostile political climate that obstructs accountability and because of a population at odds about the past. Sanford and Debra Rodman demonstrate how the genocide has been either at the forefront or in the background of Guatemalan consciousness. Whereas the residents of Plan de Sánchez struggled to recover the remains of their slaughtered relatives, the people of San Pedro Pinula seemed incredulous about the Mayan genocide in western Guatemala.

The people of eastern Guatemala accept violence as an inevitability of life, while at the same time doubting the genocide of two hundred thousand Maya in other parts of the country. Eastern Guatemala had its brush with political violence in the 1960s when a small insurgency was quickly squelched. The region did not suffer any major massacres in the 1980s, but it was kept under tight military control and saw numerous assassinations. The denial of eastern Guatemalans seems caused by the population's own role in the repression. The region supplied many troops for the genocidal campaigns, but it has never examined this involvement openly. What did the combatants come home with? Injuries? Traumas? Stories of massacres? Or did they lock away their memories as they listened in silence to their neighbors who dismissed the news reports about the massacres of entire communities?

The use of the concepts of denial, genocide, gray zone, collaboration, and betrayal by Sanford, Rodman, and Drexler steers the imagination toward new representations. Terms developed in one historical context have led to new perspectives on other outbreaks of mass violence. Ethnic cleansing is yet another concept with such interpretive potential. Pamela Ballinger describes how this concept was forged around the armed conflict in Bosnia-Herzegovina in the 1990s and has come to redirect both research and self-reflection on historical events involving the forced resettlement of minorities throughout Europe and the Soviet Union.

Ballinger demonstrates how ethnic Italians displaced from Istria to Italy during the mid-1940s and 1950s began to mirror their predicament in the 1990s civil war in Bosnia-Herzegovina. The imagination of the Istrian exodus changed through this new conceptualization. What had been regarded as the voluntary and semivoluntary migration from Istria to Italy was suddenly seen as ethnic cleansing, with all the associations of violence and suffering it entailed. In a second move, the displacement no longer remained contextualized in the Cold War but described as a clash of irreconcilable ethnic cultures. However, Ballinger's superb deconstruction of the ethnic cleansing concept in the Istrian context reveals a layered migratory history of force and agency during 12 years of frequently changing international relations between Italy and the former Yugoslavia. The ethnic cleansing concept thus became an analytic straitjacket that smothered the diverse experiences and motivations of its historical subjects and even inflated the tragic but incidental rape of one woman into the image of a massive sexual and strategic assault on women, resembling that of Bosnia-Herzegovina.

The imagination is for Sanford, Rodman, Drexler, Burnet, and Ballinger principally about representation. They want to reconstruct as complete a picture as possible about mass violence by recovering hitherto unrecorded or unacknowledged experiences, giving attention to gender, allowing all victims their due share of suffering, disclosing ambiguous relations to undermine Manichaean analyses, and introducing concepts developed in other historical contexts. These authors do not aim to capture mass violence in comprehensive and complete descriptions, if that were ever possible, but they are moved by empathy, justice, and memory politics. They want to help the powerless reclaim their past, acknowledge their gendered agency and diverse subjectivities, contest and nuance the official stories, and ultimately contribute to mourning, emotional recovery, and reconciliation. The imagination of genocide is for them a moral imperative reached through improved narrative representation.

SUBLIMATING GENOCIDE

Arguably no other people in the world have done more to come to grips with their complicity in genocide than West Germans. Several decades after World War II, the Holocaust became the object of an obsessive soul-searching. Museums, memorials, exhibitions, commemorations, books, films, documentaries, debates, reparation payments, and a repeated mea culpa were public manifestations of this national self-analysis. The (West) German people have not yet finished mourning the past and, deep down, they seem not to have shed their morbid fascination with death that characterized Nazi culture, so argues Uli Linke in a provocative and brave essay (see also Linke 1999). She wants to expose the cultural fascination with death that unmade empathy in the past and has resurfaced in present-day Germany. Genocidal imagination and emotional anesthesia meet in the artistic expression of plastinated corpses that intertwine a dark past with a technical ingenuity that invokes both Faust and Dr. Mabuse.

The Holocaust is so much part of twentieth-century world history that nobody can escape the photographs of piles of corpses that betray an intimacy with death. One image came to mind while reading Linke's intriguing essay: a picture of a boy, maybe 12 years old, who poses with an anguished look near a twisted corpse. The boy's hands are hidden in two wooden gloves with which, in another picture, he is seen lowering dead bodies into a mass grave at the Jewish cemetery of Warsaw. These photographs were taken on September 19, 1941, by Sergeant Major Heinrich Jöst who had decided to celebrate his 43rd birthday with a stroll around the ghetto (Schwarberg 1989).

There are many similar pictures of open pits with naked corpses from the Nazi era. The puzzlement therefore concerns not the pictures but the photographers. Why did they take dozens of snapshots of dying or dead Jews? Jöst wondered the same when he unlocked the drawer where he had stashed away the photos for four decades before handing them to a journalist for publication. He had observed death and dying as a spectacle, insensitive to the suffering before his eyes.

The spectacle of death and the disrespect for the dead have cropped up again in the Germany of late modernity. Linke argues that plastinated corpses bought in China, Russia, and Kyrgyzstan are echoes of the Third Reich. An emotional anesthesia comparable to the one that made ss physicians regard Jews as subhumans on which they could carry out pseudoscientific experiments underlies the art exhibit "Body Worlds." The plastinated corpses also call to mind the Nazi museum at Strasbourg University Hospital, which collected specimens of "inferior" human types, whose preservation began when the murdered bodies were "still warm, the eyes . . . wide open and shining" (Lifton 1986:285).

The plastinated bodies are a disturbing combination of anatomy, kinesiology, and technology. The defaced, depersonalized, and technomanipulated corpses make one wonder about the difference between organism and artifice. Authenticity dissolves in both directions, leaving the observer with an uncanny feeling about life in dead matter, and death in organic tissue. This deception is enhanced by the deliberate violation of the body's threshold. The membrane that separates people's inner and outer anatomy is removed, then sometimes draped across the arm of its plastinated owner. A body without a protective skin dies within days because of infection. The plastinated body negates this reality, striking as it does an active pose holding its own skin as if it were a deposable life.

The plastination of the anonymous corpses also has a troubling ethical dimension because of the display of what Linke calls "death without mourning." The exhibition of corpses as art suggests that these deceased were without relatives desiring to administer last rites, thus stigmatizing the world's peripheries as populated by uncaring people who sell their dead for money. Jöst commented about his picture of a dying woman that he saw her die in front of his eyes, and that nobody helped or could help her. He took no initiative either and read mourning as a sign of civilization absent among the ghettoized Jews. Personhood becomes nonexistent and corpses turn into subspecimens when such dehumanizing inability to mourn is attributed to stigmatized groups. The plastinated bodies in the exhibit are treated as mere organic matter devoid of the identity and culture that made them human. They ended up on the trash heap of history and thus became available for Western exploitation and profit making.

Linke's imagination of genocide is not about representation but about sublimation. She wants to show that the German preoccupation with the body as corpse, which found expression in the Holocaust, is displaced on a seemingly harmless artistic creation. From a Freudian perspective, Linke seems to suggest that the most hidden of desires—hidden below half a century of soul searching and guilt confessions—is disguised in "socially acceptable forms of gratification, not as satisfying as direct physical pleasure, but a reasonable compromise with necessary social constraints" (Mitchell and Black 1995:191). Sublimation operates in Germany as a defense against more pernicious manifestations of deeper motives and involves a numbing of emotions that accompanies this displacement. Psychological defense restricts the unbridled imagination of genocide. Genocide is no longer conceivable and telling signs are dismissed as unrelated.

Such defenses may also occur in fact-finding missions and human rights monitors intended to ascertain whether or not genocide is taking place. Findings that threaten the world order or endanger the mission are downplayed when those defenses are up, as has been the case in various violent conflicts in Sudan. Whereas the U.S. government denounced the mass violence of Sudanese government militias against the local population of Darfur as genocide, the United Nations did not go beyond the label "ethnic cleansing." This was not a nominalist quibble, but a political dispute with serious consequences. The predicate *genocide* would oblige armed intervention, while the milder designation *ethnic cleansing* would involve only diplomatic negotiation with the Sudanese government about the stationing of peacekeepers, a response comparable to the one concerning the ethnic violence in Bosnia-Herzegovina.

Sharon Hutchinson analyzes precisely such psychological and political defenses in her insightful essay about a human rights monitoring mission in southern Sudan that either stood by or was forced to stand by powerless in the face of violence. The October 2002 deployment of the Civilian Protection Monitoring Team–Sudan was hailed as an important step toward halting the military violence against civilians in southern Sudan. However, Hutchinson concludes that between October 2002 and June 2003, "the mission did more to excuse and perpetuate military violence against civilians than to curtail or remedy it." In retrospect, one might argue that these violations were the price to pay for sealing the 2005 Comprehensive Peace Agreement between the north and the south, but Hutchinson suggests that this lackluster approach might undermine the six-year implementation following the peace accords. A more robust and proactive mission enforcing compliance with the cease-fire would have been preferable.

Caught between the Sudanese government and the Sudan People's Liberation Movement/Army, the mission was unable and unwilling to intervene in ongoing hostilities, afraid to endanger the delicate peace negotiations. However, militias linked to the Sudanese government did not feel obliged to honor any agreement between the two official parties to the conflict and thus continued with their territorial expansion and violence toward civilians under the wings of the government. Under the guise of strict neutrality, the foreign monitors pretended evenhandedness in dealing with violations, but in effect they favored the Sudanese government. Hutchinson reveals how the micropolitics of diplomacy—the compromises, the turning a blind eye, the disregard of proportionality, and the desire to be evenhanded in an uneven situation—resulted in a bias favoring the Sudanese government, using neutrality as an excuse for inaction.

Michael Ignatieff has argued that neutrality often implies complicity because otherwise sovereign governments would not admit human rights monitors to their countries (cited in Hutchinson, this volume). However, this state bias might also be viewed as a defensive move in a process of sublimation. It is the desire for peace that guides the imagination of violence, thus sublimating the reality on the ground into an imaginary future while ignoring any violations that undermine the fulfillment of that wish. Offensive actions, deliberate bombings, and persistent attacks are dismissed as accidents, incidents, mistakes, misunderstandings, misjudgments, and unintentional violations because mass violence cannot be imagined under the spell of diplomacy and the desire for peace.

Silence may also occur among the survivors of genocide and mass violence as a deliberate strategy or a defensive reaction against experiences too painful to admit to consciousness. Leslie Dwyer addresses this silence in her deep-felt analysis of the 1965–66 nationalist purge in Bali in which 80,000 to 100,000 people suspected of communist sympathies were disappeared and assassinated. The Balinese do not want to talk about these troubled times because, according to many scholars, they have forgiven the perpetrators, have forgotten about the past, are only looking toward the future, or have worked through their losses. Yet Dwyer demonstrates that silence can be a form of agency. The Balinese silence is not the manifestation of repression or unawareness but is consciously negotiated and actively maintained behind the official story about the massacres and the facade of a peaceful, romanticized tourist paradise.

What emotional price do people pay for silencing their past, or is there a price to pay at all? The idea that people and societies have to work through traumatic experiences through elaboration and narrative interpretation seems a distinctly Western, psychoanalytic notion that does not necessary apply to Bali. Balinese suffering is unacknowledged by the Indonesian state and has sublimated in active silences, ritual practices, gender relations, local politics, trance, and messages from the dead. Silence is not the inability to articulate the inexpressible or a form of unconscious resistance to insight, as classic psychoanalysis would have it, but a muteness that emphasizes remembrance, truth, and accountability. In this case, sublimation might prove a more powerful political means to question mass violence than loud public protest.

ANTICIPATING GENOCIDE

Sublimation and anticipation stand at the opposite ends of the imagination of genocide. Genocidal imagination as anticipation requires deliberate planning and action to be fulfilled. The realization of this macabre fantasy is frightening because it foreshadows violence and conceives of a total annihilation. The imagination of genocide consists of either demonstrating that the perpetrators' fantasy is already materializing or showing that the seed is in place and rapidly growing into reality.

Drexler describes how victims of mass violence substantiate their conviction that what others may anticipate as taking place in the near future is already real. Timorese independence fighters asked corrupt Indonesian officers to photograph their torture and assassination of captives to prove to the world that gross human rights violations were happening in East Timor. Oral testimony could be discredited, but pictures grounded the verbal imagination in reality.

The imagination of that which is not yet but is soon to be reveals another side of anticipation. Dwyer describes how Balinese survivors of the 1965–66 purge fear that a casual remark about someone being a communist might spark a new round of massacres, while Conerly Casey shows how globalization allows people to feel so injured by world events that they resort to violent vengeance. Muslims in northern Nigeria developed a belief in an imagined community of victims and an imagined community of perpetrators, a belief fed by an unending stream of images from around the world broadcast by national and international media.

In 2004 Muslims in Kano identified deeply with fellow believers assassinated months earlier in Nigeria's Plateau State, as well as with the Palestinians Ahmed Yassin and Abdul-Azeez Rantisi eliminated by Israeli troops and the Iraqi detainees in Abu Ghraib prison brutalized by American soldiers. Empathy turned into injury, and these feelings were fed through identification and remembrance. Their membership in the imagined community of victims of Western aggression enlarged their collective identity as victimized Muslims, thus experiencing an injury to a brother-in-faith as a personal infliction. Rumors about more harm done to fellow believers developed into rage-inspired riots against threatening others (see Kakar 1996; Tambiah 1996). Humiliations endured during British colonial times and Nigeria's late 1960s civil war were recontextualized in more recent suffering, imbuing all three with interconnected meanings that were projected into the future and therefore had to be dealt with to prevent further harm.

Collective violence was believed to undo the harm of all three periods. Nigerian Muslim youths called themselves Taliban and identified with Osama bin Laden and Saddam Hussein, while Nigerian Christians were blamed for the violence against fellow Muslims worldwide and believed to have been incited by the presidents of Nigeria, Israel, and the United States as the leaders of an imagined community of perpetrators. State borders vanish under the weight of transnational identifications and imagined communities become more important than national identities thanks to the flows of information and of inflaming images in a globalized world. Rodman also describes the effects of globalization on the imagination of genocide. The awareness of Mayan men from eastern Guatemala about the genocide was raised only after their migration to the United States, where they met Mayan refugees from heavily affected regions, thus finding a common identity as Mayan survivors of repression. This globalized identification process occurs also in other regions of the world, leading to empathy and compassion—but possibly also violence, as Casey shows revealingly.

The killing of Christian neighbors and fellow residents in Kano on May 11, 2004, did therefore not come about suddenly but had been preceded by a steady buildup of images in the media documenting deadly Christian violence against Muslims in northern Nigeria and in other parts of the world. These images were reinforced by the remembrance of violent outbreaks in Nigeria's past such as the civil war. The thousands of killings foreshadowed a genocidal imagination of much larger proportions. The riots were planned in advance, victims included babies and the aged, and address lists with the names of Christians in the area were compiled. Globalization and the news media extended these ties—that Casey calls affective citizenships and that I would call an imagined community of victims— beyond national borders and forged relations based on ethnic, religious, and regional identities.

The comprehension of genocide is so multifaceted and layered that there will always remain new perspectives, insights, interpretations, and areas of knowledge to be discovered. We can never fathom genocide all the way through, and therefore we will search continuously for new meanings and explanations—all of which will eventually turn out to be incomplete. We speak with survivors, read testimonies, try to uncover hidden traces, and attempt to place events in a political, historical, and cultural context, but some pieces are forever missing, while what remains never seems to fit entirely into the mold we have designed with such care.

The incomprehension of genocide is cognitive and emotional. The events and experiences of genocide and mass violence are so varied and overwhelming that they can never be remembered, recorded, or captured in full. There will always remain gaps of knowledge. The anthropological imagination displayed in this book struggles with these unknowns, the silences, the repressed, the inexpressible, the ambiguities, and the bafflement. The authors wander off the beaten track in search of new ways to wrest a piece of understanding away from the incomprehensible. This is by no means a futile effort because each enlightening thought and solid explanation will chip away at the unknown, as this volume does so superbly.

Genocide is also emotionally difficult to grasp. The awareness that people can turn on one another without restraint is hyperreal during its occurrence, but it becomes incomprehensible after the fact because of its emotional unacceptability. Just as traumatized people cannot integrate, after the killing has stopped, their terrifying experiences into their regular lives with their everyday routines and taken-for-granted trust in the benevolence of fellow human beings, as Yolanda Gampel (2000) has shown, so societies traumatized by genocide and massive violence encounter the greatest difficulties in reconciling the horror they went through with the treadmill of ordinary living. Imagination operates both before the genocide—when plans are made, weapons are stockpiled, perpetrators are chosen and prepared, and lists of victims are drawn up—and after the genocide, when many wrestle with ways to understand that dark imagination. People are continuously reminded of past atrocities as survivors step forward to tell their stories and mass graves are opened to reveal what was hushed up for years.

The imagination and incomprehension of genocide are thus tied together in a struggle about the unknown, where the first tries to discover through different cognitive and creative perspectives what the second conceals. Representation, sublimation, and anticipation have been the three principal elaborations of imagination that stand out in this collection. The authors here have found new pathways through the labyrinth, and have enhanced our cognitive understanding, an understanding that temporarily suspends our deeper anxieties. Yet in a sober moment of reflection we have to admit that the labyrinth and our scholarly imaginations rest on a quicksand of emotions and meanings that continue to shift our interpretations into the realm of the incomprehensible.

REFERENCES

Gampel, Yolanda
2000   Reflections on the Prevalence of the Uncanny in Social Violence. *In*
            Cultures under Siege: Collective Violence and Trauma. Antonius C. G.
            M. Robben and Marcelo M. Suárez-Orozco, eds. Pp. 48–69. Cambridge:
            Cambridge University Press.

Hinton, Alexander Laban, ed.
2002   Genocide: An Anthropological Reader. Malden, MA: Blackwell.

Kakar, Sudhir
1996   The Colors of Violence: Cultural Identities, Religion, and Conflict. Chicago: University of Chicago Press.

Levi, Primo
1988   The Drowned and the Saved. Raymond Rosenthal, trans. New York:
            Summit.

Lifton, Robert Jay
1986   The Nazi Doctors: Medical Killing and the Psychology of Genocide. New
            York: Basic Books.

Linke, Uli
1999   Blood and Nation: The European Aesthetics of Race. Philadelphia: University of Pennsylvania Press.

Mitchell, Stephen A., and Margaret J. Black
1995   Freud and Beyond: A History of Modern Psychoanalytic Thought. New
            York: Basic Books.

Nora, Pierre
1978   Mémoire collective. *In* La nouvelle histoire. Jacques Le Goff, Roger
            Chartier, and Jacques Revel, eds. Pp. 398–401. Paris: Retz.

1984   Entre mémoire et histoire: La problématique des lieux. *In* Les lieux
            de mémoire, vol. 1: La république. Pierre Nora, ed. Pp.xvii–xlii. Paris:
            Gallimard.

Robben, Antonius C. G. M.
2005a   How Traumatized Societies Remember: The Aftermath of Argentina's
            Dirty War. Cultural Critique 59:120–164.
2005b   Political Violence and Trauma in Argentina. Philadelphia: University of
            Pennsylvania Press.

Schwarberg, Günther
1989   Das Getto. Göttingen: Steidl.

Tambiah, Stanley J.
1996   Leveling Crowds: Ethnonationalist Conflicts and Collective Violence in
            South Asia. Berkeley: University of California Press.

CONTRIBUTORS

PAMELA BALLINGER is an associate professor of anthropology at Bowdoin College. Her research interests include historical memory, displacement, coastal issues, Italy, and Croatia. She is currently studying the return of Italian nationals from those territories Italy lost after World War II.

JENNIE E. BURNET is an assistant professor in the Department of Anthropology at the University of Louisville. Her research interests include gender, ethnicity, war, genocide, and reconciliation in postconflict societies. She has been conducting research in Rwanda since 1997.

CONERLY CASEY is an associate professor in the anthropology and psychology programs at the American University of Kuwait. She has published several articles and book chapters about violence in northern Nigeria, including " 'Policing' through Violence: Fear, Vigilantism and the Politics of Islam in Northern Nigeria" in *Global Vigilantes: Anthropological Approaches to Vigilantism* (2007) and "Marginal Muslims": Politics and the Perceptual Bounds of Islamic Authenticity in Northern Nigeria," *Africa Today* (2008).

ELIZABETH F. DREXLER teaches anthropology at Michigan State University. Her research in Indonesia and East Timor explores how societies address the legacies of past violence, emphasizing the relationships among institutions, transnational interventions, historical narratives, and memory. She is the author of *Aceh, Indonesia: Securing the Insecure State* and co-editor of a forthcoming volume on institutions of truth and memory in the aftermath of violence. Her current research considers impunity in Indonesia.

LESLIE DWYER teaches anthropology and coordinates the peace and conflict studies program at Haverford College. She has conducted research in Indonesia since 1993, most recently on the cultural and political implications of the state-sponsored anti-communist violence of 1965–66. She is currently completing a book entitled *A World in Fragments: Violence and Its Aftermath in Bali*, in collaboration with the Balinese anthropologist Degung Santikarma, and beginning a new project on the social and political life of discourses of trauma in Indonesia and their emergence within contexts of clinical practice, humanitarian intervention, democratization, and the transnational war on terror.

ALEXANDER LABAN HINTON is an associate professor of anthropology and global affairs and the director of the Center for the Study of Genocide and Human Rights at Rutgers University, Newark. He is the author of *Why Did They Kill? Cambodia in the Shadow of Genocide* (2005) and four edited or co-edited collections: *Night of the Khmer Rouge: Genocide and Justice in Cambodia* (2007), *Annihilating Difference: The Anthropology of Genocide* (2002), *Genocide: An Anthropological Reader* (2002), and *Biocultural Approaches to the Emotions* (1999). He currently serves as the second vice-president of the International Association of Genocide Scholars, as an academic advisor to the Documentation Center of Cambodia, and on the international advisory boards of the *Journal of Genocide Research* and *Genocide Studies and Prevention*.

SHARON E. HUTCHINSON is a professor of anthropology and the director of African studies at the University of Wisconsin, Madison. She is the author of *Nuer Dilemmas: Coping with Money, War and the State* (1996) and numerous scholarly articles tracing the devastating impact of Sudan's Second Civil War (1983–2005) on Nuer and other southern Sudanese communities. She is currently drafting a book manuscript that reflects upon the ethical and methodological challenges of conducting long-term, ethnographic research in a war zone.

ULI LINKE is a professor of anthropology at the Rochester Institute of Technology. She has taught at the Central European University in Budapest, the University of Tübingen in Germany, Rutgers University, and the University of Toronto. Her research interests include visual culture and violence, the political anthropology of the body, and the cultural politics of memory.

KEVIN LEWIS O'NEILL is an assistant professor in religious studies and American studies at Indiana University. A trained cultural and social anthropologist, he has conducted ethnographic research in postgenocidal Guatemala City that addresses the relationship between neo-Pentecostal Christianity and efforts at democratization. He has been conducting research in Guatemala City since 2001.

ANTONIUS C. G. M. ROBBEN is a professor of anthropology at Utrecht University and past president of the Netherlands Society of Anthropology. Three of his most recent books are *Death, Mourning, and Burial: A Cross-Cultural Reader* (2004), *Ethnographic Fieldwork: An Anthropological Reader* (2007, with Jeffrey A. Sluka), and the award-winning ethnography *Political Violence and Trauma in Argentina* (2005).

DEBRA H. RODMAN is an assistant professor of anthropology and women's studies at Randolph-Macon College. She has received a Fulbright fellowship and a RAND/ Andrew W. Mellon grant for her research on the impact of transnational migration on gender and ethnic relations among the Maya and Ladinos of the Eastern Highlands of

Guatemala. She currently serves as an expert witness on Guatemalan political asylum cases in U.S. immigration courts.

VICTORIA SANFORD is an associate professor of anthropology at Lehman College and the Graduate Center, City University of New York. Her works include *Buried Secrets: Truth and Human Rights in Guatemala* (2003), *Violencia y genocidio en Guatemala* (2003), *La masacre de Panzós: Etnicidad, tierra y violencia en Guatemala* (2008), and *Engaged Observer: Anthropology, Advocacy, and Activism* (2006, co-edited with Asale Angel-Ajani). She is currently writing "The Land of Pale Hands: Feminicide and Impunity in Guatemala."

INDEX

Cold War, 221, 238 n. 9, 286, 301, 321; fear of communism and, 7; globalization and, 43

Collaboration: betrayal and, 220–21, 230, 232–37, 319, 321

Colonialism, 3, 15, 98, 117, 141 n. 11, 195–96; as genocide, 248–51; jihad and, 256–57, 269; Muslims and, 261, 263, 266–69; Rwanda and, 84, 320, 328

Commemoration, 15; loss of humanity and, 175, 177; national, 319–20, 322; in Rwanda, 87–88, 94, 97, 99, 105 n. 30; as symbolic control of history, 115–16

Commission for Historical Clarification (CEH), 3, 7–8, 41, 45, 193–94

Concentration camps, 1, 30, 33, 150, 167, 180, 298, 318–19

Congo, Democratic Republic of, 82, 85–86, 96–97, 102 n. 6

Cultural relativism, 305–6

Danforth, John, 59
Daniel, Valentine E., 10, 134
Darfur, 5, 55–57, 61, 76 n. 2, 77 n. 4, 325
Das, Veena, 43
Death Squad, 199
De Certeau, Michel, 155
Dehumanization, 17, 150, 176–77
Democratic Kampuchea, 5
Democratic Republic of Congo, 82, 85–86, 96–97, 102 n. 6
Denial, 2, 5–6, 17; of genocide, 302, 318, 320–21; in Guatemala, 150, 194, 200–203, 208, 210; historical, 29, 37
Douglass, William, 10

East Timor, 12, 220–28, 231–32, 236–38, 239 n. 8; postconflict, 18–19, 319–20, 327
El Salvador, 34, 43

Empathy: emotional anesthesia and, 16, 147, 151, 323, 327–28; limits of, 16–17, 147–50, 175–77, 182

"Epistemic murk" (Taussig), 10

Erotic Art Museum, 17, 167

Ethnic cleansing, 19–20, 318, 321–25; definition of, 280–81; as euphemism, 281; genocide and, 280–82

Ethnic conflicts, 203, 208–9, 279, 301

Ethnicity: in Guatemala, 211–12 n. 6; in Nigeria, 203, 205–6, 248, 250–51, 264–65; as a product of colonialism, 320; in Rwanda, 80, 82–86, 89, 93–94, 100, 104 n. 18

Ethnocide, 3, 308 n. 5

Eugenics, 172, 175

Falla, Ricardo, 30, 32
Fein, Helen, 22, 92
Feldman, Allen, 10, 169, 171, 248
Fonds d'Assistance pour les Rescapés du Génocide (FARG), 93–94
Forces Armées Rwandaises (FAR), 81, 85, 88
Forgetting, 16–20, 174–76; as emotional anesthesia, 16, 147, 151, 323; genocide and, 12, 114, 117, 133, 135, 150; institutionalized, 39–40, 42–43; reconciliation and, 6; silence and, 120–21, 182, 234
Fundación de Antropología Forense de Guatemala (FAFG), 41, 44–45, 49

Geertz, Clifford, 117, 141
Geneva Convention (1949), 58, 65–66, 68, 92, 283
Genocide, definitions of, 2–3, 21–22 n. 2, 50 n. 6, 58, 92, 104 n. 22, 237, 249, 285, 307–8 n. 5
Genocide Survivor Funds (FARG), 93–94
Germany, 11, 16–17, 101 n. 2, 147–50

Globalization, 9, 43, 117, 140 n. 9, 154–55; genocide and, 327–28; modernity and, 11

Gray zones, 8, 13–14; genocide and, 318–19, 321; in Guatemala, 20, 29, 34–37

Green, Linda, 100, 200–202, 211 n. 1–2, 212 n. 9

Grief, 4, 148

Guatemala, 12–14, 17–18, 100, 318–21, 328

Guatemalan Forensic Anthropology Foundation (FAFG), 41, 44–45, 49

Gurr, Ted Robert, 92

Habyarimana, Juvénal, 81, 84–85, 90, 102 n. 5, 102 n. 7, 104 n. 19

Harff, Barbara, 92

Hayden, Robert, 279, 282–87, 289, 303, 306, 307 n. 1

Hitler, Adolf, 285

Holocaust, 32–33, 236, 285, 296–97, 303, 322–24; Lemkin and, 2, 9, 13; post-Holocaust, 16–17, 147–48, 150, 176, 181

Horkheimer, Max, 163

Human Rights Watch, 101 n. 1, 231

Hussein, Saddam, 262, 266, 328

Hutu, 80–100

Ideology, 84–85, 87, 140 n. 9, 163, 172, 286, 288

Ignatieff, Michael, 55, 76, 326

Imagination, 16, 20–21, 127; Christian, 8, 19; of genocide, 8–11, 317, 321–24, 326–30; national, 80, 91, 95, 100–101; public, 114; scholarly, 330; social, 118

Imagined community, 327–28

Indigenous peoples, 1, 3, 13, 208–9; in Guatemala, 17, 35, 41; languages of, 196–97, 211–12 n. 6; rights movements of, 305

Indonesia, 1, 16, 305, 319, 326–27; civil war of, 221, 228, 236; history of genocide

in, 114–22; military of, 18, 140 n. 9, 220–21, 224, 226, 319; special forces of, 231

Ireland, 10

Islam, 19, 140 n. 9, 248–50

Jewish Cemetery of Warsaw, 327

Jews, 33, 308 n. 5, 327; ghettoized, 323; Italian, 297; killed in the Holocaust, 1, 148, 162, 180; Roma and, 308 n. 5; seen as individuals, 170; as the subject of experiments, 323–24

Jung, Carl, 46

Justice, 5–7, 48–49, 320, 322; global, 262; restorative, 238 n. 2; social, 249, 256; transitional, 238 n. 1

Khmer Rouge, 5–6

Kleinman, Arthur, 43

Kosovo, 279, 281, 291

Kuper, Leo, 21 n. 1, 249–50, 270 n. 2, 308 n. 5

LaCapra, Dominick, 13, 29, 32–33, 37, 39

Ladinos, 7, 17, 196, 334

Laub, Dori, 33

Lemkin, Raphaël, 2–3, 29–30, 249

Lethen, Helmut, 147, 178

Levi, Primo, 13, 29–30, 34–38, 40, 42–43, 46–47, 318

Malkki, Liisa, 10, 105 n. 28, 305

Mamdani, Mahmood, 251, 258

Masculinity, 164–67, 175, 256, 262

Maya, 3, 7–8, 13, 17, 321, 328; of eastern Guatemala, 195, 201; ex-soldiers, 206–7, 210; migrants, 208–9; movement, 209; Pokomam, 197, 208–9, 212 n. 6; soldiers, 210; survivors, 13, 29–30, 328; of western Guatemala, 195

Mead, Margaret, 117

ALEXANDER LABAN HINTON is an associate professor in the Department of Sociology and Anthropology and the director of the Center for the Study of Genocide and Human Rights at Rutgers University, Newark. He is the author of *Why Did They Kill? Cambodia in the Shadow of Genocide* (2005). He is also the editor of *Annihilating Difference: The Anthropology of Genocide* (2002) and *Biocultural Approaches to the Emotions* (1999).

KEVIN LEWIS O'NEILL is an assistant professor in religious studies and American studies at Indiana University.

Library of Congress Cataloging-in-Publication Data
Genocide : truth, memory, and representation /
edited by Alexander Laban Hinton and Kevin Lewis O'Neill.
p. cm. — (The cultures and practice of violence series)
Includes bibliographical references and index.
ISBN 978-0-8223-4388-2 (cloth : alk. paper)
ISBN 978-0-8223-4405-6 (pbk. : alk. paper)
1. Genocide. I. Hinton, Alexander Laban. II. O'Neill, Kevin Lewis, 1977–
III. Series: Cultures and practice of violence series.
HV6322.7.G4518 2009
304.6′63—dc22   2008048056